THERE IS
A BALM
IN GILEAD

# THERE IS A BALM IN GILEAD

## THE CULTURAL ROOTS OF

## MARTIN LUTHER KING, JR.

# Lewis V. Baldwin

FORTRESS PRESS                    MINNEAPOLIS

For our slave forebears
who taught us how to hope,
to struggle, and to die,
and
for the poor black stranger who sat near
Martin Luther King, Jr.'s tomb in Atlanta,
requesting money to buy food,
May 22, 1986.

THERE IS A BALM IN GILEAD
The Cultural Roots of Martin Luther King, Jr.

Interior design: Jim Gerhard

Cover design: Jim Gerhard

Library of Congress Cataloging-in-Publication Data

Baldwin, Lewis V., 1949–
    There is a balm in Gilead : the cultural roots of Martin Luther
King, Jr. / Lewis V. Baldwin.
        p.    cm.
    Includes bibliographical references (p.   ) and index.
    ISBN 0-8006-2457-2 (alk. paper)
    1. King, Martin Luther, Jr., 1929–1968.  2. King, Martin Luther,
Jr., 1929–1968—Philosophy.  3. Afro-Americans—Southern States.
4. Afro-Americans—Southern States—Religion.  5. Southern States—
Civilization—20th century.  I. Title.
E185.97.K5B35   1991
323'.092—dc20                                             90-13837
                                                              CIP

The paper used in this publication meets the minimum requirements of
American National Standard for Information Sciences—Permanence of
Paper for Printed Library Materials, ANSI Z329.48-1984.    ∞™

Manufactured in the U.S.A.                               AF 1-2457

95    94    93    92    91    1    2    3    4    5    6    7    8    9    10

# ACKNOWLEDGMENTS

Excerpts from *Stride toward Freedom* by Martin Luther King, Jr. Copyright © 1958 by Martin Luther King, Jr., renewed © 1986 by Coretta Scott King, Dexter King, Martin Luther King, III, Yolanda King and Bernice King. Reprinted by permission of HarperCollins, Publishers, Inc. and Joan Daves.

Excerpts from *Why We Can't Wait* by Martin Luther King, Jr. Copyright © 1963, 1964 by Martin Luther King, Jr. Reprinted by Permission of HarperCollins, Publishers, Inc. and Joan Daves.

Excerpts from *Where Do We Go From Here? Chaos or Community* by Martin Luther King, Jr. Copyright © 1967 by Martin Luther King, Jr. Reprinted by permission of HarperCollins, Publishers, Inc. and Joan Daves.

Excerpts from *Daddy King: An Autobiography* by Martin Luther King, Jr. Copyright © 1980 by the Reverend Tori Martin Luther King, Sr. Reprinted by permission of William Morrow & Co. and Joan Daves.

Excerpts from *My Life with Martin Luther King, Jr.*, by Coretta Scott King. Copyright © 1969 by Coretta Scott King. Reprinted by permission of Henry Holt and Company, Inc. and Joan Daves.

Excerpt from letter to Martin Luther King, Jr., 11-28-56. Reprinted by permission of Gil Burton Lloyd.

83/54

# CONTENTS

# PREFACE

This book was made possible by the assistance and encouragement of many persons. In addition to my own research in archives and libraries, I have benefitted from the insights of other scholars who have written important works on Martin Luther King, Jr. Dr. Kenneth L. Smith first sparked my interest in scholarship on King while I was a student at the Colgate-Rochester Divinity School/Bexley Hall/Crozer Theological Seminaries from 1971 to 1975. Dr. Smith, who taught the only course I ever took on King's life and thought and who served as my master's thesis advisor, suggested early in 1983 that I write a book assessing the impact of the black experience and the black church on King. Having taught King at Crozer Theological Seminary in the late 1940s, and having coauthored one of the few major works on King's intellectual sources with Ira G. Zepp, Jr., Dr. Smith has been in a position to offer advice and insight that few others can give.

I would like to acknowledge my debt to Professors James H. Cone, David J. Garrow, and Charles R. Wilson. Dr. Cone, the eminent black theologian who teaches at Union Theological Seminary, and I have had many friendly and stimulating conversations concerning our research on King since 1982. I have learned much from him about King, and we have freely shared the fruits of our research with each other. Dr. Garrow, a King scholar at the City College of the City University of New York, has been a constant source of information and insight, despite the fact that we differ substantially in our approaches to King. We have talked several times by phone, have had face-to-face conversations, and have communicated occasionally by mail. Dr. Wilson, who teaches at the University of Mississippi, has helped me more than he realizes. On December 8, 1984, Professors Wilson, Garrow, Cone, and myself presented papers on Martin Luther King, Jr., at the annual American Academy of Religion meeting in Chicago. Their papers gave me many new ideas, some of which are incorporated into this volume.

Professor Lawrence N. Jones of Howard University's School of Religion offered warm words of advice and support. At the very beginning of my work on this book, he suggested some leading queries that would make my research distinctive and contribute to an innovative perspective on King. A special word of thanks is due him for his assistance.

Several of my colleagues at Vanderbilt University read portions of the manuscript and offered constructive criticisms, helpful suggestions, and encouragement. They include Drs. Daniel Patte and Susan F. Wiltshire. Professor Jimmie L. Franklin, another Vanderbilt colleague, read the entire manuscript and made suggestions and critical analyses that were quite useful. His judgments regarding major parts of this work were immensely important, especially since he ranks among the best southern historians in the country. I am also grateful to another colleague, Peter J. Paris, who frequently reminded me of the necessity of completing this work, and whom I regard as one of the most brilliant King scholars around.

Former students in my courses on Martin Luther King, Jr., at Colgate University and Vanderbilt University contributed indirectly to the unfolding of this manuscript by the kind of intellectual excitement and stimulation they provided. Ron Liburd, a doctoral student at Vanderbilt who assisted me in one of my King courses, affected this work in very positive ways by the penetrating questions he raised from time to time.

I must express my deepest appreciation to a number of persons who shared information and insights with me through taped interviews. Emma Anderson and Sara V. Richardson, who had some association with Martin Luther King, Jr., during his student days at Crozer Theological Seminary and Calvary Baptist Church in Chester, Pennsylvania, had much to tell me about the private side of his life. Interviews with close friends and associates of King and the King family—the Reverends Ralph Abernathy, Charles Boddie, Michael E. Haynes, Robert Graetz, Bernard Lee, and Philip Lenud—added significantly to the substance and vitality of this book. Interviews with Ann Romaine, Director and Co-founder of the Southern Folk Cultural Revival Project in Nashville, Tennessee, and John Egerton, a Nashville writer who has published extensively on southern folkways and culture, enhanced my ability to treat King within a southern context. Romaine, one of the very few southern whites to function as a singer in some of the civil rights campaigns, offered rich information concerning the historical background of civil rights songs in the South. Egerton offered probing insights into how Dr. King's dietary habits related to his southern roots.

My thanks go to Louise Cook, Diane Ware, and Samantha McCoy, all of whom worked in the archives of the Martin Luther King, Jr., Center for Nonviolent Social Change during my research and writing. Cook, an archivist who has done valuable work in building a collection with the trove of King's unpublished sermons and speeches, gave me permission to look at these materials. Ware and McCoy assisted me in locating documents and in photocopying materials. I shall always remember their kindness and generosity.

I am also highly indebted to Dr. Howard Gotlieb and his staff in Special Collections at Boston University's Mugar Memorial Library for making available to me the many boxes of King papers there. They seemed particularly interested in my research and were always willing to help in any way they could.

I owe a special word of gratitude to the late Dr. John A. Hollar, who served as Editorial Director of Fortress Press. Dr. Hollar expressed a strong interest in my work from the beginning, and on many occasions reminded me of the importance of completing this book. I shall always remember his vision and his relentless commitment to the advancement of scholarship in religious studies.

I am grateful to Russell G. Hamilton and the University Research Council at Vanderbilt for furnishing financial assistance for me to do research at the King Center and at Boston University. It is great that the Vanderbilt Research Council has committed itself to supporting the research of young Vanderbilt scholars like myself.

I owe a special word of gratitude to Pat Mundy, who spent many hours typing this manuscript. She is a person of outstanding character and ability, and I was blessed to benefit from her work.

The book has received substance and spirit from my charming wife, Jacqueline, who has been my loving critic and companion. Her love and warmth helped me endure the many long nights I spent writing this manuscript.

With such debts of gratitude I offer this book to the reader, hoping that it will help students, scholars, and persons in other walks of life to understand better the faith and the culture to which Martin Luther King, Jr., was heir. I realize that it is not the final word on Dr. King's cultural roots. It really was never intended to be other than a preliminary word. If it succeeds in awakening interest and stimulating serious questions among a few of the many admirers and followers of King, I shall feel more than sufficiently rewarded. I am sure that those who worked closely with me in this effort would say the same.

Lewis V. Baldwin
Nashville, Tennessee

# INTRODUCTION

Is there no balm in Gilead?
Is there no physician there?
Why then is not the health
of the daughter of my people recovered?

Jeremiah 8:22

There is a balm in Gilead,
To make the wounded whole.
There is a balm in Gilead,
To heal the sin-sick soul.

Slave spiritual

Early in 1965, Martin Luther King, Jr., addressed a small crowd of black people outside the Antioch Baptist Church in Camden, Alabama, a town located in the heart of the so-called Alabama Blackbelt. He had only recently received the Nobel Peace Prize and was beginning to expand his vision and crusade beyond integration to issues of political rights, economic justice, and international peace. Tremendous pride and excitement filled the atmosphere in Camden on that occasion as King, often glancing at the white policemen who nervously circled the crowd, spoke eloquently and fearlessly of the need for a voting rights bill. One young woman, after shaking Dr. King's hand, declared that she would never wash her hands again. Her action was indicative of how blacks regarded the civil rights leader in the South. Black southerners recognized King as one of their own—one who shared their cultural roots and experiences, spoke their language, reflected their profound spirituality and rhythmic consciousness, possessed their gift for storytelling and deep laughter, embraced their festive and celebrative approach to life, and symbolized their strong optimism regarding the possibility of actualizing an inclusive human community within history.[1]

Though the subject of King's roots in southern black culture has occupied my thought for more than a decade, it was not until eight years ago that I began to reflect on it in entirely new ways. Actually, the conceptual framework for this study developed gradually as I examined the trove of King's unpublished papers, particularly his spontaneously delivered sermons in black churches and his speeches at black community rallies. The theoretical grounding for the study was first set forth in my 1987 essay, "Understanding Martin Luther King, Jr. within the Context of Southern Black Religious History." That essay's argument—that the black experience and the black Christian tradition were the most important sources in the shaping of King's life, thought, vision, and efforts to translate the ethical ideal of the beloved community into practical reality—is advanced here with greater interpretive depth and clarity. The main contention here is that we cannot possibly understand King's interpretation and appropriation of the Bible, of Gandhian ideas and methods, of Western philosophical categories, of the principles of American participatory democracy, of Reinhold Niebuhr's Christian realism, and of Personal-

---

1. Lewis V. Baldwin, "Family and Church: The Roots of Martin Luther King, Jr.," *National Baptist Union-Review* 91, no. 1 (January 1987): 1, 3.

istic and Social Gospel concepts without carefully considering how the black experience of oppression and the traditions of the black church influenced him.[2]

The failure of many scholars to recognize that King's genius was "folk, black, and southern" may be attributed in large measure to racism and to some extent an anti-southern bias.[3] Many books and articles on King reflect a narrow, elitist, and racist approach that assumes that the black church and the larger black community are not healthy and vital contexts for the origin of intellectual ideas regarding theology and social change.[4] The consequence of that approach has been to abstract King's intellectual development from his social and religious roots—family, church, and the larger black community— and to treat it primarily as a product of white Western philosophy and theology.[5] This approach not only minimizes the importance of the sociohistorical context that produced King, but it also overlooks much of the power and creativity he brought to his task as a preacher, theologian, and social activist. Though King was deeply influenced by his training at Crozer Theological Seminary and Boston University, it is a mistake to conclude that his revolt was rooted in white political and theological sources.

2. James H. Cone, "Martin Luther King, Jr., Black Theology—Black Church," *Theology Today* 40, no. 4 (January 1984): 409–12; and Lewis V. Baldwin, "Understanding Martin Luther King, Jr. within the Context of Southern Black Religious History," *Journal of Religious Studies* 13, no. 2 (Fall 1987): 9–10.

3. Julius R. Scruggs, *Baptist Preachers with Social Consciousness: A Comparative Study of Martin Luther King, Jr. and Harry Emerson Fosdick* (Philadelphia: Dorrance and Company, 1978), vii; and James W. McClendon, Jr., *Biography as Theology: How Life Stories Can Re-make Today's Theology* (Nashville: Abingdon Press, 1974), 67–85.

4. Cone, "Martin Luther King, Jr., Black Theology—Black Church," 411.

5. If scholars can keep Martin Luther King, Jr., within a lily-white intellectual tradition, they do not have to deal seriously with his blackness and his significance as an international symbol. Typical of what appears to be a surreptitious design to relegate King's black cultural heritage to a marginal position are Kenneth L. Smith and Ira G. Zepp, Jr., *Search for the Beloved Community: The Thinking of Martin Luther King, Jr.* (Valley Forge, Pa.: Judson Press, 1974); and John J. Ansbro, *Martin Luther King, Jr.: The Making of a Mind* (Maryknoll, N.Y.: Orbis, 1982).

Three central themes run through this book, giving it continuity and determining its direction. The first is *sense of place in a southern context*—a quality that was apparently high on King's scale of values. Sense of place is the notion that our humanness is closely related to our actual rootedness in a particular environment. The argument here is that King was *quintessentially southern*, not only because he was born and raised in the South, but also because his identity, commitment, sense of purpose, and quest for meaning were intimately associated with that region.[6] The South was a place filled with memories of life that linked him to a past and to a particular people in their struggle for freedom and human dignity. King felt an attachment to southern black life and the whole cultural spectrum in the South that was intimate and profound. The vital and nourishing symbols of that culture, which revolved around family, religion, and a system of ideas, values, and customs, meant so much in terms of his own personal growth, social awareness, and spiritual development. Although King often identified himself as a southern black preacher concerned about the redemption and transformation of southern society, that does not preclude his standing as a world figure with a universal message.[7]

*Community* is a second theme coursing through this book. A completely integrated society based on love and justice, and that transcends race, sex, class, religion,

6. Lewis V. Baldwin, "'Let Us Break Bread Together': Martin Luther King, Jr. and the Black Church in the South (1954–1968)" (Paper presented at the Southern Historical Association Meeting, New Orleans, La., 13 November 1987), 1–31; Martin Luther King, Jr., "An Autobiography of Religious Development" (Unpublished document from The King Papers, Mugar Memorial Library, Boston University, Boston, Mass., n.d., circa 1950), 1–15; and James Baldwin, "The Dangerous Road before Martin Luther King," *Harper's Magazine* (February 1961): 38.

7. Baldwin, "'Let Us Break Bread Together'," 3–4; Baldwin, "The Dangerous Road before Martin Luther King," 38; Martin Luther King, Jr., *Stride toward Freedom: The Montgomery Story* (New York: Harper & Brothers, 1958), 21–22; and King, "An Autobiography of Religious Development," 1–15; Lewis V. Baldwin, ed., *Toward the Beloved Community: Martin Luther King, Jr. and South African Apartheid* (unpublished manuscript), 1–20, 275–317.

nationality, and other artificial human barriers, was the most pervasive theme in King's sermons and writings. King's earliest understanding of community was developed within the contexts of family, church, and the larger black community of Atlanta, Georgia.[8] His beloved-community vision had a particular relevance for the South, but it also included the whole of humankind.[9]

The third theme permeating this volume is *Christian optimism*, which is descriptive of King's outlook on the future of humanity and the world. His Christian optimism, rooted in a cultural heritage stemming back to his slave forebears, affirmed that in spite of human suffering and the tragic circumstances of life, God will ultimately emerge triumphant over evil and bring liberation and salvation to all people.[10] This conception of hope, "expressed in terms of the Christian doctrine of the Kingdom of God," undergirded King's vision of the beloved community and sustained him in his efforts for the realization of that ideal.[11] His Christian optimism is boldly reflected in the title of this book, *There Is a Balm in Gilead*, taken from a slave spiritual that evolved from an incurable faith in God and a belief in the essential goodness of humanity. King's frequent references to this song

8. This contention is brilliantly advanced in Walter E. Fluker, *They Looked for a City: A Comparative Analysis of the Ideal of Community in the Thought of Howard Thurman and Martin Luther King, Jr.* (Lanham, Md.: University Press of America, 1989), 81–107.

9. This view is substantiated by Martin Luther King, Jr., *Where Do We Go from Here: Chaos or Community?* (Boston: Beacon Press, 1967), 1–191; and Baldwin, ed., *Toward the Beloved Community*, 1–20, 275–317.

10. King, *Stride toward Freedom*, 224; and Lewis V. Baldwin, "Martin Luther King, Jr., the Black Church, and the Black Messianic Vision," *The Journal of the Interdenominational Theological Center* 12, nos. 1 and 2 (Fall 1984/Spring 1985): 104–7. Two important sources that underscore Christian hope in the black tradition, with some emphasis on its influence on Martin Luther King, Jr., are William D. Watley, *Roots of Resistance: The Nonviolent Ethic of Martin Luther King, Jr.* (Valley Forge, Pa.: Judson Press, 1985), 41–44; and Cornel West, *Prophetic Fragments* (Grand Rapids, Mich.: W.B. Eerdmans, 1988), 38–49, 161–65. West's concepts of "aggressive pessimism" and "revolutionary patience" are similar to my view of "Christian optimism."

11. Smith and Zepp, *Search for the Beloved Community*, 11–12; and Baldwin, "Martin Luther King, Jr., the Black Church, and the Black Messianic Vision," 103–7.

in sermons and speeches, especially before black audiences, evidenced his burning desire to keep hope alive in
the crusade for equal rights and social justice.

This book differs from previous scholarship on King in
that it is the first extensive treatment of his roots in black
folk culture, particularly that of the South. It shows how
King turned again and again to the black South, especially to his family and church, for purposes of identity,
orientation, affirmation, and empowerment. The Southern Christian Leadership Conference (S.C.L.C.), organized under King's leadership in 1957, was a living symbol
of his reliance on the values and institutions of black
southerners, and it also symbolized his vision of "a new
South" in which blacks and whites could live and work
together in peace and harmony, thereby serving as a
model for the rest of the nation and the entire world.[12]

Significantly, this book is not a biography of King
in the conventional sense, nor is it an attempt to explore
the full range of his intellectual sources. Numerous
books and articles have already been written by scholars
with these concerns in mind. The work here simply un-
derscores and supports the claim that King's cultural
heritage must be carefully studied before we get a full
portrait of the man, the movement, the message, and the
legacy.

Chapter 1 discusses King within the framework of
southern history and culture. The primary focus is on
his roots in the black community of Atlanta, Georgia, his
sense of place within a southern context, his assessment
of the condition of his people, and his understanding
of the roles that blacks and whites should play in transforming the political culture and socioeconomic climate
of the South and of America at large. The argument

12. A letter from Martin Luther King, Jr., to Buford Boone, 9 May
1957, The King Papers, Boston University; Martin Luther King, Jr., "An
Address to the National Press Club" Washington, D.C. (The King Papers,
Boston University, 19 July 1962), 1ff.; and Martin Luther King, Jr.,
"Transcript of a Press Conference at Liberty Baptist Church," Chicago,
Ill., (The Archives of the Martin Luther King, Jr., Center for Nonviolent
Social Change, Inc., Atlanta, Ga., 24 March 1967), 1.

here is that King's sense of reality was shaped primarily by southern culture and broadened by his exposure to and serious dialogue with other cultures with different worldviews. He spoke for the black South, but he was also an impassioned voice and servant for all humanity. The civil rights movement is discussed here as largely an effort on the part of King and his followers to revitalize the South and to prepare it for a great moral, spiritual, political, and economic prosperity.

Chapter 2 examines King's family background, with special attention to his relationships with his parents, siblings, and extended family; his family heritage of social activism; his view of the ideal family life and how that was reflected in his own life as a father and husband; and the importance of family as a support network in helping him to cope with anxiety over social reality, severe external dangers, and rapidly growing fame. An examination of King's family background and relations and their influence on his life, thought, and activities is crucial for a general consideration of his relationship to the black cultural heritage.

Chapter 3 treats Martin Luther King, Jr., within the context of the black Christian tradition—a tradition distinguished from the Western Christian tradition by its greater emphasis on egalitarian values and an inclusive vision of the faith, or by what Peter J. Paris calls "its non-racist appropriation of the Christian faith."[13] The contention here is that the black church tradition was the most important single source in the development of King's faith, thought, vision, and method to achieve equal rights and social justice. Although he sometimes criticized the emotional and anti-intellectual side of the southern black church, he nevertheless was constantly inspired by that institution's potential as a source of community, spirituality, Christian optimism, and social

13. Peter J. Paris, "The Bible and the Black Churches," in *The Bible and Social Reform*, ed. Ernest R. Sandeen (Philadelphia: Fortress Press, 1982), 134.

activism.[14] The black church in the South, with its vital mixture of fundamental meanings and institutional forms, provided King with a rich spiritual heritage that extended beyond his parents and grandparents to his slave ancestors. He returned constantly to the black church for affirmation, inspiration, courage, and hope. Although King's basic theological and ethical perspectives were rooted in the black church—an institution he both criticized and praised—they were refined and occasionally "reshaped in the midst of conflict and action," and by his openness to goodness and truth in other religious and philosophical traditions.[15]

Given the diversity within the black church community, one might wonder why "black Christian tradition" is employed here as a single or unified phenomenon. This book rests on the conviction that black Christians in America, despite the differences that separate them, have historically been the products of a cultural experience dominated by oppression and have engaged in a common quest for equal rights and social justice. Their common heritage, experiences, and tendencies have led to an emphasis on certain common values and customs that make it possible to speak of "the black Christian tradition" or "the black church" in a broad and inclusive sense.[16]

Chapter 4 explores King's view of the meaning of the black odyssey in America. His black messianic vision, which held that the intense suffering and humiliation of his people had equipped them for a special mission on behalf of humanity, is discussed against the background of similar views expressed by Sojourner Truth, Robert A. Young, David Walker, Martin Delany, Alexander Crum-

---

14. Baldwin, "Understanding Martin Luther King, Jr.," 2; and Baldwin, "'Let Us Break Bread Together,'" 2, 11, 13–16.
15. Baldwin, "'Let Us Break Bread Together,'" 11–16; and Watley, *Roots of Resistance*, 15, 17–45.
16. The problem involved in the use of "black church" as a uniform or monolithic phenomenon is referred to in Hans A. Baer, *The Black Spiritual Movement: A Religious Response to Racism* (Knoxville, Tenn.: University of Tennessee Press, 1984), 12. Baer concludes, however, that there is "a certain heuristic value" in speaking of "black church."

mell, Edward W. Blyden, John E. Bruce, W. E. B. Du Bois, Claude McKay, Paul Robeson, Jesse Jackson, and others. Particular attention is devoted to the role King assigned the black church in this messianic vocation, and to the capacity of that institution to fulfill that role in the future. King's image as a black messiah, and the distinct ways in which he articulated his black messianism, is also considered. In a unique way, his feelings about his people's identity, their relationship to America, and their role in world history presented a serious challenge to that wall of negative images the white Western world sought to project about black humanity.

The extent to which King embodied and reflected the black preaching tradition is covered in chapter 5. In his work as a preacher, pastor, priest, and prophet, he represented a tradition that extended from slave preachers like Harry Hoosier and John Jasper to generations of black preachers since slavery.[17] This chapter addresses the following questions: Why did Martin Luther King, Jr., choose the Christian ministry as a life vocation? What was the nature of his preaching prior to the Rosa Parks affair? How was his perception of ministry expressed at Dexter Avenue Baptist Church in Montgomery, Alabama, and Ebenezer Baptist Church in Atlanta, Georgia? To what extent did he combine the preaching, pastoral, priestly, and prophetic dimensions in his public ministry? What was the internal nature of his leadership in the S.C.L.C., and how did he relate to and nurture staff? Did his work as a minister, quite apart from his nonviolent philosophy, reflect the overwhelming influence of his religious past? What was the role of prayer in his movements, and what was the content of his prayers? Did he make any specific references to his ordination statement or personal creed? How did he view the Bible and its authority? How did he relate to

17. Baldwin, "Understanding Martin Luther King, Jr.," 7–8; and Lewis V. Baldwin, "The Minister as Preacher, Pastor, and Prophet: The Thinking of Martin Luther King, Jr.," *The American Baptist Quarterly* 7, no. 2 (June 1988): 89–92.

other clergy?[18] Answers to these questions are provided
largely on the basis of the testimony of King and some of
his former associates in the S.C.L.C., and they indicate
the tremendous importance that King attached to the
role of the black preacher as an advocate for justice, as
a fashioner of culture, as a symbol of hope, and as a
shaper of the spiritual destiny of his people.

*There Is a Balm in Gilead* will be followed by a second
volume, *To Make the Wounded Whole: The Cultural Legacy of Martin Luther King, Jr.*, which will treat King's
critiques of and dialogues with other more conservative
and radical black approaches to the black condition, his
influence on and legacy for black theology and ethics,
his view on the relationship between the African and
Afro-American struggles, and his vision of world community.[19] Both volumes, when considered together, will
demonstrate how King, the black intellectual, maintained continuity with black mass culture in America.[20]
They will also show that King, despite his middle-class
background, shared the pain, the struggles, the hopes,
and the aspirations of the poor and oppressed throughout the world. Generally speaking, the general thrust of
the two volumes will reveal how King's vision gradually

18. I am greatly indebted to Dr. Lawrence N. Jones, black church
scholar and Dean of Howard University's School of Religion, for assistance in the formulation of these questions. See a letter from Lawrence N.
Jones, to Lewis V. Baldwin, 26 August 1985.

19. These concerns have not been treated adequately in relation to
King. Interestingly enough, they are largely ignored even in works like
William R. Miller, "The Broadening Horizons: Montgomery, America,
the World," in *Martin Luther King, Jr.: A Profile*, ed. C. Eric Lincoln (New
York: Hill and Wang, 1986), 40–71.

20. Very few scholars have ably demonstrated the historic continuity
between black intellectual life and the culture of the black masses in the
United States. Exceptions are Sterling Stuckey, *Slave Culture: Nationalist Theory and the Foundations of Black America* (New York: Oxford
University Press, 1987), chaps. 1–6; and Lawrence W. Levine, *Black Culture and Black Consciousness: Afro-American Folk Thought from Slavery
to Freedom* (New York: Oxford University Press, 1977), chaps. 1–6. For
this observation, I am greatly indebted to Wilson J. Moses, *Alexander
Crummell: A Study of Civilization and Discontent* (New York: Oxford
University Press, 1989), 9.

transcended southern particularism to assume national and international implications.[21]

Such a two-volume work is particularly important at this point in history for two reasons. First, it deflects what was written in the 1980s by authors seemingly determined to diminish King's image as a person and as a gifted, effective, moral leader. David J. Garrow's *Bearing the Cross* (1986) and Ralph D. Abernathy's *And the Walls Came Tumbling Down* (1989) are typical of such writings.[22] The works by Garrow and Abernathy highlight King's alleged moral indiscretions and his vulnerabilities as a strategist and leader and have increased the need for more balanced treatments of King's life and work. Second, King's relevance for the continuing human struggle worldwide must be seriously studied and reassessed. Ethical dialogue with King around the issues of peace, freedom, justice, and community can be fruitful for a world seeking to overcome racism, sexism, poverty, and war.[23]

The contents of this work rest on the notion that King's published books and essays are as reliable as his largely unpublished, spontaneously delivered sermons, speeches, and mass meeting addresses for understanding him and for interpreting the evolution and changing emphases in his thought. Garrow has consistently warned scholars away from primary reliance on King's published books and essays, noting that these sources were largely ghostwritten by Al Duckett, Harris Wofford, Stanley Levison, Bayard Rustin, and other advisers to King. Garrow points specifically to *Why We*

21. This development is treated to some degree in Baldwin, ed., *Toward the Beloved Community,* introduction and concluding essay; Fluker, *They Looked for a City,* chaps. 4–6; and Miller, "The Broadening Horizons," 40–71.

22. This work was almost completed when Abernathy's book appeared in published form. For a critical but fairly objective review of the book, see Lewis V. Baldwin, "Abernathy Book Controversial, Marred by Claim," *Nashville Banner,* 18 November 1989.

23. Baldwin, ed., *Toward the Beloved Community,* 1–20, 275–317.

*Can't Wait* (1964), which was almost completely ghost-written by Duckett, to *Stride toward Freedom* (1958), and to *Where Do We Go from Here: Chaos or Community?* (1967), which include extensive pieces of material prepared by Wofford, Levison, Rustin, and others.[24] The "King" one sees in these sources, according to Garrow, "is at some considerable distance, in many particulars, from the King one sees in the largely unpublished, spontaneously delivered sermons in black churches and mass meeting addresses at Southern community rallies." Garrow establishes the reliability of the wealth of King's extemporaneous, unpublished texts on the grounds that "there's no editorial revisions or 'toning up' of the language by King advisers in these manuscript texts."[25] He concludes that the "naive over-reliance" of scholars "on the least dependable King texts, coupled with the limited usage that commentators have made of the much more dependable, and often extemporaneous, unpublished King texts, has unfortunately led to a situation in which much existing scholarship on King is of little serious, long-term value, and in which truly dependable studies of his thought are just getting underway or beginning to appear."[26]

James H. Cone has stressed as strongly as Garrow the unreliability of King's published works for providing

24. A letter from David J. Garrow, to Lewis V. Baldwin, 24 September 1984; a letter from David J. Garrow, to Lewis V. Baldwin, 2 February 1985; and David J. Garrow, "The Intellectual Development of Martin Luther King, Jr.: Influences and Commentaries," *Union Seminary Quarterly Review* 40, no. 4 (January 1986): 5–6.
25. Garrow, letter to Baldwin, 24 September 1984.
26. Garrow, "The Intellectual Development of Martin Luther King, Jr.," 5. Garrow regards King's published books as being carefully prepared "for presentation to a largely northern, largely white, and largely well-educated audience of potential contributors." Scholarly works such as Hanes Walton, Jr.'s *The Political Philosophy of Martin Luther King, Jr.* (1971) and Ansbro's *Martin Luther King, Jr.: The Making of a Mind* (1982), which have drawn heavily on King's published works, are dismissed by Garrow as "workman-like exegeses of the 'King' that he, and his advisers, thought most attractive to the northern audience whose support the movement needed, but that 'King' is a spiritual stick-figure, so to speak, compared to the actual man." See a letter from Garrow, to Baldwin, 24 September 1984.

a dependable analysis of his life and thought. Cone insists that "Working for the movement 20 hours a day, traveling 325,000 miles and making 450 speeches a year, it was not possible for King to write everything that was published under his name."[27] Like Garrow, Cone declares that the unpublished materials at Atlanta's King Center and Boston University's Mugar Memorial Library provide vastly more support, both substantively and linguistically, for the contention that King was a product of black folk culture in the South.[28]

Garrow and Cone have been engaged in a serious effort to do revisionist scholarship on Martin Luther King, Jr. However, I am not convinced of the soundness of their arguments concerning the limitations of King's published texts. In cases where ghostwriters prepared King's books, essays, and speeches, they took words out of his mouth instead of putting words into his mouth. It is unreasonable for anyone to expect a man of King's greatness and level of social involvement to write every word of his books, essays, and speeches.[29] But such works were published with his approval, and there is no evidence that he disclaimed any of these texts. I personally have found no important discrepancies between what appears in King's edited and sometimes ghostwritten works and what is included in his extemporaneous, unpublished texts. King's personality and the basic outlines of his thought are evident in both. Garrow and Cone make too

27. James H. Cone, "The Theology of Martin Luther King, Jr.," *Union Seminary Quarterly Review* 40, no. 4 (January 1986): 39 n. 30. This point is also forcefully made in Garrow, "The Intellectual Development of Martin Luther King, Jr.," 5.

28. Cone, "The Theology of Martin Luther King, Jr.," 21–39; and a letter from Garrow, to Baldwin, 24 September 1984.

29. However, King did occasionally mention in his interviews and in letters addressed to others the considerable time he spent working on his books—comments that Garrow and Cone have apparently ignored. For example, in March 1967, King said in an interview, "I spent the months of January and February completing my book" or "working on the chapters of my book," which is "entitled, *Where Do We Go from Here: Chaos or Community?*" See Martin Luther King, Jr., "Transcript of a Press Conference at Liberty Baptist Church," Chicago, Ill. (The King Center Archives, 24 March 1967), 1.

much of the fact that many of King's texts were heavily edited and ghostwritten, and if the standards and limitations they have applied to King's published works are applied to those of other great men and women in our history, the history books would have to be largely rewritten in order to be reliable. My contention is that any dependable picture of King's personality, thinking, and activities must draw on both his published and unpublished texts.

A book of this nature may invite controversy, despite my efforts at objectivity. I hope those scholars and students who recognize significant gaps in historical consciousness and interpretation will fill those gaps with supplementary research and publications. Whatever shortcomings or defects may be found in this book, I want to make two relevant observations that guided my research and writing. First, this book is by one who, like Martin Luther King, Jr., was born and raised as a black man in the segregated South, steeped in the traditions of southern black Baptist Protestantism. Having been shaped by many of the same forces that produced King, and having felt much of his pain in a very personal way, I bring to this study the distinctive sensitivity of that shared experience. Second, this work constitutes another contribution to our effort to more fully understand King, who was in some ways a complex and multifaceted personality. My hope is that it will lead to other scholarly attempts to capture the spirit of this phenomenal figure.

# CAST DOWN YOUR BUCKET 1
## BACK HOME TO AN OLD SOUTHERN PLACE

> To those of my race who depend on bettering their condition in a foreign land or who underestimate the importance of cultivating friendly relations with the Southern white man, who is their next-door neighbor, I would say, "Cast down your bucket where you are"—cast it down in making friends in every manly way of the people of all races by whom we are surrounded.
>
> Booker T. Washington, 1895[1]

> The future of the American Negro is in the South. . . . This is the firing line not simply for the emancipation of the American Negro but for the emancipation of the African Negro and the Negroes of the West Indies; for the emancipation of the colored races; and for the emancipation of the white slaves of modern capitalistic monopoly.
>
> W. E. B. Du Bois, 1946[2]

> I have a deep sense of responsibility at this point and feel, for the next few years at least, that my place is here in the deep South doing all in my power to alleviate the tensions that exist between Negro and white citizens.
>
> Martin Luther King, Jr., 1958[3]

Martin Luther King, Jr., was one of the greatest prophets and distinguished reformers to emerge from the American South. A southerner by birth and heritage, he

1. Quoted in Philip S. Foner, ed., *The Voice of Black America: Major Speeches by Blacks in the United States, 1797–1973*, vol. 1 (New York: Capricorn Books, 1975), 609.

2. W. E. B. Du Bois, "Behold the Land," *Freedomways*, 4, no. 1 (Winter 1964): 12.

3. A letter from Martin Luther King, Jr., to Dr. Dwight Loder (5 August 1958, The Collection of the Institute for Black Religious Research, Garrett-Evangelical Theological Seminary, Evanston, Ill.

spent most of his thirty-nine years in the South, strug-
gling against the narrow economic, political, and racial
divisions that kept that region from attaining its highest
potential and richest ideals. He wished for a South in
which race and class would not be considerations in the
granting of rights, privileges, and opportunity. King's
distinctive understanding of truth, as well as the nonviolent methods he used in its pursuit, served as a vital
and provocative challenge to many of the South's cultural assumptions and values, and also to the general
tendency among people in our nation and throughout
the world to value materialism more than personhood,
individualism at the expense of community, and war
more than peace.

This chapter treats King's relationship to the South
and to southern culture. Special attention is devoted to
his roots in the black community of Atlanta, Georgia,
to his early experiences with racism and classism, to his
sense of regional identity and regional responsibility, to
his assessment of the condition of his people, and to his
vision of a "new South."

## GROWING UP IN THE SOUTH

King's early intellectual, spiritual, and emotional formation occurred in a climate imbued with the spirit of
southern life and culture. He was born January 15,
1929, in Atlanta, Georgia, a city known variously as "the
gateway to the South," "the New York of the South," and
"the unofficial capital of the South." He was of relatively privileged birth, despite his birth into a community that "was quite ordinary in terms of social status."
"I have never experienced the feeling of not having the
basic necessities of life," he once wrote.[4] Both of King's

4. Martin Luther King, Jr., "An Autobiography of Religious Development" (Unpublished document from The King Papers, Mugar Memorial Library, Boston University, Boston, Mass. n.d., circa 1950), 1–4;
Lenwood G. Davis, *I Have a Dream: The Life and Times of Martin Luther
King, Jr.* (Westport, Conn.: Negro Universities Press, 1969), 10; and James

parents were college trained, talented, and quite prosperous. His father, Martin Luther King, Sr., was a community leader and pastor of the Ebenezer Baptist
Church, a successful black congregation in Atlanta. His
mother, Alberta, was a school teacher and an accomplished pianist. Through his parents, Martin, Jr. (called
"Mike" and "M. L." as a child) very early had close contact with the most vital aspects of southern black culture, particularly music and religion. Thus he had a
solid cultural foundation on which he would later build
as a preacher and social activist.[5]

The Atlanta of King's childhood was similar to many
southern cities and quite typical of the South generally.
It was not the rural South, but many of its black and
white residents had come from rural areas and tended
to reflect a folksy, rural southern life-style. It was larger
and more industrialized and commercialized than most
southern cities, but it still had its share of maids, farmers, and other types of common laborers. Atlanta also
had more educated, prosperous, and sophisticated people than most southern cities, but many of its residents
were illiterate, poverty stricken, and simple minded.[6]
The lives of its citizens were dominated by the conventions of Jim Crow, blatantly symbolized in segregated
housing, churches, schools, hotels, theaters, rest rooms,
lunch counters, buses, and centers of recreation. The Ku
Klux Klan and other racist elements were visibly present,
and black Atlantans suffered emotionally and physically
from the daily routine of abusive language and mistreatment, as was the case with every black person in the

---

Haskins, *The Life and Death of Martin Luther King, Jr.* (New York:
Lothrop, Lee and Shepard, 1977), 13.

5. "Daddy King: 'There's No Hate in My Heart'," *The Chicago Tribune* (December 23, 1980): Section 2, 1, 4; and Martin Luther King, Sr.,
with Clayton Riley, *Daddy King: An Autobiography* (New York: William
Morrow, 1980), foreword, introduction, and 127–31.

6. Davis, *I Have a Dream*, 10; King, "An Autobiography of Religious
Development," 4–5; and *Atlanta: A City of the Modern South*, compiled by
workers of The Writer's Program of The Work Projects Administration in
the State of Georgia (New York: Smith and Durrell, 1942), 5.

South. This was the South with which King became familiar from early childhood.[7]

The black population of Atlanta consisted of some 90,000 persons, or thirty-three percent of the city's total population at the time of King's birth, and it was sharply divided along class lines and scattered in large and small pockets throughout the city.[8] King recalled that "Most of the Negroes in my home town who had attained wealth lived in a section of town known as 'Hunter Hills'." Many professional blacks—bankers, contractors, college professors, morticians, doctors, real estate agents, and ministers—also maintained attractive homes along Ashby Street and in the vicinity of the Atlanta University complex.[9]

The Auburn Avenue section on the northeast side of Atlanta, where King lived, was described in the 1940s as "a quiet Negro business district of decorous hotels and office buildings."[10] According to King, this section comprised blacks of average income who shared a sense of community and spiritual values that created very strong bonds of emotional security:

> The community in which I was born was characterized with a sort of unsophisticated simplicity. No one in our community was in the extremely poor class. This community was not the slum district. It is probably fair to class the people of this community as those of average income. Yet I insist that this was a wholesome community, notwithstanding the fact that none of us were [sic] ever considered members of the

7. King, *Daddy King*, chap. 9; King, "An Autobiography of Religious Development," 11–13; and "Face to Face: John Freeman of B.B.C. Interviews Martin Luther King, Jr.," U. K., London, (Transcribed from a TV telediphone recording, The Archives of the Martin Luther King, Jr., Center for Nonviolent Social Change, Inc., Atlanta, Ga., 29 October 1961). 1–5.
8. See Chalmers A. McMahan, "A Demographic Study of Atlanta, Georgia," Ph.D. diss., Vanderbilt University (Spring 1949), 263.
9. King, "An Autobiography of Religious Development," 4; *Atlanta: A City of the Modern South*, 5; and David L. Lewis, *King: A Critical Biography* (New York: Praeger Publishers, 1970), 8–10.
10. *Atlanta: A City of the Modern South*, 5.

"upper, upper class." Crime was at a minimum in our community, and most of our neighbors were deeply religious.[11]

Despite the comfort and security of his own home and neighborhood, King developed an early awareness of and sensitivity to the impact of poverty on large numbers of his people in the 1930s and 1940s. His neighborhood on Auburn Avenue was located up the hill from a poor black ghetto area.[12] Poor blacks lived squalidly along streets in many parts of the city where, as one Atlanta historian reported, "the ramshackle wooden shanties and rooming houses are crowded with many families and the streets are noisy with the cries of little ragged brown children." In the early 1940s, a considerable number of poor blacks often gathered on Decatur Street, which ran "eastward between rows of pawnshops with crowded windows, restaurants emitting the sharp smell of frying fish, and clothing stores with suits and overcoats hung over ropes along the pavements." Here a lively scene existed "full of animation" with "an eternal symphony of gay noises—the crack of rifles in the shooting galleries, the wooden clatter of balls in the poolrooms, the thin, fast music of sidewalk phonographs, and always the voices, loud but musical."[13] King did not escape the impact of this side of black life. He wrote on one occasion, "I could never get out of my mind the economic insecurity of many of my playmates and the tragic poverty of those living around me."[14]

The extent and painful effects of poverty among both blacks and whites in Atlanta became particularly evident to young King during the Great Depression. "I was much too young to remember the beginning of this depression," he declared, "but I do recall how I questioned my parents

11. King, "An Autobiography of Religious Development," 4–5.
12. Haskins, The Life and Death of Martin Luther King, Jr., 14; and Martin Luther King, Jr., *Stride Toward Freedom: The Montgomery Story* (New York: Harper & Brothers, 1958), 90.
13. *Atlanta: A City of the Modern South*, 5.
14. King, *Stride toward Freedom*, 90.

about the numerous people standing in bread lines when I was about five years of age."[15] Living in close proximity to the poor, King witnessed very early the cutthroat competition and selfish ambition that caused the wealthy to prosper at the expense of the less fortunate. "I saw economic injustice firsthand," he said, "and realized that the poor white was exploited just as much as the Negro."[16] Experiences of this nature later helped keep him from losing his sense of values despite his own economic security and growing fame.[17] Indeed, such childhood experiences accounted in large measure for King's openness to Karl Marx's and Walter Rauschenbusch's critiques of capitalism in later years.[18]

The relationship between economic injustice and racial injustice in the South had emerged clearly in King's mind by the time he reached his teens. Environmental factors and the experience of being black in the segregated South were primary in the shaping of his consciousness at this level.[19] "As far back as I could remember," he wrote, "I had resented segregation, and had asked my parents urgent and pointed questions about it. While I was still too young for school I had already learned something about discrimination. . . . I had grown up abhorring not only segregation but also the oppressive and barbarious acts that grew out of it."[20] King saw how the system of racism in the South was designed to secure white power and domination over virtually all areas of black life—economic, political, religious, social, and intellectual:

> I remember as a child seeing problems of police brutality, and this was mainly aimed at Negro children

15. King, "An Autobiography of Religious Development," 1.
16. King, *Stride toward Freedom*, 90.
17. *Ibid.*, 90–95; and King, "An Autobiography of Religious Development," 1.
18. King, *Stride toward Freedom*, 90; King, "An Autobiography of Religious Development," 1; and King, *Daddy King*, 23–128.
19. King, *Stride toward Freedom*, 90; and King, "An Autobiography of Religious Development," 1–15.
20. King, *Stride toward Freedom*, 18–19; and "Face to Face," 1–5.

and Negro adults. I can remember also the organization that is known as the Ku Klux Klan—this is an
organization that, in those days, even used violent
methods to preserve segregation and to keep the Negro in his place, so to speak. Now I can remember
seeing the Klan actually beat Negroes on some of the
streets there in Atlanta.[21]

Such experiences undoubtedly increased King's sense
of the bonds and obligations he shared with even the
poorest and most illiterate black people in the South.
Their pain was his pain, and their struggle was inevitably
his struggle. This sense of a shared experience of suffering and struggle was also heightened by King's own personal bout with racism. He recounted that as a child
restrictions barred him from the swimming pools, the
public parks, the white high schools, the theaters, and
the lunch counters at many of the stores in downtown
Atlanta.[22] At six years of age, he witnessed vicious attacks
upon his father's manhood by white policemen and mer-
chants.[23] In his adult life, King frequently alluded to two
other racist incidents during his childhood which "still
live with me a great deal":

When I was about eight years old I was in one of
the downtown stores of Atlanta, and all of a sudden
someone slapped me, and the only thing I heard was
somebody saying, "You're that nigger that stepped on
my foot." And it turned out to be a white lady, and of
course I didn't retaliate at any point. I finally went
and told my mother what had happened and she was
very upset about it, but at that time the lady who

---

21. "Face to Face," 4; and King, *Stride toward Freedom*, 18–22, 90.
22. "Face to Face," 1–5; and Martin Luther King, Jr., "A Speech to
Blacks," Grenada, Miss. (The King Center Archives, June, 1966), 3.
23. King, *Stride toward Freedom*, 19–20; King, *Daddy King*, 107–9;
Martin Luther King, Jr., "A Talk to a Seventh Grade Class at George A.
Towns Elementary School" Atlanta, Ga. (The King Center Archives,
11 March 1964) 1; and "Excerpts from an Interview with Martin Luther
King, Jr.," in Robert P. Warren, *Who Speaks for the Negro?* (unpublished manuscript from The King Center Archives, 18 March
1964) 1 ff.

slapped me had gone, and my mother and I left the store almost immediately.[24]

At age fourteen, King was forced to surrender his bus seat to a white passenger on a trip from Dublin, Georgia, to Atlanta. "That night will never leave my memory," he declared. "It was the angriest I have ever been in my life."[25] This incident was marked with a twist of irony for two reasons. First, because King was traveling from a high school oratorical contest where he had spoken on "The Negro and the Constitution," a speech that apparently won the first-place prize. Second, the incident had some of the earmarks of another situation which would later catapult King to leadership in the Montgomery Bus Boycott.[26]

The experience of having to swallow frustration and anger in the face of emotional and physical abuses from white racists was not an easy one for the sensitive child. "All of these things had done something to my growing personality," King explained. "I had come perilously close to resenting all white people."[27] In time, he was able to overcome his bitterness toward whites mainly because of the nurturing values and reinforcement of his family, the black church, and the larger black community, which instilled in him a sense of his own inherent worth and dignity that nothing in his experiences with southern white society could destroy. However, these support systems could not completely shield him from the deep inner tension that every black child in the South faced:

> As I look back over those early days, I did have something of an inner tension. On the one hand my mother

24. "Face to Face," 4–5; and Lawrence D. Reddick, *Crusader Without Violence: A Biography of Martin Luther King, Jr.* (New York: Harper and Brothers, 1959), 59–60. Reddick reports that King was eleven years old when this incident occurred—a report that does not agree with King's recollection.

25. James M. Washington, ed., *A Testament of Hope: The Essential Writings of Martin Luther King, Jr.* (San Francisco: Harper and Row, 1986), 342–43.

26. *Ibid.*; and King, *Stride toward Freedom*, chap. 3.

27. King, *Stride toward Freedom*, 90; and King, "An Autobiography of Religious Development," 12–13.

taught me that I should feel a sense of somebodiness.
. . . On the other hand, I had to go out and face the
system, which stared me in the face every day saying,
"you are less than," "you are not equal to." So this was
a real tension within me.[28]

King's childhood experiences with economic and
racial injustices in the South were of fundamental significance not only for his career as a preacher and social
activist but also for the basic orientation of his thinking.
They helped him to determine who and what he was,
and why it was necessary for him to devote his life to
the search for genuine human community. Furthermore,
these experiences convinced him that authentic selfhood
is impossible outside of a life-long quest for human community, which involves a recognition of the intrinsic
worth and dignity of all human personality. To be sure,
this yearning for total human community and the experience of being black in America were always held in creative tension by King, calling to mind the dual nature of
Afro-American consciousness as expressed in W. E. B. Du
Bois's *The Souls of Black Folk*.[29]

The harsh facts of life in a segregated society did not
stifle young King's desire to grow, achieve, and enjoy life.
He had the usual growing boy's love for the outdoors,
and the warm and balmy weather in the South did much
to encourage this feeling. Physically, he was small for his
age but was strong, active, and athletic. He had a great
love for sports that was cultivated chiefly through contact with the black community, where sports were essential to a consideration of culture. He also had the typical
child's desire to know and understand, and he often
raised questions to his parents about race, religion, and
other matters. Martin Luther King, Sr., characterized
young Martin as "a curious youngster who really did
wonder constantly about this peculiar world he saw all

28. "Face to Face," 3.
29. *Ibid.;* and John Hope Franklin, ed., *The Souls of Black Folk in Three Negro Classics* (New York: Avon Books, 1965), 215.

around him." The boy sensed things "that southern men must be aware of if they are black: the subtle moods and shifts of violent disposition, the low-burning flame of rage that never seems to go away in the deep South."[30]

King's high school experience contributed substantially to his knowledge and understanding of the world around him. In the fall of 1942, at age thirteen, he entered Booker T. Washington High School, which was "the only Negro high school in Atlanta." He vividly remembered his daily routine of riding a segregated city bus from the Fourth Ward over to the West Side to the high school. "I would get on that bus day after day, and I would end up having to go to the back of that bus with my body," he recounted. "But every time I got on that bus, I left my mind up on the front seat. And I said to myself, one of these days I'm gonna put my body up there where my mind is."[31] Although King excelled in subjects like history and mathematics, the overall curriculum of Booker T. Washington High School could not completely satisfy his desire for knowledge, though it did contribute to his growing awareness of the dialectic that had been at work in his experience as far back as he could remember. Rarely had King experienced anything without also encountering its opposite. His family, church, and neighborhood constantly dinned into his mind the idea that he was as significant as anyone else, whereas white society conspired to instill in him the corroding notion that he was worthless. His father preached and struggled against segregation, whereas his white childhood friend's father worked to keep him and his friend apart. He had an economically secure and comfortable childhood, but his playmates and workmates lived in poverty and insecurity. He saw men in the church preaching with moving fervor the need for a prophetic and relevant ministry and mission but noticed how some congregations refused to disturb the status

30. King, "An Autobiography of Religious Development," 5; and King, *Daddy King*, 127–31.
31. King, "A Speech to Blacks," Grenada, Miss., 3.

quo. He was taught the egalitarian principles embodied in the United States Constitution and the Declaration of Independence but saw his people verbally and physically abused almost daily because of their blackness. All of these experiences, which might have broken the spirit of the average perceptive and sensitive child, produced an individual so driven to think and learn that King left high school at the end of his sophomore year and entered college at the age of fifteen.[32]

A vital part of King's intellectual and spiritual formation occurred from 1944 to 1948 during his matriculation at Atlanta's Morehouse College. When he entered Morehouse College in the fall of 1944, that all-black institution had already received wide recognition for its work toward the improvement of the race. It had established a tradition of great black leadership in the South dating back to 1906, when John Hope, the school's first black president, strongly opposed Booker T. Washington's view that education for black Americans should stress agricultural and mechanical skills more than the liberal arts. Many prominent doctors, lawyers, ministers, and teachers in various parts of the nation were "Morehouse men." In the 1940s Morehouse College was like other black colleges in that it stressed humanitarian values, and young men who studied there were expected to succeed despite segregation and to become leaders of their people. The school's credo explained its mission: "Whatever you do in this hostile world, be the best." King was determined to become a living embodiment of this credo. He majored in sociology and minored in English, and these two subjects combined proved of enormous value to him as he later sought to understand his people's condition and to articulate their concerns at all levels of society.[33]

32. Krue Brock, "The Dialectical Perspective of Dr. Martin Luther King, Jr." (unpublished paper, Vanderbilt University, Spring, 1988), 4–5.

33. Linda Williams, "Molding Men: At Morehouse College, Middle Class Blacks Are Taught to Lead," *The Wall Street Journal* (May 5, 1987): 1, 25; and Christine King-Farris, "The Young Martin: From Childhood through College," *Ebony*, 41, no. 3 (January 1986): 58.

Several well-known black professors greatly influenced King's intellectual and spiritual development at Morehouse College. Under Gladstone L. Chandler, the professor of English, he learned the art of precise and lucid exposition, knowledge essential to his development as a speaker and writer. Samuel Williams, a formally trained minister and professor of philosophy, introduced King to Plato, Socrates, Kant, Machiavelli, Henry David Thoreau, and other Western philosophers, thus preparing the foundation for his graduate work in philosophical theology. It was in Williams's class that King first read Thoreau's *Essay on Civil Disobedience*, a treatise that he said afforded "my first intellectual contact with the theory of nonviolent resistance."[34] George D. Kelsey, a minister and director of the department of religion at Morehouse, helped King work through his skepticism about religion generally, and his problems with fundamentalism in particular, thereby fertilizing his mind for the seeds of Protestant liberalism that would later fall upon it at Crozer Theological Seminary and Boston University. King called Benjamin E. Mays—preacher, theologian, and President of Morehouse—"my spiritual and intellectual father."[35] Mays, along with Williams and Kelsey, stimulated King's belief in the power of ideas, and convinced him that any relevant ministry should embrace intellectual as well as social and spiritual concerns. Some scholars have argued that the most penetrating and lasting influence on King came from Walter Chivers, his sociology advisor, who taught him that racial and economic injustices were perennial allies. Chivers helped King to understand the dialectic at work in the

34. King, *Stride toward Freedom*, 91; Farris, "The Young Martin," 58; Walter E. Fluker, "A Comparative Analysis of the Ideal of Community in the Thought of Howard Thurman and Martin Luther King, Jr." (Ph.D. diss. Boston University, Winter, 1988), 267–70; and King, "A Talk to a Seventh Grade Class," 1.
35. Williams, "Molding Men," 1, 25; and Martin Luther King, Jr., "Statement Regarding the Retirement of Benjamin E. Mays," (The King Center Archives, Atlanta, Ga., 1967), 1.

black experience, a lesson that proved immensely valuable when King later studied Hegel's dialectical process at Boston University. Drs. C. B. Dansby, N. P. Tillman, and Lucius M. Tobin were among the other black scholars who guided King to new intellectual achievements at Morehouse College.[36]

In summary, the experience at Morehouse College influenced King's life and thought at several levels. First, it increased his awareness of the social, economic, and political forces that contributed to the oppression of his people, particularly in the South, and started him on an intellectual and pragmatic quest for a method to achieve racial and economic justice—a quest that became more serious when he entered Crozer Theological Seminary in 1948.[37] While a student at Morehouse College, King joined the National Association for the Advancement of Colored People (NAACP) and sought, between semesters, types of employment that would expose him to the conditions of the masses. He spent one summer working on the Cullman Brothers' Tobacco Plantation in Simsbury, Connecticut, another at Atlanta's Railway Express Company unloading trains and trucks, and still another working in the stockroom at the Southern Spring Bed Mattress Company in Atlanta. Observing that black men received drastically less pay than white men for identical jobs, King saw firsthand the reality of much of what Professor Walter Chivers had taught him in sociology classes. The fact that he chose the work of a common laborer is indeed remarkable, especially since, being the son of a prominent pastor and civic leader, he could have easily gotten less demanding jobs in any of the

36. William D. Watley, *Roots of Resistance: The Nonviolent Ethic of Martin Luther King, Jr.* (Valley Forge, Pa.: Judson Press, 1985), 18; Stephen B. Oates, *Let the Trumpet Sound: The Life of Martin Luther King, Jr.* (New York: Harper and Row, 1982), 18, 21, 26; and Farris, "The Young Martin," 58.

37. King, *Stride toward Freedom*, 90–91; Oates, *Let the Trumpet Sound*, 18, 21, 26; and Fluker, "A Comparative Analysis of the Ideal of Community," 268–70.

numerous black-owned businesses in Atlanta.[38] Furthermore, King's family resources were such that he could
have chosen not to work at all, a decision that would not
have bothered his father, who especially opposed his
children working for white people. King's decision to do
common labor evidenced his determination to maintain
a sense of communal values—values that were consistently nurtured by his ties to his family, the church, and
the larger black community, which included Morehouse
College.[39]

Morehouse College had a very important impact on
King in terms of his relationship with white people. His
feeling of potential resentment of all whites had first
surfaced at age six, when racism severed his friendship
with a white playmate. Referring specifically to that incident, King commented: "I was greatly shocked, and
from that moment on I was determined to hate every
white person. As I grew older and older this feeling continued to grow."[40] Although his family and the church
sought to impress on him how hatred destroyed the human spirit, these teachings could not have the impact
that only close and wholesome association with whites
could bring. King himself recognized this fundamental
truth after he entered Morehouse College, and he reflected on how his experiences at that institution, which
brought him in "contact with white students through
working in interracial organizations," helped him to
overcome the anger and sense of alienation that had
clouded his view of life as a child.[41]

38. Davis, *I Have a Dream*, 21; Mervyn A. Warren, "A Rhetorical
Study of the Preaching of Doctor Martin Luther King, Jr., Pastor and
Pulpit Orator" (Ph.D. diss., Michigan State University, 1966), 30–33;
and Farris, "The Young Martin," 58.

39. King, *Stride toward Freedom*, 90; Warren, "A Rhetorical Study of
the Preaching of Doctor Martin Lurther King, Jr.," 31; and King, "An
Autobiography of Religious Development," 1–15.

40. King, *Stride toward Freedom*, 90; and King, "An Autobiography
of Religious Development," 12–13.

41. King, "An Autobiography of Religious Development," 12–13;
and Fluker, "A Comparative Analysis of the Ideal of Community,"
268–69.

The Morehouse College years also inspired King to choose the ministry as a life vocation and supplied him with the oratorical skills and the basic theological and hermeneutical principles to make his ministry spiritually and socially relevant. His abilities as a public speaker, which he had been developing from his early childhood, were sharpened by his exposure to Gladstone Chandler, Samuel Williams, George Kelsey, Benjamin Mays, and Lucius Tobin, and also by his participation in the annual J. L. Webb Oratorical Contest at Morehouse College, which he won for at least two years.[42] Surrounded by trained ministers, whose teaching and preaching had a strong theological and hermeneutical base as well as a social and prophetic character, it is understandable that King became a powerful and effective preacher.

Finally, King's Morehouse College years provided him with the intellectual power, the openness, the self-discipline, and the self-confidence to succeed in his studies at Crozer and Boston. Without his exposure to strong black intellectuals at Morehouse, and his background in the black church and the black religious experience, his receptivity to and appropriation of the liberal Protestantism and personal idealism to which he was exposed at Crozer and Boston would have been virtually impossible.[43] Because of his background in black folk culture and his experiences growing up in the South, King eventually forged a creative synthesis with the most enlightened ideas and concepts from the black religious tradition, Protestant liberalism, personal idealism, and Gandhian thought. This synthesis constituted his most distinctive contribution as a preacher, thinker, and social activist.[44]

42. Watley, *Roots of Resistance*, 18; Lewis V. Baldwin, "The Minister as Preacher, Pastor, and Prophet: The Thinking of Martin Luther King, Jr.," *American Baptist Quarterly* 7, no. 2 (June 1988): 79–93; and Warren, "A Rhetorical Study of the Preaching," 30.

43. Watley, *Roots of Resistance*, chapter 1; Warren, "A Rhetorical Study of the Preaching," 30–31; and Fluker, "A Comparative Analysis of the Ideal of Community," 269–70.

44. Lewis V. Baldwin, "Understanding Martin Luther King, Jr. Within the Context of Southern Black Religious History," *Journal of Religious Studies* 13, no. 2 (Fall 1987): 13.

## SENSE OF PLACE

King's life and thought are incomprehensible without
seriously considering his *sense of place* in a southern context. His attraction to the South as a whole ran deep, but
the black community of Atlanta, Georgia, particularly
along Auburn Avenue, was his very special place. His parents and maternal grandparents had lived there together
before his birth, in an old two-story house that was occupied at various times by aunts, uncles, cousins, friends
of the family, and boarders.[45] It was a place well filled
with memories of King's early life and of the people with
whom he grew up, played, and worshipped. The Ebenezer
Baptist Church, with which he was affiliated from his
earliest remembrance, stood less than two blocks from
his home. The black community was a world virtually
sealed off from the white world—a world in which the
folk had their own language, customs, traditions, and
ways of thinking and living, and in which family, church,
and neighborhood were linked together in a chain of interdependence and mutual need. The Auburn Avenue of
King's childhood, then, had cultural and historical meanings that oriented him in space and spirit, established his
identity, and gave him a sense of shared experience and
community with black people across generations and geographical boundaries. Within his southern place, King
also came very early to the realization of a shared history
and culture with whites around him, despite the physical
barriers imposed by racial segregation.[46]

Religion was the foundation of black culture in the
South in the 1930s and 1940s, and was therefore central to
King's early sense of place. From his childhood, Ebenezer
Baptist Church was for him and his family a sacred place

45. King, *Daddy King,* 81–82. In conceptualizing the notion of "sense
of place" in relation to King, I drew heavily on the insights of Jimmie L.
Franklin, "Beyond the Constitution: Black Southerners and Sense of Place,
with a Special Note on Oklahoma," unpublished paper delivered at Oklahoma State Univ., Stillwater and Oklahoma City, Oklahoma (February 13,
1987), 1–14.
46. King, "An Autobiography of Religious Development," 1–15.

to which they returned down through the years to worship, to participate in festive occasions, and to bury their dead. While growing up in Atlanta, King could see that the church and religion provided perhaps the central assurance to his family and community of their identity and history, and of their actual foundation in a particular time and place. These expressions of culture united the life of his people with God, with each other, and, in spirit, with generations of their forebears stemming back to slavery and even to Africa. This offers a hint as to why the Georgia environment of King's childhood was such a fertile place for exploring elements of African culture in America, especially in the spiritual realm.[47] A significant number of ex-slaves and their immediate offspring, including relatives and friends of the Kings, lived there. The richness of that culture in King's own family and church was such that he witnessed variants of the African ring shout, such as "shouting" and the "holy dance," during his father's sermons. When he reached manhood, he often shared with his friend Ralph D. Abernathy how his father would prance and "walk the benches." "He would start preaching at the front of the church and walk the benches at the back."[48] Given the Reverend King's inclination for this type of religious behavior, it is conceivable that members of his church also shouted and danced during worship services at Ebenezer. Although young King admitted embarrassment by such emotional displays of religiosity, he nevertheless developed insight into some of the most vital cultural forms of black people in the deep South. He came to see that the church and religion, more than anything else, served to define the very essence of words like "place" and "community."[49]

47. King, *Daddy King*, 23–128; and King, "An Autobiography of Religious Development," 1–15.

48. A private interview with the Rev. Ralph D. Abernathy, Atlanta, Ga., 7 May 1987; and King, "An Autobiography of Religious Development," 1–15.

49. King, "An Autobiography of Religious Development," 1–15; Zelia S. Evans and J. T. Alexander, eds., *The Dexter Avenue Baptist Church, 1877–1977* (Montgomery, Ala.: Dexter Avenue Baptist Church, 1978), 69; and a letter from Martin Luther King, Jr. to the Rev. Jerry M. Chance, 9 May 1961, The King Papers, Boston University.

King's attachment to place at an early age was reflected most profoundly in his love for the music of his people, much of which was marked by strong African rhythms. The idea of place was inconceivable to him without music, mainly because of his closeness to the church and to the larger black community of Atlanta, which exposed him to black music in various forms, vocal and instrumental. According to his father, King could sing "in a fine, clear voice" even "as a young boy," and he had "the feeling for ceremonies and ritual, the passionate love for Baptist music."[50] "Baptist music" in this case included black gospel songs, the spirituals, and the great hymns of the Christian church. King had very early a deep passion for the spiritual songs of his slave forebears, the phrasing and rhythms of which he undoubtedly heard many times in his father's sermons, and which were sung, frequently with the accompaniment of piano, in the King home and in church by his mother and others. King's mother Alberta, the pianist at Ebenezer church, may have influenced the boy's love for black gospel songs and the spirituals more than anyone else. His mother's music and his father's preaching were enormously important in the shaping of his rhythm-consciousness—a sense of rhythm later reflected on a high level in the melodic sounds of his preaching. At any rate, young King carried his passionate love for music with him to Morehouse College, where he was a member of both the Glee Club and the Atlanta University-Morehouse-Spelman Chorus.[51]

King's early ties to the church and with the black middle class did not shelter him from the so-called secular music commonly associated with the lives of Atlanta's poor black masses. The streets of Atlanta in the 1930s and 1940s were often filled with the sounds of work songs coming from the lusty throats of black chain-gang workers, and at times grim-faced black men could be seen strumming musical instruments of almost every variety

---

50. King, *Daddy King*, 127.
51. *Ibid.*; and Davis, *I Have a Dream*, 13, 21.

and singing blues that rose to the dizzy heights of emotion. The sounds and rhythms of jazz sometimes flowed
from the taverns to the streets—a music of sorrow and
joy, of trials and triumph. Such scenes had a tremendous
impact on King during his childhood. He vividly recalled
his occasional walks down to "Buttermilk Bottle," the
chief slum area in Atlanta, to see an old black man play
his guitar and sing songs like "I've Been Down So Long
That Down Don't Bother Me."[52] King's early sense of
place and of his people as a whole was informed by this
art, despite his inability at that time to understand it
in theoretical terms. While a student at Morehouse, he
was known to dance to the tunes of secular music, a habit
frowned upon by his father and others in Ebenezer
church.[53] The language King used in his adult life to describe both secular and sacred black folk music suggests
that he saw it all as the product of a single cultural and
aesthetic tradition—as an expression of his people's
yearning to be and to belong.[54]

The same is true for the rich wit and humor that per-
vaded King's world early on and helped shape his notion
of place. He grew up among blacks who, like their slave
ancestors, fully employed wit and humor as a way of dealing with their oppression and exerting some control over
their environment. The folkwit and stories the youngster
heard in the King home and from other black people in
his community constituted a means of direct and continuing contact with speech patterns and a folkloric tradition that extended back to slavery and beyond.[55] King

52. *Atlanta, A City of the Modern South*, 5, 132–33; King, *Stride to-
ward Freedom*, 212; and King, "A Speech to Blacks," Grenada, Miss., 2.
    53. Farris, "The Young Martin," 57–58.
    54. King, *Stride toward Freedom*, 212; Martin Luther King, Jr., *Why
We Can't Wait* (New York: The New American Library, 1964), 61; Martin
Luther King, Jr., "Address at a Mass Meeting," Clarksdale, Miss., (The
King Center Archives, 19 March 1968), 7; and Martin Luther King, Jr.,
"Rally Speech on the Georgia Tour 'Pre-Washington Campaign'" Albany,
Ga., (The King Center Archives, 22 March 1968), 1, 5, 8–9.
    55. King, "An Autobiography of Religious Development," 2; and a
private interview with the Rev. Bernard S. Lee, Washington, D.C., 9 July
1986.

acquired a sense of the cultural essence of place by listening to the southern dialect of his people, to their quick wit and deep simplicity, to the content of the tales they told, and to the hearty laughter that was at once a reflection of their pain and a symbol of their capacity to hope and to dream in spite of the contradictions of life. King found here a rich mine of wisdom and a strength of spirit that afforded almost unlimited sources of insight and inspiration—sources that later enabled him to master the preaching art with relative ease.[56]

Equally important in the shaping of King's sense of place was the social significance of food and eating. His early development occurred in a place where food and eating played a central part in creating and maintaining community. Notions of good food were intimately linked to family reunions, funerals, revivals, and gatherings with friends, visitors, and church members. Many of the King family's prayer meetings, discussions, and major decisions took place around the table. King's mother Alberta was known for her delicious "down-home" cooking, especially "soul food," and so was his maternal grandmother, Jennie C. Parks Williams.[57] The boy always took great delight in partaking of their succulent fried chicken, chitterlings, ham, collard greens, black-eyed peas, cornbread, and biscuits. King remembered how he and his brother and sister would run around Auburn Avenue telling their playmates about their grandmother's great biscuits.[58]

The symbolic significance of food and eating and their relationship to place in a southern context must have struck King with great force for a number of reasons,

56. A private interview with the Rev. Bernard S. Lee, 9 July 1986; Baldwin, "The Minister as Preacher, Pastor, and Prophet," 81–83; and Baldwin, "Understanding Martin Luther King, Jr.," 7–8.

57. A private interview with the Rev. Bernard S. Lee, 9 July 1986; A private interview with Dr. Philip Lenud, Nashville, Tennessee, 7 April 1987; and Martin Luther King, Jr., "Prelude to Tomorrow: An Address" The Chicago Operation Breadbasket Meeting, Chicago, Ill., (The King Center Archives, 6 January 1968), 4–5.

58. King, "Prelude to Tomorrow," 4–5; Oates, *Let the Trumpet Sound*, 4; and a private interview with Dr. Philip Lenud, 7 April 1987.

aside from the simple fact that feasts strengthened communal values and social relationships. First, he was raised in an environment in which significant spiritual and ritualistic value was attached to food. References to food were very much a part of the religious heritage of the folk, as indicated by the slave practice of putting food on the graves of the deceased, and by songs like "Dwelling in Beulah Land" and "I'm Gonna Sit at the Welcome Table One of These Days."[59] Second, the South of King's childhood was the poorest section of the country, as had been the case for decades. In this context, food was viewed as a precious commodity—as something for which to be thankful—especially at a time when the effects of the Great Depression were forcing large numbers of blacks and whites into bread lines. Viewing this situation firsthand, it was difficult for King, even as a small boy, to be oblivious to food and eating as basic to life and related to a love of life. In their social significance, food and eating were quite similar to the music, folklore, sermons, and other expressions of black art that were such a vital part of King's early cultural experience.[60]

It is clear, then, that King's conception of place as a child, had more to do with a sense of peoplehood than with a physical place. It involved an attachment to a particular home, kinship network, and peoplehood where there was a sense of identity, security, and belonging. It was impossible for King the youngster, given the realities of black oppression in the South, to have the same sentimental attachment to and identification with the land

59. A private interview with John Egerton, Nashville, Tenn., 27 June 1986. For interesting and brilliant insights on the social significance of food and eating and their relationship to "place" in a southern context, see John Egerton, *Southern Food: At Home, on the Road, in History* (New York: Alfred A. Knopf, 1987), especially 175–342; Norma Jean and Carole Darden, *Spoonbread and Strawberry Wine: Recipes and Reminiscences of a Family* (New York: Fawcett Crest Books, 1978), introduction; and Vertamae Smart-Grosvenor, *Vibration Cooking or the Travel Notes of a Geechee Girl* (New York: Ballantine Books, 1970), especially 5–32.

60. King, "An Autobiography of Religious Development," 1; King, "Prelude to Tomorrow," 4–5; King, *Stride Toward Freedom*, 90; and Reddick, *Crusader without Violence*, 3.

as whites. Although he and his people shared an interesting intertwined life-style with southern whites in the
areas of diet, language, religion, value orientation, and
folkways and culture, there were values and institutions
rooted in the white-dominated South that limited black
opportunities in many ways. Owing to this situation,
King very early developed an ambivalent loyalty to the
region that was as intense as the inner tension and psychological paradox he felt over the condition of his people. Nevertheless, he had positive experiences growing
up in the South that kept him from dismissing the area
as merely a way station enroute to some better and more
permanent place. In later years, King would associate
the South with a certain hope that centered on the possibility of a new and richer human society—a hope
which was reflected in a supreme way in his people's
religion and in the way they ate, danced, sang, told tales,
and laughed.[61]

King carried with him his own cultural legacy
and southern sense of place when he moved to Chester,
Pennsylvania, to attend the predominantly white Crozer
Theological Seminary in 1948. Although he had worked
with white students in interracial organizations during
his Morehouse College years, he was not accustomed
to the type of integrated education he was to receive at
Crozer.[62] However, King was able to escape loneliness
and a feeling of homelessness in this new environment
mainly because life in Chester's essentially segregated
black community renewed in him a sense of the South.
Many of the residents there had come from the South and
had managed to recreate a southern sense of place in this

61. See King, *Stride toward Freedom*, 189–224; Martin Luther King,
Jr., "The Case Against Tokenism," *The New York Times Magazine* (August
5, 1962): 11; and Coleman B. Brown, "Grounds for American Loyalty in a
Prophetic Christian Social Ethic—With Special Attention to Martin
Luther King, Jr.," (Ph.D. diss. Union Theological Seminary in New York
City, April, 1979), 52–55.
62. King, "An Autobiography of Religious Development," 12–13;
Oates, *Let the Trumpet Sound*, 24; and Haskins, *The Life and Death of
Martin Luther King, Jr.*, 29–30.

small town. Homes shook with a deep genuine laughter; patches of peas, corn, collard greens, okra, and tomatoes crowded backyards; the rhythms and sounds of secular music could be heard on sidewalks; and churches rocked under the impact of powerful preaching, lively music, and shouting. All these elements called to mind the Atlanta of King's childhood. The Calvary Baptist Church, with which King was affiliated during his three-year sojourn in Chester, put him in close touch with many people who had deep roots in the South and who epitomized the cultural ethos of the black South with its characteristic life-style and taboos. This whole atmosphere, which drew heavily on the resources of church, family, and a complex of ideas, values, traditions, and experiences, reinforced in King a feeling of "at homeness"—of being fundamentally "southern."[63]

Blacks who knew King in Chester recall a young man who exemplified so many qualities, some of them stereotypical, generally associated at that time with the southern Negro—a quiet nobility, a vital capacity for religious feeling, bold mannerisms of language, an eloquence of style, and a fun-loving, down-to-earth approach to life. "He always seemed in deep thought, but he also had a very human side," reminisced Sara V. Richardson, who assisted King with youth groups at Chester's Calvary Baptist Church. "He loved to smile, laugh, joke, and have a good time," she continued in a 1987 interview. "He could tell jokes so dry and then burst out laughing himself, and then you had to laugh."[64] Emma Anderson, a fifty-year member at Calvary, nodded her head in agreement, and added: "He made you feel comfortable around him. He was very easy to meet." Anderson also remembered King

63. A private interview with Emma Anderson, Chester, Pa., 29 May 1987; and a private interview with Sara V. Richardson, Chester, Pa., 29 May 1987. The view that King experienced no racial discrimination at Crozer Seminary in Chester is not persuasive, especially given the fact that racism, though subtle in many cases, was such a prominent feature of life in the North at that time. See Haskins, *The Life and Death of Martin Luther King, Jr.*, 30.
64. A private interview with Sara V. Richardson, 29 May 1987.

as one who "was very interested in elderly people," probably because of the honest joy of laughter and the rich reservoir of experience and wisdom he felt they had to share with him.[65]

King displayed other habits and codes of conduct in Chester that reflected his relationship with place and the more general culture in the South. According to Sara Richardson, "He loved the old-time spirituals, and would sit for hours listening to Calvary's choirs singing them. He also loved the blues. Bessie Smith was one of his favorites."[66] Richardson declared that King's appreciation for music was clearly matched by his tremendous appetite for the southern-style food he found in the homes of many of Calvary's members. "He really loved soul food," she recalled. "He would eat chitterlings, cornbread, black-eyed peas, rice, spareribs, fried chicken, and especially lemon meringue pie. He would eat with his fingers." Emma Anderson had similar recollections, noting that King "loved anything that was 'soul.' He really enjoyed my sweet potato pie."[67]

In a way, King was adopted by the people who fed and nurtured him in other ways in Chester, an experience that undoubtedly reminded him of the extended family support network he knew so well in the South. "He would go from house to house looking for food and fun," Anderson recounted. "He was very fond of the Talley family who attended our church, and he called Esther Talley 'mother'." Sara Richardson, smiling softly, quickly echoed the claim that everyone considered King one of their own. "I would always leave my key under a brick so he could get into my house when I was away," she explained. "He would come here and cook. Having a love for sports, he would come to my house on Wednesday nights to watch boxing matches and to eat with his friends." Such positive relationships

65. A private interview with Emma Anderson, 29 May 1987.
66. A private interview with Sara V. Richardson, 29 May 1987.
67. *Ibid.*; and a private interview with Emma Anderson, 29 May 1987.

explain why King returned to Chester several times after reestablishing his base in the South.[68]

King's sense of the South was also replicated in
Boston when he moved there in 1951 to pursue a Ph.D.
at Boston University. Boston was much larger than
Chester, but he found in the Twelfth Baptist Church and
in the larger black community the same feeling of belonging and fulfillment. Many of the black people in
Boston had migrated from the South and were steeped
in the values and traditions of southern black culture.
King soon became known in the community surrounding Twelfth Baptist Church as the young man from the
South who "carried himself with dignity, but yet with
humility and a sense of humor." The Reverend Michael
E. Haynes, who served with King on the ministerial
staff at Twelfth Baptist, was immediately struck by his
humility, a spirit that had been well cultivated by his
experiences with racism and with victims of poverty in
the South. Haynes remarked:

> For a guy who was distinctly middle class and bour-
> geois, comparatively speaking, and better off than
> many of the other guys who were here, Martin carried
> himself in a very, very humble manner. He made me
> feel completely at ease, although we were in two dif-
> ferent theological and intellectual worlds.[69]

King went to Boston with a genuine emotional and
spiritual security which had grown out of his contact
with the black communities in Atlanta and Chester.
Philip Lenud, who was his friend at Morehouse College
and his roommate in Boston, viewed this as the basis for
the spirit of compassion, generosity, and patience King
displayed in his dealings with people:

> We were like brothers. This is the only man I have
> lived around or with, and never had a quarrel with
> him. Martin and I were very much alike, I suppose, in

68. A private interview with Emma Anderson, 29 May 1987.
69. A private interview with the Rev. Michael E. Haynes, Boston,
Mass. 25 June 1987.

some areas—in terms of grasping and seeking for
knowledge, and a craving to make a difference in the
world for people. He was totally passive. He was just a
born pacifist. People would just take advantage of him
because he was so good-natured. People would come
by and want him to do things or drive them places, not
realizing that Martin had to study. They put so much
work on him at Boston. He would come home sometimes with twelve to fifteen books to read, and he
really didn't have time to be doing things for people.
But he was always willing to do what he could to help
people.[70]

King discovered in Boston, as he had in Chester,
a black community that afforded so much of what he
needed for his material well-being and spiritual sustenance. The people there had an intense sensitivity to
family and spiritual values, the gifts of wit and laughter,
an appreciation for music and sports, and a festive and
feeling-oriented approach to life—values and virtues
King instinctively appreciated as a black southerner.
When he was not studying or fulfilling ministerial duties, he sometimes found pleasure in philosophical and
theological discussions with fellow students, or in visiting and chatting with the elderly. Occasionally, King
played basketball and shot pool with the youngsters in
the Social Service Center across the street from Twelfth
Baptist Church.[71] At other times he would make his way
to Barbara's Chef, Mother's Lunch, The Western Lunch
Box, or other black soul-food places for a hefty meal. He
enjoyed meeting and dating beautiful young ladies, and
frequently joined friends for a night of fun at The Totem
Pole and other night spots in Boston's black section,
"which rocked with brazzy jazz."[72] Despite the otherwise
cool and cautious New England atmosphere, Boston's

70. A private interview with Dr. Philip Lenud, 7 April 1987.
71. *Ibid.;* and a private interview with the Rev. Michael E. Haynes, 25
June 1987.
72. A private interview with the Rev. Michael E. Haynes, 25 June
1987; and Oates, *Let the Trumpet Sound,* 41.

black community gave King a sense of being spiritually located in the South.

There was a direction to King's studies at Crozer Theological Seminary and Boston University that grew out of his encounter with place and the folk in the South. His desire was to "go back home" and contribute the fruits of his training in the North toward redefining and reshaping the values and institutions that, after all, made him what he was; namely, a southern black Baptist preacher. According to Coretta Scott King, who became his wife in mid-June, 1953, in Marion, Alabama, King "felt that he should go South immediately. His intense dedication compelled him toward the harder rather than the easier solution. He had warned me of this long ago during our courtship, and now he said to me, 'I am going back where I am needed'."[73] King's marriage to Coretta was quite consistent with this sentiment, because she shared his sense of place and particularly his sensibilities on those subjects of southern religion, music, food, and other aspects of culture.

King felt the same pull toward the South that Booker T. Washington and numerous other blacks had felt before him. He believed he had something vital to offer toward the creation of a better South for blacks and whites. The region evoked powerful emotions in him— the land, the people, the strange sounds of animals, the sight of agricultural produce, the smell of down-home cooking, and the tremendous potential for growth and development—despite the widespread poverty and segregation. In every way, the need to return to the South became an ethical concern for King. "We came to the conclusion that we had something of a moral obligation to return—at least for a few years," he wrote. He commented further:

> The South, after all, was our home. Despite its short-
> comings we loved it as home, and had a real desire to

73. Coretta Scott King, *My Life with Martin Luther King, Jr.* (New York: Avon Books, 1969), 107.

do something about the problems that we felt so keenly as youngsters. We never wanted to be considered detached spectators. Since racial discrimination was most intense in the South, we felt that some of the Negroes who had received a portion of their training in other sections of the country should return to share their broader contacts and educational experience in its solution. Moreover, despite having to sacrifice much of the cultural life we loved, despite the existence of Jim Crow which kept reminding us at all times of the color of our skin, we had the feeling that something remarkable was unfolding in the South, and we wanted to be on hand to witness it. The region had marvelous possibilities, and once it came to itself and removed the blight of racial segregation, it would experience a moral, political, and economic boom hardly paralleled by any other section of the country.[74]

The South for which King yearned was a place where black people could live as first-class citizens, not as exiles or resident aliens. Having grown up in the South, he understood the exile's lot, which explains in part why he was touched so deeply by the songs of his slave forebears. He often alluded to how America had accepted, nurtured, and granted full rights and privileges to immigrants from various parts of the world but had "never demonstrated the same kind of maternal care for her black exiles who were brought here in chains from Africa." "It is no wonder," he continued, "that in one of our sorrow songs, our forebears could sing out, 'Sometimes I Feel Like a Motherless Child.' What a great sense of estrangement, rejection, and hurt that could cause people to use such a metaphor."[75] Although his people in

74. King, *Stride toward Freedom*, 21–22. Lerone Bennett caught the significance of "place" for King in Chapter I of his book, which is entitled "Soil," and so did Lenwood Davis in Chapter V of his book, called "Go South Young Man, Go South." See Lerone Bennett, Jr., *What Manner of Man: A Memorial Biography of Martin Luther King, Jr.* (New York: Pocket Books, 1968), 1–24; and Davis, *I Have a Dream*, 33–37.
75. Martin Luther King, Jr., "A Knock at Midnight," a sermon delivered at the All Saints Community Church, Los Angeles, Calif., (The King Center Archives, 25 June 1967) 14–16; Martin Luther King, Jr., "The

the South and throughout the nation were outsiders in many ways, having little economic and political power, King had a real sense of their being on the way to the promised land of freedom, justice, and equality, and that, in his view, changed their sojourn. Thus, the symbolic significance of the promised land, as taken from Biblical language, was inextricably linked to his southern sense of place.[76]

This discussion suggests that King's ideal of the beloved community also included the inherent notion of sense of place. The South as a place was quite significant in his emerging vision of and quest for the beloved community, which he defined as a completely integrated society characterized by brotherhood, love, and justice. As a youngster, King associated the South with paradoxical notions of community and noncommunity. He experienced community within the context of family, church, and the larger black Atlanta community, but he experienced noncommunity in the form of racism and discriminatory practices imposed by white society. The inner tension he experienced as a result of this paradox or dialectic caused him to struggle very early in life with the nature and meaning of community.[77]

As he looked seriously at southern life during and after his Morehouse College years, King could see that something important had always occurred between blacks and whites that transcended the narrow considerations

Crisis of Civil Rights," an address delivered at an Operation Breadbasket Meeting, Chicago, Ill., (The King Center Archives, 10 July 1967), 10; and Martin Luther King, Jr., "An Address at a Mass Meeting," Maggie Street Baptist Church, Montgomery, Ala., (The King Center Archives, 16 February 1968),4.

76. "The Birth of a New Nation: Transcript of an Interview with Martin Luther King, Jr.," WILD SOUND, Atlanta, Ga., (The King Center Archives, April 1957), 1; Martin Luther King, Jr., "Address at the National Bar Association Meeting," Milwaukee, Wis. (The King Center Archives, 20 August 1959), 3; and Martin Luther King, Jr., "The Church in Frontiers of Racial Tension," a speech delivered at Southern Baptist Theological Seminary, Louisville, Ken. (The King Center Archives, 19 April 1961), 2–3.

77. Fluker, "A Comparative Analysis of the Ideal of Community," 200–424.

of race and the lack of civil rights for his people. He could see that within the southern environment blacks and whites, by some strange historical circumstances, had been pulled to the center by a cultural vortex that had made it possible for them to influence each others' lives, thoughts, emotions, and destinies at almost every point. The interdependence and cultural exchange between them and the experiences and struggles they shared in a region stunted by poverty and racism helped to define for King the very essence of place in a southern context, and was in his view a possible foundation for creating genuine community. His view that the full humanity of blacks and whites could be realized only within the context of an authentic human community is germane to a consideration of his southern sense of place. The South, and particularly the black community of Atlanta, Georgia, was the initial context for the shaping of this vision of community—a vision that was in time broadened and refined as a result of King's personal contacts and training in the North, his involvement in the civil rights movement, and by the global focus he brought to his work as a Christian minister and activist.[78]

## A VIEW OF THE BLACK CONDITION

In the tradition of black leaders and thinkers before him, Martin Luther King, Jr. devoted considerable attention to assessing the impact of oppression on his people. His most serious reflections on this matter appeared in books and articles from 1957 to the time of his death eleven years later. Those reflections were based largely on King's experiences over the years in the black communities of Atlanta, Chester, and Boston, but he also drew heavily on the works of numerous poets and writers,

78. *Ibid.*; James H. Cone, "Martin Luther King, Jr. and the Third World," *The Journal of American History*, 74, no. 2 (September 1987): 455–67; and Lewis V. Baldwin, ed., *Toward the Beloved Community: Martin Luther King Jr. and South African Apartheid* (unpublished manuscript): 1–20, 275–317.

primarily black, whose insights into the black condition were profound and searching. He found probing literary expressions of his people's pain and struggle in the writings of James Baldwin, Countee Cullen, W. E. B. Du Bois, Paul Lawrence Dunbar, Ralph Ellison, Frantz Fanon, E. Franklin Frazier, Langston Hughes, James Weldon Johnson, John Killens, Claude McKay, Richard Wright, and others.[79] King read extensively the books of Du Bois, particularly *The Suppression of the African Slave Trade* (1896), *The Philadelphia Negro* (1899), *The Souls of Black Folk* (1903), and *Black Reconstruction in America* (1935). He characterized Du Bois as "an intellectual giant" who recognized and insistently taught that his people's oppression and deprivation resulted from "a poisonous fog of lies that depicted them as inferior."[80] Of equal significance for King were E. Franklin Frazier's *The Negro Family in the United States* (1939), which underscored the tremendous impact of oppression on the black family, and *Black Bourgeoisie* (1957), which influenced his perspective on the behavior, values, and attitudes of the black middle class.[81] James Baldwin's *Nobody Knows My Name* (1961) was also one of King's favorite books—a book that he thought provided rich "insights into the racial situation from the viewpoint of the oppressed."[82] *An American Dilemma* (1944), written by the Swedish economist Gunnar Myrdal, was one of the few books written by a white scholar that King found authoritative with regard to the black condition. In his estimation, this study was "probably the most definitive work on the Negro question in

79. A private interview with Dr. Philip Lenud, 7 April 1987; Martin Luther King, Jr., *Where Do We Go from Here: Chaos or Community?* (Boston: Beacon Press, 1967), 29, 53, 55, 59–61, 65–66, 106, 110–11, 121, 127; and a letter from Martin Luther King, Jr. to James Baldwin, 26 September 1961, The King Papers, Boston University.

80. Martin Luther King, Jr., "Honoring Dr. Du Bois," *Freedomways*, 8, no. 2 (Spring 1968), 104–11.

81. King, *Where Do We Go from Here?*, 106; Warren, *Who Speaks for the Negro?*, 14–15; and Martin Luther King, Jr., "Negroes are Not Moving too Fast," *The Saturday Evening Post* (November 7, 1964), 10.

82. A letter from Martin Luther King, Jr., to Harold Courlander, 30 October 1961, The King Papers, Boston University.

the United States that has been written."[83] Myrdal's work helped him to understand the dialectic that so poignantly characterized the Afro-American experience.

King described black people as the most battered, bruised, and defeated group in the American society—a group paralyzed by glaring forms "of political, psychological, social, economic, and intellectual bondage."[84] "The central quality of the Negro's life is pain," he declared, "a pain so old and so deep that it shows in almost every moment of his existence. It emerges in the cheerlessness of his sorrow songs, in the melancholy of his blues, and in the pathos of his sermons."[85] In King's opinion, the black condition was largely the consequence of more than two centuries of slavery and slave-trading, during which "more than 75 million black people were murdered." Furthermore, "families were torn apart, friends separated," and "cooperation to improve their condition carefully thwarted." "Considering what our forebears went through," he observed, "it is a miracle that the black man still survives."[86] King flatly rejected all explanations of his people's plight that ignored the brutality and the traumatizing effects of the slave system.

King was convinced that the plight of blacks in the segregated South was but a measure of the tremendous evil they endured throughout America. "Nobody in the history of the world has suffered like the black man," he argued. To those who charged that other immigrants had come to America under difficult circumstances and had succeeded where blacks had failed, he offered a direct rejoinder: . . .

> the situation of other immigrant groups a hundred years ago and the situation of the Negro today cannot

83. A letter from Martin Luther King, Jr., to Ada de Bichiacchi, 11 January 1960, The King Papers, Boston University; and King, *Where Do We Go from Here?*, 84–85.

84. King, *Why We Can't Wait*, 23.

85. King, *Where Do We Go from Here?*, 102–103; and Sidney M. Wilhelm, "Martin Luther King, Jr. and the Black Experience in America," *Journal of Black Studies*, 10, no. 1 (September 1979), 3–19.

86. Martin Luther King, Jr., "The Meaning of Hope," a sermon delivered at the Dexter Avenue Baptist Church, Montgomery, Ala. (The King Center Archives, 10 December 1967), 1–2.

be usefully compared. Negroes were brought here in chains long before the Irish decided *voluntarily* to leave Ireland or the Italians thought of leaving Italy. Some Jews may have left their homes in Europe involuntarily, but they were not in chains when they arrived on these shores. Other immigrant groups came to America with language and economic handicaps, but not with the stigma of color. Above all, no other ethnic group has been a slave on American soil, and no other group has had its family structure deliberately torn apart.[87]

The condition of blacks in the South presented a special problem for King, mainly because of the blatant racism and the visible signs of segregation that existed there. He noted that in the South "the scars of the slave system remained more visible and law and custom became one," thereby exposing his people to disfranchisement and other problems that were not so clearly evident in other parts of the country. "Many Americans are aware of the fact that, on the crooked scales of 'southern justice,' the life, liberty and human worth of a black man weigh precious little," King complained. The physical abuse, verbal insults, and numerous cases of reprisal to which southern blacks were subjected on a daily basis caused him a great deal of agony and frustration and confirmed his view, held at least as far back as his Morehouse College years, that the greatest challenge to American democracy would be met in the South.[88]

The extent to which racism and segregation had hurt his people emotionally and psychologically was keenly understood by King, and he gave it attention consonant with its seriousness. Life in the South provided an excellent vantage point from which he could observe and study this situation. He attributed the pervasiveness of

87. *Ibid.;* and King, *Where Do We Go from Here?,* 103.
88. Martin Luther King, Jr., "Who is Their God?," *The Nation* (October 13, 1962): 210; Martin Luther King, Jr., "When a Negro Faces Southern Justice," *New York Amsterdam News* (April 16, 1966), 31; and Martin Luther King, Jr., "A Statement Regarding the Mississippi Freedom Democratic Party at the C.O.F.O. Rally," Jackson, Miss. (The King Center Archives, 22 July 1964), 1.

ignorance and self-hatred among his people—a condition that caused many to respect their oppressors more
than they respected themselves and their own kind—
to centuries of oppression that had instilled into their
minds a sense of inferiority. In King's view, this condition became manifested in a variety of ways among middle-class blacks, whose obsession with identifying "with
the white middle class" tended to be such that many
"reject psychologically anything that reminds them of
their heritage" or "of the masses of Negroes."[89] Such
persons were often cultivated as black leaders by "the
white establishment," King thought, but their poor self-
image and "absence of faith in their people" rendered
them susceptible to becoming partners with whites in
the subjugation of the black community:

> This kind of Negro leader acquires the white man's con-
> tempt for the ordinary Negro. He is often more at home
> with the middle-class white than he is among his own
> people, and frequently his physical home is moved up
> and away from the ghetto. His language changes, his
> location changes, his income changes, and ultimately
> he changes from the representative of the Negro to
> the white man into the white man's representative
> to the Negro. The tragedy is that too often he does not
> recognize what has happened to him.[90]

The fact that some middle-class blacks were "un-
touched and unmoved by the agonies and struggles
of their underprivileged brothers" was for King further
evidence of their damaged ego. He considered this kind
of "selfish detachment" shameful and inexcusable, especially since so many well-to-do blacks owed their success
to the support of underprivileged blacks:

89. King, *Where Do We Go from Here?*, 131, 160; and Warren, *Who
Speaks for the Negro?*, 14–15. In some versions of his sermon, "A Knock
at Midnight," which was preached in black churches, King strongly criticized those blacks "who are ashamed that their forebears came from
Africa."
90. King, *Where Do We Go from Here?*, 131, 160; and Warren, *Who
Speaks for the Negro?*, 14–15.

How many Negroes who have achieved educational
and economic security have forgotten that they are
where they are because of the support of faceless, unlettered and unheralded Negroes who did ordinary
jobs in an extraordinary way? How many successful
Negroes have forgotten that uneducated and poverty-
stricken mothers and fathers worked until their eyebrows were scorched and their hands bruised so that
their children could get an education? For any middle-
class Negro to forget the masses is an act not only of
neglect but of shameful ingratitude.[91]

This analysis, offered by one who was himself a middle-
class black leader, is nothing short of remarkable. The
fact is that King was able to escape this kind of psychological condition because he refused to absorb wholeheartedly and uncritically the mentality and values of
the white elite. He recognized the paradox facing the
typical middle-class black—a paradox that kept him confused and set against himself, thus making it impossible
for him to find true happiness and inner peace:

. . . and what happens so often is that this individual finds himself caught in the middle with no cultural roots, because he is rejected by so many of the
white middle class. . . . He ends up, as E. Franklin
Frazier says in a book, unconsciously hating himself,
and he tries to compensate for this through conspicuous consumption.[92]

The disastrous sense of worthlessness that slavery and
segregation instilled in blacks was such that many resorted to resenting and fighting each other, a problem
that revealed to King the enormous work that had to be
done before his people were ready for a unified struggle:

Too many Negroes are jealous of other Negroes' suc-
cesses and progress. Too many Negro organizations
are warring against each other with a claim to absolute truth. The Pharoahs had a favorite and effective

91. King, *Where Do We Go from Here?*, 131–32.
92. Warren, *Who Speaks for the Negro?*, 14–15.

strategy to keep their slaves in bondage: keep them fighting among themselves. The divide-and-conquer technique has been a potent weapon in the arsenal of oppression.[93]

King held that the depth and intensity of black oppression could be explained largely through an analysis of the Euro-American temperament. The essence of that temperament was for him an inflated egotism linked to an insatiable love for power and wealth, a disposition that accounted for white America's need to demean and exploit black human beings.[94] King detested egoism and exploitation as much as he loved freedom and community. As he assessed the history of Euro-Americans, he saw people so bent on dominating and exploiting others for selfish gain that they transformed their own self-professed and self-created standards into lies. "The ultimate contradiction is that the men who wrote the Constitution owned slaves at the same time," King observed, "and it has been this terrible ambivalence in the soul of white America that has led us to the state we are in now." He felt that "The Negro is the most glaring evidence of white America's hypocrisy."[95] King's sentiments surged up from an antipathy for the principles on which capitalism, slavery, and racism are based.

When King turned to the white South, he witnessed the worst aspects of the Euro-American temperament in magnified form. He saw people who, motivated by an intense individualism, had fashioned a culture with its own racist ethos—a set of values that affirmed the existence of superior and inferior races and that gave one race the right to brutalize and exploit another. The constant abuse visited on the bodies and minds of southern blacks and the methods used to keep them in a general

93. King, *Where Do We Go from Here?*, 124.
94. *Ibid.*, 173–91.
95. Martin Luther King, Jr., "An Address at a Mass Meeting," Maggie Street Baptist Church, Montgomery, Alabama, 3; *The St. Louis Post-Dispatch*, St. Louis, Missouri (August 25, 1963), 1 ff.; and King, *Where Do We Go from Here?*, 102–34.

state of poverty and powerlessness were for King the most pervasive evidence of the demonic nature of capitalism and racism. Hence, it was not surprising that his native South had been the chief source of America's racism, an historical fact that made him grimace:

> The South was the stronghold of racism. In white migrations through history from the South to the North and West, racism was carried to poison the rest of the nation. Prejudice, discrimination and bigotry have been inextricably embedded through all the institutions of southern life—political, social, and economic. There could be no possibility of life transforming change anywhere so long as the vast and solid influence of southern segregation remained unchallenged and unhurt.[96]

Of all the shortcomings of white southerners, the one that seems to have disturbed King most was their stubborn determination to sanction segregation in the life of the church. "Segregation in the Christian Church is the most tragic form of segregation," he declared, "because it is a blatant denial that we are all one in Christ Jesus." He brooded over the fact that "eleven o'clock Sunday morning is the most segregated time in America," and that "The Sunday Schools are the most segregated schools in the nation."[97] King believed that segregation in the white churches in the South resulted in part from "a glaring misrepresentation of what the Scripture teaches," particularly with respect to "The 17th Chapter and 26th Verse of the Book of Acts," and "Noah's curse upon the children of Ham in the Book of Genesis."[98] In

96. King, *Where Do We Go from Here?*, 13–14; and Martin Luther King, Jr., "Civil Rights at the Crossroads," an address to the Shop Stewards of Local 815, Teamsters and Allied Trades Council, New York, N. Y. (The King Center Archives, 2 May 1967),4.

97. Lerone Bennett, Jr., "Rev. Martin Luther King, Jr., Alabama Desegregationist, Challenges Talmadge," *Ebony* (April 1957): 81; *The Capitol Times*, Madison, Wis. (March 31, 1962), 1 ff.; and Martin Luther King, Jr., "An Address to the National Press Club," Washington, D.C. (The King Papers, Boston University, 9 July 1962), 6.

98. A letter from Martin Luther King, Jr., to Mr. William E. Newgent 20 October 1959, The King Papers, Boston University.

his view, "the passages of Scripture that the segregation-
ists use in an attempt to justify their position" were indicative of the great moral and ethical dilemma that
afflicted the religion of white southerners—a dilemma
that was reflected in a profound way in the Southern
Baptist Convention, "the largest Protestant denomina-
tion in the South." "My church could never join the
Southern Baptist Convention," King remarked, "because
it's an all-white convention." For him, it was beyond reason that that body could "send thousands and millions of
dollars to Africa for the cause of missions" while barring
Africans and American blacks from its congregations.[99]

King recognized that one of the great tragedies of segregation and other forms of oppression was the manner
in which they created feelings of distrust in his people
toward whites—a distrust that often bordered on the
excessive, thus frustrating efforts to build harmonious
and working relationships between the races:

> The oppression of Negroes by whites has left an un-
> derstandable residue of suspicion. Some of this suspi-
> cion is a healthy and appropriate safeguard. An excess
> of skepticism, however, becomes a fetter. It denies
> that there can be reliable white allies, even though
> some whites have died heroically at the side of Ne-
> groes in our struggle and others have risked economic
> and political peril to support our cause.[100]

In his writings, King observed that his people confronted their oppression "in three characteristic ways."
Some chose "the way of acquiescence," tacitly adjusting
"themselves to oppression," and thereby becoming "con-
ditioned to it." He insisted that some blacks had been re-
duced to a state so low that they preferred "the fleshpots
of Egypt to the challenge of the Promised Land."[101] King

---

99. *Ibid.;* and King, "A Knock at Midnight," 7–9.
100. King, *Where Do We Go from Here?*, 51.
101. King, *Stride toward Freedom*, 211–12; Martin Luther King, Jr.,
"Our Struggle," *Liberation*, 1, no. 2 (April 1956): 3; and Martin Luther
King, Jr., "Some Things We Must Do," a speech delivered in Montgomery,
Alabama (The King Papers, Boston University, 5 December 1957), 7.

found this spirit of complacency and passivity among many poor and uneducated Southern blacks, who lacked "a sense of dignity and self-respect." Having little faith in themselves and dependent in many cases on whites for food, jobs, and shelter, these blacks, according to King, were not prepared to take the necessary steps to overthrow white domination. As he understood the situation, many of them were more prone to find comfort in the belief that prayer alone would change their condition. Although he understood this passivity as a mark of his people's vulnerability, King cautioned that prayer without wise and sustained activism could never defeat the forces of oppression:

> I am certain we need to pray for God's help and guidance in this liberation struggle, but we are gravely misled if we think the struggle will be won only by prayer. God, who gave us minds for thinking and bodies for working, would defeat His own purpose if He permitted us to obtain through prayer what may come through work and intelligence. Prayer is a marvelous and necessary supplement of our feeble efforts, but it is a dangerous substitute. When Moses strove to lead the Israelites to the Promised Land, God made it clear that He would not do for them what they could do for themselves. "And the Lord said unto Moses, Wherefore criest thou unto me? Speak unto the Children of Israel, that they go forward."[102]

King found this spirit of "acquiescence" or "passive resignation" reflected in other ways in the indifference of many middle-class blacks. Throughout his pilgrimage from Montgomery to Memphis, he encountered considerable numbers of well-to-do blacks who remained silent in the face of injustice for fear of losing what little economic security and social status they had. "Many of these Negroes," King argued, "are occupied in a middle class struggle for status and prestige. They are more concerned

102. King, "Some Things We Must do," 7; and King, *Strength to Love*, 131–32.

about 'conspicuous consumption' than about the cause of justice, and are probably not prepared for the ordeals and sacrifices involved in nonviolent action."[103] King was convinced that many privileged blacks had absorbed the white Western model of the radically autonomous individual to the point of abandoning completely the communal values that had long undergirded their people's struggle for liberation and survival:

> All too often the Negro who gets a little money and a little education, ends up saying, "I've got mine and it doesn't matter what happens to anybody else." What I want to see in the black community is a middle class of substance, a middle class that is concerned about the problems of the masses of people. For let me assure you that we all go up together, or we all go down together.[104]

King's major problem with "acquiescence" or "passive resignation" was that it caused the oppressed not only "to accept passively an unjust system" and "to cooperate with that system," but also to allow "the conscience of the oppressor to slumber." Such a response, then, was at best immoral and self-defeating:

> To accept injustice or segregation passively is to say to the oppressor that his actions are morally right. It is a way of allowing his conscience to fall asleep. At this moment the oppressed fails to be his brother's keeper. So acquiescence—while often the easier way—is not the moral way. It is the way of the coward. The Negro cannot win the respect of his oppressor by acquiescing; he merely increases the oppressor's arrogance and contempt. Acquiescence is interpreted as proof of the Negro's inferiority. The Negro cannot win the respect of the white people of the South or the peoples of the world if he is willing to sell the future of his

103. King, *Where Do We Go from Here?*, 131–32; and Martin Luther King, Jr., "The Negro in America: The End of Jim Crow?" (a transcription of a taped speech, The King Center Archives, (n.d.) 5.
104. Martin Luther King, Jr., "Address at a Mass Meeting," Selma, Ala. (The King Center Archives, 16 February 1968), 8; and King *Where Do We Go from Here?*, 132.

children for his personal and immediate comfort and safety.[105]

King identified "physical violence and corroding hatred" as "a second way" his people sometimes adopted in response to their condition. Believing that violence "is both impractical and immoral," he insisted that such an approach merely continued the cycle of hatred and oppression, thus making wholesome and productive relationships between blacks and whites impossible:

> An oppressed group will seek to rise from a position of disadvantage to one of advantage, you see, thereby subverting one tyranny for another. Now, I think our danger is that we can get so bitter that we revolt against every thing white, and this becomes a very dangerous thing because it can lead to the kind of philosophy that you get in the Black Nationalist movements—the kind of philosophy that ends up preaching black supremacy as a way of counteracting white supremacy. . . . This would be bad for our total society.[106]

Elijah Muhammad's Black Muslim movement was for King representative of the extremes of hatred and violence in the black community. His characterization of this group was to some extent excessive, especially since its members preached counter-violence or self-defense rather than the aggressive, institutionalized violence used by whites against blacks. However, while condemning the Black Muslim philosophy on the one hand, King also admitted that "I can well understand the kind of impatience that leads to this kind of reaction." Furthermore, he warned that "as long as doors are closed in the faces of millions of Negroes and they feel dejected and disinherited, an organization like this will appeal to some."[107]

---

105. King, *Stride toward Freedom*, 212.
106. *Ibid.*, 212–13; and Warren, *Who Speaks for the Negro?*, 1–5.
107. A letter from Martin Luther King, Jr., to Mr. Kivie Kaplan, 6 March 1961, The King Papers, Boston University; Oates, *Let the Trumpet Sound*, 252; and Warren, *Who Speaks for the Negro?*, 3–5.

A third approach followed by some blacks in seeking to ameliorate their condition was nonviolent direct action— an approach symbolized by King and the civil rights movement. "Like the synthesis in Hegelian philosophy," he wrote, "the principle of nonviolent resistance seeks to reconcile the truths of two opposites—acquiescence and violence—while avoiding the extremes and immoralities of both." By embracing the way of love and nonviolent protest, King saw himself as representing a middle way between the "do-nothingism" of the complacent and "the hatred and despair of the black Nationalist."[108]

Though disturbed by the complacency, passivity, indifference, and bitterness that often engulfed the lives of his people in certain sectors of the black community, King did not lose faith in their capacity to cooperate and to rise above their menial social and economic condition. Like black leaders before and after him, he could be very critical of his people while, at the same time, believing in their inherent worth and redeeming qualities. "He may be uneducated or poverty-stricken," King said of the average black man, "but he has within his being the power to alter his fate."[109] Though frequently used against one another by the oppressor, black people, he believed, had almost a natural inclination to come together against forces that threatened their existence:

> Negroes are almost instinctively cohesive. We band together readily, and against white hostility we have an intense and wholesome loyalty to each other. In some of the simplest relationships we will protect a brother even at a cost to ourselves. We are loath to be witnesses against each other when the white man seeks to divide us. We are acutely conscious of the need and sharply sensitive to the importance of defending our own. Solidarity is a reality in Negro life, as it always has been among the oppressed. Sometimes, unfortunately, it is

108. King, *Stride toward Freedom*, 213–14; and King, *Why We Can't Wait*, 87.
109. King, *Where Do We Go from Here?*, 159 ff.

mis-applied when we confuse high status with high
character.[110]

King also pointed to other qualities in his people that
he felt enhanced their power and potential. Quoting
W. E. B. Du Bois, he noted that out of their pain and
struggle black people had "learned to sing that most
original of all American music, the Negro spiritual," an
observation that proves that he recognized their artistic
and spiritual genius.[111] King apparently thought that a
recognition and celebration of such gifts and qualities
were essential for an appreciation of the positive and
unique aspects of black culture and, therefore, important for "a confirmation of our roots and a validation of
our worth."[112]

King's diagnosis of the black condition led him to
propose certain prescriptions for the afflictions of his
people—prescriptions that were set forth in some detail
in his published works. "One positive response to our
dilemma," he wrote, "is to develop a rugged sense of
somebodyness," which "means the refusal to be ashamed
of being black."[113] He knew that until his people revolu-
tionized their thinking about themselves, the black movement would be at best abortive or spasmodic:

> Our children must be taught to stand tall with their
> heads proudly lifted. We need not be duped into pur-
> chasing bleaching creams that promise to make us
> lighter. We need not process our hair to make it appear
> straight. Whether some men, black and white, realize it
> or not, black people are very beautiful. Life's piano can
> only produce the melodies of brotherhood when it is
> recognized that the black keys are as basic, necessary
> and beautiful as the white keys.[114]

110. *Ibid.*
111. King, "The Meaning of Hope," 16.
112. King, *Where Do We Go from Here?*, 53 and 122–23; and King,
*Why We Can't Wait*, 61.
113. King, *Where Do We Go from Here?*, 122–23.
114. *Ibid.*

In King's judgment, inspiring pride and confidence in the black past was necessarily a part of this effort to secure "a majestic sense of self-worth" in his people. "We have a rich and noble heritage," he remarked, and "I think it's absolutely necessary for the Negro to have an appreciation of his heritage." King sensed that an important part of that heritage was reflected in the spiritual strength and values of the slaves—resources that could be quite useful to his people in their drive for self-acceptance and self-appreciation:

> Something of the inner spirit of our slave forebears must be pursued today. From the inner depths of our being we must sing with them: "Before I'll be a slave, I'll be buried in my grave, and go home to my Lord and be free." This spirit, this drive, this rugged sense of somebodyness is the first and most vital step that the Negro must take in dealing with his dilemma.[115]

A second significant step that black people could take, according to King, involved transcending disunity within their ranks—a tragic disunity that had long been fueled by oppression. He challenged his people to "work passionately for group identity" and "group trust," asserting that "only by being reconciled to ourselves will we be able to build upon the resources we already have at our disposal."[116] Convinced that black people should not confine themselves to a single methodological approach in their struggle, King insisted that "This plea for unity is not a call for uniformity." He further declared: "There must always be healthy debate. There will be inevitable differences of opinion. The dilemma that the Negro confronts

115. *Ibid.;* Martin Luther King, Jr., "Address at the Chicago Freedom Movement Rally," Chicago, Ill. (The King Center Archives, 10 July 1966), 4; King, "The Crisis of Civil Rights," 1–10; Martin Luther King, Jr., "In Search of a Sense of Direction," a sermon delivered at the Vermont Avenue Baptist Church, Washington, D.C. (The King Center Archives, 7 February 1968), 4–5; King, *Where Do We Go from Here?*, 43–44; and "Doubts and Certainties Link: An Interview with Martin Luther King, Jr.," SYNC SOUND, London, England (The King Center Archives, Winter, 1968), 8.
116. King, *Where Do We Go from Here?*, 123–24.

is so complex and monumental that its solution will of
necessity involve a diversified approach. But Negroes can
differ and still unite around common goals."[117]

For King, this quest for solidarity among black people
necessarily required a return to the basic communal
values of their slave foreparents. He believed that the
church and other black institutions, which were the traditional arenas for the preservation and legitimation of
those values, afforded the best foundation for forging a
black "united front," although they had not always
devoted the full weight of their resources to the struggle:

> There are already structured forces in the Negro com-
> munity that can serve as the basis for building a power-
> ful united front—the Negro church, the Negro press,
> the Negro fraternities and sororities, and the Negro
> professional associations. We must admit that these
> forces have never given their full resources to the
> cause of Negro liberation. There are still too many Ne-
> gro churches that are so absorbed in a future good
> "over yonder" that they condition their members to ad-
> just to the present evils "over here." Too many Negro
> newspapers have veered away from their traditional
> role as protest organs agitating for social change, and
> have turned to the sensational and the conservative in
> place of the substantive and the militant. Too many Ne-
> gro social and professional groups have degenerated
> into snobbishness and a preoccupation with frivolities
> and trivial activity. But the failures of the past must not
> be an excuse for the inaction of the present and the
> future. These groups must be mobilized and motivated.
> This form of group unity can do infinitely more to lib-
> erate the Negro than any action of *individuals*. We
> have been oppressed as a group and we must overcome
> that oppression as a group.[118]

As a third step in overcoming the black condition, King
spoke of the need for his people "to aspire to excellence"
in every field of endeavor—"not excellence as a Negro

117. *Ibid.*
118. *Ibid.*

doctor or lawyer or a Negro craftsman, but excellence
per se." "This is particularly relevant for the young Negro," he thought, for whom "doors of opportunity are
gradually opening now that were not open to our mothers and fathers." He urged black youngsters not to "adjust
patiently" to the mediocrity encouraged by racism and
segregation but to "work assiduously" to improve their
educational and cultural standards. Moreover, King
called on blacks as a whole to raise the moral climate in
their neighborhoods, an effort that for him was essential
in refuting white assertions of black inferiority. "Our
crime rate is far too high" and "our level of cleanliness is
frequently far too low," he complained. "Even the most
poverty-stricken among us can purchase a ten-cent bar of
soap; even the most uneducated among us can have high
morals."[119] King believed that through a united thrust
to "improve their general level of behavior," blacks could
"convey to one another that our women must be respected, and that life is too precious to be destroyed in a
Saturday night brawl, or a gang execution."[120] Although
King recognized that crime, family disorganization, illegitimacy, and other problems in the black community
were the tragic by-product of racism and segregation, he
nevertheless thought that the primary responsibility for
changing these conditions rested squarely on the shoulders of black people. However, he also recognized the
need for government assistance in dealing with such
problems.[121]

King casually dismissed arguments that suggested that
his people were incapable of elevating themselves in vital
areas of life—cultural, economic, moral, political, religious, and intellectual. "We already have the inspiring
examples of Negroes who with determination have broken through the shackles of circumstance" and risen "to
the heights of genius" in many areas, he declared. He

119. *Ibid.*, 125–27; and King, *Stride toward Freedom*, 223.
120. King, *Where Do We Go from Here?*, 125.
121. *Ibid.*; and John J. Ansbro, *Martin Luther King, Jr.: The Making of a
Mind* (Maryknoll, N. Y.: Orbis Books, 1982), 131–37.

pointed to Booker T. Washington, who rose "from an old
slave cabin in Virginia's hills to become one of America's
great leaders," and to George Washington Carver, who
emerged "from crippling beginnings" to create "for himself an imperishable niche in the annals of science."[122]
King also mentioned numerous others who, in various
ways, had built on the cultural foundations established by
the slaves in their music, folklore, and dance—singers
and musical artists like Roland Hayes, Marian Anderson,
Leontyne Price, Harry Belafonte, Sammy Davis, Mahalia
Jackson, Ray Charles, and Duke Ellington; poets and
writers such as James Weldon Johnson, Paul Lawrence
Dunbar, Countée Cullen, Claude McKay, Langston
Hughes, W. E. B. Du Bois, Richard Wright, Ralph Ellison,
and James Baldwin; and athletic figures like Henry
Aaron, Roy Campanella, Muhammad Ali, Althea Gibson,
Joe Louis, Jack Johnson, Jackie Robinson, James Brown,
Bill Russell, Wilt Chamberlin, Jesse Owens, Buddy
Young, and Arthur Ashe.[123] Recognizing that not all of his
people could be in "specialized or professional jobs,"
King encouraged even those "called to be laborers in fac-
tories, fields and streets" to make their contributions to
the life of the nation. "All labor that uplifts humanity has
dignity and worth," he wrote, "and should be pursued
with respect for excellence." He felt that common laborers in the black community who aspired to excellence
had a great source of inspiration in their slave ancestors,
"who refused to be stopped" in spite of "the sizzling heat,
the rawhide whip of the overseer, and long rows of cotton," and who risked life and limb "to learn to read and
write."[124]

King identified as a fourth challenge the need for
blacks to "unite around powerful action programs" of an
economic and political nature to better their condition.
In his view, such programs held the best possibilities for

122. King, *Where Do We Go from Here?*, 126–27.
123. *Ibid.*
124. *Ibid.*, 127–28; and King, "The Meaning of Hope," 13–18.

achieving fair housing, equal job opportunities, voting rights, and other privileges guaranteed to all Americans under the Constitution.[125] Although King acknowledged that "Negroes have been far more cruelly exploited and suffer an intensity of discrimination Jews have never felt," he nonetheless thought that "the lesson of Jewish determination to use educational and social action on a mass scale to attain political representation and influence is worthy of emulation."[126] However, he scoffed at the idea that his people should "lift themselves up by their own bootstraps"—an idea he felt was promoted mostly by the very people determined to maintain black oppression:

> There again, we hear a lot of talk about the fact that the Negro should lift himself by his own bootstraps. Now, I believe in a certain aspect of that. And this is what we try to do. I do always point out the other side—that the problem is that Negroes have not always had the resources in many ways to just do it by themselves. And its a cruel jest to say to a bootless man that he ought to lift himself by his own bootstraps. And its even worst if you have a boot, and somebody's standing on the boot, and they're telling you to lift yourself by your own bootstraps.[127]

"A final challenge that we face as a result of our great dilemma," King said, "is to be ever mindful of enlarging the whole society, and giving it a new sense of values as we seek to solve our particular problem."[128] In short, he believed that his people should transcend the artificial barriers of race and ethnicity and engage in dialogue, mutual support, and working coalitions with Puerto

125. King, Where Do We Go from Here?, 128–66; and King, Why We Can't Wait, 67.
126. King, Where Do We Go from Here?, (unpublished draft, The King Center Archives, 1967), 17–18.
127. Martin Luther King, Jr., "Speech at Operation Breadbasket Meeting," Chicago Theological Seminary, Chicago, Ill. (The King Center Archives, 25 March 1967), 5.
128. King, Where Do We Go from Here?, 132–33.

Ricans, Mexican-Americans, Native Americans, Hispanic-Americans, Appalachian whites, and others who suffered under similar oppressive conditions in this country. King also suggested that such structures of dialogue, sharing, and cooperation be created between black Americans and Third World peoples, who were also victims of racism, poverty, and the institutionalized violence of Western imperialists. For him, black freedom was not attainable independently of the freedoms of other peoples in this country and abroad. This was the truth of the beloved community ideal he articulated and projected—an ideal he sought to bring to fruition through the Poor People's Campaign and in his dialogue and working relationships with leaders in the so-called Third World.[129]

## VISION OF A "NEW SOUTH"

Three points must be established if one is to understand King's vision of a redeemed, transformed, and inclusive southern society. First, that vision was shaped and informed in primal terms by his sense of place in a southern context or by a deep sense of "regional identity and regional responsibility." Second, King's vision was grounded in a Christian optimism and a deep faith in justice. Finally, his vision for the South was essentially the same vision he had for the nation and the world.[130]

King was convinced that the creation of a more peaceful, just, and inclusive South demanded a persistent struggle against the demonic forces of injustice and an unswerving devotion to the ideals and values embodied in the American democratic heritage and the Judeo-Christian faith. The modern civil rights movement was a vehicle through which King and his people sought to

129. *Ibid.;* "James Cone Interview: Liberation, Black Theology, and the Church," *Radix Magazine* (September–October 1982): 9; Cone, "Martin Luther King, Jr. and the Third World," 455–67; and Baldwin, ed., *Toward the Beloved Community,* 1–20, 275–317.

130. Watley, *Roots of Resistance,* 36; Brown, "Grounds for American Loyalty," 48–55; and Baldwin, ed., *Toward the Beloved Community,* 1–20, 275–317.

translate this vision of a "new South" into practical reality. The fact that the movement was concentrated primarily in the South, where racial injustice existed in its most glaring forms, was for King an indication of how a people can be "pulled into the mainstream by the rolling tide of historical necessity." It was also evidence of the mysterious workings of divine providence. "God still has a mysterious way to perform His wonders," King said in a speech toward the end of the Montgomery Bus Boycott in 1956. "It seems that God decided to use Montgomery as the proving ground for the struggle and triumph of freedom and justice in America. It is one of the ironies of our day that Montgomery, the cradle of the Confederacy, is being transformed into Montgomery, the cradle of freedom and justice."[131] The notion that God was somehow using the South to trigger a movement for social change throughout the nation was at the core of King's understanding of the civil rights campaigns in Montgomery, Albany, Birmingham, Selma, Memphis, and other southern cities—campaigns that, as he put it, "were geared toward attacking the system of legal segregation and the syndrome of deprivation surrounding that system."[132]

From the time of the Montgomery Bus Boycott in 1955–56, King insisted that black people should be the vanguard in this quest for a new South. This view was based on the idea that oppressed people generally have a greater propensity for moral and spiritual values than their oppressors, and also on the traditional Christian belief in the redemptive power of suffering. King held

131. Martin Luther King, Jr., "An Announcement of His Decision to Move from Montgomery to Atlanta," Dexter Avenue Baptist Church, Montgomery, Ala. (The King Papers, Boston University, 29 November 1959), 2; and Martin Luther King, Jr., "Address at the First Annual Institute on Nonviolence and Social Change under the Auspices of the Montgomery Improvement Association," Holt Street Baptist Church, Montgomery, Ala. (The King Center Archives, 3 December 1956), 1–2.

132. Martin Luther King, Jr., "Why We Must Go to Washington," a speech delivered at the S.C.L.C. Retreat, Ebenezer Baptist Church, Atlanta, Ga. (The King Center Archives, 15 January 1968), 2.

that the dismantling of political, cultural, and structural barriers to complete equality in the South depended largely upon his people's skillful and persistent adherence to nonviolent principles. Nonviolence, in this case, was viewed as a strategy with many tactical manifestations, such as mass marches, demonstrations, civil disobedience, boycotts, sit-ins, prayer vigils, and community organization. King embraced nonviolent direct action as a major method because of its moral consistency with the vision of Jesus of Nazareth and because he saw it as the most practical and moral way of confronting and transforming racist personalities, structures, and institutions, especially in the South.[133]

Although King had learned much about nonviolence from the Indian leader Mohandas K. Gandhi, from social critics such as Henry David Thoreau and A. J. Muste, from long-time social activists like Bayard Rustin and Glenn Smiley, and from Jesus' Sermon on the Mount in the New Testament, it is much more important to understand his concept of nonviolence in relation to the southern black Christian tradition.[134] Three of his mentors—Mordecai Johnson, Benjamin E. Mays, and Howard Thurman—all of whom came out of black Baptist Protestantism in the South, had either visited Gandhi in India or had incorporated aspects of his nonviolent philosophy into their thought. Furthermore, King was surrounded by southern black Christians whose traditional form of nonviolence had long represented moderation in the midst of the violence of white America. It is clear that his decision to embrace nonviolence as a personal and social ethic resulted more from

133. King, *Stride toward Freedom*, 102–07 and 212–13; and *The Daily Cardinal*, Madison, Wisconsin (March 31, 1962), 1 ff.
134. Nathan I. Huggins, "Martin Luther King, Jr.: Charisma and Leadership," *The Journal of American History*, 74, no. 2 (September, 1987): 480; King, *Stride Toward Freedom*, 95–107; and Juan Williams, et al., *Eyes on the Prize—America's Civil Rights Years, 1954–1965: A Companion Volume to the PBS Series*. (New York: Viking Penguin, 1987), 125–26.

his experiences with the practical application of that method among black southerners than from any other source:

> The experience in Montgomery did more to clarify my thinking than all the books that I had read. As the days unfolded, I became more and more convinced of the power of nonviolence. Nonviolence became more than a method to which I gave intellectual assent; it became a commitment to a way of life. Many issues I had not cleared up intellectually concerning nonviolence were now resolved within the sphere of practical action.[135]

King regarded education, religion, legislation and court action, and effective interracial alliances as meaningful and necessary supplements to nonviolent direct action. He suggested that education constituted one means of changing internal feelings of fear, prejudice, and hate in whites and of preparing blacks for heightened self-esteem and a wise use of economic and political power.[136] King emphasized a dependence on religion to change the hearts of whites and to compel them to incorporate the Christian norms of love, justice, freedom, and equality into law. "Something must happen to touch the hearts and souls of men that they will come together," he wrote, "not because the law says it, but because it is natural and right."[137] King noted that some of the major achievements of the civil rights struggle would come through legisla-

135. Martin Luther King, Jr., *Strength to Love* (Philadelphia: Fortress Press, 1981), 151–52.
136. King, *Stride toward Freedom*, 32–34; Watley, *Roots of Resistance*, 15, chapters 2–4; James H. Evans, "'To Study War No More': Martin Luther King, Jr. and Nonviolent Resistance," *The A.M.E. Zion Quarterly Review*, Vol. 97 no. 4 (January 1988): 6. Evans examines King's aproach in relation to the long history of nonviolent resistance as practiced by major activists in the United States. Also see King, "An Address at the National Bar Association Meeting," Milwaukee, Wis., 1; King, "An Address to the National Press Club," Washington, D.C., 5; Ansbro, *Martin Luther King, Jr.*, 135; A letter from Martin Luther King, Jr., to Thurgood Marshall, 6 February 1958; and "The Martin Luther King Story," *Sepia Magazine* (March 22, 1957): 2–3.
137. King, *Stride toward Freedom*, 219–20.

tion and court action, as had previously been the case. He viewed the formation of effective alliances between blacks and other racial and ethnic groups, based on common respect and interests, as still another approach to transcending the barriers to freedom, justice, and community. The Southern Christian Leadership Conference (S.C.L.C.), organized under King's leadership in Atlanta in 1957, became the operational base from which he sought to mobilize the resources of both all-black and interracial protest organizations. King's advocacy of these various approaches suggests that he saw the road to moral, social, political, and economic prosperity in the South as requiring many avenues.[138]

King's vision for the South developed and matured in the midst of the conflict and crisis situations that characterized campaigns such as Montgomery, Albany, Birmingham, and Selma. The successful outcome of the Montgomery Bus Boycott did much to stimulate his great hopes for the South in the late 1950s. In December, 1956, toward the end of the boycott, King spoke of "great resources of goodwill in the Southern white man that we must somehow tap."[139] In the spring of 1957, he wrote: "I still have faith in the South. The days ahead are bright. Something is unfolding in the South. We stand on the threshold of the most constructive and creative period in our nation's history. An old order is passing away and a new order is coming into being." King was convinced at that point that "the great majority of white Southerners are prepared to accept and abide by the supreme law of the land. They, like us, want to be law-abiding citizens." He estimated that it was only "a small but determined minority" of white southerners who "resort to threats, bodily assaults, cross-burnings,

138. King, "An Address at the National Bar Asssociation Meeting," Milwaukee, Wis., 1; King, "An Address to the National Press Club," Washington, D.C., 5; and King, *Stride toward Freedom*, 34.
139. King, "An Address at the First Annual Institute on Nonviolence and Social Change," 1–3.

bombings, shootings and open defiance of the law in an attempt to force us to retreat."[140] By 1958, King was even more specific about his vision, noting that "We are convinced that in our time the South can be a peaceful and integrated society."[141] To those who seriously doubted the possibility of the realization of the beloved community in the South, he explained: "The South has a heart, but it just has a little heart trouble now."[142] In short, the South in the late 1950s was for King "a land of terror and painful anxiety today but a land of prosperity and peace for tomorrow."[143]

It is notable and rather ironic that King's hopes for the South came to center largely and peculiarly on Alabama and Mississippi, the two southern states with the worst records in race relations at that time, and in which most of his greatest struggles occurred. "Maybe the idea of freedom in the Southland will be born right here in Montgomery, the cradle of the Confederacy," he exclaimed in

140. King, "Some Things We Must Do," 3; A letter from Martin Luther King, Jr., to Buford Boone, 9 May 1957, The King Papers, Boston University; Martin Luther King, Jr., "An Address at the Freedom Fund Report Dinner, N.A.A.C.P.'s 53rd Annual Convention," Atlanta, Ga. (The King Center Archives, 5 July 1962), 3; and Martin Luther King, Jr., "A Statement to the South and Nation," Atlanta, Ga. (The King Center Archives, 10–11 January 1957), 2–3.

141. Martin Luther King, Jr., "A Speech at the Fourth Anniversary of the Montgomery Improvement Association," Montgomery, Ala. (The King Center Archives, 3 December 1959), 1 ff.; Martin Luther King, Jr., "When Peace Becomes Obnoxious," *The Louisville Defender*, Louisville, Kentucky (March 29, 1956), 1; King, "An Address at the First Annual Institute on Nonviolence and Social Change," 2–3; and A letter from Martin Luther King, Jr., to H. E. Tate, 20 February 1958, The King Papers, Boston University.

142. See *The New York Times* (March 26, 1956): 27.

143. Reddick, *Crusader Without Violence*, 22–23. From the time of the Montgomery Bus Boycott, King's vision of the "New South" was expressed in terms of the coming of the Promised Land. In 1957 he declared: "If I die tomorrow, I'll be happy. I've been up on the mountain. I've seen the Promised Land. Its not here yet, but it's coming. If I don't see it, my daughter, Yokie, will. Nothing can stop it." These words are strikingly similar to those used by King in his last major speech on April 3, 1968, a day before his death. See Bennett, "Rev. Martin Luther King, Jr., Alabama Desegregationist," 81; and Flip Schulke, ed., *Martin Luther King, Jr.: A Documentary—Montgomery to Memphis* (New York: W. W. Norton, 1976), 224.

1956.[144] He later prophesied that "The future of America may well be determined here, in Mississippi, for it is here that democracy faces its most serious challenge."[145] The fact that King envisioned the possibility of Alabama and Mississippi playing such an historic role should not be surprising, especially since most of the redemptive and transforming activity through the civil rights movement was occurring in those states.

By the early 1960s, King had begun to advance the idea of the "new South" with greater certainty. In an address before the National Press Club in Washington, D.C., on July 19, 1962, he insisted that "The old South has gone, never to return again. Many of the problems that we are confronting in the South today grow out of the futile attempt of the white South to maintain a system of human values that came into being under a feudalistic plantation system and which cannot survive in a day of democratic egalitarianism."[146] He noted how some southern communities, confronted with clear and demanding legal decisions, were making readjustments in the old and seemingly unalterable patterns of life:

> Here and there churches are courageously making attacks on segregation, and actually integrating their congregations. Several parochial and church-related schools of the South are throwing off the traditional yoke of segregation. As the church continues to take a forthright stand on this issue, the transition from a segregated to an integrated society will be infinitely smoother.[147]

Apparently, the failures of the movement in Albany, Georgia in 1962 did not alter King's conviction that the South was inevitably on a new and changing course. This was because he refused to view the Albany

144. King, "When Peace Becomes Obnoxious," 1; and King, "An Address at the First Annual Institute on Nonviolence and Social Change," 1.
145. King, "A Statement Regarding the Mississippi Freedom Democractic Party at the C.O.F.O. Rally," 1.
146. King, "An Address to the National Press Club," 4.
147. *Ibid.*, 6.

campaign, which resulted in the addition of thousands of blacks to the voting-registration rolls, as "an unqualified failure."[148] If the Albany experience, which amounted to an unsuccessful across-the-board, full-scale offensive against segregation, shook King's confidence in the capacity of the South for lasting, positive change in race relations, the Birmingham campaign in 1963, which ended with the white business community meeting black demands for desegregated facilities and nondiscriminatory hiring practices, did much to reinforce his confidence. King was very pleased and encouraged not only with the negotiated settlement in Birmingham but also with how events there helped make civil rights a priority in the national consciousness.[149] This explains in part why, during the great march on Washington in August, 1963, he could speak so confidently and eloquently of his dream for the South:

> I have a dream that one day on the red hills of Georgia, the sons of former slaves and the sons of former slaveowners will be able to sit down together at the table of brotherhood. I have a dream that one day even in the state of Mississippi, a state sweltering with the heat of injustice, sweltering with the heat of oppression, will be transformed into an oasis of freedom and justice. . . . I have a dream that one day down in Alabama—with its vicious racists, with its Governor [Wallace] having his lips dripping with the words of interposition and nullification—one day right there in Alabama, little black boys and black girls will be able to join hands with little white boys and white girls as sisters and brothers. This is our hope. This is the faith that I go back to the South with. . . .[150]

It is difficult to avoid the conclusion that King underestimated the depth of racism in the South and in the nation

148. King, *Why We Can't Wait,* 43–44; and Watley, *Roots of Resistance,* 68–69.
149. Watley, *Roots of Resistance,* 79; and King, *Why We Can't Wait,* 59–75, 96–109.
150. Schulke, ed., *Martin Luther King, Jr.,* 218.

in general in the late 1950s and early 1960s. The experience in Montgomery had given him an exaggerated sense of the power of nonviolence and of the capacity of the South for change.[151] In 1958, he actually expressed the hope that racial reconciliation would be achieved in the South in ten to twenty years, a hope that has not yet materialized. He even accepted the possibility of white moderates entering the ranks of the movement throughout the South, a thought that resulted from a combination of naive optimism and a desire to be prudent.[152] Despite King's great faith in the South, by 1963 he began to admit that "Perhaps I was too optimistic; perhaps I expected too much. I suppose I should have realized that few members of the oppresssor race can understand the deep groans and passionate yearnings of the oppressed race, and still fewer have the vision to see that injustice must be rooted out by strong, persistent and determined action."[153] From the Birmingham jail in April, 1963, he complained that "our beloved Southland" is still "bogged down in a tragic effort to live in monologue rather than dialogue."[154] From that point, and notably after 1965, according to Coleman B. Brown, King experienced "a growing sobriety":

> a sobriety that emerged especially after 1965—not as a judgment that earlier southern victories had been dismantled, or rendered meaningless: There simply is no evidence of that in King. Rather, there seems in him a growing grief that the New South—which he was confident had somehow arrived—had, despite everything, so much resistance to itself. Moreover, he seems to have been grieving that the New Negro—for whom the sense

151. King, *Why We Can't Wait,* 89–90; and Watley, *Roots of Resistance,* 68. Coleman Brown's contention that King "never minimized that 'neurosis' of Southern racism" is not persuasive. See Brown, "Grounds for American Loyalty," 49.

152. Brown, "Grounds for American Loyalty," 49–52; and Martin Luther King, Jr., "An Address at the Prayer Pilgrimage for Freedom," The Lincoln Memorial, Washington, D.C. (The King Papers, 17 May 1957), Boston University, 2.

153. King, *Why We Can't Wait,* 89.

154. *Ibid.,* 80.

of inferiority and even the experience of overt segregation were increasingly dead things—would nonetheless have to bear, even as a new people, continued
injustice and struggle in the South, and in the North.[155]

Although he was convinced that the civil rights
achievements that had begun in Montgomery were essentially secure, King had come to see by 1966 that his magnificent dream of human solidarity was not shared by the
vast majority of white southerners.[156] He also realized
increasingly that his people did not have the economic
power to take full advantage of gains already made
through the Civil Rights Act of 1964, the Voting Rights Act
of 1965, and other types of civil rights legislation.[157]
King's realization of these problems had come into sharp
focus by mid-1966, when Stokely Carmichael's and Willie
Rick's cry of "black power" echoed throughout the nation. Under the influence of black power advocates, King
began to place more emphasis on economic justice for
black people. He insisted in a speech in Frogmore, South
Carolina, in May, 1967, that the beloved community
would not materialize in the South as long as whites
thought of integration "in esthetic and romantic terms"
rather than in terms of inclusivity, egalitarian values, and
a sharing of power:

> Now when you think of integration merely in esthetic
> or romantic terms, it may easily be a system that merely
> adds color to a still predominantly white power struc-
> ture. . . . Integration in its true dimension is shared

155. Brown, "Grounds for American Loyalty," 54. In 1965, King
wrote: "Yet in 1965 there is a new South, still far from democratic consistency or harmony, but equally distant from the plantation-overseer
South." See Martin Luther King, Jr., "Next Stop: The North," in Washington, ed., *A Testament of Hope*, 194.
156. Watley, *Roots of Resistance*, 89; Lewis V. Baldwin, "The Emerging Vision of Martin Luther King," *The Vanderbilt Hustler*, Nashville,
Tennessee (January 20, 1989): 8; Adam Fairclough, "Was Martin Luther
King a Marxist?," *History Workshop*, 15 (Spring 1983): 120; and Adam
Fairclough, "The Southern Christian Leadership Conference and the Second Reconstruction, 1957–1973," *The South Atlantic Quarterly*, 80, no. 2
(Spring 1981): 187–90.
157. Martin Luther King, Jr., "Why We Must Go to Washington," 2;
and Watley, *Roots of Resistance*, 88–110.

power. And it is a two-way road. So often we think of integration as Negroes being taken out of Negro institutions, or agencies and forces, and moved into white forces. They think of integration as having a white principal moved to a predominantly Negro school rather than a Negro principal moved to a predominantly white school. Now this means that we have to see integration in political terms, and see that integration is mutual acceptance, true inter-group and inter-personal living where there is shared power.[158]

In King's opinion, there was no need for blacks, any more than for whites, to abandon all of their institutions, values, and traditions with the coming of integration to the South. For him, integration did not mean total assimilation into white culture or a loss of black identity. He felt that the very idea of whites defining integration and then applying it to blacks implied a continuation of white dominance. King hoped that as black people were fully incorporated into southern life and institutions, they would bring in black-oriented institutions, perspectives, and interests. He wanted ultimately to see a society in which black power and white power intersected, and in which the positive features of black life and culture would be valued as much as those of whites.[159]

King also realized by 1966 that he had made a mistake in assuming that "there would be direct and major derivative benefits for the northern ghettoes from the southern campaigns."[160] The riots that occurred in the black communities of Harlem, Rochester, Watts, and Chicago between 1964 and 1966 were for King a clear indication of the frustration and rage resulting from slum conditions. His involvements in the Chicago campaign in 1966 and the Memphis strike early in 1968 were designed to

158. Martin Luther King, Jr., "To Chart Our Course for the Future," an address delivered at an S.C.L.C. Retreat, Frogmore, S. C. (The King Center Archives, 29–31 May 1967), 4–5; and Watley, *Roots of Resistance*, 89–91.

159. King, "An Address at a Mass Meeting," Clarksdale, Miss. 7–10; and Martin Luther King, Jr., "Address at a Mass Meeting," Eutaw, Ala. (The King Center Archives, 20 March 1968), 3–4.

160. Brown, "Grounds for American Loyalty," 53.

mobilize national opinion and to encourage federal support for open housing policies, improved educational opportunities, affordable health care, increased wages, and
other issues of economic justice for poor blacks.[161] As
King deepened his involvement in the struggle for economic justice, he was confronted with several harsh realities. First, he discovered the great difficulty whites had
in even entertaining the idea of sharing power with black
people. He suffered an erosion of support from white lib-
erals, who found the idea of economic equality much
more frightening and difficult to accept than the issue of
civil rights. The vicious attacks visited on King and his
followers by whites in the Marquette Park, Gage, Bogan,
and Jefferson Park communities of Chicago in 1966, and
the growing white backlash in the face of black riots and
demands for economic justice throughout the country,
served as vivid reminders that white America was not as
receptive to the actualization of the beloved community
as King initially assumed. This caused King much anxiety
and frustration, compelling him to conclude in 1966 that
"the vast majority of white Americans are racists."[162]

Second, King increasingly came to see that the
problem of economic inequality and injustice was not
confined to blacks—that Puerto Ricans, Mexican-
Americans, Appalachian whites, and other groups were
victimized in various ways by the same problem. This
led King to become involved in the planning of the
Poor People's Campaign in late 1967 and early 1968, a
campaign designed to solidify these various racial and
ethnic groups in a struggle for economic justice.[163] This

161. Watley, *Roots of Resistance*, 94–100; and Joan T. Beifuss, *At the River I Stand: Memphis, the 1968 Strike, and Martin Luther King* (Memphis: B & W Books, 1985), 135, 190–96, 211–25.

162. Watley, *Roots of Resistance*, 89, 96–99; Baldwin, "The Emerging Vision of Martin Luther King," 8; Kenneth L. Smith, "Equality and Justice: A Dream or Vision of Reality," *Report from the Capital* (January 1984): 4–5, 7; and Fairclough, "Was Martin Luther King A Marxist?," 120.

163. Watley, *Roots of Resistance*, 89; and Adam Fairclough, *To Redeem the Soul of America: The Southern Christian Leadership Conference and Martin Luther King, Jr.* (Athens, Ga.: The University of Georgia Press, 1987), 357–83.

was reflective of his conviction that the beloved community would never be realized as long as considerable numbers of his people limited their thinking to the particularity of the black experience of oppression in the South. It was also proof of King's belief that America could transcend racism and classism to become truly one nation in fulfillment of the Constitution and the Declaration of Independence. This is one reason why he opposed the vision, advanced at various times in our nation's history, of a separate nation for black people.[164]

Finally, King's increased involvement in the movement for economic justice convinced him of the need for a radical restructuring of the American economy and a refocusing of the entire national purpose. As King became more deeply aware of the relationship between racial oppression, class exploitation, and militarism, he advocated basic structural changes within the capitalistic system, calling for the nationalization of basic industries, massive federal expenditures to enhance deprived communities and to provide jobs for ghetto residents, and guaranteed housing, medical care, and annual incomes for the poor. By the time of his death, then, King had moved beyond the dream of integrated buses, schools, and lunch counters in the South to envision a truly democratic society for everyone without racism, economic exploitation, and wars of aggression.[165]

Despite his expanding vision, King remained primarily concerned with the moral, social, political, and economic prosperity of his native South. Nothing disturbed him more than the methods used by southern racists to keep the South from its proper ascendancy. He criticized white southerners who consistently dismissed every attempt at interracial peace and harmony through the civil

164. King, *Where Do We Go from Here?*, 53; Martin Luther King, Jr., "See You in Washington," a speech given at the S.C.L.C. Retreat, Ebenezer Baptist Church, Atlanta, Ga. (The King Center Archives, 17 January 1967), 3–4; and "James Cone Interview," 9.
165. Baldwin, "The Emerging Vision of Martin Luther King," 8; and Smith, "Equality and Justice," 4–5, 7.

rights movement as Communist-inspired and controlled.
King vowed that "We will not allow [James] Eastland,
[Ross] Barnett, or the George Wallaces to use the 'Red'
issue to block our efforts, to split our ranks, or confuse
our supporters."[166] He insisted that those who turned to
"planned and institutionalized tokenism" as "a new carefully constructed roadblock" to social progress in the
South were doomed to failure:

> Many areas of the South are retreating to a position
> which will permit a handful of Negroes to attend all-
> white schools or the employment in lily-white factories
> of one Negro to a thousand white employees. Thus
> we have advanced in some areas from all-out, unre-
> strained resistance to a sophisticated form of delay em-
> bodied in tokenism. In a sense, this is one of the most
> difficult problems our movement confronts. But I am
> confident that this tactic will prove to be as vain a hope
> as the earlier quest to utilize massive resistance to in-
> hibit even a scintilla of change.[167]

King's belief in the South's potential for growth and
change remained strong even as he confronted white
resistance and the horror of America's military role in
Vietnam. By the time of his death he was speaking of the
"difficult days ahead," but he still insisted that "we will
reach the promised land."[168] This struck a responsive

166. Martin Luther King, Jr., "A Response to J. Edgar Hoover's
Charge that Communists Have Infiltrated the Civil Rights Movement,"
Atlanta, Ga. (The King Papers, Boston University, 23 April 1964), 1–3;
Martin Luther King, Jr., "A Statement in Response to *The Atlanta Consti-
tution's* Article Alleging Communist Ties," Atlanta, Ga. (The King Center
Archives, 25 July 1963), 1–2; and "A Transcript of the Martin Luther
King, Jr. Interview on 'Face the Nation,'" broadcast over CBS Television
Network (The King Papers, Boston University, 10 May 1964), 18–20. Al-
though it is generally accepted that King was not a true Marxist, the
emerging contention is that he was by 1966 an advocate of Democratic
Socialism. See Fairclough, "Was Martin Luther King A Marxist?," 117–
25; Manning Marable, "King's Ambiguous Legacy," *WIN Magazine*, 18,
no. 7 (April 15, 1982): 15–19; Paulette Pierce, "From Mythical Symbol to
Socialist," *New York Democratic Socialist* (n.d.), 1A; and *Workers Viewpoint: Newspaper of the Communist Workers Party*, 8, no. 25 (August 17–
August 30, 1983), 1 ff.
167. King, "An Address to the National Press Club," Washington,
D.C., 3.
168. Schulke, ed., *Martin Luther King, Jr.*, 224.

chord in the hearts of black people whose very determination and *will to struggle* depended on a strong belief in the possibility of a more peaceful, just, and inclusive South and nation.

What was the source of King's optimism regarding the South? It was his cultural heritage as a black American. Deeply rooted in that heritage was a Christian optimism that upheld two views. The first view was that "God is on our side," a view that runs like a thread through the whole fabric of black history. King and his people in the South, like their slave foreparents, subscribed unquestionably to the providential view that God controls history and the universe, and that God's plan for all humanity would ultimately be fulfilled. "This is why our movement is often referred to as a spiritual movement," King once said. "We feel that the universe is on the side of right."[169] This Christian optimism, which he articulated in terms of the Social Gospel doctrine of the Kingdom of God, was the driving force behind the movement in the South—a Christian optimism that brought together his people's concern for individual salvation and their social vision of a redeemed and transformed society. For King, this Christian optimism was as evident in Langston Hughes' poem, "Mother to Son," as it was in songs like "We Shall Overcome," "There is a Balm in Gilead," and "The Negro National Anthem."[170]

Second, this Christian optimism upheld the view that the natural inclination of human beings to altruism could always be appealed to with positive results.[171]

169. Martin Luther King, Jr., "An Address at the 47th N.A.A.C.P. Annual Convention," San Francisco, Calif. (The King Papers, Boston University, 27 June 1956), 8–9.
170. *Ibid.*, 13; Martin Luther King, Jr., "An Address at a Mass Meeting," Waycross, Ga. (The King Center Archives, 22 March 1968), 5–6; Martin Luther King, Jr., "Draft of a Statement Regarding the Passage of the 1964 Civil Rights Act" (The King Center Archives, June 1964), 1–4; and Martin Luther King, Jr., "A Great Challenge Derived from a Serious Dilemma," a speech delivered in Atlanta, Ga. (The King Center Archives, 15 December 1965), 14.
171. Kenneth L. Smith and Ira G. Zepp, Jr., *Search for the Beloved Community: The Thinking of Martin Luther King, Jr.* (Valley Forge, Pa.: Judson Press, 1974), 11–12.

This is why King and his people could believe even in the capacity of the Jim Clarks, Bull Connors, and George Wallaces to change for the better, especially when appeals were made to their consciences through nonviolence based on love. The Christian realism of Reinhold Niebuhr, which insisted on the reality of sin on every level of human existence, was probably at this point the greatest sobering influence upon King's optimistic anthropological assumptions—assumptions that reflected the influence of his black church roots as well as the evangelical liberalism of George Davis, L. Harold DeWolf, Walter Rauschenbusch, and others.[172] This optimistic anthropology, coupled with the idea of a God-controlled history, sustained black hopes of a new South, and gave King and his followers the fortitude to face vicious racists, police dogs, cattle-prods, and other symbols of brutality without resorting to violence.

King's feeling and hope for the South were encouraged somewhat by what he saw as positive, distinguishing features in the character of southerners, black and white. He spoke with pride of the "new Negro" who, through love and nonviolence, was challenging the South, perhaps the most violent area in the country, with a broader concept of democracy.[173] While he recognized that black southerners were generally more humane than their white counterparts, he believed, nevertheless, that white southerners had a capacity for honesty and commitment to principle that surpassed that of white northerners—a capacity that, if properly cultivated, could contribute to a transforming impulse:

> You know, when you can finally convert a white South-
> erner, you have one of the most genuine, committed
> human beings that you'll ever find. Did you ever notice
> that? You see, what the white South has going for it

172. Watley, *Roots of Resistance*, 69; and Ansbro, *Martin Luther King, Jr.*, 151.
173. Washington, ed., *A Testament of Hope*, 76; and King, "An Address to the National Press Club," Washington, D.C., 6–7.

that the North doesn't have is that the average white Southerner has at least had individual contact with Negroes. It hasn't been person-to-person contact, but he's at least had individual contact with Negroes. Now, the thing to do is to transform that lord-serving relationship into intergroup, interpersonal living. And when that happens, do you know that I really feel that the South is going to get ahead of the North. Because one thing about this brother down here is that he doesn't like us, and he lets us know it. . . . You do at least know how to deal with it. I've been up North, and I've found that you don't know how to deal with it, because you can't quite get at your target. He'll (white Northerner) sit up there and smile in your face. You go down to see the officials and they'll serve you cookies and tea, and shake your hand and pose for pictures with you. And at the same time, keeping Negroes in ghettoes and slums. But down here, they won't take no pictures with us, they won't give us no tea and cookies, and they tell us on television that they don't like us. They don't hide it.[174]

It would be a mistake to reduce King's thoughts at this point to chauvinism or romanticism. Like Julian Bond, Charles Evers, Ralph Ellison, Bayard Rustin, and other black leaders involved in the movement, he was genuinely "more optimistic about the South than the North," believing that the South could in the long run prove the better environment for the kind of society he envisioned.[175] Recognizing that race relations in the South were not characterized by the hypocrisy and false sympathy so typical of the North, King declared that "The South has a problem and knows it." He concluded that the South, despite its rigid system of segregation,

174. Martin Luther King, Jr., "An Address at a Mass Meeting," Marks, Miss. (The King Center Archives, 19 March 1968), 5–6.

175. Frederick L. Downing, "A Review of David J. Garrow's *Bearing the Cross: Martin Luther King, Jr., and the Southern Christian Leadership Conference*," in *Theology Today* (October 1987): 391; and F. Garvin Davenport, Jr., *The Myth of Southern History: Historical Consciousness in Twentieth Century Southern Literature* (Nashville: Vanderbilt University Press, 1970), 196–97.

had much to teach the North about human communication between the races.[176]

During his thirteen years as a civil rights leader, King became associated with a considerable number of southern white moderates whose moral authority and communal vision transcended their loyalty to, and institutional connections in, that region. These experiences undoubtedly helped sustain his belief in the human potential of white southerners. During the Montgomery Bus Boycott, King worked with southern-born white ministers such as Robert Hughes, Glenn Smiley, and Ray Wadley, whose efforts to bring about reconciliation between the races were for him a great source of encouragement. King was tremendously inspired by the activities of white southern-based spiritual and moral leaders such as Myles Horton and Clarence Jordan. He found in Horton's Highlander Folk School (a unique embodiment of unionism, democracy, and Christian socialism) and in Jordan's Koinonia Farm (a pioneering interracial farming community in Americus, Georgia) living examples of the kind of interracial amity he envisioned for the "new South."[177]

Moreover, King expressed great respect and admiration for southern white writers like Sarah P. Boyle, Ann Braden, James M. Dabbs, Harry Golden, Ralph McGill, and Aubrey Williams, who "have written about our struggle in eloquent and prophetic terms." King was also very fond of Buford Boone of *The Tuscaloosa News*, Tuscaloosa, Alabama, whose editorials constantly addressed the need for peaceful change in the South in the late 1950s. When Boone received a Pulitzer Prize

176. Quoted in Pat Watters, "The Spring Offensive," *The Nation*, 198, no. 6 (February 3, 1964): 119–20.

177. King, *Stride toward Freedom*, 32, 108–109, 163, and 173. Virtually nothing exists on King's views on and relationships with figures like Hughes, Smiley, Wadley, Horton, and Jordan. Such a study would enhance our understanding of how King related to whites in the South, particularly white moderates who shared much of his perspective on interracial harmony and cooperation. A study of this nature would have to draw on the many letters King exchanged with persons like Hughes, Wadley, and Jordan. Such sources can be found at the King Center in Atlanta and at Boston University.

for his writings, King sent him a congratulatory note, praising the "moral courage and profound dignity" he had "evinced in so many situations," and insisting that he was eminently representative of the type of leadership needed among white southerners:

> I have just read that you received the 1957 Pulitzer Award for outstanding editorials. May I extend my congratulations to you for such a noble achievement. It is my hope that many other persons in the white South will rise up and courageously give the type of leadership that you have given. I share with you your conviction that our difficult problems can be solved only by attitudes founded upon patience, tolerance and loving understanding of the frailties and imperfections of man. That you have been able to follow and promote such an attitude speaks most highly of you and, in my judgment, accounts for the success with which your efforts have met.[178]

King recognized similar qualities of leadership in southern white moderates like Lillian Smith, who wrote extensively on "race as the central reality of southern life," and Richmond Flowers, the Alabama attorney general. Knowing that Smith was an early and ardent supporter of the 1954 Supreme Court decision on school integration and of his nonviolent philosophy and methods, King referred to her as "a radiant spirit" and as "one of my dearest friends."[179] Smith had a high regard for King's wisdom and compassion, and she shared his view that "Only through persuasion, love, goodwill, and firm nonviolent resistance can the change take place in our

---

178. King, *Stride toward Freedom*, 32, 108–109, 163, 173; A private interview with the Rev. Robert Graetz, Cincinnati, Ohio, 26 July 1988; and King, *Why We Can't Wait*, 89. King's view of southern writers like Boyle, Braden, Dabbs, Golden, McGill, Williams, and Lillian Smith was considerably more positive than his view of the great southern writer William J. Faulkner, who urged the NAACP to "stop now for a moment," and who "encouraged Negroes to accept injustice, exploitation and indignity for a while longer." See Washington, ed., *A Testament of Hope*, 80, and a letter from Martin Luther King, Jr., to Buford Boone, 9 May 1957.

179. Richard H. King, *A Southern Renaissance: The Cultural Awakening of the American South, 1930–1955* (New York: Oxford University Press, 1968), pp. 173, 176; and King, "The Meaning of Hope," 13.

South." She felt that King's nonviolent approach "would stir the consciences of white southerners because it employed religious symbols that they shared with blacks and that they responded to 'on a deep level of their hearts and minds'." "Being a deep South white, reared in a religious home and the Methodist Church," she told King on one occasion, "I realize the deep ties of common songs, common prayer, common symbols that bind our two races together on a religio-mystical level, even as another brutally mythic idea, the concept of White Supremacy, tears our people apart."[180]

As was the case with Smith, King recognized in Flowers one of that fascinating breed of southern moderates who were not afraid to challenge the artificial barriers that separated the races. In 1965, Flowers sought to prosecute the accused assassins of Viola Liuzzo, the civil rights worker from Detroit, and, one year later, in his effort to become Governor of Alabama, he became "the first major white candidate in modern times to campaign directly among the Negro people in a deep South state."[181] This impressed King to the degree that he actually appealed to black Alabama voters on behalf of Flowers.[182] He saw how Flowers endured ostracism from fellow whites and even physical abuse from the Ku Klux Klan because of his opposition to George Wallace and the forces of racism in Alabama. Flowers and other southern white moderates were always a reminder to King that the white South was not a monolithic community when it came to the question of race.[183]

One cannot help but believe that King's hope for and faith in the South also stemmed in large measure from

180. Anne C. Loveland, *Lillian Smith: A Southerner Confronting the South* (Baton Rouge, La.: Louisiana State University Press, 1986), 62, 139, 155–56; and Louise Blackwell and Frances Clay, *Lillian Smith* (New York: Twayne Publishers, 1971), 90, 95.
181. *The New York Times* (April 14, 1966): 27; and *The New York Times* (April 30, 1966): 1, 14.
182. *The New York Times* (April 30, 1966): 1, 14.
183. King, "A Statement to the South and Nation," Atlanta, Ga., 2–3; and King, "An Address at the First Annual Institute on Nonviolence and Social Change," 2–3.

his deep love for that region of the country. It was his knowledge of and love for the South that made it possible for him to speak to the best rather than to the worst qualities in his fellow southerners. As stated previously, King's "strong sense of identity as a southerner," and his "critical loyalty to the South," explain why he adopted "the policy of spending more time in this section of the country."[184] "Knowing the pressing demands and problems in the South, and the many requests that come from depressed communities," King said repeatedly, "I always feel a real sense of guilt when I don't spend enough time here."[185] Indeed, "he remained, up to his assassination," as Coleman B. Brown has written, "preoccupied with evaluating the southern scene, and with maintaining a heavy personal involvement in the social struggle there."[186] Herein lies further proof not only of King's enduring loyalty to place in a southern context but also of his belief that his leadership and sacrifices were indissolubly tied to the destiny of his people. Although his vision became more truly national and international after he was awarded the Nobel Peace Prize in 1964, the South remained his "crucial matrix."[187]

King was particularly attracted to the beauty of the South and its abundance of untapped resources. "Some of the most beautiful land to be found anywhere, rich in natural resources, is in the South," King observed. "The problem is the white folk want it all for themselves."[188] Such greed was for him an indication of white southerners' refusal to accept the simple fact that "The earth is the Lord's, and the fullness thereof."[189] Considering the

184. King, *A Southern Renaissance*, 170; James Baldwin, "The Dangerous Road Before Martin Luther King, Jr.," *Harper's Magazine* (February, 1961): 38; Brown, "Grounds for American Loyalty," 48–55; and a letter from Martin Luther King, Jr., to Mrs. Wayne A. Dockhorn, 29 September 1960, The King Papers, Boston University.
185. A letter from Martin Luther King, Jr., to Mrs. Uvee Mdodana, 13 February 1963, The King Papers, Boston University.
186. Brown, "Grounds for American Loyalty," 54.
187. *Ibid.*, 55.
188. King, "An Address at a Mass Meeting," Clarksdale, Miss., 6.
189. *Ibid.*

tremendous possibilities for development and change in the South, King deemed it unconscionable that its inhabitants allowed segregation to keep the region in poverty, ignorance, and deprivation:

> Even the most casual observer can see that the South has marvelous possibilities. It is rich in natural resources, blessed with the beauties of nature, and endowed with a native warmth of spirit. Yet, in spite of these assets, it is retarded by a blight that debilitates not only the Negro but also the white man. Poor white men, women, and children, bearing the scars of ignorance, deprivation, and poverty, are evidence of the fact that harm to one is injury to all. Segregation has placed the whole South socially, educationally, and economically behind the rest of the nation.[190]

In King's view, segregation stood as undeniable proof of the failure of white southerners to face the clear fact that the very future and destiny of the country were tied up with what answer would be given to southern blacks. He called on whites to recognize that black people would be a primary force in determining the future and destiny of the South. "Since the largest segment of the Negro population lives in the South," he wrote, "the problem must be solved in the South or it cannot be solved anywhere."[191]

King believed that as the South became more industrialized, improvements would automatically occur in its social, educational, and economic stature, thus leading to a better quality of life for black and white alike:

> . . . if the South is to grow economically it must continue to industrialize. We see signs of this vigorous industrialization, with a concomitant urbanization, throughout every Southern state. Day after day, the South is receiving new multi-million dollar industries.

190. Martin Luther King, Jr., "A Speech at a Dinner Honoring Him as a Nobel Prize Recipient," Dinkler Plaza Hotel, Atlanta, Ga. 27 January 1965, 6–7.

191. Martin Luther King, Jr., "Suggested Preamble for the S.C.L.C.," Atlanta, Georgia (n.d.), The King Center Archives, 1–2.

With the growth of industry the folkways of white supremacy will gradually pass away. . . . This growth of industry will also increase the purchasing power of the Negro, and this augmented purchasing power will result in improved medical care, greater educational opportunities, and more adequate housing.[192]

King did not live to see the fulfillment of his vision of "a new South." His declining influence as a spokesman for black America in the late 1960s, coupled with white resistance to black demands for economic justice and the corrosive effect of the Vietnam war on the civil rights movement, aborted and distracted much of the momentum and also the national financial resources needed to ensure the full realization of his vision. However, King did witness significant limited steps taken in the direction of a more peaceful, just, and inclusive South. Black people won the right to service in public restaurants, to stay in public hotels, to use public restrooms, to use public transportation on a nondiscriminatory basis, and to vote. In schools, universities, law firms, and major corporations, some of the barriers to black advancement crumbled, paving the way for the emergence of a new black middle class.[193] King pointed to such achievements as evidence that, "We have broken aloose from the slavery of Egypt, we have moved through the wilderness of separate but equal, and now we stand on the borders of the Promised Land of integration."[194]

King attributed the dynamism and achievements of the southern civil rights movement to many factors. First, its employment of nonviolence as a method of social action. This method, rooted in the Christian optimism of the folk, and supremely symbolized in the life and work of King,

192. King, "An Address to the National Press Club," Washington, D.C., 4.
193. Smith, "Equality and Justice," 4–5.
194. Martin Luther King, Jr., "Excerpts from a Speech," delivered at the Ford Hall Forum, Boston, Mass. (The King Papers, Boston University, 11 December 1960), 1; King, "An Address to the National Press Club," Washington, D.C., 1 ff.; King, "An Address at the National Bar Association Meeting," Milwaukee, Wis. 3; and King, "The Church in Frontiers of Racial Tension," 3.

cemented black southerners and gave them the determination to act despite fear. Furthermore, nonviolence was the force around which the S.C.L.C., NAACP, the Urban League, Congress of Racial Equality (CORE), the Student Nonviolent Coordinating Committee, and other local, state, and national civil rights organizations combined their resources and efforts in search of a more optimistic and humane South.[195]

Second, King viewed the movement's power and accomplishments as stemming largely from its reliance upon the spiritual and cultural values of the folk. Black southerners' armament for the struggle, which King called "soul force," came from within, not from without. The writings of W. E. B. Du Bois, James Baldwin, Langston Hughes, Maya Angelou, Ruby Dee, and numerous other black intellectuals, playwrights, poets, and novelists were as much a part of the cultural and spiritual thrust of the southern civil rights movement as the slave spirituals, the gospel songs of Mahalia Jackson and Thomas Dorsey, the soul music of Aretha Franklin and James Brown, and the sermons of black preachers.[196] King himself, who was very much in touch with the spirituality of his people and who represented to the fullest the wedding of the secular and sacred in black life, found innovative and sustaining power through an appeal to these folk sources.

195. King, "A Response to J. Edgar Hoover's Charge," 2; King, "A Statement in Response to *The Atlanta Constitution's* Article," 2; Aldon D. Morris, *The Origins of the Civil Rights Movement: Black Communities Organizing for Change* (New York: The Free Press, A Division of Macmillan, 1984), chapters 1–3; Fairclough, *To Redeem the Soul of America*, 4–5; and Clayborne Carson, "Civil Rights Reform and the Black Freedom Struggle," in Charles W. Eagles, ed., *The Civil Rights Movement in America* (Jackson: University Press of Mississippi, 1986), 19–32. King symbolized more than anyone else the unity, optimism, and victories of the movement. He was a symbol of unity in that he not only encouraged unity and a commonality of purpose among black civil rights organizations, but also took conservative black preachers, laypersons, and progressive-minded whites and brought them together in the struggle. See "James Cone Interview," 9.

196. King, "An Address at the 47th N.A.A.C.P. Annual Convention," San Francisco, Calif., 8–9; King, "Some Things We Must Do," 20; and King, *Where Do We Go from Here?*, 102–103.

Equally important for the dynamism and victories of the movement were the sources and symbols of the American democratic heritage, which embodied some of the same values that flowed from the black cultural heritage. King and his people found in "The Battle Hymn of the Republic," in the heritage of the Constitution and the Declaration of Independence, and in the American tradition of dissent in general, echoes of the same fundamental principles and norms that permeated black literature, songs, and sermons. This is why King constantly reaffirmed and reappropriated these aspects of culture as a way of inspiring his people to greater heights in the struggle.[197]

The civil rights movement was a necessary step in the maturation of both blacks and whites, particularly in the South. King observed that perhaps its greatest impact was evident in the creation of "a new Negro" in the South, a development that suggested to him that the self-doubt that had so long afflicted his people would not be permanent. In other words, the movement brought "the Southern Negro new visibility" and demonstrated "to him that many stereotypes he has held about himself and other Negroes are not valid":

> The most important thing in this whole movement is what has happened to the Negro. For the first time, the Negro is on his own side. This has not always been true. But today the Negro is with himself. He has gained a new respect for himself. He believes in himself. World opinion is on his side. The law is on his side and, as one columnist said, all the stars of heaven are on his side. It seems to be historically true that once an oppressed people rise up there is no stopping them

197. Lewis V. Baldwin, "Martin Luther King, Jr., the Black Church, and the Black Messianic Vision," *The Journal of the Interdenominational Theological Center*, 12, nos. 1 and 2 (Fall 1984–Spring 1985): 98; James H. Cone, "A Review of John J. Ansbro's *Martin Luther King, Jr.: The Making of a Mind* (1982)," *Fellowship*, 50, no. 1 (January–February, 1984): 33; and King, *Why We Can't Wait*, 76–95. Perhaps the best and most extensive discussion of how King drew on the sources and symbols of American participatory democracy is found in Brown, "Grounds for American Loyalty," 1 ff.

short of complete freedom. The Negro is eternally through with segregation; he will never accept it again, in Mississippi, Georgia, or anywhere else.[198]

In King's view, this "new Negro" represented the best hope for a truly redeemed and transformed South. He believed that this new sense of self and of destiny among his people in the South found its most profound expression "in the words of the old Negro slave preacher that were uttered in the form of a prayer":

> Lord we ain't what we ought to be;
> We ain't what we want to be;
> We ain't what we gonna be;
> But thank God, we ain't what we was.[199]

King's assessment of how the movement affected white southerners has seldom been noted in the literature on southern history and culture. In King's estimation, the very presence of a new sense of values and of social mission had made "the leaders of the most backward, inhumane governments" in the South "say *yes* when they wanted to say *no*." He envisioned the white South becoming more humane and optimistic because of the nonviolent revolution and the way the media projected it to the nation and the world.[200] Indeed, the racial attitudes of many whites, southern and northern, were affected in significant ways. The entire nation was eventually forced to reconsider its attitudes and priorities as they related to issues of race, class, and foreign policy.

---

198. Bennett, "Rev. Martin Luther King, Jr., Alabama Desegregationist," 79; King, "An Address to the National Press Club," Washington, D.C., 6–7; and Washington, ed., *A Testament of Hope*, 76–77.

199. King, "A Speech at a Dinner Honoring Him as a Nobel Peace Prize Recipient," Atlanta, Ga., 16; and Oates, *Let the Trumpet Sound*, 253.

200. King, "A Speech to Blacks," Grenada, Miss., 2; and "Covering the South: A National Symposium on the Media and the Civil Rights Movement," *The Southern Register: The Newsletter for the Center for the Study of Southern Culture*, 5, no. 1 (Spring 1987), The University of Mississippi: 1–11. The extent to which King and his followers helped alter the consciousness of that once insular component of American religion known as southern Fundamentalism has not been recognized and sufficiently treated by scholars of American religion.

King's idea of a redeemed and transformed South is one part of his dream of the 1950s and 1960s that remains unfulfilled in the 1980s. Race, poverty, and anti-intellectualism are still keeping the South from reaching its potential as a modern, progressive industrialized society. At least twenty-five percent of the children in kindergarten who graduated to first grade in 1988 lived in poverty, and the South's malnutrition rate and infant mortality rate still exceed those of any civilized country. Black southerners are still more the victims of poverty and lower levels of education than white southerners. Despite the basic civil or constitutional rights achieved under King's leadership, the majority of blacks in the South still live in poverty largely because of discrimination and the poor economic conditions of the region. The poor quality of education and the high rate of poverty, which breed an economy based on low-skill, low-wage manufacturing, explain why most southern states have either stagnated or declined in recent years.[201]

While he obviously could not foresee exactly how southern life and history would unfold in the 1970s, 1980s, and 1990s, King, in his last public speech on April 3, 1968, a day before he was gunned down in Memphis, Tennessee, used symbolism to convey a profound vision of what he felt the South and the nation as a whole would become. He spoke of having "been to the mountaintop," of having "seen the promised land," and of having seen "the glory of the coming of the Lord."[202] It was not a simple statement of bright, shallow optimism or telescopic idealism. He was talking about a society that ought to exist—that would exist. At that point, the future event of liberation had broken into the present for King. He was happy—not in some blithesome, ephemeral sense—but happy in the conviction

201. See Susan McDonald, "South's Traditions a Hindrance," *Vanderbilt Register* (June 3, 1988): 1, 3.
202. Schulke, ed., *Martin Luther King, Jr.*, 224.

that he and his people possessed a freedom that could not be defined or confined by anything that existed in the larger society. With this conviction, King, like generations of his forebears, died on southern soil. The blood he shed raised to further awareness the deep tension between a complex, stubborn southern past that would not die and a more modern, creative South that could not be denied.

# WALK TOGETHER, CHILDREN
## FAMILY HERITAGE

2

My parents taught me something very early. Somehow they
instilled in me a feeling of somebodyness, and they would say
to me over and over again that you're just as good as any child
in Atlanta, Georgia.

Martin Luther King, Jr., 1966[1]

Those who stand tall in our presence appear to be of unusual
height because, in most cases, they stand on the shoulders of
giants who have preceded them.

John Hope Franklin, 1986[2]

Walk together, children,
Don't you get weary,
Talk together, children,
Don't you get weary,
Sing together, children,
Don't you get weary,
There's a great camp meeting
in the Promised Land.

Negro Spiritual[3]

The home and family setting was basic to the environment in which Martin Luther King, Jr., lived, matured,
and struggled. His early emotional, intellectual, moral,

1. Martin Luther King, Jr., "A Speech to Blacks," Grenada, Miss.
(The Archives of the Martin Luther King, Jr. Center for Nonviolent Social
Change, Inc., Atlanta, Georgia, 16 June 1966) 3.
2. John Hope Franklin, "The Forerunners," *American Visions: The
Magazine of Afro-American Culture*, 1, no. 1 (January–February 1986):
26, 35.
3. Quoted in John Lovell, Jr., *Black Song: The Forge and the
Flame—The Story of How the Afro-American Spiritual Was Hammered
Out* (New York: Paragon House Publishers, 1972), 276, 278.

and spiritual development occurred largely within a family that included parents, grandparents, and a wide circle of aunts, uncles, cousins, and members of the church family.[4] In this setting of the extended family, we find not only the seedbed for the cultivation of much of King's early life and thought but also a support system that nurtured and sustained him in the course of his work as a minister and social activist. A serious study of King's home and family environment is useful for a general consideration of his relationship to the black cultural heritage, and also for an understanding of how his vision moved gradually beyond southern particularism to assume national and even international implications.[5]

This chapter deals with King's home and family environment as the chief source of his personal and intellectual development, and as a stabilizing force that helped him fulfill a range of responsibilities as husband, father, minister, and social activist. This discussion enables us to venture an answer to one of the most perplexing questions concerning King: How did he stabilize himself sufficiently to carry out his work, faced with severe external dangers and with equally severe narcissistic challenges

4. Martin Luther King, Jr., "An Autobiography of Religious Development" (Unpublished document from The King Papers, Mugar Memorial Library, Boston University, Boston, Mass. n.d., circa 1950), 1–15; Martin Luther King, Jr., *Stride toward Freedom: The Montgomery Story* (New York: Harper & Brothers, 1958), 18–21; Robert P. Warren, "An Interview with Martin Luther King, Jr.," in *Who Speaks for the Negro?* (Unpublished manuscript, The King Center Archives, 18 May 1964), 1 ff.; and Walter E. Fluker, *They Looked for a City: A Comparative Analysis of the Ideal of Community in the Thought of Howard Thurman and Martin Luther King, Jr.* (Lanham, Md.: University Press of America, 1989), 191–92. Given the tremendous importance of home and family as a support mechanism and as the nucleus for King's early personal and intellectual development, it is strange that scholars have devoted so little attention to these settings. This pattern of omission is reflected even in works that treat King's roots in black culture, such as William D. Watley, *Roots of Resistance: The Nonviolent Ethic of Martin Luther King, Jr.* (Valley Forge, Pa.: Judson Press, 1985), 17–45; and James H. Cone, "Martin Luther King: The Source of His Courage to Face Death," *Concilium* (March 1983): 74–79.

5. Fluker, *They Looked for a City*, 191–92; Lewis V. Baldwin, "Understanding Martin Luther King, Jr. Within the Context of Southern Black Religious History," *Journal of Religious Studies*, 13, no. 2 (Fall 1987): 9–10; and Lewis V. Baldwin, "Family and Church: The Roots of Martin Luther King, Jr.," *National Baptist Union-Review*, 91, no. 1 (January 1987): 1, 3, 7, 9, 12.

(e.g., leadership versus grandiosity, fatherhood versus sainthood, vision versus paranoia, insight versus egocentrism, conviction versus delusions, self-respect versus messiahship)?

## HISTORICAL BACKGROUND OF THE KING FAMILY

King's family history in America began with the forcible capture and transporting of millions of black people from Africa to these shores. His ancestors lived for several generations under brutal conditions of oppression in the South, denied the most basic human rights and freedom. They were proud and courageous men and women who were bought, sold, exchanged, and violated, and who worked in the fields until their eyebrows were scorched and their hands bruised. They were bearers of rich African cultures that became the source of both their resistance and their quest for community.[6]

Much of what King knew about his ancestors came through the medium of folktales commonly told in the King home during his childhood.[7] In a home where great importance was attached to the subject of genealogy, it was only natural for him to hear stories about the struggles and achievements of his great-grandparents, grandparents, and parents. It was in this setting that King heard stories about his maternal great-grandfather, the Reverend Williams, who served as a "slave exhorter" on a Georgia plantation. A slave himself, the Reverend Williams shared in the pain and joy of the slave community, reflected its rich expressive culture and values, and undoubtedly became a source of spiritual

6. Lerone Bennett, Jr., *What Manner of Man: A Memorial Biography of Martin Luther King, Jr.* (New York: Pocket Books, 1968), 4–5, and 7.

7. King, "An Autobiography of Religious Development," p. 2; Stephen B. Oates, *Let the Trumpet Sound: The Life of Martin Luther King, Jr.* (New York: Harper & Row, 1982), 5; Coretta Scott King, *My Life with Martin Luther King, Jr.* (New York: Avon Books, 1969), 92; and Frederick L. Downing, *To See the Promised Land: The Faith Pilgrimage of Martin Luther King, Jr.* (Macon, Ga.: Mercer University Press, 1986), 44–45, 49.

strength for fellow slaves and for generations of family members who descended from him. Memories of the Reverend Williams' struggles and of his role as spiritual leader among his people in Greene County, Georgia, lingered with King's maternal grandfather, Alfred D. Williams, and his mother, Alberta Christine Williams King, figuring prominently in the shaping of their sense of identity and family values.[8]

Through his father, A. D. Williams had the most direct contact with slavery possible short of having been a slave himself. He almost certainly heard Reverend Williams talk about slavery, and the emotional and physical scars left by that system were probably the best indication to A. D. of its brutal character. Furthermore, A. D. lived among other ex-slaves in Greene County who bore the marks of slavery and embodied aspects of slave culture. After settling in Atlanta, A. D. Williams, like his father, established himself as a preacher, and in 1894 became pastor of the Ebenezer Baptist Church in that city.[9] In that environment, A. D. continued to encounter black people and social, political, and economic realities that reflected the tragic legacy of slavery. In the fall of 1899, he married Jennie C. Parks, a beautiful young woman who also traced her ancestral roots back to slavery, and who also knew from experience what it meant to be black in the South at that time. The couple's sense of the depth of southern racism was probably heightened as they lived through the Atlanta race riot of 1906, when at least ten blacks and two whites were killed. Memories of family traditions and of black life in the South were passed down by them to their only child, Alberta, who would later pass them on to her son, Martin Luther King, Jr.[10]

8. King, *Stride toward Freedom*, 19; Downing, *To See the Promised Land*, 47; and Martin Luther King, Sr., with Clayton Riley, *Daddy King: An Autobiography*, (New York: William Morrow, 1980), 84 ff.

9. Bennett, *What Manner of Man*, 3, 7; King, *Daddy King*, 84 ff.; and Downing, *To See the Promised Land*, 45–50.

10. King, *Daddy King*, 85–86; Oates, *Let the Trumpet Sound*, 6–8; and Taylor Branch, *Parting the Waters: America in the King Years, 1954–63* (New York: Simon and Schuster, 1988), 30–40.

A. D. Williams possessed an iron-like strength and a dignity of character that reflected the influence of his father and other ex-slaves around him, and that he passed on to his daughter and grandchildren. At a time when scores of black men were lynched, he absolutely refused to allow his spirit to be broken by the forces of racism and discrimination. Commonly referred to as "one of Atlanta's most prominent and respected ministers," A. D. was the first president of the local NAACP.[11] In the 1920s, he led Atlanta's black community in a boycott of stores and other businesses that supported *The Georgian,* a newspaper known to use racial epithets in its references to black people. On another occasion, A. D. took the lead in stopping a municipal bond issue because it contained no provisions for black high school education. From the time he assumed the pastorate of Ebenezer Church until his death in 1931, he vigorously pursued his vision of a better day for his people, and in doing so provided broad shoulders on which later generations in his family could stand.[12]

This family tradition of protest against injustice was also exemplified by King's paternal grandparents, James A. King and Delia Lindsay King, who were themselves the children of slave parents in rural Georgia, and who in the 1880s found themselves enmeshed in a cruel and exploitative system of sharecropping in Stockbridge, about twenty miles from Atlanta.[13] Described as "a lean, tough little fellow, very wiry and strong," James King clashed numerous times with white landlords who sought

11. King, *Daddy King,* 13, 84–86; Coleman B. Brown, "Grounds for American Loyalty in a Prophetic Christian Social Ethic—With Special Attention to Martin Luther King, Jr." (Ph.D. diss., Union Theological Seminary in New York City, April, 1979), 66; and Fluker, *They Looked for a City,* 82.
12. King, *Daddy King,* 84–86; and Esther M. Smith, *A History of Ebenezer Baptist Church, Atlanta, Georgia* (Atlanta: Ebenezer Baptist Church, Publisher, 1956), 3.
13. King, *Daddy King,* 23–79; King, *My Life with Martin Luther King, Jr.,* 88–89; King, *Stride toward Freedom,* 19; and Bennett, *What Manner of Man,* 4–5.

to exploit and degrade him and his family.[14] The landlords for whom he worked provided land, shelter, seed,
fertilizer, mules, and sometimes food for his family,
which included his wife Delia and the children—
Woodie, Lenora, Cleo, James, Jr., Henry, Joel, Lucille,
Ruby, and Michael, who would later become Martin
Luther King, Sr. Year after year the entire family worked
diligently to produce good crops. When the crops were
harvested and sold, the landlords unjustly claimed most
of the profits, forcing James King deeper and deeper
into debt. Although he was unable to read or write, he
lived daily with a keen awareness of the extent to which
he was being exploited, and with the knowledge that he,
despite honorable intentions and hard work, would
never fulfill his dream of buying his own home and
farm.[15] Devoid of the spirit of nonviolence that would
later pervade the life of his famous grandson, and seldom in a position to strike at the system which labeled
him "a nigger" and "a boy," James was driven to alco-
holism and to the verbal and physical abuse of his wife
Delia and the children.[16] His story was the same as that
of so many black men in the South in his day—loyal,
hardworking men who were forced to turn their torment
and frustration inward by circumstances beyond their
control. Fully aware of his grandfather's struggles, Martin Luther King, Jr., once described this tragic dilemma
in these terms:

> The rage and torment of the Negro male were fre-
> quently turned inward because if it gained outward ex-
> pression its consequences would have been fatal. He
> became resigned to hopelessness and he communicated
> this to his children. Some, unable to contain the emo-
> tional storms, struck out at those who would be less
> likely to destroy them. He beat his wife and his children
> in order to protest a social injustice, and the tragedy

14. King, *Daddy King*, 23–24, 35–43.
15. Bennett, *What Manner of Man*, 5; and King, *Daddy King*, 58–59.
16. King, *Daddy King*, 23–48.

was that none of them understood why the violence exploded.[17]

An incident occurred between James King and his son Michael that helped the son to discipline himself. Michael, a teenager at the time, was angered when his intoxicated father struck his mother, a situation that led to a fight between the father and the son. Having a strong belief in the scriptures, which said "Honor thy father and thy mother," young Michael was left with a feeling of emptiness and shame that he never forgot.[18] He loved his father, and the thought of having hurt him caused Michael to pray aloud to God for forgiveness. In any case, he and his father never fought again, and the experience became a tremendous source of discipline that influenced Michael's relationship years later with his own children, one of whom would become the greatest civil rights leader in this century.[19]

Despite his personal problems, James King was filled with a strength of spirit and a desire for success that seemed unsullied by his years of sharecropping—a quality passed on to his children and, eventually, to his grandchildren. Though he never wanted to be exactly like his father, Michael saw in him noble qualities that he and his brothers and sisters deeply admired and respected. Many years after his father's death, Michael, then known as Martin Luther King, Sr., wrote:

> I knew James King was a man who wanted more than he could ever have. And what he wanted wasn't really that much—a decent home for his family, a day's pay for a day's work, the freedom to be judged as a human being and not a beast, a nigger, a nightmare in the white mind. But for him, these things were never to happen. *Maybe tomorrow, just maybe*—Papa must have

17. Martin Luther King, Jr., "The Dignity of Family Life: An Address at Abbott House," Westchester County, N.Y. (The King Center Archives, 29 October 1965), 7–8.
18. King, *Daddy King*, 46–53, 66–67.
19. *Ibid.*

thought that so many, many times. And every time he
did, it had to cut through his soul—the fact that, for no
reason that could ever make sense, he would not live to
see, to feel, to *be* a part of that new day.[20]

Michael vividly recalled those times when the fires of
liberty burst forth into an ardent flame in the bosom
of his father, causing him to resist the oppressive system
even at the risk of his life. One day while on an errand for
his mother, Delia, Michael was beaten by a white millowner who resented the boy's refusal to get water for his
millworkers. That incident enraged James King, causing
him to go in search of the millowner with a rifle. Unable
to find the millowner at his mill, he informed the millworkers that he would shoot any man who touched his
son. James refused to surrender or to leave Stockbridge
even as a mob threatened to kill him, and the incident
was soon forgotten.[21] Michael remembered another occasion when his father protected him from the wrath of a
man named Graves, a dishonest and racist landowner,
who was trying to cheat the Kings out of cotton seed
money. When the boy reminded his father and Graves
about the money, the landowner reacted angrily, insisting that "You better get that sassy little nigger outta here,
Jim, 'fore I kick his little butt." James King immediately
responded: "Don't nobody touch my boy, Mr. Graves.
Anything need to be done to him, I'll take care of it." "I
could see that Papa wasn't about to back off from him,"
Michael recalled, "and it looked like there'd be some
trouble." Only the intervention of other farmers in the
dispute prevented what probably would have been a fight
between James and Mr. Graves. Michael discovered in
his father a spirit of resistance that left him proud as he
grew to manhood.[22]

The fires of liberty in James King's blood burned with
the same intensity in the bosom of Delia King. It is

20. *Ibid.*, 58–59.
21. *Ibid.*, 35–36.
22. *Ibid.*, 40–42.

reported that her temper was even worse than her husband's, in some ways, "because it was so deep in her that anything bringing it out was bringing out some real trouble."[23] Her hot temper was sobered only by her abiding faith in God and her feeling of being at peace with herself. But at times these virtues were not enough to contain the anger and frustration she experienced over the oppressive conditions in Stockbridge, Georgia. It was Delia's hatred for racial injustice that caused her to confront violently the millowner who physically abused her son Michael. Michael would later describe the incident in terms compelling enough to deserve extensive quotation:

> I had never seen my mother move so quickly. She leaped at this man, dug her shoulder into his middle and knocked him back against the side of the mill shed. My mother had worked all her life, she was powerfully built and had the strength of any man. The millowner was shocked. He tried to grab hold of her, but she tripped him up and he fell to the ground. Oh, Lord, what did he do that for? Mama jumped down on him, pounding away at his face. Some of the mill hands tried to get her off the man, but she punched one of them right in the mouth so hard he spun around and stumbled back, looking as if he'd never been hit that hard in his life. The millowner pushed and turned, but he couldn't get Mama off him. She raised up and brought both her fists down across his nose, and blood spurted out of his face all over the ground. Then she got up. The other men had moved back a little. She stared at them. Her eyes were like coals blazing out of their sockets. "You can kill me!" she shouted. "But if you put a hand on a child of mine, you'll answer."[24]

The spirits of Delia and James King were never broken by the forces of racism, a fact that filled their children with amazement as they grew up in the emotionally charged climate of Stockbridge, Georgia. Even "in her

23. *Ibid.*, 25, 33–34.
24. *Ibid.*, 34.

times of great suffering," Delia "never surrendered to
self-pity or doubt," mainly because of her faith in a God
who would find vindication.[25] In his final years, James
struggled for inner peace and for a more constructive
relationship with his family. "He had tried so hard
to change," according to his son Michael. "He quit drinking, came to church, and seemed to make peace with
himself and with his God."[26] His deep love for his family,
which had been denied its fullest expression by a vicious
system based on racism, was revealed in a powerful way
when Delia succumbed to cancer in 1924. Michael would
later write about his father's reaction to the loss:

> Papa was just ruined by Mama's death. She'd suffered
> so much, and he'd been able to do nothing, offer no
> comfort. It cut into him. He took it hard and thought
> that whiskey would help. His grief just broke him
> down at the graveside, and none of us could do any-
> thing to help. And in the sound of his pain I heard
> Papa's love for Mama, and I heard the years they'd
> spent trying to build a life in a place where the Negro
> wasn't regarded as a human being.[27]

Michael went on to describe his own response to the
loss—a response that was probably shared by all of
the children of James and Delia King:

> During those final nights, when she was slipping away
> from us, I cursed the whites who took so much away
> and inflicted so much hatred and violence on people
> whose color they didn't happen to share. I told Mama,
> as I had years ago, that I'd hate every white face I ever
> saw, but she made me promise I'd never let that hap-
> pen. "Hatred," she told me, "makes nothin' but more
> hatred, Michael. Don't you do it."[28]

In the midst of her pain, Delia King had come to a
profound understanding of the meaning and significance

25. *Ibid.*, 25, 74.
26. *Ibid.*, 88.
27. *Ibid.*, 74.
28. *Ibid.*

of the love ethic. The advice she offered her son while on her deathbed was the same Michael would give years later to his own son, Martin Luther King, Jr., who also came very close to hating all white people during his boyhood. But Michael wondered if he could honor the promise he made to Delia about not hating whites. "As I looked at my father that day we buried Mama, and saw so many of the scars that had been left on my parents," he declared, "I really didn't know how I could keep that promise."[29] Although he would eventually overcome the bitterness he felt toward white people, Michael developed a hatred for systems of oppression that would remain with him throughout his entire life.[30]

On Thanksgiving Day, November 25, 1926, Michael King married Alberta Christine Williams, the daughter of the Reverend A. D. Williams and Jennie C. Parks Williams. The wedding took place at the Ebenezer Baptist Church in Atlanta, a church that was closely associated with the Williams family history, and that Michael would later serve as pastor. The presence of Michael's father at the wedding was indicative of the closer relationship that had been developing between the two men since Delia King's death. That relationship improved to the point where James King, just prior to his death in 1933, requested that Michael officially change his name to Martin Luther, a request the son accepted without hesitation. This was an important gesture because James, at the time of the boy's birth in 1899, had actually named him after two of his brothers, Martin and Luther. Delia had insisted at the time that their son be called Michael, after the archangel, and her wish prevailed.[31] When James King requested that the name be changed, he never envisioned that the name Martin Luther King would one day assume great spiritual significance, and would become

29. *Ibid.*; and "Daddy King: 'There's No Hate in My Heart,'" *The Chicago Tribune* (December 23, 1980): Section II, 1, 4.

30. "Daddy King: 'There's No Hate in My Heart,'" 1, 4; and King, *Daddy King*, 107–9.

31. King, *Daddy King*, 80–81, 87–88.

identified with the very souls of the King family and of black America generally.

After their marriage, Michael and Alberta King moved into the upstairs portion of A. D.'s and Jennie Williams's home at 501 Auburn Avenue in Atlanta, and began their life together. In a culture where much value was attached to the extended family network, it was common at that time for young black, recently married couples to live with parents and in-laws until they established themselves financially. Three children were born to the couple. The first was a daughter, Willie Christine, born in the fall of 1927. She was given the same middle name as her mother. Christine, as she was called, was followed by Michael, Jr., born in the winter of 1929, and Alfred Daniel, born in the summer of 1930. The birth of Michael, Jr., commonly called Mike or M. L., so pleased his father that he "leaped to touch the ceiling in an upstairs bedroom in celebration." The child was only five when he took his father's name, becoming Martin Luther King, Jr. Alfred Daniel, referred to as A. D., was named after his maternal grandfather.[32] The fact that the children were named after close relatives and ancestors was not insignificant. From the time of slavery, black people had often associated a person's name with that person's very soul and often with the souls of relatives and ancestors.[33] This custom clearly reflected African traditions brought over by slaves, many of whom were the ancestors of Martin, Sr., and Alberta King. Both the Kings and the Williams had apparently been deeply influenced by these traditions.[34] By naming their children for relatives and ancestors, Martin, Sr., and Alberta heightened the spiritual significance of their names, and revealed the power of their sense of family unity and family values.

32. *Ibid.*, pp. 81–87; and Christine King Farris, "The Young Martin: From Childhood through College," *Ebony*, 41, no. 3 (January 1986): 56.

33. For a brilliant discussion of the spiritual significance of names in Afro-American culture, see Sterling Stuckey, *Slave Culture: Nationalist Theory and the Foundations of Black America* (New York: Oxford University Press, 1987), 193–244.

34. *Ibid.*; King, *Daddy King*, 87–88; and King, *My Life with Martin Luther King, Jr.*, 118.

## THE KING HOME AND FAMILY

The images of family that emerge from the books, essays, letters, speeches, and personal interviews of Martin Luther King, Jr., are enormously important for understanding his personal and intellectual formation. King recalled a family setting that included loving relationships and an abundance of good food, books, and talent undergirded with prayer.[35] "I was born in a very congenial home situation," he remembered, in which "our parents themselves were very intimate, and they always maintained an intimate relationship with us." According to King, the relationship between his father and mother was such that "I can hardly remember a time that they argued (my father happens to be the kind who just won't argue), or had any great fall out."[36] That relationship between his parents became a metaphor for King's relationship to his own wife and children.

The intimacy between Martin Luther King, Sr., and Alberta Williams King was reflected on a high level in their children's relationships with each other. Of his relationship with his sister Christine and brother A. D., Martin, Jr., wrote: "Because of our relative closeness of ages we all grew up together, and to this day there still exists that intimate relationship which existed between us in childhood."[37] Although the three had numerous playmates and friends while growing up in Atlanta, most of their time was spent playing, studying, and eating together in their home on Auburn Avenue. Martin, Jr. was a typically aggressive boy who competed with his sister and brother, and who was sometimes hurt doing mischievous and daring things with them.[38] He was known

35. King, "An Autobiography of Religious Development," 1–15; and James Haskins, *The Life and Death of Martin Luther King, Jr.* (New York: Lothrop, Lee and Shepard, 1977), 14–15.
36. King, "An Autobiography of Religious Development," 3.
37. *Ibid.*, 1–2.
38. Alberta King, "Dr. Martin Luther King, Jr.: Birth to Twelve Years Old by His Mother," Ebenezer Baptist Church, Atlanta, Ga. (A King Center Recording, 18 January 1973); Farris, "The Young Martin," 56–57; and Downing, *To See the Promised Land*, 39–45.

to sneak downtown without his parents' permission, and to make excuses to avoid household chores. On one occasion he, Christine, and A. D. locked themselves in the hall cabinet and almost broke it. Martin, Jr. also occasionally teased his sister and brother, and one day clubbed A. D. on the head with a telephone for antagonizing Christine to the point of tears.[39] The closeness of the King family was such that no matter what the children did, they were always expected home in time to join the family at the evening meal. On such occasions, Martin, Sr., or "Daddy King" as he was called, and Alberta, affectionately referred to as "Mother Dear," would read from the Bible, offer prayers, and engage Martin, Jr., Christine, and A. D. in conversation around the dinner table. Not only would they share ideas and family values with the children but would be interested in what they had to say as well.[40] This closely knit family, in which a concern for family unity, loyalty, and interfamily cooperation was consistently expressed, was a chief source of King's early understanding of community.[41]

With this intimacy came security—a security generated in the King household by a wonderful sense of strong, positive parenting. Growing up in a middle class home, Martin, Jr., Christine, and A. D. always had the basic necessities of life. "These things were always provided by a father who put his family first," Martin, Jr. recounted. He further noted:

> My father has always been a real father. This is not to say that I was born with a silver spoon in my mouth; far from it. My father has never made more than an ordinary salary, but the secret is that he knows the art of saving and budgeting. He never wasted his money at the expense of his family. He has always had sense

39. King, *Daddy King*, 109, 127; Farris, "The Young Martin," 56–57; Oates, *Let the Trumpet Sound*, 8–13; Downing, *To See the Promised Land*, 41–43.

40. Farris, "The Young Martin," 56–57; Oates, *Let the Trumpet Sound*, 5; King, *Daddy King*, 127–31.

41. Fluker, *They Looked for a City*, 82.

enough not to live beyond his means. So for this reason he has been able to provide us with the basic necessities of life with little strain.[42]

Martin, Jr.'s reflections bear out author Jim Bishop's claim that Daddy King was "one of the most profound father figures in the black South."[43] Daddy King's dedication to the survival and welfare of his family was the best evidence for this claim. He often said that he protected and provided for his children "with a mother's heart."[44] "My prayer," he once remarked, "was always—Lord, grant that my children will not have to come the way I did. . . . I equipped myself to give them the comforts of life. Not to waste, not to keep up with the Joneses, but just to be comfortable." Even during the worst years of the Great Depression, Daddy King made sure that his home remained warm and secure. He once boasted that by 1935 "I'd become a prosperous young pastor, a husband and father whose family had never lived in a rented home or driven a car on which a payment was ever made late. We dressed well, we ate well, we enjoyed great respect among the people of our community."[45] Young Martin saw very early that Daddy King was strong, secure, and self-reliant, and he adored and respected him. The boy dreamed of becoming like his father—tall, muscular, resolute, and a good provider. King's "single-minded determination, faith and forthrightness," according to his sister Christine, "unquestionably came from Dad."[46] The spiritual bond between him and Daddy

42. King, "An Autobiography of Religious Development," 3–4.
43. Jim Bishop, *The Days of Martin Luther King, Jr.* (New York: G. P. Putnam's Sons, 1971), 469.
44. A private interview with the Rev. Ralph D. Abernathy, Atlanta, Ga., 17 March 1987.
45. James Baldwin, "The Dangerous Road before Martin Luther King, Jr.," *Harper's Magazine* (February 1961); 37; and King, *Daddy King*, 98.
46. A private interview with Dr. Philip Lenud, Nashville, Tenn., 7 April 1987; and Farris, "The Young Martin," 57. The best source on King's relationship to his father is King, *Daddy King*, 80–214. Another brilliant treatment of this subject, written in classic storytelling style, is David R. Collins, *Not Only Dreamers: Martin Luther King, Sr. and Martin Luther King, Jr.* (Elgin, Ill.: Brethren Press, 1986), chap. 1 ff.

King was symbolic of how he would later relate not only to his own children but to his people as a whole.

Although the King home was traditional with Daddy King considered the head of the family, Alberta also played a vital role in making it comfortable and secure. "Our mother has also been behind the scene setting forth those motherly cares," Martin, Jr. once observed, "the lack of which leaves a missing link in life."[47] Alberta was always there when questions were being asked by the children, and she nurtured their minds and spirits when Daddy King was away for revivals, church conferences, or other church or community-related activities. King's love and respect for his mother equaled that which he had for his father, and he saw many qualities in her that he felt worthy of emulation. Concerning her brother, Martin, Jr., Christine wrote: "I'd have to say that he got his love, compassion and ability to listen to others from mother."[48] Philip Lenud, who was King's classmate at Morehouse in the late 1940s, and who often ate pancakes in the King home on Saturday mornings, agreed with this claim, noting that Alberta King, in contrast to her hot-tempered, stubborn, and often abrasive husband, "was an absolute angel. She was so sweet."[49] Daddy King once reflected on how his wife, whom he affectionately called "Bunch," related to their children with a rare combination of gentleness and firmness, and on how she, more than anyone else, soothed and reinforced the tender spirit of Martin, Jr.:

> Bunch was very gifted with children. She raised all of ours with great love and respect for their feelings. . . . She could be strict, in her way, and the kids learned early on that as gentle as their mother was, they couldn't get up early enough in the morning to fool her, any day of the week. She knew each of her children almost as well as she knew herself. M. L.

47. King, "An Autobiography of Religious Development," 4.
48. Farris, "The Young Martin," 57; King, *My Life with Martin Luther King, Jr.*, 92.
49. A private interview with Philip Lenud, 7 April 1987.

came along with sensitivities only she could investigate and soothe.[50]

Martin, Jr. also inherited other features and qualities from his mother, such as his short build (only five feet, seven inches), high forehead, full lips and nose, humility, and great sense of humor. These features and qualities were matched only by the firm and broad torso the boy inherited from Daddy King. Apparently, King's relationship with his parents was both physical and spiritual in nature. The images of the strong father and mother, always a prominent feature of the King household, created in young Martin and his siblings a sense of the family as coherent, solid, and secure.[51]

This sense of intimacy and security was also enhanced by the presence of other relatives and friends in the King home. The house was always filled with aunts, uncles, cousins, friends of the family, boarders, and others who were not actual relatives at all, and this contributed to the King children's early sense of the vitality of the extended family model as an instrument of black survival in the South.[52] Among those who lived with the Kings were Ida Worthem, an aunt to the children, and Jennie C. Parks Williams, the maternal grandmother, who was variously and affectionately called "Mama," "Big Mama," and "Grandmother Jennie." "Aunt Ida" spent many hours reading to Martin, Jr., Christine, and A. D. from newspapers, books, and encyclopedias. Christine recalled that the things Martin, Jr., heard from his aunt "whetted his curiosity about the world around him, and helped him to develop into an inquisitive child and an avid reader."[53]

50. King, *Daddy King*, 131.
51. Lawrence D. Reddick, *Crusader without Violence: A Biography of Martin Luther King, Jr.* (New York: Harper & Brothers, Publishers, 1959), 2; A private interview with Philip Lenud, 7 April 1987; King, "An Autobiography of Religious Development," 1–15; A private interview with the Rev. Bernard S. Lee, Washington, D.C., 9 July 1986; and King, *My Life with Martin Luther King, Jr.*, 92.
52. King, *Daddy King*, 81, 109; Farris, "The Young Martin," 56–57; and Fluker, *They Looked for a City*, 191–92.
53. King, "An Autobiography of Religious Development," 2; Farris, "The Young Martin," 56–57; and Oates, *Let the Trumpet Sound*, 8–9.

The children were influenced significantly by both their aunt and grandmother. Concerning their relationship to Grandmother Jennie, Martin Jr., reported:

> In our immediate family there was also a saintly grandmother (my mother's mother) whose husband had died when I was one year old. She was very dear to each of us, but especially to me. I sometimes think that I was her favorite grandchild. I can remember very vividly how she spent many evenings telling us interesting stories.[54]

The family history, tales, and vivid Biblical stories shared by Aunt Ida, Grandmother Jennie, and Alberta, all of whom stood in the best tradition of black storytellers in the South, served a didactic purpose in that the King children were informed of the values of family, church, and the larger black community. It was here that the children got their first lessons in the art of storytelling— lessons that later enhanced Christine's qualities as a teacher and King's and A. D.'s gifts as preachers.[55]

It is impossible to understand Grandmother Jennie's role in the King household without a keen knowledge of the role that the grandmother has played in the black family since slavery, especially in the South. The sociologist E. Franklin Frazier once wrote:

> During slavery the Negro grandmother occupied in many instances an important place in the plantation economy and was highly esteemed by both the slaves and the masters. In the master's house she was very often the "mammy" whom history and tradition have idealized because of her loyalty and affection. Because of her intimate relations with the whites, all family secrets. . . were in her keeping; she was the defender of the family honor. The tie of affection between her and her charges was never outgrown. Often she was the confidential adviser of the older members of the

54. King, "An Autobiography of Religious Development," 2.
55. *Ibid.;* Farris, "The Young Martin," 56–57; Oates, *Let the Trumpet Sound,* 5; and Downing, *To See the Promised Land,* 89–93.

household. To young mothers she was an authority on first babies. Age added dignity to her position, and her regime extended frequently through two generations, occasionally through three. . . . She was the repository of the accumulated lore and superstition of the slaves. . . . When emancipation came, it was often the old grandmother who kept the generations together.[56]

The prestige and importance of Jennie C. Parks Williams in the King home were essentially as great as that of the black grandmother during slavery. She was a strong spiritual force, a bearer of culture, and a pillar of strength. She was held in high regard, even reverence, as a pillar in the family, church, and larger black community of Atlanta. She was a wise teacher whose advice or counsel the young and elderly alike took seriously.[57] Grandmother Jennie's pivotal role is clearly substantiated when her relationship to Martin, Jr., is studied. The boy took great delight in freely throwing himself into his grandmother's lap, in listening to her wise counsel, and in eating large quantities of her delicious "soul food."[58] One day when the King boys were playing in the upstairs portion of their two-story Victorian-style home on Auburn Avenue, A. D. slid down the banister and accidentally knocked Grandmother Jennie to the ground. When she did not move, Martin, Jr., stood there in shock, convinced that he and A. D. had killed her. Little Martin was so distraught that he ran upstairs and hurled himself out of a bedroom window, falling about twelve feet to the ground. He stayed there motionless until his grandmother was declared alive. Family members and friends were incredulous when they realized that Martin, Jr.,

56. E. Franklin Frazier, *The Negro Family in the United States* (Chicago: The University of Chicago Press, 1968), 114–116.

57. Farris, "The Young Martin," 56–57; Downing, *To See the Promised Land*, Chapter 5; and King, *My Life with Martin Luther King, Jr.*, 91.

58. King, "An Autobiography of Religious Development," 2; Martin Luther King, Jr., "A Prelude to Tomorrow: An Address," The Chicago Operation Breadbasket Meeting, Chicago, Illinois (The King Center Archives, 6 January 1968), 4–5; Downing, *To See the Promised Land*, 97–120.

had actually tried to kill himself because of his deep love for his grandmother.[59] Much of the child's early life centered on Grandmother Jennie, who helped instill in him a strong sense of identity, self-esteem, and mission. Martin, Jr., represented perfection in her eyes, and her love for him was such that she could not stand to see him cry. Christine would later describe her brother's relationship with Grandmother Jennie in these terms:

> She and M. L. were extremely close. Whenever Daddy had to discipline M. L., Grandmother always had a hug, kiss or kind word to help the hurt go away. She often told Dad that she hated to see him spank Martin because "the child looked so pitiful" when he did.[60]

Grandmother Jennie's death in May, 1941, was a severe blow to Martin, Jr., who was only twelve at the time. His grandmother died suddenly of a heart attack at a church where she was to have spoken. Martin, Jr., had sneaked downtown Atlanta to see a parade, something strictly forbidden by Daddy King on Sunday, and was not present when Grandmother Jennie died.[61] When informed of the incident, the boy virtually exploded with feelings of anger, guilt, and sorrow. "I was particularly hurt by this incident mainly because of the extreme love I had for her," Martin, Jr., later wrote.[62] Daddy King recalled that the boy "cried off and on for several days afterward, and was unable to sleep at night."[63] Christine recounted how her brother convinced himself that their grandmother's death "was God's way of punishing him for having disobeyed Dad by going to the parade." This experience helped young Martin discipline himself. Once he got over his grandmother's death, according to

59. Downing, *To See the Promised Land*, 98–99; and Oates, *Let the Trumpet Sound*, 8–9.
60. Farris, "The Young Martin," 56–57; King, *Daddy King*, 109; King, *My Life with Martin Luther King, Jr.*, 91; and Oates, *Let the Trumpet Sound*, 8.
61. King, *Daddy King*, 109; and Farris, "The Young Martin," 56–57.
62. King, "An Autobiography of Religious Development," 10.
63. King, *Daddy King*, 109.

Christine, "a number of people commented on how mature he seemed to have become."[64]

Martin Jr., Christine, and A. D. were taught to work assiduously to aspire to excellence. They found inspiring examples in their parents, who with determination had overcome great odds in the South to achieve excellence in their fields of endeavor. Daddy King had settled in Atlanta in 1916, "a raw, strapping country boy," determined not "to be a slave" or "to plow another mule." By 1930, he had received a degree from Atlanta's Morehouse College and had emerged as a successful pastor and a respected and admired community leader. Alberta had completed her training at Spelman Seminary in Atlanta, and had become an accomplished musician and a school teacher, other professions highly respected among blacks in the South at that time.[65] Considering their successful careers, it is not surprising that Daddy King and Alberta started preparing their children for rich and productive lives while they were still very young. "I'd begun thinking about the future of my youngsters," Daddy King commented, "and in the rush to help them grow up a little faster than they wanted to—especially the boys—I began easing them toward a special attention to the ministry."[66] "I really saw the boys becoming ministers and Christine a teacher," paths pursued by the parents.[67] Although this turned out the case, the King children, especially Martin, Jr. and A. D., initially had little interest in pursuing the future that their father wanted for them. According to Daddy King, "A. D. just backed away from this. He was a child who was determined from his earliest days not to be what his father was. At times he got so dramatic about it that we had a few run-ins over the matter, even while he was still very young." Of Martin, Jr.,

64. Farris, "The Young Martin," 56–57.
65. Baldwin, "The Dangerous Road Before Martin Luther King, Jr.," 37; King, *My Life with Martin Luther King, Jr.*, 89; King, *Daddy King*, 59, 66–67; and Haskins, *The Life and Death of Martin Luther King, Jr.*, 14.
66. King, *Daddy King*, 127.
67. *Ibid.*, 127–28.

Daddy King wrote: "For his part, M. L. said very little about preaching as his life's work, and—unreasonably, I guess—that made me believe through his earliest years that he would evolve more naturally than A. D. to a place in the pastorate of Ebenezer."[68] Although Alberta shared Daddy King's dream for their children, she was not in favor of pressuring them to choose a certain profession. She constantly warned her husband: "Don't push the boys too hard, King. It's easy to turn children away from things that you want so much. Let them be who they'll be."[69]

This concern for excellence led Martin, Sr., and Alberta King to exercise strict discipline in raising their children. Martin, Jr., often reminisced about having grown up "in a relatively strict home—strict enough for me to develop certain disciplinary principles as I came up."[70] Daddy King was so powerful and domineering that he shaped his children's personalities in decisive ways. Martin, Jr., apparently adjusted quite well to his father, Christine became an introvert, and A. D., who had his father's temper, often argued with and rebelled against him and was asked to leave the King home on several occasions.[71] Daddy King recalled that his hot temper made it very difficult at times for him to discipline his children with patience:

> My impatience made it very hard for me to sit down with the boys and quietly explain to them the way I wanted things done. With M. L. and A. D., I found that a switch was usually quicker and more persuasive, although I never had to use this form of punishment with Christine. She was the exceptionally well-behaved, serious, and studious member of the trio.[72]

68. *Ibid.*
69. *Ibid.*
70. "Face to Face: John Freeman of B.B.C. Interviews Martin Luther King, Jr.," U.K., London (Transcribed from a TV telediphone recording, The King Center Archives, (29 October 1961), 2.
71. King, *Daddy King*, 127, 131; A private interview with the Rev. Ralph D. Abernathy, 17 March 1987; and Farris, "The Young Martin," 56–58.
72. King, *Daddy King*, 130.

Reflecting on his father's image as a disciplinarian, Martin, Jr., once said with a laugh: "Whippings must not be so bad, for I received them until I was fifteen."[73] Daddy King's approach to discipline inspired awe in his children. "With his fearless honesty and his robust, dynamic presence," Martin, Jr. said of his daddy, "his words commanded attention."[74] Alberta was always a sobering influence on her husband when the need to discipline the children arose. Daddy King wrote:

> Bunch insisted, though, as the children grew older, that any form of discipline used on them by either of us had to be agreed upon by both parents. This often curbed my temper, but it also helped Bunch to understand the things that made me angry. We talked a lot about the future of the kids, and she was able to understand that even when I got very upset with them, it was only because I wanted them to be strong and able and happy.[75]

As a way of steering their children toward excellence, Martin, Sr., and Alberta King stressed values that have traditionally been upheld by the black family. They emphasized education as the path to competence, culture, and economic security.[76] Daddy King is said to have preached education and economic security "as though his law included twelve commandments which black people need to obey for these times: 'Thou shalt get thy children to college,' and 'Thou shalt own thy own home.'"[77] Alberta also constantly reminded their children of the importance of learning, earning a little money through odd jobs, and practicing "the King home's three S's—

73. Quoted in Reddick, *Crusader without Violence*, 5.
74. King, *Stride toward Freedom*, 19.
75. King, *Daddy King*, 131.
76. Reddick, *Crusader without Violence*, 51; Haskins, *The Life and Death of Martin Luther King, Jr.*, 14; Lenwood G. Davis, *I Have A Dream: The Life and Times of Martin Luther King, Jr.* (Westport, Conn.: Negro Universities Press, 1969), 13; Farris, "The Young Martin," 56–58; and King, *Daddy King*, 127–31.
77. King, *Daddy King*, 10; and "Daddy King: 'There's No Hate in My Heart,'" 1, 4.

Spending, Saving, and Sharing."[78] Both Martin, Sr., and
Alberta had been taught these same values from their
earliest childhood. Although Martin, Sr.'s, mother Delia
never learned to read or write herself, she had a great
sense of the value of education, and although his father
James never saw the value of education, he did teach his
children the importance of thrift and economic security.[79] Alberta had come from a family with a strong intellectual tradition and in which, therefore, a college
education was a matter of course. Alberta's mother Jennie had been educated at Spelman Seminary in Atlanta,
and her father, Alfred Daniel, had received a degree from
Morehouse College. Thus, it is not surprising that Martin, Sr., and Alberta studied at Morehouse and Spelman,
respectively, and eventually sent their children to these
predominantly black institutions.[80]

Martin, Jr., Christine, and A. D. were required to follow
a simple daily schedule that would not interfere with their
studies. Daddy King and Alberta made sure that the children got to school on time every morning and that they
did their homework and chores as soon as they reached
home in the afternoon. After supper, there would be family conversation, more studying, family prayers, and bed-
time.[81] When the King children left school each day, they
went home to educated parents who reinforced what they
had learned in the classroom. This was not the case for
the average black child in Atlanta and in the South generally in the 1930s and 1940s. Martin, Jr., would later recall
that "I was exposed to the best educational conditions in
my childhood."[82] He entered nursery school at age three
and kindergarten at age five, before moving on to the first
grade at Atlanta's David T. Howard Elementary School.
After his graduation from sixth grade, Martin, Jr., joined
his sister Christine at Atlanta University's Laboratory

78. King, *Daddy King*, 131.
79. *Ibid.*, 37–38.
80. *Ibid.*, 13, 20, 88; Baldwin, "The Dangerous Road before Martin
Luther King, Jr.," 37; and Branch, *Parting the Waters*, 30.
81. King, *Daddy King*, 131; and Farris, "The Young Martin," 56.
82. King, "An Autobiography of Religious Development," 5.

High School, a private, experimental school at which he studied for two years before attending Booker T. Washington, a public high school. These institutions provided a liberal educational environment for black students during the period when segregation was most blatant.[83] Martin, Jr., performed well in both elementary and high school with a modicum of effort, and read numerous books about black history and the black experience. The youngster also developed a love for music and poetry, and was fascinated by the sounds and power of words.[84] According to Daddy King, young Martin's "schoolwork, in both the private and public institutions he attended, was always of a high caliber." This caused the black community and the King family to expect greatness from the boy, and Daddy King and Alberta cultivated him with this expectation.[85]

The notion that Martin, Jr., had an extraordinary destiny became more pronounced when he entered Morehouse College at age fifteen. Family members, neighbors, and members of Ebenezer Baptist Church added an extra measure to the affection they lavished on the young man. Morehouse at that time was a very special part of Atlanta's black community and of the King family's history, so it was only natural for Martin, Jr., to matriculate there. His studies were supervised by his parents and professors, giving further evidence of how family and community combined to have an impact on his early life. The educational environment provided by King's family was complemented by the rich educational tradition in Atlanta, where several black colleges and seminaries constituted the largest center for black training in the country. King's sense of self-worth and mission was strengthened in this atmosphere, and by the many black college professors, insurance executives,

83. *Ibid.*; and Farris, "The Young Martin," 57–58.
84. King, *Daddy King*, 127; Haskins, *The Life and Death of Martin Luther King, Jr.*, 18–19; Oates, *Let the Trumpet Sound*, 10–13; and Farris, "The Young Martin," 56–58.
85. King, *Daddy King*, 127–31.

ministers, morticians, physicians, and other symbols of progress and success that surrounded him. Although young Martin was not an exceptional student at Morehouse, he did display flashes of brilliance, insight, and leadership, qualities that later catapulted him to the forefront of his people's struggle for freedom. In terms of intellectual acumen and ability, he was quite similar to his mother. Daddy King, by his own admission, was not particularly gifted in this regard.[86]

It was the King family's deep belief in the value of learning that set King's educational course through Morehouse College, Crozer Theological Seminary, and Boston University, culminating in his attainment of a doctoral degree.[87] His experiences with the depersonalizing effects of racism, his religious heritage, and his family's strong intellectual tradition were the links that fostered a kind of natural openness to the liberal philosophy and theology he studied at these institutions.[88] The young man's good academic performance at Crozer Theological Seminary and excellent classroom record at Boston University were not only a testimony to the strength of his own family, but also an illustration of how the black family, despite tremendous odds, has been "a bulwark of black achievement." Furthermore, King's impressive classroom records further reinforced the notion that he was destined to do great things for his family and for black people in general.[89]

Martin, Sr., and Alberta King also taught their children the value of respecting themselves as well as others. Declaring on one occasion that "I have never believed that anybody was better than I," Daddy King's entire life of service to his family, church, and community was

86. Farris, "The Young Martin," 58; *Daddy King*, 17–22; and Fluker, *They Looked for a City*, 85.

87. King, *Daddy King*, 10; and "Daddy King: 'There's No Hate in My Heart,'" 1, 4.

88. Watley, *Roots of Resistance*, 36.

89. Robert B. Hill, *The Strengths of Black Families: A National Urban League Research Study* (New York: Emerson Hall Publishers, 1972), X (Preface); King, *Daddy King*, 141–43; and Farris, "The Young Martin," 58.

developed around this concept of respect for personality. He never wanted Martin, Jr., Christine, and A. D. to work for white people, fearing that such exposure would inevitably damage their young personalities.[90] Alberta was a source of comfort and strength for the children as they confronted the powerful effects of racism at an early age. One day, after being told by the parents of his white playmate that he could no longer associate with their son because he was black, Martin, who was only six years old at the time, turned to his mother for an explanation. "Why don't white people like us, Mother Dear?," he asked. The answer Alberta gave to her son's wounded spirit and youthful curiosity lingered with him:

> My mother took me on her lap and began by telling me about slavery and how it ended with the Civil War. She tried to explain the divided system of the South—the segregated schools, restaurants, theaters, housing; the white and colored signs on drinking fountains, waiting rooms, lavatories—as a social condition rather than a natural order. Then she said the words that almost every Negro hears before he can yet understand the injustice that makes them necessary: "You are as good as anyone."[91]

Daddy King's and Alberta's often repeated message to their children—"You must never feel that you are less than anyone else"—largely explains why Martin, Jr., was such a healthy child from a physical and emotional standpoint.[92] This message gave the boy a sense of his own significance that nothing in his experiences with racism and segregation could destroy. Thus, he was not driven to the neurotic stage of having to prove himself. He knew who he was and what he was because of his

90. Quoted in Baldwin, "The Dangerous Road before Martin Luther King, Jr.," 38; King, *Stride toward Freedom*, 90; and King, *Daddy King*, 141–42.

91. Fluker, *They Looked for a City*, 83; King, *Stride Toward Freedom*, 19; King, "An Autobiography of Religious Development," 11–13; King, *Daddy King*, 126, 130; and Farris, "The Young Martin," 57.

92. King, "A Speech to Blacks," Grenada, Miss., 3; and "Face to Face," 3.

parents. The King family's emphasis on self-worth, pride, and dignity provided a foundation for the abiding faith, optimism, and self-confidence that Martin, Jr., would later display in his efforts to transform and redeem human society.[93]

In an environment in which racial discrimination and class exploitation were so intense, Martin, Sr., and Alberta King constantly reminded their children of the importance of loving and respecting all human beings. They had heard the same message from their own parents years earlier. Martin, Jr., Christine, and A. D. were taught to view the poor, the elderly, and even whites as persons with dignity and worth.[94] Martin, Jr., like his father before him, found it very difficult to love and respect whites as a child, particularly after racism severed his relationship with his white playmate:

> My parents would always tell me that I should not hate the white man, but that it was my duty as a Christian to love him. At this point the religious element came in. The question arose in my mind—"how could I love a race of people who hated me and who had been responsible for breaking me up with one of my best childhood friends?" This was a great question in my mind for a number of years.[95]

Daddy King's and Alberta's teachings concerning the dignity and worth of other selves rooted young Martin in a significance of the whole of life. It was here that he got not only his first notion of the inherent worth of human personality but also of the social nature of human existence—of the interrelatedness and interdependence of all life—ideas for which he later received a metaphysical grounding in Boston Personalism. This offers a clue as to

93. A private interview with Dr. Philip Lenud, 7 April 1987; and Baldwin, "Understanding Martin Luther King, Jr. within the Context of Southern Black Religious History," 6.

94. Reddick, *Crusader without Violence*, 51; King, "An Autobiography of Religious Development," 12; King, *Daddy King*, 53; and Davis, *I Have A Dream*, 13.

95. King, "An Autobiography of Religious Development," 12–13.

why Martin, Jr., was able to relate so well with people of all backgrounds in the more public arenas in which he lived and acted, especially after he emerged as a famous civil rights leader.[96]

The King home was also a place in which high moral and spiritual values were upheld. It was a superb example of a Christian household in which disciplined devotional and moral training was emphasized along with high educational standards. Many of the folktales and Bible stories Martin, Jr., Christine, and A. D. heard as children were infused with direct moral messages—messages about the value of integrity, about the importance and obligations of friendship, about the obligations of parents and children to one another, and about the responsibilities of the truly moral person toward his or her community.[97] Smoking, drinking alcoholic beverages, dancing, lying, cursing, and cheating were completely forbidden. When he reached manhood, Martin, Jr., frequently referred jokingly to his father's high moral standards, noting that "My old man has always been a moralist. He doesn't drink liquor, and he doesn't chase women."[98] Biblical training, genuine and simplistic piety, and rigid discipline were the means by which Martin, Sr., and Alberta King instilled spiritual values in their children. The children were taught to value prayer, meditation, fasting, and other expressions of spirituality, and this led them to an early understanding of the moral order and the religious idea.[99] The necessity for a close relationship to the personal God of love and reason was stressed, an idea for which Martin, Jr., found support in the black church and later in the liberal theology he studied at Crozer Theological

96. Watley, *Roots of Resistance*, 31–36; and Kenneth L. Smith and Ira G. Zepp, Jr., *Search for the Beloved Community: The Thinking of Martin Luther King, Jr.* (Valley Forge, Pa.: Judson Press, 1974), 99–118.

97. Farris, "The Young Martin," 56; Downing, *To See the Promised Land*, 97–120; and King, *My Life with Martin Luther King, Jr.*, 92.

98. Coretta Scott King, "An Address at the National Conference on Civil Rights," Fisk University, Nashville, Tenn. (5 April 1986), 1 ff.

99. King, "An Autobiography of Religious Development," 8; and Ervin Smith, *The Ethics of Martin Luther King, Jr.* (New York: The Edwin Mellen Press, 1981), 1.

Seminary and Boston University. In a revealing statement in his "Autobiography of Religious Development," written after he graduated from Morehouse College, young Martin attributed his basic Christian optimism primarily to the spiritual values he inherited from a loving family and a safe and comfortable environment:

> It is quite easy for me to think of a God of love mainly because I grew up in a family where love was central and where lovely relationships were ever present. It is quite easy for me to think of the universe as basically friendly mainly because of my uplifting hereditary and environmental circumstances. It is quite easy for me to lean more toward optimism than pessimism about human nature mainly because of my childhood experiences.[100]

Social consciousness and a sense of social responsibility were also among the values that Martin, Sr., and Alberta King instilled in their children. Martin, Jr., Christine, and A. D. were consistently taught that they had a moral obligation to resist both individual and social evil, and to help uplift the poor and the oppressed. Daddy King, described as "a voice for the voiceless" before "black people in Atlanta had access to City Hall," taught his children through his proud and compelling example.[101] "For more than forty years," wrote a newspaper columnist, "black people in Atlanta knew that M. L., Sr., was the man to see when you wanted to go to school, to get a job, buy a house, or get out of trouble. . . . They came because they knew he cared, that he was fearless, and that he would take action."[102] After assuming the pastorate of Atlanta's Ebenezer Baptist Church in 1931, Daddy King followed his father-in-law's example by leading boycotts, a voting rights march, and by fighting for full-arrest powers for black policemen.

---

100. King, "An Autobiography of Religious Development," 6.
101. Farris, "The Young Martin," 57–58; King, *Stride Toward Freedom*, 17–21; "Daddy King: 'There's No Hate in My Heart,'" 1, 4.
102. "Daddy King: 'There's No Hate in My Heart,'" 1, 4.

Martin, Jr., remembered his father as one who "always stood out in social reform," especially during his years of service as president of Atlanta's NAACP:

> From before I was born, my father had refused to ride the city buses, after witnessing a brutal attack on a load of Negro passengers. He had led the fight in Atlanta to equalize teachers' salaries, and had been instrumental in the elimination of Jim Crow elevators in the courthouse. As pastor of Ebenezer Baptist church, . . . he had wielded great influence in the Negro community, and had perhaps won the grudging respect of the whites. At any rate, they had never attacked him physically, a fact that filled my brother and sister and me with wonder as we grew up in this tension-packed atmosphere.[103]

Two incidents occurred in young Martin's childhood that helped him understand the intensity of his father's spirit of resistance to racism. At age six, he saw Daddy King storm out of a shoe store after a white clerk insisted that he sit in the black section before being served. "This was the first time I had ever seen my father so angry," Martin, Jr., recalled years later. "I still remember walking down the street beside him as he muttered, 'I don't care how long I have to live with this system, I will never accept it.'"[104] Daddy King later assessed the impact of this incident on young Martin:

> M. L. was looking up at me. I could see he was confused by what was going on. After all, he only wanted a pair of shoes to wear. When I told him we were leaving, he seemed ready to cry. In trying to explain, I became angry—not at him, but the little fella didn't know that and became very frightened. As we drove back toward Auburn Avenue, I was able to speak quietly about the whole episode in the store, but the questions, the confusions, remained in his eyes. . . . M. L. just couldn't understand why it was all right to buy

103. "Face to Face," 1; King, *Daddy King*, 23–136; and King, *Stride toward Freedom*, 17–21.
104. King, *Stride toward Freedom*, 19.

shoes in the back of a store and not in the front.
. . . And I said to him that the best way to explain it
was to say that I'd never accept the stupidity and cruelty of segregation, not as long as I lived. I was going
to be fighting against it in some way or other as long
as there was breath in me. I wanted him to understand that. He still looked puzzled. But he nodded
his head and told me that if I was against it, he would
help me all he could. . . . M. L. seemed so thoughtful
and determined on this matter that I felt certain he
wouldn't forget his promise to help.[105]

On another occasion, Martin, Jr., witnessed his father's courageous stand against a white policeman who,
after charging him with a traffic violation, arrogantly
called him "a boy." Daddy King replied indignantly, "I'm
no boy. . . . I'm a man, and until you call me one, I will
not listen to you." The policeman was so surprised that
he wrote the ticket up nervously, and quickly left the
scene.[106] The fact that this and other incidents involving
his father remained indelibly etched in King's memory is
worthy of special note. Daddy King's example of courage,
at a time when even blacks in U. S. Army uniforms were
beaten and lynched, strongly influenced his son's later
views about how the younger generations of black people
might meet the challenge of racism in this country.

Alberta King shared her husband's healthy and active
concern for social conditions, although her spirit of resistance found a somewhat different expression. Viewing
firsthand the impact of capitalism on the poor and especially on poor blacks, she cautioned her children against
an uncritical acceptance of the capitalistic ethic and
the materialistic ingredients associated with it. Philip
Lenud, a friend of the King family, related a story about
how Alberta lashed out at materialism and elitism one
Saturday morning after seeing her car, Daddy King's car,
and the cars of Martin, Jr., Christine, and A. D. parked on
the front driveway. With a sense of shame, she said to her

105. King, *Daddy King*, 108–109.
106. King, *Stride toward Freedom*, 20.

husband: "King, come here. Look at all of these cars out here. This is a sin because we're supposed to be serving the people. All of you—King, M. L., Christine, A. D.—move these cars out back somewhere so I can't see them." "This has grown up in me," Lenud declared, "her rebellion against materialism over against what she saw as their mission and purpose as a family in the ministry serving the people, and especially the poor."[107] When it came to the evils of capitalism, Martin, Jr., was more in agreement with his mother than with his father, whom the young man once described as "a thoroughgoing capitalist."[108] As Martin, Jr., grew to manhood, his sense of the evils of the capitalist ethic was reinforced by the knowledge that his great-grandparents had been slaves, that his paternal grandparents had been shamefully exploited as sharecroppers, and that his own father had been a farm laborer from age twelve until he reached manhood. Young Martin's sensitivity to this part of his family heritage helped make it possible for him to identify with a world larger than anything he experienced or imagined in black middle-class Atlanta.[109]

Through his mother, Martin, Jr., had his first and most direct contact with pacifism prior to his matriculation at Morehouse College. According to Philip Lenud, "His mother was the strong pacifist in the family, and he took that from her."[110] Alberta's pacifism stemmed from her profound emotional and spiritual security, on which young Martin appears to have drawn heavily. "He was just secure," Lenud observed, "and when you're secure you don't have to fight, particularly when you are secure in spiritual ways and have a sense of divine purpose."[111] Although Martin, Sr., was also strong and

107. A private interview with Dr. Philip Lenud, 7 April 1987.
108. King, *My Life with Martin Luther King, Jr.*, 71; Watley, *Roots of Resistance*, 110; and King, *Daddy King*, 147.
109. King, *Stride toward Freedom*, 19.
110. A private interview with Dr. Philip Lenud, 7 April 1987. Lenud's recollections concerning Alberta King call into question Coretta Scott King's claim that "the spirit of nonviolence was not inherited from Martin's family." See King, *My Life with Martin Luther King, Jr.*, 88–89.
111. *Ibid.*

secure in many ways, he was too much like his parents, James and Delia King, to adopt the nonviolent ethic with ease. On one occasion he is said to have "beaten up" a fellow minister who owed him money and refused to settle the debt.[112] Young Martin found virtually nothing in Daddy King's personality to inspire his early tendency toward nonviolence.

Martin, Jr., did inherit from both of his parents a sense of mission that later propelled him to the forefront of a national and international struggle for freedom and human dignity. Considering his roots in that heritage of struggle that was embodied in A. D. Williams, James and Delia King, and Martin, Sr., and Alberta King, it is not difficult to understand why Martin Luther King, Jr., became the greatest civil rights leader on the American scene in this century. When he spoke, he was speaking not only his own words but also the words of his parents and grandparents. Their dream became his dream, and their struggle, his struggle. Young Martin himself, referring specifically to his father's image as a civil rights leader, but certainly with a broader knowledge of the struggles of other family members who preceded him, insisted that "With this heritage, it is not surprising that I had also learned to abhor segregation, considering it both rationally inexplicable and morally unjustifiable." "I could never adjust to the separate waiting rooms, separate eating places, separate rest rooms," he continued, "partly because the separate was always unequal, and partly because the very idea of separation did something to my sense of dignity and self-respect."[113]

King's close ties to family and to the general culture of the South helped him maintain a sense of values during his studies at Crozer Theological Seminary and Boston

112. *Ibid.* Martin Luther King, Jr. once said of his father: "My father never advocated violence as a way to solve the problem. Though, I grant you that at points my father did not come up under the discipline of the nonviolent philosophy." See Warren, *Who Speaks for the Negro?*, 1–2.
113. Fluker, *They Looked for a City*, 83; King, *Daddy King*, xi–xiv; and King, *Stride toward Freedom*, 20–21.

University. The fact that he was only nineteen when he left Atlanta to attend Crozer Theological Seminary was a matter of great concern for his parents, who worried about the effect that the cold, impersonal, and rapidly-paced northern social environment could have on their son.[114] To offset the possible negative effect of such an environment on their son, Daddy King and Alberta entrusted him to the care of the Reverend and Mrs. J. Pius Barbour in Chester, Pennsylvania, and later to the supervision of the Reverend and Mrs. William H. Hester in Boston, all of whom were old friends of the King family. In a way, Martin, Jr., was adopted by the Barbours, the Hesters, and other black families with whom he associated, and this made his studies in the northeast all the more interesting and rewarding. In the homes of these people, Martin, Jr., discovered essentially what the black extended family afforded him in the South—nourishing food, folk wit and story, deep genuine laughter, spiritual sustenance, and a general feeling of being accepted and loved.[115] Without this kind of support and reinforcement, the transition from essentially black educational institutions in the South to predominantly white schools in the North would have been a spiritually painful experience for the youngster.

The frequent expressions of love and concern that came from close family members in the South were also a sustaining force for Martin, Jr., in the North. He continued to look primarily to Daddy King and Alberta for advice, support, and encouragement, and his communication with them through the mail and telephone always brought a renewal of spirit. Martin, Jr., was especially uplifted on those occasions when his parents traveled from Atlanta to visit him. Philip Lenud recalled that the

114. King, *Daddy King*, 144–45; King, *My Life with Martin Luther King, Jr.*, 100.
115. King, *My Life with Martin Luther King, Jr.*, 72; King, *Daddy King*, 147–49; A private interview with the Rev. Michael E. Haynes, Boston, Mass. (25 June 1986); A private interview with Dr. Philip Lenud (7 April 1987); A private interview with Sara V. Richardson, Chester, Pa. (29 May 1987); and A private interview with Emma Anderson, Chester, Pa. (29 May 1987).

young man always found security and strength of spirit in knowing that Daddy King would be there when he needed him:

> Martin always had this idea that his daddy would take care of him. His daddy bought him a new green Chevrolet when he got out of Crozer in 1951, and he took it to Boston. After about a year, the car started giving him problems, and I said, "Martin, let me help you." He said, "No Phil, I'll just wait for my daddy to come." He found such awesome security in his father because his father was such a strong man, like my father was.[116]

While at Crozer Theological Seminary, Martin, Jr., related how his father "had the tremendous responsibility of keeping all of us in school (my brother in college, my sister in graduate school, and me in the seminary), and although it has been somewhat a burden from a financial angle, he has done it with a smile."[117] Daddy King provided support for Martin, Jr., with the understanding that the youngster was being trained to follow him as pastor of Ebenezer Baptist Church. This partly explains why he often urged his son to remain firm in spiritual values in the face of the liberal idealism he was studying at Crozer Theological Seminary and later at Boston University. In December, 1954, after Martin, Jr., completed the residential requirements for the doctorate at Boston University, his father said to him in a letter: "You are becoming very popular. As I told you, you must be much in prayer. Persons like yourself are the ones the devil turns all his forces aloose to destroy."[118] Although Martin, Jr., came to disagree theologically with Daddy King on a range of concerns, such differences never interfered with the young man's desire to seek and abide by his father's spiritual advice. For him, Daddy King was the best symbol of the

116. A private interview with Dr. Philip Lenud (7 April 1987).
117. King, "An Autobiography of Religious Development," 4–5.
118. King, *Daddy King*, 127–28, 147; and A letter from Martin Luther King, Sr., to Martin Luther King, Jr. (2 December 1954), The King Papers, Boston University.

rock-like strength and dignity so characteristic of the King family.[119]

## MARTIN, JR., AS HUSBAND AND FATHER

King's experiences in Boston were rich and rewarding in many ways. Aside from providing him with excellent academic training and a keen sense of how southern black culture merged with the culture of the black North, those experiences set him on a course that would eventually lead to his assuming the roles of husband and father. In 1952, during his second year at Boston University's School of Theology, King met Coretta Scott, a music student at the New England Conservatory, who would eventually become his wife. The couple met through a mutual friend named Mary Powell, who had known King in Atlanta when he was at Morehouse College and she was at Spelman, and who was married to a nephew of Dr. Benjamin E. Mays, the president of Morehouse College. This is another indication of how King's southern roots continued to affect his life in a northern context. In any case, the similar backgrounds of Martin, Jr., and Coretta seemed to make them a perfect match. "Martin and I both had a heritage deeply rooted in southern soil," Coretta recalled.[120] Both were products of parents who had struggled against monumental odds to achieve economic security in the South. Coretta had been born early in 1927 in Marion, Alabama, where her forebears had owned land since the Civil War, and where her parents, Obadiah and Bernice M. Scott, owned a farm and a considerable estate by the 1950s.[121] Martin, Jr., and Coretta also knew the pain of oppression and shared a common desire to help make the nation, and particularly the South, a better place for both black and white people.

119. King, "An Autobiography of Religious Development," 14; and King, *My Life with Martin Luther King, Jr.*, 76, 81–82.
120. King, *My Life with Martin Luther King, Jr.*, 34, 64–67.
121. *Ibid.*, chap. 2; Bennett, *What Manner of Man*, 31–32; and King, *Daddy King*, 23–79.

They strongly believed in the value of education as an avenue to freedom. Furthermore, both were deeply religious but were moving away from the rigid fundamentalism to which they had been exposed in many southern black churches.[122] These commonalities were ultimately more important than any differences that might have kept Martin Luther King, Jr. and Coretta Scott apart.

Despite what they shared in terms of background, interests, and perspectives, there were factors from the beginning that threatened the possibility of Martin, Jr. and Coretta becoming husband and wife. One was Coretta's stereotypical impression of ministers, which she shared with her friend Mary Powell before her introduction to King. She later recounted:

> The moment Mary told me the young man was a minister I lost interest, for I began to think of the stereotypes of ministers I had known—fundamentalists in their thinking, very narrow, and overly pious. Genuine piety is inspiring, but many of the ministers I had met went around wearing a look of sanctity that they seemed to put on like their black suits.[123]

"The fact that young King was a Baptist also prejudiced me," wrote Coretta, whose roots were in the African Methodist Episcopal Zion Church. She perceived Baptist churches as being "overly emotional," and found the Methodist custom of baptism by sprinkling to be more in line with her thinking than the Baptist practice of total immersion. For these reasons, Coretta had vowed never to become a Baptist, to say nothing of marrying a Baptist preacher. "I thought about how circumscribed my life might become," she said. Moreover, she was very

122. "Martin Luther King, Jr.: A Personal Portrait," a videotaped interview (Goldsboro, N.C.: Distributed by Carroll's Marketing and Management Service, 1966–67); and King, *My Life with Martin Luther King, Jr.*, 64, 66, 71, 76–77, 103; and King, "An Autobiography of Religious Development," 13–15.
123. King, *My Life with Martin Luther King, Jr.*, 66; and King, "An Address at the National Conference on Civil Rights," Nashville, Tenn., 1 ff.

concerned at that time about her musical career and believed that marriage would have interfered with it.[124] Coretta's reservations about dating and eventually marrying a minister faded almost from the moment she met Martin Luther King, Jr. "He radiated charm," she remembered. "When he talked he grew in stature. Even when he was so young, he drew people to him from the very first moment with his eloquence, his sincerity, and his moral stature. I knew immediately that he was very special."[125] Coretta found that young Martin "was just different" from other ministers she had known. "I liked him as a man and as a person," she declared, "and pretty soon I forgot the fact that he was a minister and I would be a minister's wife."[126] Martin, Jr., apparently developed strong feelings for Coretta on their first date, for he assured her: "You have everything I have ever wanted in a wife. The four things I look for in a wife are character, intelligence, personality, and beauty. And you have them all." Coretta was somewhat flurried by this remark, which suggested to her that young Martin was quite consciously looking for a wife.[127]

Coretta sensed very early that marriage to Martin, Jr., would not take place without the involvement of his family, and especially his father. "Martin's big problem in deciding whom to marry was his great love and respect for his father," she observed years later:

> Whatever he might say about deciding for himself, I recognized that his father might be the determining factor, because of the strong influence he had on his son. I wondered whether, if his father said "no," Martin would give in to him. Mary Powell had told me that she believed Rev. King, Sr., wanted his son to marry the girl in Atlanta, and she doubted if Martin would make the final

124. King, *My Life with Martin Luther King, Jr.*, 66, 77; and Baldwin, "The Dangerous Road before Martin Luther King, Jr.," 39.

125. King, *My Life with Martin Luther King, Jr.*, 68.

126. King, "An Address at the National Conference on Civil Rights," Nashville, Tenn., 1 ff.

127. King, *My Life with Martin Luther King, Jr.*, 68–69.

decision himself. As I fell more deeply in love with him, this worried me a great deal.[128]

When Martin Luther King, Sr., first met Coretta in November, 1952, he had serious doubts about her as a wife for his son. "She was planning a career on the concert stage," he later explained, "which I hardly thought was appropriate for a young woman seeing a young man from a strict Baptist upbringing and background. Perhaps, I suggested, she'd find much more in common with someone from her own field of interest, music."[129] This point did not slip by unnoticed, especially since Daddy King had promised to help take care of his son's wife while he was in school. However, Daddy King's doubts and objections were not strong enough to overshadow the love Martin, Jr., and Coretta developed for each other, and the couple was married on the lawn of Coretta's parents' home in Marion, Alabama, on June 18, 1953. The King family's support for the union was evident in that A. D. was Martin's best man, and Daddy King solemnized the couple's vows. Other members of the King family were also present, along with friends and members of Atlanta's Ebenezer Baptist Church.[130]

When Coretta married Martin, Jr., she looked ahead to what she thought would be the full but quiet life of a minister's wife. This was the case for the first year of their marriage. The couple spent the summer of 1953 with Martin, Sr., and Alberta King in Atlanta, an experience that afforded Coretta a deeper knowledge of the King family, the environment in which her husband had been raised, and the responsibilities involved in being a preacher's wife.[131] It could not have been a more exciting, soul-searching, and tension-free time for the couple.

128. *Ibid.*, 76.
129. King, *Daddy King*, 149.
130. *Ibid.*, 149–50; and King, *My Life with Martin Luther King, Jr.*, 73, 84–85.
131. "Martin Luther King, Jr.: A Personal Portrait," a videotaped interview; and King, *My Life with Martin Luther King, Jr.*, 87–88, 101.

On their return to Boston in September, 1953, Martin, Jr., and Coretta rented an apartment and struggled to complete their education. As had been the case before they married, their "social life in Boston was still mostly among other southern blacks who were studying at the various colleges and universities," and that association undoubtedly contributed to what became a lifelong interest in the fate of their people in the South. So much around them called to mind their southern past, with its vital resources of family, church, and friendship networks. It was in this context that Coretta became most familiar with the "southern ways" of her husband—his love for music, parties and dancing, sports, soul food, good conversation, and folk wit and laughter.[132]

Coretta's reflections on Martin Luther King, Jr., as a husband in the year prior to his emergence as a full-time pastor and civil rights leader are immensely important for sketching a complete portrait of the man. She remembered her husband as a kind, sensitive, and self-confident man who could be both playful and very serious. King often teased Coretta about her background on a farm in the rural South, and about their having spent their honeymoon at a funeral parlor because of restrictions that barred blacks from hotels in Alabama. The couple frequently went out to the beach and the amusement park in Boston, where Martin would roller-skate with his friends "until they were ready to drop, laughing and roughhousing and doing fancy turns and gyrations."[133] Most of King's time was spent studying and doing the housework. Because Coretta was so busy with her lessons at the New England Conservatory of Music, King spent one day a week doing the cooking, the dishes, the heavy cleaning, and the washing. Coretta recalled the many times she arrived home where her husband greeted her with a warm smile, a kiss, and the aroma of smothered cabbage, fried chicken, pork chops, pigs' feet, pigs' snout, pigs'

132. King, *My Life with Martin Luther King, Jr.*, 101, 105.
133. *Ibid.*, 40, 86, 101–9.

ears, ham hocks, cornbread, and other southern-style foods. "Though Martin helped so much in the house the first year we were married," she said, "all the domestic work did not make him self-conscious. He was too sure of his manhood."[134]

King's idea of the roles that husband and wife should play in a home was heavily influenced by the teachings and example of his parents. Having grown up in a family in which his father was the head of the household, he often told Coretta jokingly that "I want my wife to respect me as the head of the family. I *am* the head of the family." The couple would then laugh at the slightly pompous remark, and Martin would say: "Of course, I don't really mean that. I think marriage should be a shared relationship."[135] But the fact is that King, nurtured in a male-dominated culture, shared the common view that women should be homemakers, and he actually groomed Coretta for her role as the wife of a Baptist minister. Coretta's reflections on this matter are revealing enough to merit extensive quotation:

> Martin had, all through his life, an ambivalent attitude toward the role of women. On the one hand, he believed that women are just as intelligent and capable as men and that they should hold positions of authority and influence. But when it came to his own situation, he thought in terms of his wife being a homemaker and a mother for his children. He was very definite that he would expect whoever he married to be at home waiting for him. . . . At the same time, Martin, even in those days, would say, "I don't want a wife I can't communicate with." From the beginning, he would encourage me to be active outside of the home, and would be very pleased when I had ideas of my own or even when I could fill in for him. Yet—it was the female role he was most anxious for me to play. . . . There were also other considerations he had thought about. He would say, "I must have a wife who will be as dedicated as I am. I will

134. *Ibid.*, 102–3.
135. *Ibid.*, 103–4.

be the pastor of a large Negro church in the South. That's where I plan to live and work. I want the kind of wife who will fit into that kind of situation. . . ."[136]

Coretta essentially resigned herself to the role of the supportive wife, believing that "this is one of the most important roles that I can play."[137] "That was an adjustment I had to make," she continued, "and I believe I made it very well." Martin did not like the idea of Coretta working, insisting that "I'm supposed to earn enough money to take care of you and the family."[138] Though firm in his conviction that the major responsibilities in the home should fall on the shoulders of the husband, King had none of the psychological insecurities that beset so many black men in white America in his time—that neurotic stage that drove them to assert their authority in the home at all costs. "He always made me feel like a real woman because he was a real man in every respect," Coretta reported. Coretta found full satisfaction in seeing her husband as "a very strong man" who "wore the pants," and who was a source of strength for her and for others who met him. Coretta often said that "if I had not married a strong man, I would have 'worn the pants.'"[139]

Martin, Jr., and Coretta talked a lot about their future in the year before they moved to Montgomery, Alabama. One concern frequently discussed was their love for children and their desire to be good parents. King wanted to be the father of eight children, a desire Coretta did not readily accept. By the time they moved to Montgomery in September, 1954, to assume a full-time ministry at Dexter Avenue Baptist Church, the couple had compromised and decided on four children.[140] Although King wanted a boy for his first child, who would carry his name, he was quite pleased when Yolanda Denise,

136. *Ibid.*, 73–74.
137. *Ibid.*, 27, 83, 109, 179.
138. *Ibid.*, 103–4.
139. *Ibid.*
140. *Ibid.*, 117–18; King, "An Address at the National Conference on Civil Rights," Nashville, Tenn., 1 ff.

nicknamed Yoki, was born on November 17, 1955. Three other children followed. On October 23, 1957, Martin Luther King, III, called Marty, was born. Dexter Scott came along on January 30, 1961, and Bernice Albertine, referred to as Bunny, on March 28, 1963, after the family had moved from Montgomery to Atlanta.[141] In keeping with the family tradition and with traditions stemming back to slavery and even to Africa, Martin, Jr., and Coretta conferred the names of relatives and ancestors on their children. This was for them one means of furthering their children's personal and family identity.[142]

Yoki, Marty, Dexter, and Bunny were born during the period when their father was heavily involved in the struggle for equal rights and social justice. This posed serious problems, especially because King had looked forward to spending time with his family. The problems stemmed from King's roles as a husband and father, the leader of the civil rights movement, a preacher and pastor in his church, and a world religious figure, with equal commitments in all directions.[143] As he grew in popularity and fame, King saw how difficult it was to find a balance between the public realm of politics and social involvement and the private realm of family, intimate relationships, and the raising of children. He saw firsthand how families so often suffer in the public realm. He and Coretta were constantly in the public eye, and their children were frequently sought out and questioned by classmates, reporters, and other curious persons. In this situation, King lost so much time in which he would have found fulfillment as a father and husband. He was seldom at home when his children were raising questions and crying out for that love and security that only a father could provide.[144] He no longer had time to assist his

141. King, *My Life with Martin Luther King, Jr.*, 117–19; Octavia Vivian, *Coretta: The Story of Mrs. Martin Luther King, Jr.* (Philadelphia: Fortress Press, 1970), 60; and Reddick, *Crusader without Violence*, 6.

142. King, *My Life with Martin Luther King, Jr.*, 118.

143. "Martin Luther King, Jr.: A Personal Portrait," a videotaped interview.

144. King, "An Address at the National Conference on Civil Rights," Nashville, Tenn., 1 ff.

wife with household chores. King himself once spoke at great length about the difficulty of adjusting to the roles of husband and father in light of his other responsibilities as a national and international figure:

It is very difficult. This is one of the most frustrating aspects of my life—the great demands that come as a result of my involvement in the civil rights movement and in the whole struggle for justice and peace. I have to be away from home a great deal. I have to be out of town more than I'm in town, and this takes away from the family so much. It is just impossible to carry out the responsibilities of a father and a husband when you have these kinds of demands.[145]

Martin Luther King, Jr., always faced a choice between action in the public world and care for the concerns of the private. He also experienced an interesting daily battle in trying to run the parallel between sainthood and fatherhood. "Like all religious leaders and religious people," King said on one occasion, "I have the desire to reach the majestic heights of sainthood."[146] But marriage and the demands of his children sometimes made him appear less as a saint than a father. However, the responsibilities that came with marriage and fatherhood did not keep King from achieving the highest expression of creative self-sacrifice so often associated with sainthood. Although loyal to family, he ultimately gave his life for the improvement of the human condition. Even so, King was never able to resolve the public versus private dilemma and the fragile alliance between fatherhood and sainthood.[147]

Considering the nature and extent of his involvements, King always looked forward to occasions when the family could eat, talk, and sing together. "He wanted so badly to share with the children more," according to Coretta, "and he made sure that the time he spent with them was

145. *Ibid.*; and "Martin Luther King, Jr.: A Personal Portrait," a videotaped interview.
146. "Martin Luther King, Jr.: A Personal Portrait," a videotaped interview.
147. *Ibid;* and King, *My Life with Martin Luther King, Jr.,* 187.

*quality time."* "He wanted to be like his father," she continued, "always by his children's side." King often said
that whenever he had to say a word in a school play, to
participate in sports, or to sing in the choir—anything—
Mamma and Daddy King were sure to be in the audience
rooting for him. Daddy King always believed it was his
duty to be present whenever one of his children was doing
something special. If he could not go, Mamma King would
attend.[148] This image of Daddy King had an enormous impact on young Martin's relationship to his own children.
"There was a spiritual quality that one could feel and
sense in Martin's relationship with Yoki, Marty, and the
others," declared the Reverend Bernard Lee, who frequently dined with the family. "Spirituality was always
present, even when Martin disciplined his children.
Things were often said about him by others that would
normally break up a family unit, but that spirituality
would exude and just take over."[149] That spiritual relationship was most evident when King held his children in his
arms or took their hands as he moved among the people.

King found great pleasure in teasing and playing with
his children. He occasionally took them to playgrounds
and amusement parks, and enjoyed with them the swings,
the rides, the games, and other forms of entertainment.
King loved basketball, baseball, football, swimming, and
tennis, and he delighted in teaching his sons these sports,
sometimes to Coretta's displeasure. "Occasionally, on
rainy days, when Martin was in town and he happened
to be at home," she noted, "you could hear me saying over
and over, 'Martin please don't play ball in the house.'
The boys and he would look at me with pitiful expressions, and my husband, quite logically, would ask, 'Where
else is there for us to play?' I never did think of a satisfac-
tory answer for that question."[150] Some of King's most

148. King, "An Address at the National Conference on Civil Rights,"
Nashville, Tenn., 1 ff. and King, *My Life with Martin Luther King, Jr.*, 97.
149. A private interview with the Rev. Bernard S. Lee, 9 July 1986.
150. Reddick, *Crusader without Violence*, 3; and King, *My Life with
Martin Luther King, Jr.*, 93.

intimate moments with his children occurred on those rare occasions when he baby-sat with them in Coretta's absence:

> In spite of Martin's being away so much, he was wonderful with his children, and they adored him. When Daddy was home it was something special. Occasionally when I had to go to a church meeting, or do some shopping, Martin would baby-sit, and how they loved that! They had a wild time together. They often played on the bed. The children would roughhouse and jump on top of him. I might come into my bedroom and find all our family sitting on top of him. I must admit that I occasionally got cross about things being thrown helter-skelter in the room and the house almost dismantled, but Martin would appear surprised at my annoyance, which always completely disarmed me.[151]

Coretta remembered several games invented by her husband for the amusement of their children. One such game, called "the refrigerator game," was invented by King when his daughter Yoki was still very young. According to Coretta, he would put Yoki

> on top of the refrigerator and tell her to jump, and then he would catch her in his arms. She loved it! She would say, "let's go up," which meant being put on top of the refrigerator. It frightened me so because I thought someday he might miss his catch. But he never did—even as Marty, Dexter, and Bunny came along, they all had their turn at the game.[152]

Another game, which gave Coretta "the greatest pleasure to watch," was the "kissing game" between her husband and their youngest daughter Bunny:

> Whenever Martin came home, as soon as he entered the doorway Bunny would run and swing into his arms. He would stoop to lift her up and say, "Give me some good old sugar." With her arms around his neck,

---

151. King, *My Life with Martin Luther King, Jr.*, 221.
152. *Ibid.*

she would smack him on the mouth. He had previously taught her where the sugar spot was for each person in the family. He would then say, "I bet you don't know where Yoki's sugar is!" She would smack him on the right side of his mouth. "Where is Dexter's sugar?" There she kissed him on the right cheek. Next he would say, "I know you don't know where Marty's sugar is!" She would quickly kiss him on the forehead. "I just know you've forgotten where Mommy's sugar is!" She would kiss him in the center of his mouth. Finally, he would say, "And Bunny doesn't have any sugar." "Yes, I do!" And with a loud smack, she would kiss him on the right cheek. When she found all the designated sugar spots, which she always did quickly, the game ended.[153]

Yoki would later remember her father as one who "was as much a kid at heart as we were." "He'd get down on the floor and rock with us and roll around," she recalled, "much to the concern of my mother, who was always afraid we'd break something." Yoki also recounted how her father would "pick food from the serving bowl or platter and my mother would fuss at him about it all the time, but he did it anyway." Nothing thrilled King's children more than the jokes he shared with them, as Yoki would later observe:

> Daddy used to love to tell jokes—a whole lot of them. He could tell jokes with such a straight, poker face that it only added to the humor. One of his favorite stories was something he picked up from the late comedienne Moms Mabley. There was a guy walking up the street with a processed "do," you know, the 50s and 60s version of the curl look. Moms asks him, "Man, what is that you got on your head?" "Madame Walker," he says. Moms retorts, "You better tell Madame she better walk around them edges a little bit more." I don't think Daddy was fond of seeing men with a "do."[154]

153. *Ibid.*, 221–22.
154. "'I Remember Martin,'" *Ebony*, 39, no. 6 (April 1984), 38.

Knowing of their father's love for humor and practical jokes, Yoki and the other children sometimes made him the victim of pranks. One day they poured water in his ear as he slept, a mischievous trick that really angered King, causing him to spank Yoki and Marty. But all of this was done in the spirit of love, and it helped the children to grow and mature in a manner consistent with their father's wishes.[155]

Life in Atlanta and in the South generally in the 1950s and 1960s posed a special problem for Martin, Jr., and Coretta King as they struggled to provide for their children's health, comfort, and security. Despite all their efforts, they could not shield their children from the realities of racism and segregation. The children experienced the pain of being called "nigger" very early, and they discovered the feeling of being barred from schools, parks, and other facilities.[156] King often referred to the pain he felt when forced to explain to Yoki why Atlanta's Funtown was closed to her, an experience that marked the child's "first emotional realization and understanding of being black in a white world":

> The family often used to ride with me to the Atlanta airport, and on our way, we always passed Funtown, a sort of miniature Disneyland with mechanical rides and that sort of thing. Yolanda would inevitably say, "I want to go to Funtown," and I would always evade a direct reply. I really didn't know how to explain to her why she couldn't go. Then one day at home, she ran down stairs exclaiming that a TV commercial was urging people to come to Funtown. Then my wife and I had to sit down with her between us and try to explain it. I have won some applause as a speaker, but my tongue twisted and my speech stammered seeking to explain to my six-year-old daughter why the public invitation

155. A private interview with the Rev. Bernard S. Lee, 9 July 1986; and King, "An Address at the National Conference on Civil Rights," Nashville, Tenn., 1 ff.

156. King, *My Life with Martin Luther King, Jr.*, 217–20; and James M. Washington, ed., *A Testament of Hope: The Essential Writings of Martin Luther King, Jr.* (San Francisco: Harper & Row, 1986), 341–42.

on television didn't include her, and others like her.
One of the most painful experiences I have ever faced
was to see her tears when I told her that Funtown was
closed to colored children, for I realized that at that
moment the first dark cloud of inferiority had floated
into her little mental sky, that at that moment her personality had begun to warp with that first unconscious
bitterness toward white people. It was the first time
that prejudice based upon skin color had been explained to her. But it was of paramount importance to
me that she not grow up bitter. So I told her that although many white people were against her going to
Funtown, there were many others who did want colored children to go. It helped somewhat. Pleasantly,
word came to me later that Funtown had quietly desegregated, so I took Yolanda. A number of white persons
there asked, "Aren't you Dr. King, and isn't this your
daughter?" I said we were, and she heard them say how
glad they were to see us there.[157]

The safety and welfare of the children also accounted
for other policies adopted by King and his wife. They
agreed very early in the movement that it would not be
good for both of them to go to jail while the children were
so young, a policy that really hurt Coretta because of her
strong desire to make this sacrifice for the cause of civil
rights. For the protection of the children, the couple also
agreed never to travel by plane together, except in unusual circumstances. As threats against his life mounted,
King even opposed the idea of his wife working with him
in the more dangerous areas of the South. He felt that if
circumstances led to his assassination, Coretta should be
in a position to care for the children.[158]
Always concerned about the security of his children
from a spiritual, emotional, and economic standpoint,
King taught them values that he had learned as a child.
He instilled in them a sense of the moral order and
the religious idea, and kept before them the importance
of their own personhood as well as that of other human

beings. The Kings also taught their children the value of getting up early every morning, of studying and being on time for school, of doing their chores, and of saving and sharing with others. King even discussed sex with his daughter Yoki as a way of preparing her intellectually for the realities of womanhood. Yoki, Marty, Dexter, and Bunny learned some of these basic values through the medium of the jokes and tales their father shared with them, and also from the books from which he read to them on quiet evenings.[159] The essential message was always the same—the children "should strive for excellence in all their endeavors." "My husband often told the children that if a man had nothing that was worth dying for, then he was not fit to live," Coretta explained. "He said also that it's not how long you live, but how well you live. He knew that at any moment his physical life could be cut short, and we faced this possibility squarely and honestly."[160] King's life as an intellectual, preacher, and social activist was for his children the best and most compelling example of how life should be lived. The power of his example and teachings reflected itself in the fact that all of his children attended college and chose stimulating and challenging careers.

## THE FAMILY AS A SUPPORT MECHANISM FOR KING

Martin Luther King, Jr., could not have sustained himself in a protracted battle for freedom without a community that cared for him, embraced him, and accepted him in spite of his mistakes. Faced with many personal sufferings that involved arrests more than twenty times, physical attacks, and victimization through numerous threats against his life and family, King drew strength and courage not from the liberal theology he studied at Crozer Theological Seminary and Boston University, but from a social network built largely around his family.

159. *Ibid.*, 222; and King, "An Address at the National Conference on Civil Rights," Nashville, Tenn., 1 ff.
160. King, *My Life with Martin Luther King, Jr.*, 327.

Without the love, comfort, support, and encouragement
provided by his family, King could not have maintained
the physical strength, mental stability, and moral and
spiritual balance necessary to confront the enormous
challenges of social reality, external dangers, and
rapidly growing fame.[161]King's rise to the forefront of
the civil rights movement and the worldwide struggle
for justice and peace did not surprise or disturb his wife
Coretta, who always said that "my husband was committed to social justice and determined to be successful in
life when I met him."[162] Sharing her husband's passion
for equal rights and social justice, Coretta determined
very early that his burden was hers as well. "As Martin
was being made ready to be the leader and the symbol of
the Negro movement," she wrote, "so I was being prepared to be his wife and helpmate. It was in Montgomery that I became aware of the contribution I could
make in sustaining and helping my husband in what was
to come."[163]

For thirteen years prior to her husband's assassination,
Coretta King was a working mother and an active father
for their children. It was she who constantly explained to
the children why their father had to be away from home
so much. "I told them that daddy is doing God's work," she
explained. "He loves you all, but he also loves other people. I taught this to them in simple terms while they were
very young, and I enlarged on that definition as they got
older."[164] Coretta was the constant source of comfort and
strength for the children as they confronted the devastat-
ing consequences of racism in the South in their early
years. She also helped them see the relevance of what

161. Virtually nothing has been written about the family as a support
system for King during the civil rights era. The best and most extensive
treatments of this subject are King, *Daddy King*, chaps. 12–15; and King,
*My Life with Martin Luther King, Jr.*, 1–335.
162. King, "An Address at the National Conference on Civil Rights,"
Nashville, Tenn., 1 ff.
163. King, *My Life with Martin Luther King, Jr.*, 109.
164. *Ibid.*, 219, 249; and King, "An Address at the National Conference
on Civil Rights," Nashville, Tenn., 1 ff.

their father was doing for their own lives and futures, as well as for the destiny of black people and the nation as a whole.[165]

Coretta's support for Martin also found expression in other ways. Many nights when King arrived home after fulfilling a busy schedule, Coretta would meet him at the door with a hug and kiss. "We would often come in off the road at 10 o'clock at night," recounted King's assistant Bernard Lee, "and Coretta would be so glad to see us that she would get up and fix a major meal. Late at night we'd be sitting there eating greens and cornbread." Martin and Coretta would often tease one another and sing together on those occasions, and these times were immensely important in keeping them strong and dedicated to each other and to the cause.[166] When King met a storm of criticism from both blacks and whites because of his expressed opposition to the involvement of the United States in Vietnam, Coretta not only supported him but also made many speeches on Vietnam for him.[167] "I remember saying to him so many times, especially after he received the Nobel Peace Prize," Coretta reminisced, "'I think there is a role you must play in achieving world peace, and I will be so glad when the time comes when you can assume that role.'" It is difficult to measure the significance of this kind of support, especially when one considers that King's own father initially opposed his stance on Vietnam.[168]

Confronted daily with criticism and threats, it was never easy for Coretta to remain undaunted. At times, her concern for her husband's safety and well-being took priority over other considerations, and understandably

165. King, *My Life with Martin Luther King, Jr.*, 217–20, 248–249; and "Martin Luther King, Jr.: A Personal Portrait," a videotaped interview.

166. A private interview with the Rev. Bernard S. Lee, 9 July 1986; and King, *My Life with Martin Luther King, Jr.*, 23, 40, 86, 103, 105.

167. King, *My Life with Martin Luther King, Jr.*, 294–95; and Watley, *Roots of Resistance*, 102.

168. King, *My Life with Martin Luther King, Jr.*, 294–95; Daddy King did eventually see the wisdom of his son's position on Vietnam and supported it.

so. When officials sentenced King to six months' hard labor in Georgia's State Penitentiary at Reidsville in 1961 for allegedly violating his probation, Coretta burst into tears.[169] This was a very rare occurrence for the woman who had stood by her husband when their home was bombed in Montgomery, when he suffered a near-fatal stabbing in Harlem in 1958, and during the forty or so threatening phone calls he received each day. The pressures of family life, stemming primarily from King's frequent absences and the scarcity of financial resources, did cause tension and differences between the couple at times, but these difficulties were never permitted to fragment the family or to interfere with the movement. Coretta stood by her husband's side because she believed in the essential righteousness of his cause and personal sacrifices, and because she valued his contributions to the uplift of humanity. She was always amazed, and often disturbed, to discover that her husband cared more about his service to humanity than about money and other material values. King frequently said to her: "People who are doing something don't have time to be worried about all that," an observation to which Coretta seldom responded.[170]

King's own reflections on the supportive role of Coretta are profound and searching. He found great pleasure and consolation in knowing that his wife was aware of the whole struggle and of all his involvements in the struggle. Referring specifically to Coretta's knowledge of and participation in the struggle, King once noted that "I think at many points she educated me":

> When I met her she was very concerned about all the things that we're trying to do now. I never will forget that the first discussion we had when we met was the whole question of racial injustice, economic injustice, and peace. In her college days she had been actively engaged in movements dealing with these problems.

169. King, *My Life with Martin Luther King, Jr.*, 200–01.
170. Quoted in Baldwin, "The Dangerous Road before Martin Luther King, Jr.," 39.

> So I must admit—I wish I could say, to satisfy my mas-
> culine ego, that I led her down this path, but I must say
> that we went down together.[171]

From the time of the Montgomery Bus Boycott, King
knew that Coretta would be one of his greatest sources of
support and his most loving critic. The calmness Coretta
displayed when their home was bombed in Montgomery
in 1956 did much to reinforce this perception. After
the bombing, King said to his wife: "Well, Coretta, I don't
know what I would have done without you. You have been
a real soldier." "I realized then," Coretta recalled, "how
much it meant to him for me to continue to be strong and
to give him support, not only in terms of words, but in
terms of actually feeling this way and being this way."[172]
For King, Coretta was always "a most understanding
wife, who has given me consolation when I needed it
most." It is not an insignificant point that he dedicated his
first book, *Stride Toward Freedom: The Montgomery Story*
(1958), "To Coretta, my beloved wife and co-worker."[173]

The manner in which Coretta adjusted to the possibility of her husband's assassination was a source of inspiration and instruction for him. Death was frequently a topic
of conversation in the King home, and that helped to prepare Coretta emotionally, spiritually, and philosophically for what would be the inevitable. Shortly before he
was killed in Memphis, King alluded to his wife's amazing
adjustment to the fact that he was exposing himself to the
constant danger of assassination:

> The interesting thing is that she's adjusted to this,
> and she's adjusted by looking at it philosophically.
> She's realistic enough to know that emotions are
> high on this issue and that something can happen.
> There are many sick people in our society—people
> who are corroded with hatred, and they will
> use violence, and they will assassinate leaders of the

171. "Martin Luther King, Jr.: A Personal Portrait," a videotaped
interview.
172. *Ibid.;* and King, *My Life with Martin Luther King, Jr.,* 115, 143.
173. "Martin Luther King, Jr.: A Personal Portrait," a videotaped interview.

> movement. . . . My wife is very conscious of this, but
> it does not stop her in her commitment in going about
> her daily work. If one worried about these things all
> the time, one certainly couldn't function. So we must
> go on with the faith that the cause is right, and that if
> something happens in the process, it will serve that
> cause in a way that we may not be able to see at this
> time.[174]

Because of the understanding and support of Coretta
and other members of the King family, who believed
strongly in an afterlife, King did not have to face the
possibility of his own death alone. Others who were
very close to the King family, such as the black theologians Benjamin E. Mays and Howard Thurman, helped
King to accept the reality of death without crippling
fear through their counseling and teachings. Philip
Lenud claims that Thurman's brilliant and extensive reflections on transcendence were of great inspirational
value to King as he confronted the reality and the possible meaning of his own death.[175] The significance of
family and other black folk sources should be carefully
considered over against the common assumption that
Martin Heidegger and other existentialists were primarily responsible for King's ability to deal courageously,
creatively, and philosophically with the imminent possibility of his own death.[176]

The extent to which King received support and inspiration from his children also deserves special consideration. King frequently commented on how the birth of
Yoki, whom he called "the darling of my life," helped prepare him for the frustration, stress, and discouragement
he would experience during the Montgomery Bus Boycott, which was his first attempt at social change:

> Martin always said that Yoki came at a time in his life
> when he needed something to take his mind off the
> tremendous pressures that bore down upon him. When

174. *Ibid.;* and John J. Ansbro, *Martin Luther King, Jr.: The Making of a Mind* (Maryknoll, N.Y.: Orbis Books, 1982), 98.
175. A private interview with Dr. Philip Lenud, 7 April 1987.
176. Ansbro, *Martin Luther King, Jr.,* 96–98.

he came home from the stress and turmoil that he was suddenly plunged into, the baby was there cooing and cuddly and trustful and loving. There is something renewing about a small child—something he needed very much, because less than three weeks after Yoki was born, a seamstress named Rosa Parks refused to give up her seat on a Montgomery bus, and the Movement was born.[177]

Growing up in a family with a long and fertile tradition of social concern and involvement, it was very difficult for Yoki, Marty, Dexter, and Bunny, even as small children, to remain oblivious to their father's activities and contributions. "I think that in some ways they understand," King once said of his children, "even though it's pretty hard on them."[178] Coretta's frequent discussions with the children concerning racism and segregation, and about the need for their father to make personal sacrifices to effect change, were quite significant in heightening their consciousness. A number of interesting stories developed out of this whole effort. One day early in December, 1961, as Yoki wept out of fear that her father would not be released from an Albany, Georgia, jail in time for Christmas, Marty, only four years old then, sat on the side of the bed embracing and consoling his sister. "Don't cry Yoki," the child remarked. "Daddy will be back. He has to help the people. He has already helped some people, but he has to help some more and when he finishes, he'll be back, so don't cry, Yoki."[179] The experience was apparently enriching because a few days later, when Coretta explained to Yoki why Atlanta's Funtown was closed to black children, and how her father's jail-going would make life better, the child responded: "Well, that's fine Mommy. Tell him to stay in jail until I can go to Funtown."[180] On still another occasion as Coretta counseled the children on how to deal with being called

177. King, *My Life with Martin Luther King, Jr.*, 118–19.
178. "Martin Luther King, Jr.: A Personal Portrait," a videotaped interview.
179. King, *My Life with Martin Luther King, Jr.*, 199.
180. "Martin Luther King, Jr.: A Personal Portrait," a videotaped interview.

"nigger," Dexter, who was four at the time, gave perhaps the best answer. "Mommy, you know why some people say 'nigger'?," he asked. "Some people say 'nigger' because they don't know *how* to say 'Negro.'"[181] Responses of this nature led Martin and Coretta King to the realization that their children were being helped by their commitment to racial justice. They also convinced the couple that their children had learned to hold their heads high and believe in their father, even when he was being denounced as a liar, a Communist, and an Uncle Tom.[182]

Coretta occasionally allowed the children to accompany their father on some of his trips, sensing that such exposure would further enlighten them concerning the movement and how it related to them and to black people as a whole. Marty and Dexter accompanied King on a people-to-people tour through rural Georgia in March, 1968, an experience that left an indelible mark on the boys' memories. Following the trip, Dexter, visibly tired and in need of sleep, told his mother that "I don't see how my daddy can do so much and talk to so many people and not even get tired at all." This comment genuinely pleased Coretta, who felt that being with their father on some of these trips would also help the boys to accept his absences and to share in his commitment.[183]

The vital supportive roles assumed by King's wife and children provide solid evidence against the claim that "a man who dedicates himself to a cause doesn't need a family." "I knew that, being the kind of man he was," Coretta observed, "Martin needed us. He functioned better with a wife and children because he needed the warmth we gave him, and from the standpoint of the cause, having us gave him a kind of humanness which brought him closer to the mass of the people."[184] In appreciation for their love and support, King dedicated his book, *Why We Can't Wait* (1964), "To my children—Yolanda, Martin III,

181. *Ibid.;* and King, *My Life with Martin Luther King, Jr.,* 218.
182. King, *My Life with Martin Luther King, Jr.,* 19.
183. *Ibid.,* 307–8.
184. *Ibid.,* 187.

Dexter, and Bernice—for whom I dream that one day soon they will no longer be judged by the color of their skin, but by the content of their character."[185]

King's family support network extended beyond his wife and children to include his parents, in-laws, aunts, uncles, cousins, and members of the church family. The love and support of this extended family system helped King deal with the constant threats against his life and with the painful rejection he experienced from the federal government and from various sectors of the society. Of particular significance were the concern and the moral and spiritual support of Martin Luther, Sr., and Alberta King. Although their concern for their son's welfare sometimes took precedence over considerations regarding the movement, Daddy King and Alberta always allowed him to make his own decisions about the nature and extent of his involvement. Their desire was to remain quietly in the background while, at the same time, assisting young Martin and his wife with their children and other responsibilities that were essential to their well-being and progress.[186]

The relationship between King and his father during the movement was rooted in a mutual love and understanding that almost defies definition. In the early stages of the Montgomery struggle, when the forces of racism moved against his son with power that seemed almost invincible, Daddy King wept and advised young Martin to turn the reins of leadership over to someone else. This experience helped Daddy King discipline himself, and he never displayed such emotions in his son's presence again. From that point, he assured Martin, Jr.: "Well, son, you know that whatever you decide to do, you can count on Daddy."[187] Daddy King was very proud of his son and of the spiritual and moral power he

185. "Martin Luther King, Jr.: A Personal Portrait," a videotaped interview.

186. King, *Daddy King*, chaps. 12–14; and A Private Interview with the Rev. Bernard S. Lee, 9 July 1986.

187. King, *My Life with Martin Luther King, Jr.*, 144–145.

imparted to the family and to the entire nation. Martin, Jr., continued to view Daddy King as a profile in courage, and he once spoke of his father's role and his own role "as historical phases of the same process":

> I think my father and I have worked together a great deal in the last few years, trying to grapple with the same problem. . . . He was working in the area of civil rights before I was born and when I was just a kid, and I grew up in the kind of atmosphere that had a real civil rights concern. I do think its the same problem that we are grappling with—its the same historical process. . . .[188]

On another occasion King evoked the name of the great Protestant Reformer Martin Luther, noting that "Both father and I have fought all our lives for reform, and perhaps we've earned our right to the name."[189] Much of the power of the relationship between young Martin and Daddy King stemmed not only from the tradition of social action that bound them together but also from what they learned and experienced from each other. Martin, Jr., frequently alluded to the impelling spiritual and moral power he received from his father, a power that helped him grow in wisdom and fortitude. In a similar vein, Daddy King credited his son with introducing him to the most powerful method available to humans in their quest for social justice. "I never thought I would be nonviolent," Daddy King commented on one occasion, "but M. L. has convinced me that nonviolence is the way to deal with these white folks." On another occasion he declared that "I love what my son taught me and thousands of other people in this country about the enormous personal power of nonviolence."[190]

188. Warren, *Who Speaks for the Negro?*, 1 ff.
189. Zelia S. Evans and J. T. Alexander, eds., *Dexter Avenue Baptist Church, 1877–1977* (Montgomery, Ala.: Dexter Avenue Baptist Church, 1978), 69.
190. A private interview with the Rev. Bernard S. Lee, 9 July 1986; and "Daddy King: 'There's No Hate in My Heart,'" 1, 4.

The spiritual and moral power that drew Martin, Jr., and Alberta King together in a chain of mutual love and support took on a somewhat unique character. Alberta, with her rich and warm displays of motherly love, afforded her son an example of human energy and resourcefulness that no one else in the King family could have provided in a time of conflict and crisis. Aside from becoming one with young Martin in suffering, in struggle, and in the celebration of the liberation of humanity, Alberta shared with him nourishing food, confidential advice, and vital portions of the accumulated lore of the folk. The tie of affection that marked this mother-son relationship was revealed most profoundly during those times when King chatted with his mother by telephone. There were times when he and his brother A. D. "would both be on the phone with their mother, laughing and riding each other about their huge appetites and what they were doing to their respective waistlines." At other times they would tease and fool their mother for a while, "disguising their voices, each pretending to be the other."[191] The power that this kind of affection generated helped ease the heavy burdens King was forced to bear daily as a result of his involvement in the movement. To be sure, much of the faith and optimism with which he faced life grew out of those moments of conversation and sharing with his mother and others in the family.

The love and support King received from his family during the thirteen years of his active leadership in the civil rights movement was characteristic of the role that the black family has played since slavery. In the midst of the crises, conflict, and change that marked the 1950s and 1960s, the King family emerged as a supreme example of how the black family has functioned as a flexible and adaptable instrument of black survival.

191. A private interview with the Rev. Bernard S. Lee, 9 July 1986; A private interview with Dr. Philip Lenud, 7 April 1987; King, *My Life with Martin Luther King, Jr.*, 92, 317; and King, *Daddy King*, 188.

## KING'S REFLECTIONS ON
## FAMILY AND FAMILY VALUES

King's relationship to and experiences with his family were paramount in the shaping of his overall perspective on the family and family values. Aside from the scattered references in his books and essays, King delivered several speeches and sermons on the family, and also drafted a statement calling for voluntary family planning that was included in the United States *Congressional Record* on May 10, 1966.[192] In these sources, a particular theoretical orientation is suggested as a framework for viewing family life, and particularly black family life—an orientation that posits a direct correlation between the malfunctioning of America's social, political, and economic systems and family instability.

Convinced that human welfare and survival were intimately tied to the vitality of family life and values, King found it disturbing that so many social scientists in his day "have tended to denigrate the role of the family" by questioning its relevance and predicting its demise. He credited the Polish-English anthropologist Bronislaw Malinowski and the popular pediatrician and anti-war activist Benjamin Spock with refuting such "pessimistic and negative appraisals" with their brilliant statements on the family as "the main educational agency of mankind."[193] King strongly endorsed and built on these statements, insisting that "Family life not only educates in general but its quality ultimately determines the individual's capacity to love." He further noted that "the institution of the family is decisive in determining not only if a person has the capacity to love another individual, but in the larger social sense, whether he is capable of loving his fellow men collectively," a perspective that

192. "Martin Luther King Supports Voluntary Family Planning Legislation," *Congressional Record-Senate*, Washington, D. C. (May 10, 1966); 10161.

193. King, "The Dignity of Family Life," 1–2; and Martin Luther King, Jr., "The Negro Family: An Address at the University of Chicago," Chicago, Illinois (The King Center Archives, 27 January 1966), 1–2.

was undoubtedly enriched by King's own experiences with family.[194]

King devoted considerable attention in his speeches and writings to how black family life had been ignored and distorted in American scholarship. He complained that "the Negro family as an institution has been obscured and its special problems little comprehended," mainly because of the absence of a rigorous social science methodology that sufficiently considered the disadvantage black Americans suffered because of northern ghettos and southern segregated communities.[195] King attached great value to certain aspects of a study by Daniel Patrick Moynihan, which concluded, on the basis of charts, diagrams, and theoretical conceptualizations, that black families in the urban ghettos were crumbling and disintegrating, and which suggested that progress in social justice and tranquillity could be delayed for generations because of this alarming trend. King held that the disproportionately high rates of divorce, illegitimacy, and single-parent families among his people were not attributable to "innate weaknesses," but to the tragic legacy of slavery and segregation. Thus, he concluded that overcoming racism and the debased status of black Americans would necessarily involve all Americans, and particularly social scientists, in learning "something about the special origins of the Negro family."[196]

King displayed keen insight into the history of the black family as an institution since slavery. "The Negro family for three hundred years has been on the tracks of the racing locomotive of American history, and was dragged along mangled and crippled," he declared. He asserted that American slavery was unique in its

194. King, "The Dignity of Family Life," 2; and King, "The Negro Family," 3.
195. King, "The Dignity of Family Life," 2; and King, "The Negro Family," 4.
196. King, "The Dignity of Family Life," 2–3; and King, "The Negro Family," 5–8.

conscious dehumanization of blacks and its fragmentation of black family life. For King, the manner in which
blacks were captured in Africa and forced to endure the
horror of the Middle Passage, the selective process on
slave markets, and the sheer physical, spiritual, and psychological torture that accompanied the "breaking in"
process, explained what E. Franklin Frazier called "the
disorganization of Negro family life." The problem of
disorganization was further exacerbated, King thought,
by the slavemaster's disregard for slave marriages, by
slave breeding, and by the sexual abuse of black women
by masters and overseers. "The liberation from slavery
should have initiated a birth of stable family life" during
Reconstruction, King wrote, but "government policy
was so conflicted and disinterested that a new inferno
engulfed the Negro and his family. Thrown off the plan-
tations penniless, homeless, still largely in the territory
of their enemies and in the grip of fear, bewilderment
and aimlessness, hundreds of thousands became wan-
derers," thus giving rise to slum conditions. Although
laced with truth, King's perspective on black family
history was based too much on the myths and stereotypes projected in the writings of Moynihan, Frazier,
and others—myths and stereotypes that suggest that the
black family is "matriarchal," "unstable," and "patho-
logical."[197] Had King had the chance to read later studies by scholars such as Robert B. Hill, Herbert G.
Gutman, and Wallace C. Smith—studies that emphasize
the strengths of black families and black family values
despite oppression—his reflections on the history of the
black family as an institution may have been more profound and searching.[198]

197. King, "The Dignity of Family Life," 4–6; Frazier, *The Negro Family in the United States,* 3–49; and Daniel P. Moynihan, *The Negro Family:
The Call for National Action* (Washington, D.C.: U. S. Department of
Labor, 1967), 1 ff. Frazier's and Moynihan's studies apparently figured
prominently in the shaping of King's perspective on the black family. See
King, "The Dignity of Family Life," 1–11; and King, "The Negro Family,"
1–28.
198. See Hill, *The Strengths of Black Families,* 5–56; Herbert G. Gutman, *The Black Family in Slavery and Freedom, 1750–1925* (New York:

Much of the strength of King's perspective was evident in his assessment of what constituted ideal family life. "From both a personal and a theoretical standpoint," according to Lawrence D. Reddick, "he believes in the monogamous family. Two persons absolutely devoted to each other, he maintains, bring out the best in marriage by attaining a high standard of mutual understanding and self-fulfillment."[199] As Reddick observes, King rejected claims that the monogamous structure was the source of deeply rooted family problems: "What is wrong with the American family, he insists, is not monogamy. Much of the blame for unhappy and broken homes he places on the strains that arise out of our struggle for material possessions and prestige."[200] Given King's firm belief in the monogamous family, critical questions must be raised concerning the mounting charge that he was guilty of numerous extramarital affairs.[201] King's sexual transgressions were few and far between, and they were more indicative of the pressures on him than of his family situation. At home only about ten percent of the time, and confronted daily by women who made advances toward him, it was only natural for a passionate man like King to occasionally succumb to temptation. Although unacceptable by Judeo-Christian moral standards, King's affairs with women showed that he was *human*. Those affairs did not overshadow his deep love for his family, and nor did they undermine his view of what constituted the ideal family. King's family values remained in place even as he struggled to become the ideal husband, father, and leader.

Although it is clear that King regarded the nuclear family structure as an ideal family model, there is no

Pantheon Books, 1976), 3–460; and Wallace C. Smith, *The Church in the Life of the Black Family* (Valley Forge, Pa.: Judson Press, 1985), 21–101.

199. Reddick, *Crusader without Violence*, 5.

200. *Ibid.*

201. See David J. Garrow, *Bearing the Cross: Martin Luther King, Jr. and the Southern Christian Leadership Conference* (New York: William Morrow, 1986), especially 373–376; and Ralph D. Abernathy, *And the Walls Came Tumbling Down: An Autobiography* (New York: Harper & Brothers, 1989), 412–93.

evidence that he considered it more healthy than the
extended family model. It is better to say that he recognized vital qualities in both, a view informed by the fact
that he was a product of a confluence of both. But what
mattered most to King was not so much the family
model or structure but, rather, the extent to which a
family experience contributed to warm, loving, and secure relationships.[202]

In King's view, the survival, health, and vitality of
the family structure in America depended on some important factors. First, he advocated voluntary family planning as a way of undercutting the problems of unwanted
children and overpopulation. King insisted that problems
related to unwanted children and spontaneous population growth constituted an urgent threat to life on this
planet, and this explains why he supported the practice of
birth control based on responsible parenthood and the
economic conditions of society. "Family planning, to relate population to world resources," King argued, "is possible, practical, and necessary." He categorically rejected
the argument that those who advocated voluntary family
planning were somehow seeking to limit the proportion
of people of color in America and in the world generally.[203] Although he may have been somewhat naive at this
point, King's position was not surprising, especially since
voluntary family planning was such a crucial part of his
own family history.

Second, King advocated strong and responsible parenthood as a means of molding and training children. He
placed special emphasis on the model of the creatively
active wife and mother—an emphasis that bordered at
times on romanticism. He believed that biologically and
aesthetically, "women are more suitable than men for
keeping house" and attending children, an attitude that
had existed for generations among the men of the King

202. King, "An Autobiography of Religious Development," 1–15; King,
"The Dignity of Family Life," 1–11; and King, "The Negro Family," 1–28.
203. Smith, *The Ethics of Martin Luther King, Jr.*, 94–98; and "Martin
Luther King Supports Voluntary Family Planning," 10161.

family.[204] This is not to say that King down-played the importance of the father in the molding and nurturing of children. To the contrary, he believed that the contributions of both the mother and the father were essential to the cultivation of those higher qualities of the artistic, moral, and spiritual in children.[205]

The influence of King's own family model in his analysis of parent-children role relationships is unmistakable. He regarded strong and responsible parenthood as the key to the strict but well-organized upbringing of children. He felt that "children should be raised moderately, neither overly inhibited nor allowed to run wild." Major family problems were inevitable, he maintained, when children are allowed free expression without discipline and a sense of responsibility. Although King believed that corporeal punishment should be used to discipline children, he advocated its use only as a last resort. Children, in his view, should always respond to parents with respect, obedience, and, when possible, a recognition of family responsibility.[206]

In "What a Mother Should Tell Her Child" and "Training Your Child in Love," sermons delivered in 1963 and 1966 respectively, King spoke at length concerning motherhood in particular and parenthood in general. His primary emphasis was on motherhood as an honorable and desirable state, and as one means by which "certain eternal and abiding principles of the universe" are instilled in children.[207] One of the most important responsibilities of a mother, he insisted, is to teach her children respect for the dignity and worth of human personality. For King, this involved not only instructing children on the importance of "a positive and healthy

204. Reddick, *Crusader without Violence*, 5; and King, *My Life with Martin Luther King, Jr.*, 73, 75, 103–104.
205. Reddick, *Crusader without Violence*, 5–8; and Smith, *The Ethics of Martin Luther King, Jr.*, 94–98.
206. Reddick, *Crusader without Violence*, 5; and Smith, *The Ethics of Martin Luther King, Jr.*, 94–98.
207. Martin Luther King, Jr., "What a Mother Should Tell Her Child," a sermon delivered at Ebenezer Baptist Church, Atlanta, Ga., 12 May 1963, The King Center Archives, p. 4.

self-love" but also on the significance of loving other
selves. Children must be made to "understand that in
God's economy, the no $D$ is as significant as the Ph.D.,"
King declared, "and a person who has no house is as
significant as the person who's been to Morehouse." He
believed that such an attitude, established at an early
age, would help the child avoid the kind of negative self-
concept that leads to an unhealthy attitude toward all
people.[208]

In King's opinion, the mother's responsibility also en-
tailed instilling in the child a desire to achieve excellence in his or her field of endeavor, social awareness
and a sense of social responsibility, an intense God-
consciousness, and a world perspective that upholds the
interrelated structure of reality. "Without these principles being instilled in the minds and in the hearts of
young people today," King suggested, "we are all
doomed for destruction." The Christian home was for
him an ideal setting for the cultivation of such principles and values.[209]

Because of his roots in southern black culture, King
was able to avoid a strictly rationalistic and individualis-
tic image of the family. In other words, he refused to see
the family as merely an expanded description of the individual. Family for him was essentially communal in
nature—an institution in which persons are linked not
only by blood but by a shared history, shared pain, and a
shared hope for liberation. King viewed the family as one
of the two primary institutions that held the key to the
liberation and survival of black people. The other primary institution in this equation was the church.

208. *Ibid.*, 8; and Martin Luther King, Jr., "Training Your Child in
Love," a sermon delivered at Ebenezer Baptist Church, Atlanta, Ga. The
King Center Archives, (8 May 1966), 1–11.

209. King, "What a Mother Should Tell Her Child," 1–14; and King,
"Training Your Child in Love," 1–11. For very interesting instructions on
how children can be taught higher human values, see also a letter from
Martin Luther King, Jr. to the Student Body of Jesse Crowell School,
Albion, Mich., 1 December 1960, The King Papers, Boston University; and
a statement dictated by Martin Luther King, Jr. to Mr. L. F. Palmer, Jr.,
Chicago, Ill. (23 February 1961), The King Papers, Boston University.

# HOW I GOT OVER
## ROOTS IN THE BLACK CHURCH

# 3

> The Negro church touches almost every ramification of the life of the Negro.
>
> Carter G. Woodson, 1939[1]

> The church has always been a second home for me. As far back as I can remember I was in church every Sunday.
>
> Martin Luther King, Jr., 1950[2]

> How I got over,
> How I got over,
> My soul looks back and wonders,
> How I got over.
>
> Black Gospel Song[3]

The influence of the black church on Martin Luther King, Jr.'s, personal and intellectual formation was as

1. Carter G. Woodson, "The Negro Church, An All-Comprehending Institution," *The Negro History Bulletin*, 3, no. 1 (October 1939): 7.
2. Martin Luther King, Jr., "An Autobiography of Religious Development" (Unpublished document, The King Papers, Mugar Memorial Library, Boston University, Boston, Mass., n.d., circa 1950), 8.
3. Tony Heilbut, *The Gospel Sound: Good News and Bad Times* (New York: Doubleday Anchor Books, 1975), 65 ff.; and Martin Luther King, Jr., "Ingratitude," a sermon delivered at the Ebenezer Baptist Church, Atlanta, Ga. (The Archives of the Martin Luther King, Jr., Center for Nonviolent Social Change, Inc., Atlanta, Georgia, 18 June 1967), 8.

significant as that of his family. He became conscious very early of the vital link between family and church in his Atlanta environment—a consciousness that was heightened as the values and traditions of one reinforced those of the other in his life. King's early exposure to the richness of black culture in his family and church laid the foundation for his understanding of, and sense of solidarity with, black people in the deep South and in the nation as a whole.[4] Indeed, the coming together of these two institutions in his consciousness contributed substantially to his sense of identity, of place, and of obligation toward his people.

King's lifelong connection with the black church is the focus of this chapter. Special attention is devoted to the southern black church as a context for the development of his faith, thought, vision, and method to achieve equal rights and social justice. The discussion proceeds as follows: (1) King's background in the black church; (2) rediscovering the black church in the South; (3) King's relationship to the National Baptist Convention, U.S.A.; (4) and King's thoughts concerning the future of the black church.

## BACKGROUND IN THE BLACK CHURCH

An obvious link between Martin Luther King, Jr., and the black church tradition can be located in his ancestry. The family into which he was born had deep roots in southern black Baptist Protestantism, reaching as far back as his maternal great-grandfather, the Reverend Williams. King's maternal grandfather, Alfred D. Williams, was one of the most active and popular black Baptist preachers in the South in the early part of this century, serving as

4. King, "An Autobiography of Religious Development," 1–15; and Martin Luther King, Jr., "The Early Days," excerpts of a sermon delivered at the Mt. Pisgah Missionary Baptist Church, Chicago, Ill., (The King Center Archives, 27 August 1967), 9–12.

president of the Atlanta Baptist Ministers' Union, as moderator of the Atlanta Baptist Association, and as Treasurer, Home Mission Board Secretary, Foreign Mission Board Representative, and an Executive Board member of the National Baptist Convention, U.S.A., the largest black church organization in the world.[5] King's father, Martin Luther King, Sr., served on the Executive Board, the Board of Directors, and the Foreign Mission Board of that same organization. King's grandmothers and mother worked with female agencies in local, state, and national Baptist associations and were noted for their piety and great zeal for Christian endeavors.[6] With this heritage, it is easy to understand King's claim that "Religion has just been something that I grew up in."[7] He drank from the wellsprings of that curious mixture of African and European spirituality concocted in the southern black Baptist Church, and that institution became an important part of his religious self-understanding.[8]

The image of the Ebenezer Baptist Church in Atlanta, Georgia was particularly significant in King's developing identity and faith. This congregation had started back in 1886 with blacks who had lived close to slavery, and King's maternal grandfather had served as its second pastor. King joined that congregation at age five under the pastoral supervision of his father, and remained in that connection until his death. He once described the

---

5. Esther M. Smith, *A History of Ebenezer Baptist Church, Atlanta, Georgia* (Atlanta: The Ebenezer Baptist Church, 1956), 3; and Taylor Branch, *Parting the Waters: America in the King Years, 1954–63* (New York: Simon & Schuster, 1988), 30–40. Lerone Bennett, Jr., portrays A. D. Williams as "a keen-witted pioneer who was unusually successful in accumulating worldly goods and diffusing the spiritual insights of the Negro religious tradition." See Lerone Bennett, Jr., *What Manner of Man: A Memorial Biography of Martin Luther King, Jr.* (New York: Pocket Books, 1968), 7.

6. Smith, *A History of Ebenezer Baptist Church*, 3; and Lewis V. Baldwin, "Understanding Martin Luther King, Jr. Within the Context of Southern Black Religious History," *Journal of Religious Studies*, 13, no. 2 (Fall 1987): 8.

7. King, "An Autobiography of Religious Development," 8.

8. Martin Luther King, Jr., "The Un-Christian Christian," *Ebony*, 20, no. 10 (August 1965): 77.

situation that led him to join Ebenezer Church at such a young age:

> I well remember how this event occurred. Our church was in the midst of the spring revival, and a guest evangelist had come down from Virginia. On Sunday morning the guest evangelist came into our Sunday School to talk to us about salvation, and after a short talk on this point he extended an invitation to any of us who wanted to join the church. My sister was the first one to join the church that morning, and after seeing her join I decided that I would not let her get ahead of me, so I was the next. I had never given this matter a thought, and even at the time of my baptism I was unaware of what was taking place. From this it seems quite clear that I joined the church not out of any dynamic conviction, but out of a childhood desire to keep up with my sister.[9]

The "crisis" conversion, a process deeply rooted in the black Christian tradition, was apparently not a part of King's childhood religious experience. "Conversion for me was never an abrupt something," he once explained in an autobiographical sketch written while he was in the seminary. "I have never experienced the so-called 'crisis moment.' Conversion for me has been the gradual intaking of the noble ideals set forth in my family and my environment, and I must admit that this intaking has been largely unconscious."[10] Years later he would make a similar point, noting that "I had grown up in the church and the church meant something very real to me, but it was a kind of inherited religion and I had never felt

---

9. King, "An Autobiography of Religious Development," 7–8; and "An Historical Overview," *Program Booklet of the Centennial Celebration, 1886–1986* (Atlanta: The Ebenezer Baptist Church, 1986), 1. Frederick L. Downing has produced the first serious and comprehensive account of the maturation of King's faith, with some attention to the influence of his family and church. But Downing's discussion is heavily marred by his strong effort to make King's development of faith conform to the theories of Erik H. Erikson and James W. Fowler. See Frederick L. Downing, *To See the Promised Land: The Faith Pilgrimage of Martin Luther King, Jr.* (Macon, Ga.: Mercer University Press, 1986), 3–120.

10. *Ibid.*

an experience with God in the way that you must have it if you're going to walk the lonely path of this life."[11] These reflections further reveal how family and church became essentially *one* in King's early faith pilgrimage. The church for him was an extension of his family life and traditions. It was also an essential part of King's early experiences with the larger black community of Atlanta, a community largely held together by the church, black colleges, and other institutions. "I can well remember that all of my childhood playmates were regular Sunday School goers; not that I chose them on this basis," he reported, "but because it was very difficult to find playmates in my community who did not attend Sunday School."[12]

King's early involvement in the church extended beyond his sunday school experiences. He learned to recite passages from the Bible before he was five, an ability that was not uncommon among the children of black preachers in the South at that time. His exposure to the music of the black church was such that, at four years of age, he could sing well enough to appear before congregations and church conventions. King's parents took him to a Baptist convention about that time, and the boy sang, "with rollicking gospel beat," "I Want to Be More Like Jesus," accompanied by his mother Alberta at the piano.[13] King's early fascination with gospel music, the spirituals, and the great hymns of the church was nurtured in a black church community in which sacred music and sound musical education were a part of daily life. In the 1930s and 1940s, the Big Bethel African Methodist Episcopal Church (A.M.E.), located

11. King, "The Early Days," 9.
12. King, "An Autobiography of Religious Development," 5; and Coretta Scott King, *My Life with Martin Luther King, Jr.* (New York: Avon Books, 1969), 78.
13. Lenwood G. Davis, *I Have a Dream: The Life and Times of Martin Luther King, Jr.* (Westport, Conn.: Negro Universities Press, 1969), 13; King, *My Life with Martin Luther King, Jr.*, 93; and Martin Luther King, Sr., written with Clayton Riley, *Daddy King: An Autobiography* (New York: William Morrow, 1980), 127. Daddy King recalled that his son "loved the church, in a way I could recall in myself."

in close proximity to the Ebenezer Baptist Church and the King home, became widely known for black sacred music, and especially for *Heaven Bound*, written and performed by the members of that congregation. "Utilizing many of the old spirituals in the form of the miracle play," this piece attracted large crowds in many performances, some of which were undoubtedly attended by the Kings. Kemper Harreld, the Director of Music at Morehouse College in the early 1940s, did notable work with orchestras and glee clubs in various black churches and schools, thus adding to the richness of black Atlanta's musical tradition.[14]

It was in this context that Martin, Sr., and Alberta King provided their children with extensive music lessons, a process initially resisted by young Martin and his brother A. D., who associated such lessons with "sissy stuff." On one occasion the boys attacked the family piano with a hammer, and on another they loosened the piano's legs, causing them to collapse when their music instructor sat on it, pranks for which they were promptly whipped.[15] But these pranks resulted from an aversion for male piano players and not from any dislike for the intrinsic value of music. King's involvements with church music continued through his high school and college years and became a vital part of his experiences as a pastor and civil rights activist.[16]

King once pointed to two incidents that happened in late childhood and early adolescence that had a profound effect on his religious development. One occurred at age six, when he lost his white playmate due to racism. As his parents explained to him the reasons

14. *Atlanta: A City of the Modern South*, compiled by workers of The Writer's Program of The Works Projects Administration in the State of Georgia (New York: Smith and Durrell, Publishers, 1942), 132–33; and Christine King Farris, "The Young Martin: From Childhood through College," *Ebony*, 41, no. 3 (January 1986), 56.

15. Farris, "The Young Martin," 56.

16. James M. Washington, ed., *A Testament of Hope: The Essential Writings of Martin Luther King, Jr.* (San Francisco: Harper & Row, 1986), 348; and Martin Luther King, Jr., *Why We Can't Wait* (New York: The New American Library, 1964), 61.

for such an unfortunate occurrence and of the need for him to love white people in spite of it, King was confronted forthrightly with the radical challenge of the ethic of Christian love for the very first time, a challenge with which he was ill prepared to deal at such a young age. Although King developed an intense bitterness toward white people, that feeling, as stated previously, was tempered somewhat by his parents' teachings concerning the essence and vital necessity of Christian love—teachings that were reinforced by his sunday school experiences at Ebenezer, which "helped me to build the capacity for getting along with people."[17]

The second incident that contributed to King's religious maturation was the death of Jennie C. Parks Williams, his maternal grandmother. "It was after this incident for the first time that I talked at any length on the doctrine of immortality," King declared. "My parents attempted to explain it to me, and I was assured that somehow my grandmother still lived."[18] The explanation he heard from his parents concerning immortality was markedly African—the view that death is the high point of life because the spirit lives. King's sense of his grandmother's continued existence after death, and hence his special place as her favorite grandchild, helped sustain the boy in the midst of that painful loss. Although he later challenged and rejected certain elements of black folk religion, King remained "a strong believer in personal immortality."[19]

17. King, "An Autobiography of Religious Development," 8–9, 11–13.
18. *Ibid.*, 10–11.
19. *Ibid.*, 11. In African traditions, the extended family includes the dead as well as the living. Some relationship between West African traditions and Afro-American customs during and after slavery is suggested in this notion of surviving spirits that maintain an interest and a role in the affairs of the living. King and his parents clearly reflected these traditions in their views on immortality. For some discussion of the link between African and Afro-American traditions on this subject, see Lewis V. Baldwin, "'A Home in Dat Rock': Afro-American Folk Sources and Slave Visions of Heaven and Hell," *The Journal of Religious Thought*, 41, no. 1 (Spring–Summer 1984), 39, 46–50; and Sterling Stuckey, *Slave Culture: Nationalist Theory and the Foundations of Black America* (New York: Oxford University Press, 1987), 3–97.

While still in his early teens, King experienced some skepticism regarding "the fundamentalist line" introduced to him at Ebenezer church by "unlettered" sunday school teachers, who "had never heard of Biblical Criticism":

> I guess I accepted Biblical studies uncritically until I was about twelve years old. But this uncritical attitude could not last long, for it was contrary to the very nature of my being. I had always been the questioning and precocious type. At the age of 13 I shocked my Sunday School class by denying the bodily resurrection of Jesus. From the age of thirteen on doubts began to spring forth unrelentingly. At the age of fifteen I entered college and more and more I could see a gap between what I had learned in Sunday School and what I was learning in college. The conflict continued until I studied a course in Bible in which I came to see that behind the legends and myths of the Book were many profound truths which one could not escape.[20]

At Morehouse College, King was exposed to Benjamin E. Mays, George D. Kelsey, Samuel Williams, and others who represented a more enlightened perspective and tradition in the southern black church. "It was at this period that the shackles of fundamentalism were removed from my body," King wrote. "This is why, when I came to Crozer, I could accept the liberal interpretation with relative ease."[21] Although he accepted much of the liberal theological tradition to which he was exposed at Crozer Theological Seminary and later at Boston University, the impact of family and church on his thought remained profound. As a Crozer student he observed:

> At present I still feel the affects of the noble moral and ethical ideals that I grew up under. They have been real and precious to me, and even in moments of theological doubt I could never turn away from them. Even though I have never had an abrupt conversion experience, religion has been real to me and closely

20. King, "An Autobiography of Religious Development," 9–10.
21. *Ibid.,* 13.

knitted to life. In fact, the two cannot be separated;
religion for me is life.[22]

During his studies at Crozer Theological Seminary and
Boston University, King affiliated with black churches
that reminded him in various ways of Ebenezer church
and other black churches in the South. In Chester, Pennsylvania, he attended the Calvary Baptist Church and became known as one of "the Sons of Calvary," a distinction
he shared with William A. Jones, Samuel D. Proctor, and
others who would emerge as great preachers in the black
church. Calvary had been organized in 1879 by exslaves
from Virginia, and much of the style and ethos of the
southern black church remained evident in its worship
practices while King was there.[23] In Boston, King became
affiliated with the Twelfth Baptist Church, a congregation that developed out of a movement led by Free People
of Color in 1804 and that was active on the Underground
Railroad. Twelfth Baptist Church, like Calvary Church,
counted among its membership in the 1950s numerous
blacks with southern roots who had migrated to the
North.[24] This situation not only provided King with continuing exposure to southern black culture, but it also
reinforced his desire to eventually return to the black
church in the South.[25]

King's background in the black church made him
receptive to the Protestant liberalism and personal idealism he studied at Crozer Theological Seminary and
Boston University. Many of the major themes advanced
by Protestant liberalism and personal idealism were

22. *Ibid.*, 15.
23. "History of Calvary Baptist Church," in *Program Booklet of the
Calvary Baptist Church's Centennial Celebration, 1879–1979* (Chester, Pa.:
Linder Printing Company, 1979), 25; a private interview with Emma An-
derson, Chester, Pa., 29 May 1987; and a private interview with Sara V.
Richardson, Chester, Pa., 29 May 1987.
24. *One Hundred and Five Years by Faith: A History of the Twelfth
Baptist Church, 1840–1945* (Boston: The Twelfth Baptist Church, 1946),
9–27; "The Twelfth Baptist Church of Boston, 1840: Celebration Two,"
*Program Booklet of the Three-Fold Celebration Year* (Boston: The Twelfth
Baptist Church, 1985), 19; and a private interview with the Rev. Michael
E. Haynes, Boston, Mass., 25 June 1987.
25. A private interview with Sara V. Richardson, 29 May 1987; and a
private interview with the Rev. Michael E. Haynes, 25 June 1987.

consistent with traditional black church beliefs—beliefs that were affirmed and proclaimed in King's father's pulpit at Atlanta's Ebenezer Baptist Church. King's training at Crozer Theological Seminary and Boston University, as William D. Watley explains, served as "a refining process rather than the primary source for thoughts which were already present in King's mind— thoughts that had been implanted there by the teachings inherent in black religion and the black church."[26] In short, Protestant liberalism and personal idealism provided the intellectual framework within which King could articulate ideas and beliefs he inherited from the black church.[27] This is substantiated by the following discussion of major themes in King's thought.

One example of how King reflected the black religious heritage is implied in his concept of the personal God of love and reason, which Peter Paris describes as the most dominant theme in his writings, speeches, and sermons.[28] The basic message of King's religious heritage was that God is a God of love who creates and sustains the universe and who acts in history for the logical fulfillment of the divine purpose. King's slave forebears had affirmed, on the basis of their reading of the Bible, that this God works in history to destroy the forces of evil and oppression, and this is why they sang with power and conviction:

> He delivered Daniel from de lion's den,
> Jonah f'om de belly of de whale,
> An' de Hebrew chillun f'om de fiery furnace,
> An' why not every man.[29]

26. William D. Watley, *Roots of Resistance: The Nonviolent Ethic of Martin Luther King, Jr.* (Valley Forge, Pa.: Judson Press, 1985), 19.

27. James H. Cone, "Martin Luther King, Jr., Black Theology–Black Church," *Theology Today*, 40, no. 4 (January 1984), 409–11; and Baldwin, "Understanding Martin Luther King, Jr.," 8–10.

28. Peter J. Paris, *Black Leaders in Conflict: Joseph H. Jackson, Martin Luther King, Jr., Malcolm X, Adam Clayton Powell, Jr.* (Philadelphia: The Pilgrim Press, 1978), 71.

29. William F. Allen, et al., Compilers, *Slave Songs of the United States* (New York: Peter Smith, 1951), 94; and Watley, *Roots of Resistance*, 22–23.

With equal fervor, they sang of the human inability to transcend God's power, an idea that had strong implications for the black struggle against white oppression:

> He's so high
> You can't get over Him,
> So wide,
> You can't get around Him,
> So low
> You can't get under Him,
> You must come through by the door.[30]

These songs linked King, in matters of spirit, with his ancestry. Like his slave forebears, he drew on the symbolism of the Exodus, of Joshua and the Battle of Jericho, of the Cross and Resurrection events, and of other themes in the Bible to illustrate God's support for the helpless and the weak. Although King struggled with the reality of sin and evil in the world and with the complex and peculiar problem of black suffering, his roots in the theistic tradition of the black church kept him from denying God's existence, God's goodness, God's power, and God's justice. That tradition explains why King rejected not only the "finistic theism" of Paul Tillich, Henry Nelson Wieman, and Edgar S. Brightman, but also the "Death of God" theology advanced in the 1960s by Thomas J. J. Altizer, William Hamilton, and Paul Van Buren. While he affirmed Tillich's emphasis on God's power and Wieman's and Brightman's stress on God's goodness, King opposed Tillich's efforts to limit God's goodness and Wieman's and Brightman's insistence on God's limited power.[31] He also found Tillich's and Wieman's idea of the impersonality of God inconsistent with black church teachings concerning

30. Quoted in Gardner C. Taylor, "King Day Sermon," Colgate-Rochester Divinity School, Rochester, New York (15 January 1974), 1 ff.

31. Baldwin, "Understanding Martin Luther King, Jr.," 13–16; Watley, *Roots of Resistance*, 20–45; and Martin Luther King, Jr., "A Comparison of the Conceptions of God in the Thinking of Paul Tillich and Henry Nelson Wieman" (Ph.D. diss., Boston University Graduate School, Boston, Massachusetts, 1955), 65–320.

the personality of God, and, therefore, unacceptable.
For King, the black concept of God had a personal
meaning and relevance that could not be captured in
the language of white Western theology, and particularly Tillichian theology:

> Paul Tillich says, "He's the new being," and that's
> beautiful. But in our poetic language we've said it so
> many different ways. Sometimes when we've tried to
> see the meaning of Jesus we said, "He's a lily of the
> valley," and that "He is a bright and morning star." At
> times we've said, "He's a rock in a weary land." "He's a
> shelter in the time of storm." At times we've said,
> "He's altogether lovely." At times we've said, "He's a
> battleaxe in the time of battle." At times we've said
> "He's a mother to the motherless and a father to the
> fatherless." At times we've just ended up saying, "He's
> my everything."[32]

King admitted that the personal idealism of Brightman
and L. Harold DeWolf "gave me metaphysical and philosophical grounding for the idea of a personal God," but
his conviction about the reality of the personal God was
cultivated by the black church and black religion long
before he entered a seminary and a university.[33]

The same applies with respect to King's idea of the
redemptive power of love, a second theme that occurs
and reoccurs in his speeches and writings. Traditional
black preaching has always affirmed and proclaimed the
redemptive power of love and the idea that humans fulfill
their moral responsibility by reflecting the love of God in
their social relationships. King was exposed to these

32. Martin Luther King, Jr., "Is the Universe Friendly?" a sermon
delivered at Ebenezer Baptist Church, Atlanta, Ga. (The King Center
Archives, 12 December 1965), 9. In the black Christian tradition, as
James H. Cone rightly notes, "statements about God are not theologically
distinct from statements about Jesus Christ." See James H. Cone, *The
Spirituals and the Blues: An Interpretation* (Westport, Conn.: Greenwood
Press, 1972), 47.
33. Martin Luther King, Jr., *Stride toward Freedom: The Mont-
gomery Story* (New York: Harper & Brothers, 1958), 100; and Baldwin,
"Understanding Martin Luther King, Jr.," 15–16.

teachings at home and at Ebenezer Baptist Church long before he was able to understand them in ethical and theological terms. While at Crozer Theological Seminary and Boston University, his understanding of the love ethic was increased and refined as he studied Friedrich Nietzsche, Paul Tillich, Anders Nygren, George W. Davis, L. Harold DeWolf, Mohandas K. Gandhi, Paul Ramsey, Howard Thurman, and the New Testament.[34] But it was the practical application of that ethic in traditional black church life and in the larger black community that empowered what would have otherwise been powerless liberal ethics and theology for King.

King's sense of the inherent dignity and worth of all human beings also developed very early out of his black church experience. His parents' teachings on the sacredness of humanity were reinforced by what he heard in church concerning the Judeo-Christian view of humanity being "made in the image of God." This *imago Dei* concept in the black church developed out of the heritage of the slaves, who, despite their untutored state, caught the significance of the fact that every human soul is a part of God and is therefore dear to the heart of God.[35] King himself once observed how his slave foreparents transcended negative and distorted images of black humanity to affirm that God "was not a God that would subject some of His children, and exalt the others."[36] He saw this same concept at work in Ebenezer church and in other black churches when janitors and maids were given the same recognition, positions of influence, and respect as doctors and lawyers. This background was significant

34. Ervin Smith, *The Ethics of Martin Luther King, Jr.* (New York: The Edwin Mellen Press, 1981), 1–2; John J. Ansbro, *Martin Luther King, Jr.: The Making of a Mind* (Maryknoll, N.Y.: Orbis Books, 1982), chap. 2; and Baldwin, "Understanding Martin Luther King, Jr.," 13–16.

35. Howard Thurman, *Deep River and the Negro Spiritual Speaks of Life and Death* (Richmond, Ind.: Friends United Press, 1975), 17–18; Baldwin, "Understanding Martin Luther King, Jr.," 16–17; and Watley, *Roots of Resistance*, 33–36.

36. Martin Luther King, Jr., "The Meaning of Hope," a sermon delivered at the Dexter Avenue Baptist Church, Montgomery, Alabama (The King Center Archives, 10 December 1967), 1 ff.

in preparing King for an acceptance of the personalistic idea of the ultimate value of human life. The writings of Plato, Immanuel Kant, Edgar S. Brightman, George Kelsey, the existentialists, and others simply provided King with ways of conceptualizing this idea in philosophical and metaphysical terms.[37]

The social nature of human existence and the interrelatedness of all life are other themes King advanced in conformity with the black church tradition. These themes undergirded Kings' vision of the *beloved community*, which embodied the concepts of love, forgiveness, reconciliation, nonviolence, freedom, justice, human dignity, morality, and the personal God. This vision was based on the faith that a human community that embraces love and justice will exist in time because all life is interrelated and interdependent, and humans are, therefore, linked together by divine providence in a common destiny. Much of the language and categories used by King to describe this vision were derived from democratic and Social Gospel principles, from philosophers like Immanuel Kant, and from theologians and ethicists such as L. Harold DeWolf, Anders Nygren, Paul Ramsey, Paul Tillich, Howard Thurman, Mohandas K. Gandhi, and Reinhold Niebuhr.[38] But King's firm belief in the ideal of the *beloved community*, and his optimism regarding its realization, were deeply rooted in the Biblical view of the millennial hope as understood in the black Christian tradition.[39] Lawrence N. Jones rightly argues that "ever since blacks have been in America, they have been in search of the 'Beloved Community'—a community in which all persons can enjoy the fruits of democracy as guaranteed by the Constitution and the Declaration of

37. Ansbro, *Martin Luther King, Jr.,* 71–109.

38. Baldwin, "Understanding Martin Luther King, Jr.," 17–20; and Ansbro, *Martin Luther King, Jr.,* 1–36, 71–109, 111–97.

39. Watley, *Roots of Resistance,* 26–31; Baldwin, "Understanding Martin Luther King, Jr.," 17; and Walter E. Fluker, *They Looked for a City: A Comparative Analysis of the Ideal of Community in the Thought of Howard Thurman and Martin Luther King, Jr.,* (Lanham, Md.: University Press of America, 1989), 84–88.

Independence."[40] The slaves gave voice to their common
longing for community in spirituals like:

> Let us break bread together
> On our knees,
> As we face the rising sun.

and

> Old Zion's children marchin' along,
> Marchin' along, marchin' along,
> Old Zion's children marchin' along,
> Talking about the welcome day.[41]

This vision of community was the basis of King's spiritual bond with his ancestry, and this helps explain why he enunciated and proposed it in such graphic and eloquent language.[42]

The moral obligation to resist collective evil is yet another theme that King developed under the influence of the black church. The belief in God as a moral God and in the existence and triumph of the moral order in the universe has inspired black Americans historically to challenge social evil even at the risk of their lives.[43] When King affirmed the supremacy of the moral law, the sacred rights of the individual conscience, and the obligation of moral and rational persons to resist evil systems, he was echoing the ideas of not only Henry David Thoreau, Socrates, St. Augustine, St. Thomas Aquinas, Gandhi, and Reinhold Niebuhr, but also the convictions of Richard Allen, Harriet Tubman, Sojourner Truth, Frederick Douglass, A. D. Williams, Howard Thurman, Martin Luther

40. See Lawrence N. Jones, "Black Christians in Antebellum America: In Quest of the Beloved Community," *The Journal of Religious Thought*, 38, no. 1 (Spring–Summer 1981): 12–19; Baldwin, "Understanding Martin Luther King, Jr.," 17–18; and Fluker, *They Looked for a City*, 111.

41. Quoted in John Lovell, Jr., *Black Song: The Forge and the Flame—The Story of How the Afro-American Spiritual Was Hammered Out* (New York: Paragon House, Publishers, 1972), 264, 280, 456.

42. Baldwin, "Understanding Martin Luther King, Jr.," 18. King's quoting of the slave spiritual, "Free At Last," in his "I Have a Dream" speech in Washington, D.C. on August 28, 1963, is an indication of how he was linked to his slave forebears in matters of spirit.

43. Watley, *Roots of Resistance*, 20–24.

King, Sr., and countless other black church persons who preceded him.[44] King was mindful of the black church's long history of struggle against racism, war, and other social evils and of his place in that history. Although he found sound theological and moral support for challenging and transforming evil social structures in the Social Gospel of Walter Rauschenbusch, it was King's sense of being a part of a long, dissenting tradition in the black church that figured most prominently in his efforts to translate ideas into practical action.[45]

The foregoing discussion supports William Watley's contention that the black church and black religion were "major formative sources for King's intellectual development."[46] The intellectual sources King studied at Crozer Theological Seminary and Boston University were important in that they helped him to make the transition from fundamentalism to a more enlightened evangelical liberalism. Therefore, he was able to return to the black church in the South with a more theologically innovative and socially aware ministry—a ministry that would inspire ordinary, religious black people.

## REDISCOVERING THE SOUTHERN BLACK CHURCH

After completing the residential requirements for the doctoral degree at Boston University in the fall of 1953, Martin Luther King, Jr., began to give serious consideration to job possibilities. Two churches in the Northeast—one in Massachusetts and the other in New

44. Ansbro, *Martin Luther King, Jr.*, 110–62; and Baldwin, "Understanding Martin Luther King, Jr.," 19. A careful reading of black literature from slavery times to the present reveals the strong moral obligation black people felt to challenge collective or social evil. See Philip S. Foner, ed., *The Voice of Black America: Major Speeches by Blacks in the United States, 1797–1973*, 2 vols. (New York: Capricorn Books, 1975), 1 ff.

45. Ansbro, *Martin Luther King, Jr.*, 163–97; King, "The Meaning of Hope," 1 ff.; and a letter from Martin Luther King, Jr., to the Reverend Jerry M. Chance, 9 May 1961.

46. Watley, *Roots of Resistance*, 44–45.

York—had expressed an interest in having him as pastor, and three colleges had offered him teaching and administrative positions.[47] But King's strong desire to return to the black church in the South overshadowed these attractive and challenging job options. After competing unsuccessfully for the pastorate of a black church in Chattanooga, Tennessee, he accepted the call to pastor the Dexter Avenue Baptist Church in Montgomery, Alabama, early in 1954.[48] Dexter had been organized in 1877 by exslaves and their children, who held their first meeting "in an old shabby building where odors of the filth and signs of the horrors of slave life were evident." Apparently a southern sense of place figured prominently in King's decision to pastor this congregation. According to Coretta Scott King, her husband was convinced that serving a black church in his native South "would give him an opportunity to work toward improving the conditions of the black masses." "Though Martin's interest was broad enough to include all underprivileged peoples, whatever their race," she noted, "he most certainly felt that his place was as pastor of a Negro church in the South. He wanted this because it would bring him into close contact with the people to whom he wanted to devote his life."[49] King knew that religion was at the center of southern black life and culture—that religion, more than anything else, gave meaning and significance to spirituality and community—and that there could be no revolution for his people without the involvement of the church. He desired to work through the church to achieve better relations between black and white southerners.

47. King, *Stride toward Freedom*, 16–17 and 21–24.

48. King, *My Life with Martin Luther King, Jr.*, 106–7; a letter from the Pulpit Committee of the Dexter Avenue Baptist Church to Martin Luther King, Jr., 10 March 1954, The King Papers, Boston University; a letter from Martin Luther King, Jr., to the Dexter Avenue Baptist Church, 14 April 1954, The King Papers, Boston University; and a private interview with Dr. Philip Lenud, Nashville, Tennessee, 7 April 1987.

49. King, *My Life with Martin Luther King, Jr.*, 107; and Zelia S. Evans and J. T. Alexander, eds., *Dexter Avenue Baptist Church, 1877–1977* (Montgomery, Ala.: The Dexter Avenue Baptist Church, 1978), 10.

Despite King's attraction toward the South, the decision to move there was not easy. He struggled with the
question—"Can I return to a society that condones a system I have abhorred since childhood?"[50] Coretta shared
her husband's hesitancy on this matter, noting that:

> I wanted to go back South *someday*—it was our home,
> and we loved it—but not yet. Selfishly, perhaps, I
> wanted to breathe the freer air and the rich cultural
> life of the North a while longer and to enjoy the
> greater opportunities a northern city would give me
> for furthering my musical career.[51]

The thought of raising children in the segregated
South further complicated the decision. But Martin and
Coretta King were pulled toward the South by powerful
physical forces such as family, friends, and church—
forces that eclipsed even the worst aspects of segregation. "For several days we talked and thought and prayed
over each of these matters," King recalled. "Finally we
agreed that in spite of the disadvantages and inevitable
sacrifices, our greatest service could be rendered in our
native South."[52]

The Kings went to Dexter Avenue Church determined
to develop a spiritually enriching and socially relevant
ministry. They found the church less than imposing in
size and vitality but impressive in its "challenging possibilities." Like the typical black church in the South, "it
occupied a central place in the community," but was
somewhat unique in that many professional people
with substantial incomes were among its approximately
three hundred members.[53] There were college professors, physicians, and prosperous business people at
Dexter Avenue Church who, by their achievements, had
defied the very logic of Jim Crowism. Moreover, King
discovered that the congregation "had a long tradition
of an educated ministry"—that some of the country's

50. King, *Stride toward Freedom*, 21.
51. King, *My Life with Martin Luther King, Jr.*, 106–7.
52. King, *Stride toward Freedom*, 21.
53. *Ibid.*, 17, 25; and King, *My Life with Martin Luther King, Jr.*, 110.

best-trained and most popular black ministers had held pastorates there. Dexter Avenue Church's affluence and rich tradition of seminary-trained leadership made it a kind of symbol of black aspirations in the heart of the old Confederacy, but these features also bestowed on the church a middle-class, elitist image that bothered King:

> I was anxious to change the impression in the community that Dexter was a sort of silk-stocking church catering only to a certain class. Often it was referred to as the "big folks church." Revolting against this idea, I was convinced that worship at its best is a social experience with people of all levels of life coming together to realize their oneness and unity under God. Whenever the church, consciously or unconsciously, caters to one class it loses the spiritual force of the "whosoever will, let him come" doctrine, and is in danger of becoming little more than a social club with a thin veneer of religiosity.[54]

This notion of worship in the black church as community connected rather than class oriented determined the nature of King's ministry at Dexter Avenue Church. The role he coveted for the congregation was grounded in the idea of the church as an inclusive community in which each person is regarded as an image of God with dignity, worth, and rights derived from God. Motivated by this vision, King recommended new programs at Dexter that he believed would engender feelings of wholeness and harmony among the members. In his "Recommendations to the Dexter Avenue Baptist Church for the Fiscal Year, 1954–55," he proposed the formation of membership, courtesy, and birthday clubs and committees "in order that every member of the church shall be identified with a smaller and more intimate fellowship of the

54. King, *Stride toward Freedom*, 25–26. Martin Luther King, Jr., "Recommendations to the Dexter Avenue Baptist Church for the Fiscal Year, 1954–55," (unpublished document, The King Papers, Boston University, Boston, Mass., n.d., circa 1954), 1–7; and Evans and Alexander, eds., *Dexter Avenue Baptist Church*, 71–80.

church," and he also called for a social service committee
"to channel and invigorate services to the sick and
needy." Clearly, King's ministry at the Dexter Avenue
Church was rooted in the conviction that the church's
function as a spiritual and moral agent in the creation of
community must begin in the daily face-to-face relationships in the local congregation, and then extend to embrace persons in the rest of society.[55]

Some of the programmatic recommendations King
made at the Dexter Avenue Church were designed
specifically to uplift the members and Montgomery's
black community as a whole socially, economically, intellectually, and politically. He established a Scholarship Fund Committee "to choose each year for a
scholarship award the high school graduate of Dexter
possessing the highest scholastic rating as well as unusual possibilities for service to humanity; one who has
been actively engaged in some phase of church life and
who plans to attend college." Educational committees
were formed at King's request to inform the members of
Dexter's history and relationship to the community,
to reorganize and revitalize the sunday school and the
Baptist Training Union (B.T.U.), and to educate members concerning the Bible and other topics of interest.
A Cultural Committee was organized to encourage
promising artists, and to keep before the membership a
sense of the vitality of black culture. A Youth Council,
a Women's Council, and a Brotherhood Committee were
instituted to develop Christian leadership, and a Missionary Society to carry the church's message into the
broader community. Finally, King started a Social and
Political Action Committee to keep "the congregation
intelligently informed concerning the social, political,
and economic situation."[56]

55. King, *Stride toward Freedom*, 25–26; King, "Recommendations
to the Dexter Avenue Baptist Church, 1954–55," 1–7; and Evans and Alexander, eds., *Dexter Avenue Baptist Church*, 71–80.
56. King, *Stride toward Freedom*, 30.

After having broadened the auxiliary program of the Dexter Avenue Church, King took other steps to extend his ministry of service to the community. He became affiliated with the local branch of the NAACP and the Montgomery Chapter of the Alabama Council on Human Relations, organizations that sought to further racial justice and community through the employment of legal and educational means, respectively.[57] King led the Dexter Avenue Church to take out a life membership with the NAACP, and by early 1956 was "urging other churches in our community to do likewise."[58] Dexter was frequently the focal point of meetings held by civil rights and community organizations. For example, on March 13, 1955, several months before King emerged to lead the bus boycott, the church hosted a symposium on "The Meaning of Integration for the American Society," and several community leaders addressed the meaning of integration in education, politics, business, personality development, and the Christian church.[59] Other conferences were held at the Dexter Avenue Church at various times to explore possible solutions to the race problem and to bring into clearer focus the philosophies, aims, and methods of local social and political action groups like the NAACP, the Progressive Democrats, the Citizen's Committee, the Citizens Coordinating Committee, and the Women's Political Council.[60]

It became apparent to King very early that some black churches in the Montgomery area did not share his approach to ministry and mission. The social indifference and ineffectiveness of those churches—coupled with a lack of unity among black leaders, the indifference of

57. *Ibid.*, 31–34.

58. A letter from Martin Luther King, Jr., to Roy Wilkins, 1 May 1956, The King Papers, Boston University.

59. "The Meaning of Integration for the American Society," an unpublished bulletin of the Dexter Avenue Baptist Church, Montgomery, Alabama (The King Papers, Boston University, 13 March 1955), 1; and King, *Stride toward Freedom*, 31–35.

60. King, *Stride toward Freedom*, 25–34; and Evans and Alexander, eds., *Dexter Avenue Baptist Church*, 69–145.

educated blacks, and the passivity of many of the uneducated—almost persuaded King that "no lasting social reform could ever be achieved in Montgomery."[61] He regarded the efforts of many black churches in satisfying the spiritual cravings of persons while leaving the status quo undisturbed as grossly inadequate, and he placed the blame for this one-track approach to religion squarely on the shoulders of black preachers:

> The apparent apathy of the Negro ministers presented a special problem. A faithful few had always shown a deep concern for social problems, but too many had remained aloof from the area of social responsibility. Much of this indifference, it is true, stemmed from a sincere feeling that ministers were not supposed to get mixed up in such earthly, temporal matters as social and economic improvement; they were to "preach the gospel," and keep men's minds centered on "the heavenly." But however sincere, this view of religion, I felt, was too confined.[62]

As King's involvement in his people's struggle in the South deepened, he became increasingly critical of black churches that offered an anesthetic rather than a relevant social gospel to the masses. The uneducated leadership and the tendency toward extreme emotionalism and fundamentalism in many black churches frustrated him.[63] As a boy growing up in Atlanta some years earlier, he had failed to find full intellectual satisfaction in the church precisely for those reasons. King's decision to choose ministry over medicine and law as a life vocation had been reached only because his father's social involvements through Atlanta's Ebenezer Baptist Church and his experiences at Morehouse College had shown him a more positive side of the southern black church. Martin Luther King, Sr., Benjamin Mays, George Kelsey, and others had

61. King, *Stride toward Freedom*, 35–38.
62. *Ibid.*, 35.
63. *Ibid.*, 35–36; Evans and Alexander, eds., *Dexter Avenue Baptist Church*, 69; Fluker, *They Looked for a City*, 84; and Martin Luther King, Jr., *Strength to Love* (Philadelphia: Fortress Press, 1981), 62–63.

helped young Martin to overcome his accumulated doubts about that institution and its potential as an effective vehicle for social change. These figures also influenced his decision to return to the southern black church and to use it as a power base to liberate his people.[64]

King's study of the German philosopher Georg Wilhelm Friedrich Hegel at Boston University had also contributed to his understanding of the black church in the South.[65] Having studied Hegel's analysis of the dialectical process, he could see a dialectic at work in the black church; meaning that certain black churches were excessively otherworldly in their approach to religion, whereas some tended to give more priority to earthly concerns. Indeed, Hegel's analysis was enormously useful to King as he struggled to understand the ambivalent side of the black church and black religion throughout American history. Drawing on Hegel, King argued that an adequate understanding of religion is found neither in the thesis of this-worldliness nor in the antithesis of otherworldliness, but in a synthesis that reconciles the limited truths of both. Disturbed by the prevailing otherworldly outlook of most black preachers and churches in Montgomery, King insisted that "saving souls" and an active involvement in transforming the social order were not antagonistic but complementary callings:

> Religion deals with both earth and heaven, both time and eternity. Religion operates not only on the vertical plane but also on the horizontal. It seeks not only to integrate men with God but to integrate men with men and each man with himself. This means, at bottom, that the Christian gospel is a two-way road. On the one hand it seeks to change the souls of men, and thereby unite them with God; on the other hand it seeks to change the environmental conditions of men so that

64. Evans and Alexander, eds., *Dexter Avenue Baptist Church*, 69; Watley, *Roots of Resistance*, 18; and King, "An Autobiography of Religious Development," 9, 13–15.
65. Ansbro, *Martin Luther King, Jr.*, 119–28; and Kenneth L. Smith and Ira G. Zepp, Jr., *Search for the Beloved Community: The Thinking of Martin Luther King, Jr.* (Valley Forge, Pa: Judson Press, 1974), 114–18.

the soul will have a chance after it is changed. Any religion that professes to be concerned with the souls of men and is not concerned with the slums that damn them, the economic conditions that strangle them, and the social conditions that cripple them is a dry-as-dust religion. Such a religion is the kind that Marxists like to see—an opiate of the people.[66]

King applied the Hegelian principle in his critique of the excessive emotionalism, dogmatism, and anti-intellectualism of many black churches. He pointed to two types of black churches that he believed had failed to respond properly to the needs of the community. He wrote: "One burns with emotionalism, and the other freezes with classism. The former, reducing worship to entertainment, places more emphasis on volume than on content and confuses spirituality with muscularity," whereas the latter "develops a class system and boasts of its dignity, its membership of professional people, and its exclusiveness."[67] In King's view, both of these extremes existed in the South and in the nation as a whole. Although he rejected the southern black church's propensity toward uninhibited emotionalism, apathy, anti-intellectualism, and complacency, he, on the other hand, appreciated that institution's amazing vitality as a source of spirituality, as a symbol of hope and community, and as a potential agent of social change.[68] This is another indication of how King could be critical of black persons and institutions while, at the same time, affirming and appreciating their redeeming qualities.

When the Rosa Parks incident sparked the Montgomery Bus Boycott early in December, 1955, an opportunity arose for King to rediscover the power of the church as the emanating force of black communal life

66. King, *Stride toward Freedom*, 36. King once argued that the Hegelian dialectic, which led him to discover truth in polarities, had "the answer to many of life's problems." See Martin Luther King, Jr., "See You in Washington," a speech delivered at the S.C.L.C. Staff Retreat, Atlanta, Ga. (The King Center Archives, 17 January 1968), 3–4.
67. King, *Strength to Love*, 62–63.
68. *Ibid.;* and King, *Stride toward Freedom*, 34–35, 137–38, 177–78.

and activity in the South. Dexter Avenue Baptist Church functioned primarily as a *de facto* platform for King's activities during the boycott, and it also became "the platform for his rise to national prominence."[69] His success in bringing the Dexter Avenue Church to the forefront of the struggle owed much to the contributions and inspiration of persons who preceded him in Montgomery. One such person was Vernon Johns, the imposing, scholarly, and controversial figure who was King's immediate predecessor at the Dexter Avenue Church. Described as "one of the ten great preachers of the first half of the twentieth century," Johns had accepted the pastorate at Dexter in 1947, and had become widely known for his attacks on elitism in that congregation and on the social attitudes of southern whites. He had consistently denounced the members of Dexter church for their obsession with status and prestige and had carried on virtually a one-man protest against segregation in Montgomery—actions that won him the respect of some and the resentment of others.[70] One Dexter church historian pictured Johns as a veritable John the Baptist who prepared the way for King:

> Through his dramatic teachings, he aroused not only the Dexter family but thousands of citizens of Montgomery to the transition which was taking place in the southern way of life. He kindled a flame of thought in the citizens of Montgomery. Thus, when Rev. Martin Luther King came to pastor Dexter the foundation laid by Dr. Johns made the people receptive to the Social Gospel he promoted.[71]

69. Coleman B. Brown, "Grounds for American Loyalty in a Prophetic Christian Social Ethic—With Special Attention to Martin Luther King, Jr.," (Ph.D. diss., Union Theological Seminary in New York City, April, 1979), 45.

70. Norman W. Walton, "A Short History of Dexter Avenue Baptist Church," *Program Booklet of the Eightieth Anniversary of the Dexter Avenue Baptist Church* (Montgomery, Ala.: The Dexter Avenue Baptist Church, 1958), 3; and Branch, *Parting the Waters*, 6–25. Branch's discussion of Johns as a "forerunner" of Dr. King is important, but it does not give the subject the attention it deserves.

71. Walton, "A Short History of Dexter Avenue Baptist Church," 3.

Lay persons such as E. D. Nixon and Jo Ann Robinson also helped prepare the ground for King's success in Montgomery. King spoke of Nixon as one who had never tired of keeping the race problem before the conscience of the community—as one who "had spoken with courage" and "stood with valor and determination" when "others had feared to speak."[72] Through his roles as state president of the NAACP, as president of the Montgomery NAACP, as head of Montgomery's Progressive Democrats, and as an activist with organized labor, Nixon had "worked fearlessly to achieve the rights of his people, and to rouse Negroes from their apathy."[73] As head of the Women's Political Council in Montgomery, Jo Ann Robinson had led a group of black women in the planning of a bus boycott more than a year before the Rosa Parks incident, thus creating a movement on which King and other ministers would later build.[74] King himself recognized these important forerunners as "unknown heroes" who were more deserving "of public exposure, national and international," than him and Ralph Abernathy, his closest friend and associate in Montgomery. In King's view, the Montgomery Bus Boycott was a people's movement in which he was simply "one of the participants."[75]

The organization and general thrust of the movement in Montgomery reflected the indigenous nature of the black church. That institution's worship service became the model for the mass meeting phenomenon, and the Montgomery Improvement Association, Inc. (M.I.A.), brought into being in 1955 to lead the boycott, was based in the church and largely controlled by

72. King, *Stride toward Freedom*, 38–39.
73. *Ibid.*, 39.
74. David J. Garrow, ed., *The Montgomery Bus Boycott and the Women Who Started It: The Memoir of Jo Ann Gibson-Robinson* (Knoxville: University of Tennessee Press, 1987), ix–100. This is an important revision of the traditional account of the Montgomery boycott.
75. Martin Luther King, Jr., "Unknown Heroes," *The New York Amsterdam News* (May 12, 1962), 1 ff.; Martin Luther King, Jr., "An Address to the Ministers' Leadership Training Program," Miami, Fla. (The King Center Archives, 19, 23 February 1968), 2; and King, *Stride toward Freedom*, 9–10.

ministers.[76] As president of the M.I.A., Martin Luther
King, Jr., brought black and white ministers of various
denominations together in a common struggle to deseg-
regate Montgomery's city buses. The fact that King was
able to transcend the parochialism of his black Baptist
heritage to solidify ministers and lay persons across denominational lines further attests to his importance as
a symbol of unity in the black freedom struggle. He was
vehemently opposed to using denominational banners
as fragmentary barriers to unity, knowing that such a
practice would have undermined his people's struggle.
The ecumenical character of the Montgomery movement made possible a free and effective "car lift" service to transport protesters to and from work, a method
that had been used in a bus boycott in Baton Rouge,
Louisiana in 1953 under the leadership of the Rev.
Theodore J. Jemison.[77] King proudly reported how "the
churches have become the dispatch centers where the
people gather to wait for rides."[78] This was for him another indication of how "our church is becoming militant, stressing a social gospel as well as a gospel of
personal salvation."[79]

Beginning with the Montgomery struggle, nonviolent
direct action was institutionalized in the black church
under King's leadership. The power of that method
was verified in the crucible of struggle in and through
the church, and the church furnished the arena for the
dissemination of the Gandhian philosophy of nonviolence.[80] It was King's background in the black church

76. King, *Stride toward Freedom*, 57–188; and *The Reports of the
Montgomery Improvement Association, Inc., 1955–57* (Unpublished documents, The King Papers, Boston University).
77. King, *Stride towards Freedom*, 9–10, 43–180.
78. Martin Luther King, Jr., "Our Struggle," *Liberation*, 1, no. 2
(April 1956): 3–6.
79. Martin Luther King, Jr., "Annual Address," delivered at the First
Annual Institute on Nonviolence and Social Change Under the Auspices of
the Montgomery Improvement Association, Holt Street Baptist Church,
Montgomery, Ala. (The King Center Archives, 3 December 1956), 2.
80. Lewis V. Baldwin, "Martin Luther King, Jr., The Black Church,
and the Black Messianic Vision," *The Journal of the Interdenominational
Theological Center*, 12, nos. 1 and 2 (Fall 1984–Spring 1985): 97–98; and
Watley, *Roots of Resistance*, 15–17.

that made him receptive to Gandhian philosophy and methods. He stood squarely in the tradition of William Whipper, Frederick Douglass, the NAACP, and the National Urban League, all of whom had emphasized nonviolence and moral suasion as the most practical methods for achieving integration and basic constitutional rights for black Americans.[81] King was conscious of this tradition, as evidenced by his claim that nonviolence "is consistent with the deeply religious traditions of Negroes."[82] Nathan I. Huggins's comment on the power and effectiveness of King's nonviolent strategy among black Christians in Montgomery and in the South generally is searching and persuasive:

> But the tactic worked in the Southern setting because of the deep tradition of Christian stoicism in the black community. Blacks had long appreciated the moral superiority of those who continued to do right despite violence and oppression. When King repeated again and again that "undeserved suffering is redemptive," he was merely iterating a value that his Southern black audiences had lived their lives by. Christian stoicism was the traditional base on which southern blacks engrafted King's message of nonviolence.[83]

For King, the genius and power of the black church and black religion were evident not only in how they

81. James H. Cone, "The Theology of Martin Luther King, Jr.," *Union Seminary Quarterly Review*, 40, no. 4 (January 1986): 22; John Hope Franklin, "The Forerunners," *American Visions: The Magazine of Afro-American Culture*, 1, no. 1 (January–February 1986): 26–35; and Peter J. Paris, *The Social Teaching of the Black Churches* (Philadelphia: Fortress Press, 1985), 14–15, 50, 111. Paris convincingly argues that "the dominant strand" of the black Christian tradition "has always viewed violence as self-contradictory, as a logical deduction from the idea that all persons are equal under God."

82. Martin Luther King, Jr., "The Burning Truth in the South," *The Progressive*, Madison, Wis. (May 1960), 3. King once noted that "It is important to recall that Negroes created the theory of nonviolence as it applies to American conditions." See Martin Luther King, Jr., "Negroes Are Not Moving Too Fast," *The Saturday Evening Post* (November 7, 1964), 10.

83. Nathan I. Huggins, "Martin Luther King, Jr.: Charisma and Leadership," *The Journal of American History*, 74, no. 2 (September 1987): 480–81.

incorporated and appropriated elements of Gandhian thought, but also in how they provided the moral and spiritual disciplines needed to sustain black people in their struggle. The crisis created by the Montgomery Bus Boycott forced King to constantly return to these resources for spiritual sustenance, courage, and hope. In times of distress, uncertainty, and discouragement, he sought relief through a personal, existential appropriation of black faith.[84] Perhaps the most striking example of this occurred on January 27, 1956, in the early stage of the boycott, when King received a telephone call at midnight from a racist who called him a nigger and threatened to kill him and to bomb his home. In the midst of that experience, King found relief, strength, and determination not in the Western theology and philosophy he had studied at Crozer Theological Seminary and Boston University, but through an encounter with the personal God about whom he had learned through his church and his parents. He described that experience in words full of eloquence and searching detail:

> . . . I never will forget one night, very late—it was around midnight. And you can have some strange experiences at midnight. The telephone started ringing and I picked it up. On the other end was an ugly voice. That voice said to me, in substance, "nigger, we are tired of you and your mess now, and if you aren't out of this town in three days, we're going to blow your brains out and blow up your house." I'd heard these things before, but for some reason that night it got to me. I turned over and I tried to go to sleep, but I couldn't sleep. I was frustrated, bewildered. Then I got up and went back to the kitchen and started warming some coffee, thinking that coffee would give me

84. *Ibid.*: Bennett, *What Manner of Man*, 55–56; James H. Cone, "Martin Luther King, Jr., Black Theology, and the Black Church," *The A.M.E. Zion Quarterly Review*, 507, no. 2 (July 1986): 5; James H. Cone, "A Review of John J. Ansbro's *Martin Luther King, Jr.: The Making of a Mind* (1982)," *Fellowship* (January–February 1984): 32–33; and Lewis V. Baldwin, "Family, Church, and the Black Experience: The Shaping of Martin Luther King, Jr.," *The A.M.E. Zion Quarterly Review*, 98, no. 4 (January 1987): 6.

a little relief. Then I started thinking about many things—I pulled back on the theology and philosophy that I had just studied in the universities, trying to give philosophical and theological reasons for the existence and the reality of sin and evil, but the answer didn't quite come there. I sat there and thought about a beautiful little daughter who had just been born about a month earlier. . . . She was the darling of my life. I'd come in night after night and see that little, gentle smile. And I sat at that table thinking about that little girl and thinking about the fact that she could be taken away from me any minute. And I started thinking about a dedicated, devoted and loyal wife who was over there asleep. And she could be taken from me. I could be taken from her. And I got to the point where I couldn't take it any longer—I was weak. And something said to me, "You can't call on Daddy now, he's up in Atlanta, a hundred and seventy-five miles away. You can't even call on Mamma now. You've got to call on that something and that person that your Daddy used to tell you about—that power that can make a way out of no way." And I discovered then that religion had to become real to me and I had to know God for myself. And I bowed down over that cup of coffee, I never will forget it. Oh yes, I prayed a prayer, and I prayed out loud that night. I said, "Lord, I'm down here trying to do what's right. I think I'm right. I think the cause that we represent is right. But Lord, I must confess that I'm weak now, I'm faltering, I'm losing my courage, and I can't let the people see me like this because if they see me weak and losing my courage, they will begin to get weak."

And then came the vision which renewed King's courage, strength, and determination—a vision to which he would refer again and again to lift his spirit and to inspire and motivate his people in the midst of struggle:

And it seemed at that moment that I could hear an inner voice saying to me, "Martin Luther, stand up for righteousness. Stand up for justice. Stand up for truth. And lo I will be with you, even until the end of the world. . . ." I heard the voice of Jesus saying still to fight on. He promised never to leave me, never to leave me alone. No, never alone. No, never alone. He promised never to leave me, never to leave me alone.[85]

This "vision in the kitchen," as David J. Garrow calls it, must be understood in relationship to King's religious heritage. As far back as slavery and beyond, his forebears had talked and sung about walking and talking with God in times of trouble—that God who was "as intimate, personal, and immediate as the gods of Africa had been." "I'm gonna tell the Master all about my trouble," "Massa Jesus is my bosom friend," and "I'm goin' to walk with [talk with, live with, see] King Jesus by myself, by myself," were refrains that echoed through the slave spirituals.[86] King was an heir of this tradition. The fact that he experienced the "vision in the kitchen" after his liberal training at Crozer Theological Seminary and Boston University shows that the spiritual resources of his heritage in the South became eminently more important than his theological education in preparing him to lead his people against the evil forces of racism. Given his background in the black church, it is conceivable that King had many "crisis moments" similar to the "vision in the kitchen"—experiences that he had not had in the years prior to the Montgomery Bus Boycott.[87] However, it was the "vision in the kitchen" that led him to a profoundly religious understanding of his leadership and mission.

85. King, *Stride toward Freedom*, 58–63, 134–36; King, "Early Days," 9–12; and David J. Garrow, *Bearing the Cross: Martin Luther King, Jr. and the Southern Christian Leadership Conference* (New York: William Morrow, 1986), 57–58.

86. Garrow, *Bearing the Cross*, 57–58; and Lawrence W. Levine, *Black Culture and Black Consciousness: Afro–American Folk Thought from Slavery to Freedom* (New York: Oxford University Press, 1977), 35. I agree wholeheartedly with Preston N. Williams' contention that "the kitchen experience to which Garrow repeatedly points to explain King's moments of depression and his persistence in the face of great odds is never interpreted in depth or linked to King's religious heritage." See Preston N. Williams, "The Public and Private Burdens of Martin Luther King, Jr.," *The Christian Century* (February 25, 1987); 198–99.

87. David J. Garrow fails to point to the possibility that King's "vision in the kitchen" was simply one of many such experiences he had during his thirteen years as a civil rights leader. Garrow's unfamiliarity with the black church and the black religious experience undoubtedly accounts for this oversight. See Garrow, *Bearing the Cross*, 57–58.

From that point on, King accepted that mission as the cross he had been ordained to bear.[88]

It was that "vision in the kitchen" that gave King the courage and calmness to face the worst when his home on Jackson Street in Montgomery was bombed on January 30, 1956, three days later. In the wake of that incident, he stood on his porch and consoled the angry, panicky crowd of black supporters who had gathered there, urging them that "If you have weapons, take them home; if you do not have them, please do not seek to get them. We cannot solve this problem through retaliatory violence. We must meet violence with nonviolence." King went on to say: "Remember, if I am stopped, this movement will not stop, because God is with the movement. Go home with this glowing faith and this radiant assurance."[89] It was at that moment that King discovered anew the tremendous potential of the southern black church as a source of community, spirituality, Christian optimism, and social activism. "As I finished speaking there were shouts of 'Amen' and 'God bless you,'" he remembered. "I could hear voices saying: 'We are with you all the way, Reverend.' I looked out over that vast throng of people and noticed tears on their faces."[90] The black church provided one of the most reliable support mechanisms for King when he was plagued by violent attacks and by criticism and questions concerning the legitimacy of his civil rights activities.

The successful outcome of the Montgomery protest and the wave of white-on-black violence that followed afforded still other occasions for King to witness and experience the vitality of southern black religion and culture. Many blacks were verbally abused, jailed, and beaten, and black churches, as had been the case during the Reconstruction period, increasingly became objects of suspicion and contempt among whites. In a report issued on January 14, 1957, three weeks after the Supreme

88. Garrow, *Bearing the Cross*, 57 ff.
89. King, *Stride toward Freedom*, 135–38.
90. *Ibid.*

Court declared bus segregation illegal in Montgomery, eight Baptist Churches, one African Methodist Episcopal Church, one African Methodist Episcopal Zion Church, one Christian Methodist Episcopal Church, and one Lutheran Church in the city were listed as being most vulnerable to attacks from racists, and so were the homes of King, Ralph Abernathy, and a dozen other black preachers.[91] These statistics alone testified to the enormous importance of the black church in the movement. By the end of January, 1957, four black Baptist Churches in Montgomery—Bell Street, Hutchinson Street, Mt. Olive, and First Baptist—had been hit by explosions and so had the home of Ralph Abernathy.[92] "Discouraged, and still revolted by the bombings," King declared, "for some strange reason I began to feel a personal sense of guilt for everything that was happening." He continued:

> In this mood I went to the mass meeting on Monday night. There for the first time, I broke down in public. I had invited the audience to join me in prayer, and had begun by asking God's guidance and direction in all our activities. Then, in the grip of an emotion I could not control, I said, "Lord, I hope no one will have to die as a result of our struggle for freedom in Montgomery. Certainly I don't want to die. But if anyone has to die, let it be me." The audience was in an uproar. Shouts and cries of "no, no" came from all sides. So intense was the reaction, that I could not go on with my prayer. Two of my fellow ministers came to the pulpit and suggested that I take a seat. For a few minutes I stood with their arms around me, unable to move. Finally, with the help of my friends, I sat down.[93]

Here was an occasion when the traditional prayer meeting served to solidify an abused and exploited people around a common faith, hope, purpose, and strategy

91. "The Montgomery Improvement Association's List of Persons and Churches Most Vulnerable to Violent Attacks" (Unpublished document, The King Center Archives, 14 January 1957), 1.
92. King, *Stride toward Freedom*, 175–78.
93. *Ibid.*, 177–78.

for change.[94] Though caught in the web of guilt and emotion, King did not stand alone, for the sense of being a part of a suffering community was indeed overwhelming for all who participated. The emotive qualities of the black church experience, which King had previously frowned on, took on a new and more personal dimension for him. The songs of slavery came alive, prayer rose to sermon, tears gave way to rejoicing, hope triumphed over sorrow, and King learned another lesson about the spiritual power of the black church in the South that he would never forget.[95] To be sure, experiences of this nature deepened his understanding of spirituality and its vital relationship to social transformation.

The spirit of cooperation between black churches and ministers through the Montgomery Improvement Association helped make possible the Southern Christian Leadership Conference (S.C.L.C.), a more permanent and broadly based civil rights organization with branches across the South. S.C.L.C. was organized by about one hundred church persons at Atlanta's Ebenezer Baptist Church in January, 1957, and King was elected its first president. The new organization was led by black ministers and was firmly rooted in the black church in the South. According to King, S.C.L.C.—variously referred to as "a church," "a faith operation," "the social action arm of the black church," and "the black church writ large"—"was organized to serve as a channel through which local protest organizations in the South could coordinate their protest activities, and give the total struggle a sense of Christian and disciplined direction."[96]

94. *Ibid.* For brief but perceptive discussions of how the black prayer tradition took on a new dimension during the civil rights movement, see Harold A. Carter, *The Prayer Tradition of Black People* (Valley Forge, Pa.: Judson Press, 1976), 21, 65–67, 94, 106–13, 129–30; and O. Richard Bowyer, et al., *Prayer in the Black Tradition* (Nashville: The Upper Room, 1986), 64–67.
95. King, *Stride toward Freedom,* 177–78.
96. Adam Fairclough, "The Southern Christian Leadership Conference and the Second Reconstruction, 1957–1973," *The Southern Atlantic Quarterly,* 8, no. 2 (Spring 1981): 178; Adam Fairclough, *To Redeem the Soul of America: The Southern Christian Leadership Conference and*

King's commitment to nonviolent direct action became the operating philosophy of S.C.L.C., and that organization remained his primary base of activities until his death.[97]

It was King's increasing devotion to S.C.L.C. and to the black freedom movement as a whole that led him to resign from the pastorate of Dexter Avenue Baptist Church in January, 1960. He realized that the quality of his pastorship at the Dexter Church was being increasingly diminished by the growing demands of the movement across the South, and this disturbed him greatly. Furthermore, his father, who had pressed him for years to leave the dangers of Montgomery and return to Atlanta, also urged him to resign.[98] At the same time, King was driven by the conviction that he was the instrument of a special destiny—that his future was somehow linked to God's unfolding plan of liberation for his people. "I have a sort of nagging conscience that someone will interpret my leaving Montgomery as a retreat from the civil rights struggle," he speculated. "Actually, I will be involved in it on a larger scale. I can't stop now. History has thrust something upon me from which I cannot turn away."[99] Not surprisingly, King's decision to resign was met with

---

*Martin Luther King, Jr.* (Athens, Ga.: University of Georgia Press, 1987), 1–2; Garrow, *Bearing the Cross*, 122–25; and a private interview with Rev. Bernard S. Lee, Washington, D.C., 9 July 1986. In his statement of resignation, submitted November 29, 1959, King asserted: "The time has come for a broad, bold advance of the Southern campaign for equality. . . . Not only will it include a stepped up campaign of voter registration, but a full-scale approach will be made upon discrimination and segregation in all forms. . . . We must employ new methods of struggle involving the masses of our people." See Evans and Alexander, eds., *Dexter Avenue Baptist Church*, 141; and a letter from Martin Luther King, Jr., to Dr. P. J. Ellis, 6 February 1960, The King Papers, Boston University.

97. Fairclough, *To Redeem the Soul of America*, 1–9.

98. Evans and Alexander, eds., *Dexter Avenue Baptist Church*, 141; and Garrow, *Bearing the Cross*, 122–25.

99. Quoted in Garrow, *Bearing the Cross*, 125. King's prediction proved accurate as more radical streams of protest in the black community, specifically the Black Muslims, interpreted his departure from Montgomery as flight from "the portals of death in Alabama." See *Los Angeles Herald-Dispatch*, Los Angeles, California (January 9, 1960): 1 ff.; and C. Eric Lincoln, *The Black Muslims in America* (Boston: Beacon Press, 1973), 161.

considerable sorrow and disapproval from the members at the Dexter Avenue Church, but these feelings were tempered by the general perception that God had greater responsibilities for the dynamic young minister. One elderly member undoubtedly spoke for the entire congregation when he declared that King, despite his departure from Montgomery, would always be identified in a special way with the history and struggles of black people in that city:

> Reverend King will not truly be leaving us, because part of him always will remain in Montgomery, and at the same time, part of us will go with him. We'll always be together, everywhere. The history books may write it that Reverend King was born in Atlanta and then came to Montgomery, but we feel he was born in Montgomery in the struggle here, and now he is moving to Atlanta for bigger responsibilities.[100]

At the beginning of 1960, King's deepest desire was to be more accessible to S.C.L.C. while retaining a pastoral role in some local black congregation in the South. After giving the matter his most prayerful and serious consideration, he agreed to return to his native Atlanta, Georgia, and to accept the co-pastorship of Ebenezer Baptist Church along with his father.[101] By that time, fame had opened many other options for him, but these were overshadowed by his enduring commitment to the southern black church and to the struggle of his people. The move to Atlanta was significant not only because S.C.L.C. was headquartered there but also because of the symbolic importance of Ebenezer Baptist Church. As stated earlier, Ebenezer church was intimately

---

100. Evans and Alexander, eds., *Dexter Avenue Baptist Church*, 141; and "A Response to Martin Luther King, Jr.'s Announcement that He Is Moving from Dexter to Atlanta" (Unpublished statement, The King Papers, Boston University, 29 November 1959), 1–2.

101. Evans and Alexander, eds., *Dexter Avenue Baptist Church*, 141; a letter from the Ebenezer Baptist Church to Dr. Martin Luther King, Jr., 17 November 1959, The King Papers, Boston University; and a letter from Martin Luther King, Jr., to the Ebenezer Baptist Church, 19 November 1959, The King Papers, Boston University.

connected with King's sense of place and of regional identity and responsibility. He had had very special experiences of community there and felt an attachment to that church that was both physical and spiritual in nature. As had been the case with Dexter Avenue Baptist Church in Montgomery, King related to the people at Ebenezer church without feelings of alienation and without a sense of theological besiegement and betrayal, despite his liberal theological training and rapidly growing fame. For King, Ebenezer church would eventually serve the same function as the Dexter Avenue Church—a *de facto* platform from which he sought to explain and to launch his movement for human liberation. In a letter to a fellow clergyman, King stated: "In order to be true to my work in the South, and my position as co-pastor of the Ebenezer Baptist Church in Atlanta, I have had to adopt a policy of not being out of the pulpit more than twice a month."[102] Although his mounting responsibilities and fame as a civil rights leader and an international figure made it virtually impossible for him to maintain this policy, King nevertheless retained a strong sense of commitment to the ministry and mission of Ebenezer Church.[103]

From 1960 until his death eight years later, King devoted much time, energy, and resources to expanding the role of the southern black church in the civil rights movement. Numerous activities occurred during that period that gave him an opportunity to assess the impact of that institution on the struggle. In 1962, King and

102. Lewis V. Baldwin, "'Let Us Break Bread Together': Martin Luther King, Jr. and the Black Church in the South," a paper presented at the Southern Historical Association Meetings, New Orleans, La., 13 November 1987, 2, 18–19; a letter from Martin Luther King, Jr., to P. O. Watson, 19 November 1959, The King Papers, Boston University; a letter from Martin Luther King, Jr., to the Rev. W. H. McKinney, 31 March 1960, The King Papers, Boston University; a letter from Martin Luther King, Jr., to Mrs. Wayne A. Dockhorn, 29 September 1960, The King Papers, Boston University; a private interview with the Rev. Ralph D. Abernathy, Atlanta, Ga., 17 March 1987; and a private interview with the Rev. Michael E. Haynes, 25 June 1987.
103. King, *My Life with Martin Luther King, Jr.*, 78–79, 169; King, *Daddy King*, 168–69; Garrow, *Bearing the Cross*, 123; and a letter from Martin Luther King, Jr., to Mrs. Wayne A. Dockhorn, 29 September 1960.

S.C.L.C. joined local black college students, community leaders, and members of the newly formed Student Non-violent Coordinating Committee (S.N.C.C.) in an across-the-board, full-scale offensive against the entire system of segregation in Albany, Georgia. The effort did not meet with an unqualified success, mainly because of poor planning and timing, rifts between S.C.L.C. and S.N.C.C. workers, and the lack of a focus on a single, clearly defined target of injustice. But the Albany campaign did evoke memories of the Montgomery experience in that it demonstrated that there was no disjunction between the black church and the black community.[104] In Albany, black congregations provided funds, staff, demonstrators, food, meeting space, and lodging for the movement. Shiloh Baptist Church and other churches were the focal points of mass meetings and prayer vigils, and black clergymen were jailed while demonstrating alongside their parishioners. One of the most notable features of the Albany campaign was the frequent and widespread singing of the spirituals and other freedom songs, which were so much a part of the black church and the black religious experience in the South. Many of these songs were created during mass meetings, public demonstrations, and while demonstrators stood crowded in jails, suggesting a close connection between art and struggle, and art and life. Traditional songs like "Sometimes I Feel Like My Time Ain't Long," "This Little Light of Mine," and "Swing Low Sweet Chariot Let Me Ride" were most often heard, but frequently newly created songs like "Oh Prichett, Oh Kelley," composed to the tune of "Oh Mary, Oh Martha," were used as powerful statements against Police Chief Laurie Prichett, Mayor Asa D. Kelley, Jr., and other Albany officials who symbolized opposition to justice and racial harmony.[105] Bernice J. Reagon has

104. Watley, *Roots of Resistance*, 65–70; and Howard Zinn, *Albany: A Special Report* (Atlanta: The Southern Regional Council, 1962), 1–34.
105. "Why Our Prayer Vigil," a group statement of the Negotiating Committee of the Albany Movement and Chief Consultants, Dr. Martin

described these songs as "group participation" songs that reinforced bonds of community and reflected how black art emerged out of a collective experience of suffering and struggle:

> Here song formed for the first time a basic and common language between organizers who were middle-class Black college students and older adult members of a Black Belt rural area. Albany, known as a singing movement, provided room for traditional song-leaders to re-shape and re-focus and expand the body of song brought it by organizers.[106]

Sensing the symbolic importance and tremendous potential of the black church, many white residents in Albany looked upon that institution with fear, suspicion, and contempt. The Mt. Mary Church, the Mt. Olive Baptist Church, and the Shady Grove Baptist Church were demolished by mysterious blasts and fires, incidents that clearly reminded Martin Luther King, Jr., of Montgomery.[107] On September 12, 1962, King joined the former baseball star Jackie Robinson in establishing a building fund "to rebuild these churches completely and to rescue other damaged churches involved in the civil rights struggle."[108] Despite the many problems that attended the Albany campaign, highlighted by the failure to break down the walls of segregation there, King left that city in late 1962 with the satisfaction that black

---

Luther King, Jr. and Dr. Ralph Abernathy (Unpublished document, The King Center Archives, n.d., circa 1962) 1–2; "Religious Leaders Arrested in Albany, Georgia" (Unpublished document, The King Center Archives, 28 August 1962), 1–2; *Newsweek* (December 25, 1961), 17–18; and Bernice J. Reagon, "Songs of the Civil Rights Movement, 1955–1965: A Study in Culture History" (Ph.D. diss., Howard University, Washington, D.C., May 1975), 132–38.

106. Reagon, "Songs of the Civil Rights Movement," 178.

107. A letter from Martin Luther King, Jr., to the Rev. Leroy Freeman, 8 October 1962, The King Papers, Boston University; and "Dr. King and Jackie Robinson Head Rebuilding for Burned Churches," a news release from the S.C.L.C., Atlanta, Ga. (The King Center Archives, 12 September 1962), 1–2.

108. "Dr. King and Jackie Robinson Head Rebuilding for Burned Churches," 1–2.

congregations had responded well to the appeal of non-violence.[109]

The Albany movement produced a new body of experiences that King and other ministers in S.C.L.C. drew on as they extended their campaign of nonviolent direct action into Birmingham, Alabama in September, 1962.[110] In contrast to Albany, they identified a specific target of protest in Birmingham and gave serious thought and attention to planning, timing, legal matters, and potential threats to black unity. S.C.L.C.'s specific objective was to upset the patterns of racial segregation in Birmingham through a series of boycotts and demonstrations aimed at the white business community. As in the case of Montgomery and Albany, King and other ministers appealed to the black church community for financial contributions, moral support, and spiritual sustenance. From the outset, many black pastors refused to actively support the movement and some even criticized S.C.L.C.'s strategy and tactics when the sit-in demonstrations began on April 3, 1963.[111] Some had been convinced by city officials, businessmen, and the local press in Birmingham that King was an "outsider" seeking personal glory in a struggle that should be led by local pastors. Other black ministers resented being told to support a campaign that they had no part in organizing, and complained that they had not been properly informed of the movement's starting date and plan of operation.[112] Still others charged that King and S.C.L.C. were guilty of "bad timing," especially in starting sit-in demonstrations only one day after the moderate Albert Boutwell's victory over Eugene "Bull" Connor in Birm-

109. Watley, *Roots of Resistance*, 68; and King, *Why We Can't Wait*, 43–45.

110. King, *Why We Can't Wait*, 43–45; and Watley, *Roots of Resistance*, 65–70.

111. Washington, ed., *A Testament of Hope*, 346–47; King, *Why We Can't Wait*, 43–45, 66–68; Watley, *Roots of Resistance*, 70–79; Fairclough, *To Redeem the Soul of America*, 111–39; and Garrow, *Bearing the Cross*, 173–286.

112. Washington, ed., *A Testament of Hope*, 346–47; King, *Why We Can't Wait*, 66–68; and Fairclough, *To Redeem the Soul of America*, 118–19.

ingham's mayoral election. To these preachers, it seemed churlish and provocative to begin protests at a time when the Boutwell victory offered the prospect of a trend toward racial moderation.[113] Faced with these problems and challenges, it appeared that King and S.C.L.C. would fail in their effort to attract widespread support from Birmingham's black pastors and their congregations.

The effort to secure a strong base in the black church community eventually achieved success for two reasons. First, Birmingham's white business community refused to seriously negotiate with representatives of the black community. This problem was compounded as Bull Connor, who remained Birmingham's Commissioner of Public Safety after losing the mayoral race to Boutwell, resorted increasingly to violence and other acts of intimidation, thus creating a sense of outrage in the black community. Black preachers began to denounce Commissioner Connor and other city officials from their pulpits, and sympathy and support for the demonstrators mounted. Second, King appeared before several groups of black preachers and used his powers of persuasion to explain, cajole, and pressure many of them into supporting the struggle.[114] In a speech before one hundred clergymen at the Baptist Ministers' Conference in Birmingham, King criticized some black preachers for "riding around in big cars, living in fine homes, but who are not willing to take part in the fight." "If you can't stand up with your people," King declared, "you are not fit to be a preacher." He spoke at length about the need for a socially conscious ministry in the South, a point he had made repeatedly in Montgomery and Albany. "I pleaded for the projection of strong, firm leadership by the Negro minister," King recalled, "pointing out that he is freer,

---

113. King, *Why We Can't Wait*, 66–68; and Fairclough, *To Redeem the Soul of America*, 118–19.

114. Washington, ed., *A Testament of Hope*, 346–47; King, *Why We Can't Wait*, 66–68; Watley, *Roots of Resistance*, 70–79; and Alan F. Westin and Barry Mahoney, *The Trial of Martin Luther King, Jr.: The Landmark Birmingham Case and Its Meaning for America Today* (New York: Thomas Y. Crowell, 1974), 1–198.

more independent, than any other person in the community. I asked how the Negro would ever gain his freedom without the guidance, support and inspiration of his spiritual leaders."[115]

In time, black churches became key centers in unifying and rallying the black community more forcefully to the cause of freedom in Birmingham. Local black clergymen joined King and S.C.L.C. in bringing to the struggle a vigorous, determined leadership that did much to undermine the claim that black churches were essentially otherworldly in their outlook. The most active local pastor was the Reverend Fred Shuttlesworth of the Bethel Baptist church, who had organized the Alabama Christian Movement for Human Rights (A.C.H.R.) in 1956.[116] Referred to by King as "one of the nation's most courageous freedom fighters," Shuttlesworth had conducted virtually a one-man struggle against Jim Crow in Birmingham long before S.C.L.C. arrived there. His A.C.H.R. became one of the eighty-five affiliates of S.C.L.C., and he was as instrumental as King in defeating the forces of segregation in Birmingham.[117]

Inspired by the charismatic leadership of figures like Shuttlesworth and King, the Sixteenth Street Baptist Church, the St. James Baptist Church, the New Pilgrim Baptist Church, the Metropolitan A.M.E. Zion Church, and other congregations distinguished themselves for outstanding service on behalf of the Birmingham struggle.[118] King later assessed the impact of these churches in two areas. First, he acknowledged that they had been instrumental in bringing the spiritual resources of the black heritage in the South to bear on the movement. King illustrated this by pointing to the the slave spirituals, which were sung with tremendous power in the black churches of Birmingham, reinforcing a sense of

---

115. King, *Why We Can't Wait*, 67; Washington, ed., *A Testament of Hope*, 346; and Fairclough, *To Redeem the Soul of America*, 119.
116. King, *Why We Can't Wait*, 51.
117. *Ibid.*, 51 ff.
118. Fairclough, *To Redeem the Soul of America*, 111–39.

community and a determination already seasoned by exposure to a racist society. King wrote:

> In a sense the freedom songs are the soul of the movement. They are more than just incantations of clever phrases designed to invigorate a campaign; they are as old as the history of the Negro in America. They are adaptations of the songs the slaves sang—the sorrow songs, the shouts for joy, the battle hymns and the anthems of our movement. I have heard people talk of their beat and rhythm, but we in the movement are as inspired by their words. "Woke Up This Morning with My Mind Stayed on Freedom" is a sentence that needs no music to make its point. We sing the freedom songs today for the same reason the slaves sang them, because we too are in bondage and the songs add hope to our determination that "We shall overcome, Black and white together, We shall overcome someday." I have stood in a meeting with hundreds of youngsters and joined in while they sang "Ain't Gonna Let Nobody Turn Me 'Round." It is not just a song; it is a resolve. A few minutes later, I have seen those same youngsters refuse to turn around from the onrush of a police dog, refuse to turn around before a pugnacious Bull Connor in command of men armed with power hoses. These songs bind us together, give us courage together, help us to march together.[119]

Second, King regarded the black churches in Birmingham as the principal sources from which the gospel of love and nonviolence was preached. In an address before the National Conference on Religion and Race in January, 1963, delivered while the Birmingham campaign was still in full swing, King said:

> I am happy to say that the nonviolent movement in America has come not from secular forces but from the heart of the Negro church. This movement has done a great deal to revitalize the Negro church and to give its message a relevant and authentic ring. The

---

119. King, *Why We Can't Wait*, 61; and Washington, ed., *A Testament of Hope*, 348.

great principles of love and justice which stand at the
center of the nonviolent movement are deeply rooted
in our Judeo-Christian heritage.[120]

King reiterated this point three months later as he sat in
a Birmingham jail. "I am grateful to God that, through
the Negro church, the dimension of nonviolence entered
our struggle," he wrote.[121] For King, the acceptance of
nonviolent direct action was indicative of a certain
sophistication on the part of black churches in Birmingham. After all, it was the practice of militant nonviolence by black Christians that forced Birmingham's
business and industrial community to negotiate in good
faith with the black community in May, 1963, thereby
dealing a death blow to decades of *de jure* segregation
in that city.[122]

The faithfulness and heroism displayed by black
preachers and lay persons in the face of threats and
persecution from the Ku Klux Klan and other racist
groups in Birmingham helped reinforce King's growing
faith in the power and potential of the southern black
church. He marveled at the fact that Birmingham's
black community could remain strong, unified, determined, and hopeful even as bombs destroyed churches
and the homes of ministers. The grief and bitterness
King felt as a result of these racist attacks were heightened when an explosion killed four black girls at the
Sixteenth Street Baptist Church in September, 1963, but
he found much consolation in seeing that his people
could still sing "We Shall Overcome" even as they
salved their wounds and buried their dead. "Tears came
into my eyes that at such a tragic moment, my race still
could sing its hope and faith," King told an inter-
viewer.[123] This indomitable Christian optimism led him

120. Quoted in Mathew Ahmann, ed., *Race: A Challenge to Religion*
(Chicago: Henry Regnery, 1963), 164–65.
121. Washington, ed., *A Testament of Hope*, 297; King, *Why We Can't
Wait*, 87; and Ansbro, *Martin Luther King, Jr.*, 177–78.
122. King, *Why We Can't Wait*, 37.
123. Washington, ed., *A Testament of Hope*, 346–48.

to compare the black church in the South to the ancient church of the Apostles:

> . . . the role of the Negro church today, by and large, is a glorious example in the history of Christendom. For never in Christian history, within a Christian country, have Christian churches been on the receiving end of such naked brutality and violence as we are witnessing here in America today. Not since the days of the Christians in the catacombs has God's house, as a symbol, weathered such attack as the Negro churches.[124]

King was convinced that the triumph of nonviolence over the forces of segregation in Birmingham had heightened the image of the black church in the national consciousness, thus preparing the way for subsequent nonviolent direct action campaigns in other southern towns. Between 1963 and 1968, King and S.C.L.C. expanded their movement into St. Augustine, Florida, Greenwood, Mississippi, and many other small towns in the South with the knowledge that the pride and power of nonviolence had been well established in black churches. On entering these small towns, King's first move always was to establish contact with black ministers and their congregations. Although many strong black church persons refused to become actively involved in the civil rights movement, that does not necessarily mean that they opposed its philosophy and goals. As John J. Ansbro has indicated, southern black congregations prepared considerable numbers of their

124. *Ibid.*, 346–47. King had a high regard for the normative authority of the early church. Discovery of the strict discipline of devotion among the early Christians was a source of great inspiration for his nonviolent campaigns. He once wrote: "The early Christians practiced civil disobedience to a superb degree. And often they were thrown into the lion's den, and they were placed on the chopping blocks—and they went there with the songs of Zion on their lips, and in their souls, because they had discovered that there was something so true, and so precious, that they had to follow it." King believed that the black church was more in line with this noble tradition than its white counterpart. See Martin Luther King, Jr., "Why We Must Go to Washington," a speech delivered at the S.C.L.C. Retreat, Ebenezer Baptist Church, Atlanta, Ga., (The King Center Archives, 15 January 1968), 14–15; and King, *Why We Can't Wait*, 77, 84, 91–92.

constituents for a practical commitment to nonviolence by their emphases on the dignity of self, the value of sacrificial love, the merit of undeserved suffering as exemplified in the life of Jesus, and the reality of a personal God who destroys evil and seeks justice and peace.[125]

The launching of a voting rights campaign in Selma, Alabama, in January, 1965 proved to be one of the most difficult tests for King and the black church. King entered the Selma campaign with a determination to use the moral, spiritual, and physical resources of the black church to promote the cause of freedom and justice in the realm of southern politics. Black churches became the unifying force and base of operation for the achievement of this goal. Brown Chapel A.M.E. Church, the First Baptist Church, and the Tabernacle Baptist Church were most active in this effort. King and his followers drew on the spiritual disciplines of these and other churches, uniting the prayer circle and the picket line. Consequently, they were able to confront the insults and brutality of Sheriff Jim Clark, Mayor Joe Smitherman, Colonel Al Lingo, and other racist officials and private citizens in Selma with patience and courage.[126]

Brown Chapel A.M.E. Church distinguished itself as one of the most historic landmarks of the civil rights movement in the South, sharing that distinction with the Dexter Avenue Baptist Church in Montgomery, the Sixteenth Street and the Bethel Baptist Churches in Birmingham, and the Ebenezer Baptist Church in Atlanta. Some of King's most powerful preaching on nonviolence took place at Brown Chapel, and that church was the focal point of most of the mass meetings, youth meetings, prayer vigils, classes on nonviolent self-defense, memorial services for murdered demonstrators, and negotiations between civil rights leaders and civil officials

125. See Fairclough, *To Redeem the Soul of America*, 11–137; Garrow, *Bearing the Cross*, chap. 6; and Ansbro, *Martin Luther King, Jr.*, 178.

126. Fairclough, *To Redeem the Soul of America*, 225–51; Watley, *Roots of Resistance*, 79–90; and Robert M. Bleiweiss, ed., *Marching to Freedom: The Life of Martin Luther King, Jr.* (New York: The New American Library, 1968), 124–37.

in Selma.[127] On March 21, 1965, King stood in Brown
Chapel's pulpit and offered words of hope and inspiration to the most ecumenically minded group of people to
participate in a civil rights campaign since the Great
March on Washington two years earlier—a group that
included men, women, children, rich and poor, black and
white, and Catholics, Protestants, and Jews. King captured the spirit of the moment with his eloquent oratory
as the demonstrators prepared for the long march from
Selma to Montgomery, which would end on March 25.[128]
Charles E. Fager describes how black spirituals like
"Joshua Fit the Battle of Jericho" and "Ain't Gonna
Let Nobody Turn Me Round" constantly filled the atmosphere at Brown Chapel, drawing civil rights activists
together around a common philosophy, experience,
and mission. On one occasion, writes Fager, "the worn
brown benches were packed with people clapping and
swaying to the music, which grew louder and more enthusiastic as the crowd grew steadily larger."[129] This
spirit helped make possible the Voting Rights Act in August, 1965, a piece of legislation that guaranteed black
Americans the right to vote under the protection of the
federal government.

After the victory at Selma, King sought to muster the
full resources of black churches and black ministers in
the interest of economic justice and international peace.
The central questions for King at this point were: How
can the power and resources of black congregations
be used to help change an economic system that brutally
maims not only the masses of black people but also

127. Brown Chapel is mentioned repeatedly in the four major works
on the 1965 Selma campaign. See Robert M. Mikell, Selma (Huntsville,
Ala.: Publishers Enterprise, 1965), 1 ff.; David J. Garrow, Protest at Selma:
Martin Luther King, Jr. and the Voting Rights Act of 1965 (New Haven: Yale
University Press, 1978), 1 ff.; Sheyann Webb and Rachel West Nelson, as
told to Frank Sikora, Selma, Lord Selma: Girlhood Memories of the Civil
Rights Days (New York: William Morrow, 1980), 1 ff.; and Charles E. Fager,
Selma, 1965: The March that Changed the South (Boston: Beacon Press,
1985), 1 ff.
128. Bleiweiss, ed., Marching to Freedom, 134–37; and Watley, Roots
of Resistance, 79–90.
129. Fager, Selma, 1965, 8, 40, 116.

millions of other Americans of various racial and ethnic backgrounds? What role should the black church assume in the quest for international peace? The response of the black church to these concerns was not overwhelmingly positive. A small cadre of black ministers came together in support of King's proposed Poor People's Campaign in late 1967 and early 1968.[130] When King joined the Sanitation Workers' Strike in Memphis, Tennessee in March, 1968, a strike that pushed for better wages and union recognition, he was backed by more than a hundred ministers from the Community on the Move for Equality (C.O.M.E.), a local organization.[131] However, the black church in its national institutional form never mounted a strong offensive program to mobilize black communities against poverty. The same can be said of the black church in relation to the issue of international peace. King was deeply troubled by the fact that black congregations and their leadership lagged so far behind in their responsibility to teach their young people about the choice of conscientious objection as a logical Christian alternative to military involvement abroad.[132] The failures of the black church in meeting the enormous challenges of economic justice and international peace help explain why King continued to be critical of that institution even as his faith in its power and potential mounted.

## KING AND THE NATIONAL
## BAPTIST CONVENTION, U.S.A.

King's belief in the power and potential of the black church as a unifying force and a vehicle for social change

130. Fairclough, *To Redeem the Soul of America*, 333–83; and Vincent Harding, "The Land Beyond: Reflections on King's Speech," *Sojourners* (January 1983): 18–21.

131. Bleiweiss, ed., *Marching to Freedom*, 2–9; Fairclough, *To Redeem the Soul of America*, 357–83; and Joan T. Beifuss, *At the River I Stand: Memphis, the 1968 Strike, and Martin Luther King* (Memphis: B. and W. Books, 1985), 94–95, 101–6, 117–18, 124–27, 136–37, 193–96, and 276–80.

132. Harding, *The Land Beyond*, 20.

centered largely on the National Baptist Convention, U.S.A., Inc. Founded in 1880, this black church organization consisted of some five million members and more than twenty thousand preachers at the time of the Montgomery Bus Boycott. King, following in the tradition of his father and maternal grandfather, became affiliated with this convention and so did many of his associate ministers in S.C.L.C.[133] King's goal was to turn this powerful citadel of black Protestantism into a reform vehicle, a plan he discussed obsessively prior to the convention's 1957 meeting.[134] This goal was quite consistent with his belief that the black church should be the vanguard in the struggle to redeem and transform the society. However, implementing this goal would prove much more difficult than King initially imagined, mainly because it brought him into conflict with the convention's powerful, strong-willed, and autocratic president, the Reverend Joseph H. Jackson of Chicago, who had followed a more cautious and conservative course since assuming his position in 1953.[135]

King's relationship with Jackson dated back to the late 1930s and early 1940s. As a friend of Martin Luther King, Sr., Jackson often spent time with the King family while in Atlanta for speaking engagements or church

133. Branch, *Parting the Waters,* 228; Smith, *A History of Ebenezer Baptist Church,* 2–3; and J. H. Jackson, *A Story of Christian Activism: The History of the National Baptist Convention* (Nashville: Townsend Press, 1980), 281–82.

134. Branch, *Parting the Waters,* 228.

135. *Ibid.;* Garrow, *Bearing the Cross,* 165–66; David L. Lewis, *King: A Critical Biography* (New York: Praeger Publishers, 1970), 157–58, 333, 336, 358; and Charles H. King, "Quest and Conflict: The Untold Story of the Power Struggle Between King and Jackson," *Negro Digest* (May 1967), 6–9, 71–79. Unfortunately, King scholars have largely ignored the King-Jackson feud and how it affected the role of the black church in the civil rights movement. See Owen D. Pelt and Ralph Lee Smith, *The Story of the National Baptists* (New York: Vantage Press, 1960), 1 ff.; and James M. Washington, *Frustrated Fellowship: The Black Baptist Quest for Social Power* (Macon, Ga.: Mercer University Press, 1986), 187–207. The King-Jackson feud is given considerable attention in Leroy Fitts, *A History of Black Baptists* (Nashville: Broadman Press, 1985), 100–1, 103–5. Perhaps the most extensive and controversial account of this conflict is afforded in William D. Booth, *The Progressive Story: New Baptist Roots* (St. Paul, Minn.: Braun Press, 1981), 1–93.

conventions, and he was frequently a guest in the King home when he served as president of the National Baptist Convention. Young Martin knew and revered Jackson from the time he was a small boy. The two related to each other in a friendly and cooperative manner before and during the Montgomery Bus Boycott, an experience that led King to believe that S.C.L.C. could rely on the National Baptist Convention for moral, spiritual, and material support. In September, 1955, three months before the boycott began, King invited Jackson to preach at the Dexter Avenue Baptist Church, but Jackson kindly declined because of other commitments. In a letter to King, Jackson expressed regret for his unavailability, praised the civil rights leader for his great work at Dexter Church, and called upon King and Dexter Church to join him in building a strong National Baptist Convention for future generations.[136]

Although Jackson and the National Baptist Convention had no direct involvement in the Montgomery Bus Boycott, they did support it morally and financially. "We looked with appreciation on the work of Dr. Martin Luther King, Jr. who served as president of the Montgomery Improvement Association," Jackson later wrote. He continued: "I encouraged the work of this Association and—along with other members of the National Baptist Convention—sought to give as much help as possible without seeking the spotlight or trying to take any of the credit for what the leaders in Montgomery were doing."[137] In a conference with other influential figures in the convention, Jackson initially decided to buy a bus to assist the boycott in Montgomery, but, on the advice of King, changed his mind and simply made a financial contribution. On February 14, 1956, Jackson sent letters to practically all of the state leaders in

136. A letter from Joseph H. Jackson to Martin Luther King, Jr., 28 September 1955, The King Papers, Boston University; and Branch, *Parting the Waters*, 55–56 and 101–2.
137. Jackson, *A Story of Christian Activism*, 281–84. Taylor Branch's claim that J. H. Jackson never "openly endorsed the boycott" is erroneous. See Branch, *Parting the Waters*, 195–96.

the National Baptist Convention, urging them to support the activities in Montgomery. When King and other ministers in the Montgomery Improvement Association were arrested, Jackson sent a telegram to Alabama's governor James Folsom, calling for their release, for a peaceful and just resolution of the bus dispute, and for efforts "to continue the growth of goodwill among the people of both races within your state."[138] When the National Baptist Convention met in Denver in September, 1956, Jackson presented the bus boycott idea to the delegates. In December, 1956, he delivered a rousing sermon at the first anniversary of the Montgomery movement. He later led the convention in "a bombed church drive" to rebuild black churches that had been bombed in Montgomery. Deeply appreciative for these gestures, the black ministers in that city drafted a statement declaring that "the National Baptist Convention and its President, Dr. J. H. Jackson, have been with us all the way."[139]

The selection of Martin Luther King, Jr., as the featured speaker at the National Baptist Convention's annual meeting in Denver, Colorado in 1956 further convinced the civil rights leader of the possibility of a close alliance between that body and the developing movement for civil rights. Charles H. King graphically describes how, on that occasion, "a beaming president led a shy young man down the aisles to the strains of *Onward Christian Soldiers*":

> It was in inspiring sight. President Jackson introduced young King to the Convention in glowing terms. King was at the peak of his popularity, and captivated the audience. His brilliant address on that occasion, "Letter to America," was masterfully delivered. His father, Martin Luther King, Sr., strode with pride at the back of the auditorium as he listened. His pride in his son would not allow him to sit down. He glanced

138. Jackson, *A Story of Christian Activism*, 281–85.
139. *Ibid.*

around at the delegates to see the effect his boy had upon them. What he saw there was the same thing that Joseph Harrison Jackson saw—a possible black Moses. The crowd did not want to let the young man go. From that moment, Negro Baptists had an idol. Martin Luther King had added the National Baptist Convention, U.S.A., Inc., as another of his conquests. Critics of Jackson point to this as the moment Jackson made his decision to remain at the helm of the Negro Baptists.[140]

The convention's reaction to King's speech was viewed by some as an indication of the possible threat he posed to Jackson's popularity and leadership. "In Denver, after listening to King," declared the Reverend Joseph Kirkland of Philadelphia, "Jackson felt his power slipping from his grasp."[141] The impact of King at the 1956 convention was sufficient enough to increase what was already "a ground-swell toward new leadership" among progressive ministers who discredited Jackson's leadership "as being weak on civil rights and strong on dictatorship." In a letter to King, written just two months after the 1956 convention, the Reverend Gil B. Lloyd of the Mount Zion Baptist Church in Seattle, Washington requested "permission to form a committee to sponsor your name for the presidency of the National Baptist Convention, U.S.A., Inc." The letter continued:

> As we stand at the threshold of momentous decision on Christian integration, while taking the long-range view of the future of our Negro Baptist ranks, *we must have a new leadership* which embodies religious zeal with scholarship, group loyalty with clear thinking, and administration with integrity. Across the nation, your embodiment of these virtues is a *fait accompli*. Under your leadership, our national body could develop a much-needed program of dynamic evangelism, education, missions, social action and finance. As I see it, without

140. King, "Quest and Conflict," 71–72; and Jackson, *A Story of Christian Activism*, 316. During his appearance before the 1956 National Baptist Convention meeting, King congratulated Jackson for his support of the Montgomery Bus Boycott. See Fitts, *A History of Black Baptists*, 100.
141. King, "Quest and Conflict," 71–72.

such a development at this particular insightful point of
Negro and Baptist history in this country, our Baptist
churches will miss their greatest opportunity since Reconstruction to enrich and broaden and stabilize the
future.[142]

Noting that "I have longed for a Baptist messiah like you
since 1932," the Reverend Lloyd suggested forming a
committee of 25 to 50 across the country to actively work
for King's nomination and election.[143] The plan appeared
logical and well timed, especially since Jackson had
promised to step down at the 1957 convention, and given
King's plan to use the convention as a reform vehicle.[144]
But the Reverend Lloyd's suggestions came at a moment
when King was still strongly devoted to the southern
black church and particularly to the black struggle in
Montgomery. King's reply to the Reverend Lloyd's letter
is revealing:

> After thinking over the proposition you have suggested,
> I have concluded that I have an obligation to continue
> to devote my undivided attention to the situation here
> in Montgomery. I feel that the confidence that the peo-
> ple have in me and their readiness to follow my leader-
> ship have thrust upon me a responsibility that I must
> follow through with. I do hope that you understand that
> I am deeply appreciative of your interest in me and in
> the situation here.[145]

The progressives' clamor for King as a possible president of the National Baptist Convention did not go unnoticed by Joseph H. Jackson and his supporters. This
effort contributed to a mild tension between King and
Jackson that had been developing since King's celebrated address at the 1956 Denver convention, an

142. *Ibid.*, 72; and a letter from the Rev. Gil Burton Lloyd to Martin
Luther King, Jr., 28 November 1956, The King Papers, Boston University.
143. A letter from the Rev. Gil Burton Lloyd to Martin Luther King,
Jr., 28 November 1956.
144. Branch, *Parting the Waters*, 228; and King, "Quest and Conflict,"
9–10, 71–79.
145. A letter from Martin Luther King, Jr., to the Rev. Gil Burton
Lloyd, 7 January 1957, The King Papers, Boston University.

address that attacked "gradualism" in the civil rights movement.[146] Despite this growing tension, King tried to maintain a friendly and cooperative relationship with Jackson. In the period between 1956 and 1958, the two men continued to communicate on friendly but distant terms. In December, 1957, King asked Jackson to serve on the National Advisory Committee of the newly formed S.C.L.C., noting that "your name will lend prestige in helping us carry out the objectives of the *Crusade for Citizenship*," a campaign that sought to increase black voters in the South.[147] If Jackson consented to King's request, he was certainly not an active member of S.C.L.C.'s National Advisory Committee, for the evidence available does not point in this direction.[148] However, Jackson did express support for S.C.L.C. when it was first organized, and he boasted that many of the ministers who planned this organization served on the Board of Directors of the National Baptist Convention. Moreover, Jackson publicly acknowledged the experience, the insight, and the high level of dedication King brought to S.C.L.C. as its first president.[149] When King suggested that Ralph D. Abernathy, an associate in S.C.L.C., be appointed to the Social Action Committee of the National Baptist Convention, Jackson declined on the grounds that a tentative agreement had been made with another appointee, but he assured King that "If this does not materialize, I shall be happy to consider the name suggested by you."[150] King had no idea at this time that he and Jackson would become involved in a

146. King, "Quest and Conflict," 72, 74; and Fitts, *A History of Black Baptists*, 100–1.
147. A letter from Martin Luther King, Jr., to Dr. Joseph H. Jackson, 17 December 1957, The King Papers, Boston University.
148. Interestingly enough, King did not mention Jackson in this connection in his *Stride toward Freedom* (1958), which appeared in published form a year after King made this request of Jackson. Taylor Branch makes a passing reference to King's letter to Jackson concerning the *Crusade for Citizenship*, but he offers no clear indication of how Jackson responded. See Branch, *Parting the Waters*, 230–31.
149. Jackson, *A Story of Christian Activism*, 285–86.
150. A letter from Dr. Joseph H. Jackson to Martin Luther King, Jr., 22 August 1958, The King Papers, Boston University.

feud that would challenge the very structure of the conventional black church and its leadership, divide millions of black church persons, and pose a threat to the success of the civil rights struggle.[151]

In 1957, at the annual meeting of the Sunday School and Baptist Training Union Congress of the National Baptist Convention, King's name was offered in nomination for the vice presidency of that body. His popularity was such that all candidates for that position withdrew in his favor.[152] "It was apparent to all," wrote Charles H. King, "that King was being groomed to take over the Convention." As time passed, progressive ministers in the convention increasingly pitted King against Jackson. Many who supported King "were bitter, fading ministers who feared that Jackson would destroy their own ambitions for leadership. The young supporters of King began a campaign against Jackson on the charge that he was like 'Uncle Tom.'"[153] On the other side were Jacksonian conservatives, some of whom insisted that King was too much involved in civil rights issues "to enter factional denominational considerations." As an internationally known figure, they argued, King "was diminishing his standing by playing the part of a 'conventional' churchman." They further contended that King did not "need the Convention; nor did the Convention need him."[154]

Relations between King and Jackson grew worse after 1958. Two concerns separated the Jacksonian conservative members from the progressive members who supported King. One was Jackson's "strange position" on civil rights, and the other was his refusal to relinquish his office even in violation of the tenure provision in the Constitution of the National Baptist Convention. The first concern struck at the heart of King's plan to bring the full resources of the black church into the civil rights movement. In both a theoretical and practical sense,

151. King, "Quest and Conflict," 6–8, 72–79.
152. *Ibid.*, 72.
153. *Ibid.*
154. *Ibid.*

Jackson came down on the side of Booker T. Washington, stressing the agricultural and mechanical arts as a pre-requisite to economic independence, and flatly rejecting King's nonviolent direct action campaigns.[155] This has led some to suggest that "The King-Jackson feud was, in spirit, a replay of the Booker T. Washington–William E. B. DuBois conflict."[156] In any case, Jackson urged the National Baptist Convention to buy farmland and to aid black farmers in gaining independence from whites, a proposal that, coming at any other time in history, might have been unanimously approved.[157] In opposing King, Jackson claimed that the role of a preacher involved spreading the Gospel to the flock, saving souls for Jesus, and effecting change by exemplary conduct. He dis-missed nonviolent direct action campaigns as premedi-tated actions designed to cause social disruption, and charged that King was using this technique to gain con-trol of the National Baptist Convention.[158] This suggests that the problem between the two men had as much to do with power as with ideological differences. For the most part, King quietly ignored the attacks of Jackson on his personality, philosophy, and methods, mainly because of his feeling that a constant public airing of differences would reflect badly on the black church and its role in the movement. Furthermore, King knew that the media

155. *Ibid.*, 73; Lewis, *King*, 336; Garrow, *Bearing the Cross*, 165–66; Branch, *Parting the Waters*, 195–96, 228, 505–7, 515, 848, 872; and Gayraud S. Wilmore, *Black Religion and Black Radicalism: An Interpre-tation of the Religious History of Afro-American People* (Maryknoll, N.Y.: Orbis Books, 1983), 233.

156. King, "Quest and Conflict," 7; and Wilmore, *Black Religion and Black Radicalism*, 233.

157. King, "Quest and Conflict," 73.

158. Lewis, *King*, 158, 336; and Jackson, *A Story of Christian Ac-tivism*, 428. Jackson went as far as to characterize King's nonviolent strategy as "not far removed from open crime." See Garrow, *Bearing the Cross*, 491. Contrary to what Jackson believed, King had no desire to take over the National Baptist Convention, to be president of that body, or to undermine the president's position. His concern for the National Baptist Convention was two-fold. First, he wanted that body to maintain its insti-tutional and constitutional integrity with regard to the tenure issue. Sec-ond, he wanted that body to be more in tune with the civil rights thrust of that time.

would exploit such differences, much as it did with his disagreements with Malcolm X, thus distracting attention from the real issues.[159]

The issue of tenure in office was a very emotional one for the National Baptists between 1957 and 1962, causing thousands of ministers to join either the pro-Jackson or anti-Jackson forces. King sided with the anti-Jackson forces during this period. According to Charles H. King, the tenure issue was closely related to the struggle for civil rights and with the whole history of the National Baptist Convention:

> The story of tenure in the National Baptist Convention, U.S.A., Inc., was, oddly enough, closely allied with the fight for civil rights. From the organization of the Convention in 1880, and for a period of 73 years, only 11 men had served as president. Of these 11, five had served one year, one had served two years, and one had served three years. The remaining 63 years found four men in strong control of the Negro Baptists: Rev. W. J. Simmons, 1886–1890; Rev. E. C. Morris, 1894–1921; Rev. L. K. Williams, 1923–1940; and Dr. D. V. Jemison, 1941–1953.[160]

Determined to "free themselves from one-man domination," many of the preachers of the National Baptist Convention had insisted that Joseph H. Jackson's term as president be limited to four years. A new article was included in the convention's constitution in 1952, a year before Jackson assumed leadership, stating that "A President of this Convention shall not be eligible for re-election after he has served four consecutive terms, or until at least one year has elapsed."[161] The Jacksonians' determination to abolish this constitutional provision became evident as early as the 1955 convention, "when a Jackson supporter stood on the floor to make a motion that this

---

159. King, "Quest and Conflict," 74; and James H. Cone, *Speaking the truth: Ecumenism, Liberation, and Black Theology* (Grand Rapids, Mich.: W. B. Eerdmans, 1986), 167.

160. King, "Quest and Conflict," 8.

161. *Ibid.*, 8–9; and Booth, *The Progressive Story*, 1–2.

revision of the constitution be declared 'null and void.'"[162] One anti-Jackson preacher, Dr. L. K. Jackson of Gary, Indiana, rose to condemn the administration for tampering with the constitution. The dispute continued at the 1956 convention, and a decision was made to put the issue to rest at the 1957 convention in Louisville, Kentucky, where Jackson was supposed to step down in favor of a successor. But King's popularity in the National Baptist Convention was such that Jackson developed second thoughts about his constitutional obligation.

The central question in Louisville was: "Would J. H. Jackson be eligible for re-election? Or, would another leader be chosen?" Again, the Jacksonians declared that the tenure provision was "null and void" because it had been voted on on the wrong day and in an illegal manner. They quoted Article XIV of the constitution to illustrate their point: "This constitution may be altered or amended at any annual session by a two-thirds vote of the members present, provided that such vote is taken without regard to total enrollment, and provided further that no amendment may be considered after the second day of the session. . . ."[163] The anti-Jackson forces held firmly to the view that the spirit of the constitution, and especially its tenure provision, was as the majority directed. Taylor Branch perceptively describes what eventually transpired at the 1957 convention:

> When the moment was ripe, a Jackson lieutenant sprang up, called for a suspension of the rules to keep him on as president, and led a great shout of acclamation. It was over more quickly than a Teamsters election. Afterward, Jackson moved steadily to consolidate power against active involvement in civil rights, growing more autocratic and more conservative. The preachers close to King, joking that Billy Graham was more likely to embrace the civil rights cause than was Jackson, drifted toward insurrection within their own church.[164]

162. King, "Quest and Conflict," 9.
163. *Ibid.*, 9–10, 71; and Branch, *Parting the Waters*, 228.
164. Branch, *Parting the Waters*, 228.

Disappointed over how the Jackson forces had destroyed tenure, the progressives also moved to consolidate their power. By 1959, they were pushing Gardner C. Taylor—friend of Martin Luther King, Jr., and pastor of the 10,000 member Concord Baptist Church, Brooklyn, New York—as a candidate for president of the National Baptist Convention. Like Joseph H. Jackson, Taylor was a gifted orator and a man of deep conviction. Unlike Jackson, he was a strong supporter of King and the civil rights movement. The "draft Taylor" movement was in full swing when the convention met in Philadelphia in September, 1960. Taylor was in control of large voting blocs in the East, whereas Jackson remained strong in the South and midwest. The first step involved establishing the ground rules for the election. The electoral procedure used up to that point was as follows: "After the president would make his annual address, a vice president would make a motion that the rules be suspended and the president would be re-elected by acclamation."[165] King and other Taylorites dismissed this procedure as unfair, undemocratic, and marked with steamroller tactics. They insisted that ballots be cast by all delegates, and that votes be recorded as they voted by states, a procedure to which the Jacksonians consented.

But contrary to the supposed agreement calling for the dual submission of names by the nominating committee, the Taylorites were caught unprepared when the committee reported only the name of Joseph H. Jackson. Acting quickly, and without asking for nominations from the floor, the committee moved that its report "be adopted with a unanimous vote for the re-election of Jackson." Outmaneuvered and betrayed, the Taylorites refused to leave the convention hall when Jackson's vice president rapped the meeting into adjournment. They insisted on having an orderly election despite the absence of Jackson

---

165. King, "Quest and Conflict," 74–75; Booth, *The Progressive Story*, 21–30; and Jackson, *A Story of Christian Activism*, 484.

and most of his followers—an election that resulted in
1,864 votes for Taylor and 536 votes for Jackson. On that
note, Martin Luther King, Jr., rose and moved that the
Taylorite slate of National Baptist Convention officers be
elected.[166]

The year 1960 found both Taylor and Jackson claiming
the presidency of the National Baptist Convention. Both
sides refused to yield. Events came to a head at the convention in Kansas City in September, 1961, when the
Taylorites sought to settle the dispute through the courts.
Although King refused to become openly involved in the
court battle, he was thoroughly pleased when a court-
supervised election was ordered. To his regret, however,
King discovered later that Joseph H. Jackson had won by
a vote of 2,732 to 1,519.[167] The election set off a shouting
and shoving match between the Jacksonians and the
Taylorites, during which the Reverend Arthur G. Wright
fell and later died of his injuries. Finally triumphant over
the Taylorites, Jackson and his supporters made several
moves against King that many regarded as vengeful.
First, they removed King from the vice presidency of the
Sunday School and Baptist Training Union Congress, although he had been unanimously elected in St. Louis.
The Reverend E. C. Estell was promptly appointed to
replace King.[168] Second, Jackson accused King of master-
minding the invasion of the convention floor, which
led to the Reverend Wright's death, a blatantly false

166. King, "Quest and Conflict," 75–77; and Branch, *Parting the
Waters*, 337–38.
167. King, "Quest and Conflict," 77–78; Booth, *The Progressive Story*,
40; Garrow, *Bearing the Cross*, 166; and Branch, *Parting the Waters*,
500–2, 505.
168. Lewis, *King*, 158; Branch, *Parting the Waters*, 504–7; Garrow,
*Bearing the Cross*, 166; King, "Quest and Conflict," 72; Fitts, *A History of
Black Baptists*, 101–5; a letter from William J. Bishop to Martin Luther
King, Jr., 17 September 1961, The King Papers, Boston University; and a
letter from Martin Luther King, Jr., to the Rev. Charles W. Butler, 20
September 1961, The King Papers, Boston University. Jackson claimed
that King was not removed from the vice presidency of the Congress of
Christian Education because of fear or jealousy of his international fame
and influence, a point that is highly suspect. See Jackson, *A Story of
Christian Activism*, 483–86; and Booth, *The Progressive Story*, 42–43.

charge.[169] These actions opened a new chapter in the dispute between the Jacksonian conservatives and the progressives.

Jackson's efforts to implicate King in the fracas that resulted in the Reverend Wright's death triggered a huge uproar in the black church community and posed a serious threat to the freedom movement in the South.[170] Reactions to Jackson's accusation were swift and stern. One laywoman wrote him a long letter advising that it would be better and wiser for him to retract this statement. A letter from one of the convention's preachers characterized Jackson's charge against King as "defamatory," and expressed hope that "Dr. Jackson will speedily retract his unfounded statement and thereby demonstrate to our nation that a climate of jealousy and bitterness does not permeate the area of leadership in the National Baptist Convention of America, Inc."[171] Perhaps the strongest statement was issued by more than thirty black Baptist preachers, denouncing Jackson's actions as "vicious and un-Christian" and urging that he "immediately and publicly" refute the charges he made against King. Some of the most active and powerful ministers in the National Baptist Convention and in the civil rights movement

169. Lewis, *King*, 158; Booth, *The Progressive Story*, 40–42; Garrow, *Bearing the Cross*, 166; and Branch, *Parting the Waters*, 504–7. In his massive work on National Baptist History, Joseph H. Jackson seems to suggest that the Taylorites created the climate that led to the Wright tragedy. Interestingly enough, Jackson does not mention Martin Luther King, Jr., in connection with the tragedy. This story appeared in many major newspapers, such as *The New York Times*, *The New York Amsterdam News*, and *The Los Angeles Eagle*. The story also made the headlines in many southern newspapers, a development that upset Dr. King. See a letter from Martin Luther King, Jr., to the Rev. Charles W. Butler, 20 September 1961; a letter from Martin Luther King, Jr., to the Rev. Marvin T. Robinson, 3 October 1961, The King Papers, Boston University; and Jackson, *A Story of Christian Activism*, 458, 489.

170. Garrow, *Bearing the Cross*, 166; a telegram from Martin Luther King, Jr., to Dr. Joseph H. Jackson, 10 September 1961, The King Papers, Boston University; and a letter from Martin Luther King, Jr., to the Rev. Charles W. Butler, September 20, 1961.

171. A letter from Erma J. Hughes to Dr. Joseph H. Jackson, 16 September 1961, The King Papers, Boston University; and a letter from Richard A. Battles to Martin Luther King, Jr., 12 September 1961, The King Papers, Boston University.

attached their names to this statement, among them Ralph D. Abernathy, William Holmes Borders, Benjamin E. Mays, Sandy Ray, Fred L. Shuttlesworth, Kelly Miller Smith, and Gardner C. Taylor.[172]

In a telegram to Jackson, King dismissed the charges against him as "unwarranted, untrue, unethical," and "libelous to the core," and demanded that Jackson, in the spirit of Christianity, "retract this statement immediately and urge the press to give as much attention to the retraction as it gave to the original accusation." King further noted that he had had nothing to do with mapping the Taylorite strategy, and that he was not even in the auditorium when the Reverend Wright was injured.[173] Although Jackson insisted that he had been misunderstood and misquoted by the press, he never gave the public retraction that King demanded. Many of King's friends urged him to sue Jackson, a suggestion King promptly rejected as inconsistent with his "basic philosophy."[174] It was this mounting tension between the Jacksonians and those who supported King and the progressive agenda that led to a split within the National Baptist Convention in 1961.[175]

172. This group of ministers warned Jackson that "If this character-assassination is not righted, it will be a disservice to the Baptists, to the Christian family, to the Negro community in America, and to God." See a news release from the Southern Christian Leadership Conference, Atlanta, Ga., 12 September 1961, The King Papers, Boston University.

173. A telegram from Martin Luther King, Jr., to Dr. Joseph H. Jackson, 10 September 1961.

174. Lewis, *King*, 158; Booth, *The Progressive Story*, 40–41; a letter from Martin Luther King, Jr., to the Rev. Charles W. Butler, 20 September 1961; and Garrow, *Bearing the Cross*, 166. All of the reporters who were in the press conference insisted that Joseph H. Jackson did accuse King of master-minding the invasion of the convention floor that led to the Wright tragedy. See a letter from Martin Luther King, Jr., to the Rev. Marvin T. Robinson, October 3, 1961; and "Dr. Jackson Explains to Martin Luther King: Calls Self Victim of Press," *The New York Amsterdam News* (October 14, 1961); 1, 13. King accepted the Jackson attack as "another cross I will have to bear." See a letter from Martin Luther King, Jr., to Al Leon Lowry (September 21, 1961), The King Papers, Boston University.

175. Booth, *The Progressive Story*, 31–92; Garrow, *Bearing the Cross*, 165–66; and Branch, *Parting the Waters*, 228, 335–39, 505–7, 848.

On November 14, 1961, a group of reform-minded and anti-Jackson people, under the leadership of the Reverend L. Venchael Booth, met and organized the Progressive National Baptist Convention, Inc. at the Zion Baptist Church in Cincinnati, Ohio. This group represented fourteen states. The new body adopted tenure in its constitution, and vowed to fully support "the Negro fight for first-class citizenship." King's philosophy and methods were enthusiastically endorsed.[176] Supporting this development was not an easy decision for King, especially considering his strong belief in the need for black church unity as a precondition for black liberation. Reports that he was expelled from the National Baptist Convention along with other ministers who opposed Joseph H. Jackson's "policy of gradualism" and supported Gardner C. Taylor's election bid would seem to suggest that he had no choice but to support the formation of the Progressive National Baptist Convention.[177] King supported that body because it provided him with the strong support base and the reform vehicle he had long struggled to establish among black Baptists. His decision to do so caused many Jackson supporters to cease their active involvement in S.C.L.C.[178]

176. Booth, *The Progressive Story*, 80–82.
177. Fitts, *A History of Black Baptists*, 103–4. The nature and extent of King's role in the founding of the Progressive National Baptist Convention has been the subject of much debate. William R. Miller claims that King was a founder of this convention. Edward L. Wheeler notes that King, in the interest of black church unity, actually opposed L. Venchael Booth's call for a new convention. David L. Lewis contends that King actively supported the organization. It is more correct to say that King, while siding with the progressives, had no active role in the organization of the Progressive National Baptist Convention. Its founders, for the most part, were his followers. See William R. Miller, *Martin Luther King, Jr.: His Life, Martyrdom and Meaning for the World* (New York: Weybright and Talley, Inc., 1968), 138; Booth, *The Progressive Story*, 70, 80; Edward L. Wheeler, "Beyond One Man: A General Survey of Black Baptist Church History," *Review and Expositor: The Black Experience and the Church*, vol. 70, no. 3 (Summer 1973), 317; Lewis, *King*, 157–58; "25 Years: A Journey of Faith," *Baptist Progress* (September–November 1986): 3; and Washington, ed., *A Testament of Hope*, xvii.
178. Booth, *The Progressive Story*, 80–82; and Garrow, *Bearing the Cross*, 166.

In the meantime, King's and Jackson's different philosophies and methods remained a barrier to the full involvement of the black church in the civil rights struggle. In 1960 to 1961, Jackson publicly denounced the student sit-ins in which King was involved, arguing that "some Negroes talk too much about racial integration and not enough about racial elevation."[179] In 1962, Jackson criticized black preachers who journeyed South to support King in Albany, Georgia, suggesting that "It is hypocrisy for a delegation to leave Chicago and go to Albany to fight segregation." While his reasoning was correct in this instance, his motives were questionable.[180] In 1963, he attacked the March on Washington, highlighted by King's "I Have a Dream" speech, as "a dangerous unwarranted protest."[181]

One of the most interesting and unfortunate confrontations between King and Jackson occurred in 1966 in Chicago, where Jackson lived and pastored the Olivet Baptist Church. When King arrived in Chicago in January, 1966, to mobilize slum tenants into an army of peaceful demonstrators, Jackson joined Mayor Richard J. Daley in denouncing him as an "outsider." When King assumed "trusteeship" of one of Chicago's slum tenements, stating that he would collect rents and use the money to clean and renovate the building, Jackson increased his attack. He scoffed at the fact that King

179. Garrow, *Bearing the Cross*, 165–66; and Branch, *Parting the Waters*, 373.

180. Lewis, *King*, 158; and Paul Twine, "A Response to Remarks by Dr. J. H. Jackson," Chicago, Ill., (The King Papers, Boston University, n.d. circa 1962), 1–2. Dr. William G. Anderson, a friend of King and president of the Albany Movement, casually dismissed Jackson's point, and noted: "He's a Mississippi boy who's been away so long that he has no idea what the Negro in the Deep South is up against." See "News from the Albany Movement," released through the Public Relations Department of the Albany Movement, Albany, Ga. (1962), The King Papers, Boston University, 1. By the time of the Albany Movement, King was referring, in letters to black friends and fellow ministers, to "the conniving methods of J. H. Jackson and the shortsightedness of the National Baptist Convention." See a letter from Martin Luther King, Jr. to Dr. Gardner C. Taylor, 25 January 1962, The King Papers, Boston University.

181. Branch, *Parting the Waters*, 848.

and his aides appropriated the property of an elderly white man, refused to pay rent, and then declared these actions "supralegal."[182] When King called for a mass rally at Chicago's Soldier Field to protest slums, Jackson responded by urging blacks to stay at home. *The Chicago Tribune* gave extensive and exaggerated coverage to these attacks. Jackson's denunciation of the rally helps explain why less than half of the expected 100,000 persons attended.[183] The influence of Jackson also accounted, to some extent, for the failure of local black churches and ministers to wholeheartedly support King and the Chicago movement, a factor that undoubtedly contributed to its failure.[184] Jackson insisted that black Chicagoans needed no help from King because they already had genuine friends like Mayor Daley. Angered by such attacks, King broke his silence and declared that "I don't think Dr. Jackson speaks for one percent of the Negroes in this country."[185] King's point was probably more accurate than he realized, particularly when one considers the findings of a *Chicago Defender* survey in late 1966, which claimed that Chicago's blacks preferred him over Jackson by a margin of 21.5 to 1.[186]

The rift between King and Jackson was never healed and will always remain a sad chapter in the history of the black church and the civil rights movement. The most unfortunate part of the story is that the two men failed to achieve the solidarity needed to make the National Baptist Convention an effective moral and political force in the black struggle of the 1950s and 1960s.[187] The media, power-seeking and vengeful black preachers, and others with dishonorable motives, who pitted King and Jackson

182. Jackson, *A Story of Christian Activism*, 424; Watley, *Roots of Resistance*, 94–95; and Lewis, *King*, 333.
183. Lewis, *King*, 333; and Watley, *Roots of Resistance*, 96.
184. King scholars have written considerably on King's failures in Chicago but have tended to ignore Jackson's role as a possible factor. For example, see Watley, *Roots of Resistance*, 99–100.
185. Quoted in Garrow, *Bearing the Cross*, 491.
186. Lewis, *King*, 358.
187. Washington, *Frustrated Fellowship*, 206–7.

against each other, must share some of the blame for what happened.[188]

## ON THE FUTURE
## OF THE BLACK CHURCH

The problems Martin Luther King, Jr., encountered in the National Baptist Convention did not destroy his faith in the power and potential of the black church as a reform vehicle. His keen sense of the rich and vital aspects of the black religious heritage led him to believe that the black church would continue to be a flexible and adaptable instrument of black liberation and survival. King held that his people's struggle for freedom and human dignity had had no past without the black church, and that without it that struggle would have no enduring and promising future:

> The role of the Negro church in the present struggle of the Negro for full citizenship is a unique sociological phenomenon peculiar to the Negro community in the South. It should be mentioned that its present role is also its past and future role. The record will indicate that the civil rights interest and thrust of the Negro community has directly paralleled the development and leadership offered by the Negro church in every community without exception. This is understandably so, when you consider the social structure of the Negro community in the South.[189]

For King, the power and potential of the black church as a liberating and transforming force stemmed primarily from the fact that it is the only institution in America where black people can function with a high degree of freedom and autonomy. He characterized the black church as the "only forum owned, operated and controlled" by black people, as the vehicle that "affords the

188. Lewis, *King*, 333; Branch, *Parting the Waters*, 506–7, 872; and King, "Quest and Conflict," 72.
189. A letter from Martin Luther King, Jr., to the Rev. Jerry M. Chance, 9 May 1961, The King Papers, Boston University.

broadest opportunity for social intercourse," and as "the headquarters of the Negro's struggle for full citizenship."[190] King believed that if the black church misused its freedom and autonomy by failing to be the vanguard in the struggle for peace, justice, and community, then it would crumble from within and rob itself of a significant place in the annals of human history.[191]

In King's opinion, certain adjustments had to be made to ensure the black church's continued existence as the arena out of which all issues relating to black liberation and survival could be addressed. One of those adjustments had to do with the cultivation of responsible and charismatic leadership. King's experiences in the black church, and particularly in the National Baptist Convention, convinced him that that institution had too many narrow-minded, power-hungry, and self-serving persons in leadership and decision-making positions.[192] He pointed out that black preachers, as the freest and most independent persons in the community, were most untrue to their calling when they put their own needs and desires beyond those of the masses. The black church would achieve its greatest success as an agent of change, he believed, only when more of its leaders chose to practice, in the manner of the servant as exemplified by Jesus Christ, sacrificial forms of ministry.[193]

King also believed that the support of the masses would be necessary to guarantee the black church's survival as a nurturing and liberating institution. Toward the end of his life, he observed with frustration and

190. *Ibid.*
191. King, "The Un-Christian Christian," 80; and King, *Why We Can't Wait,* 67.
192. Martin Luther King, Jr., "Answer to a Perplexing Question," a sermon delivered at Ebenezer Baptist Church, Atlanta, Ga., (The King Center Archives, 3 March 1963), 7–8; a letter from Martin Luther King, Jr., to Rev. Marvin T. Robinson, 3 October 1961; and Fairclough, *To Redeem the Soul of America,* 119, 428 n. 26.
193. King, *Why We Can't Wait,* 65–68; King, "Answer to a Perplexing Question," 7–8; Washington, ed., *A Testament of Hope,* 41–42; and Fairclough, *To Redeem the Soul of America,* 119.

disappointment the increasing number of black people who were abandoning the church:

> I'm disturbed about the Negro. The more we start building houses, the less we see the church. The more we accumulate big bank accounts, the less we find in the pew. The more our long cars begin to deck out the highways of cities and the highways of the globe, the less we're seen around the church. I'm disturbed about the Negro. It was God that brought us over, and its God that's gonna take us through.[194]

The slave forebears were for King compelling examples of how today's black people might remain firmly rooted in religion and the church:

> There was a time that in the life of any Negro, religion had a place. Go back to the dark days of slavery. Our mothers and fathers knew that it was God that would bring them over. . . . Our mothers and fathers were able to get over the dark days of slavery and the dark days of segregation because religion gave them something within. . . . It was the only way that they were able to live with that system.[195]

The black slave's capacity to transcend the bitterness and ironies of his circumstance through song was, in King's view, both a lesson and an inspiration for blacks as they dealt with more contemporary forms of oppression:

> He would sing sometimes, when he thought about the fact that he had to go out in the fields and work with no shoes. He thought about the fact that he had to face the sizzling heat and the rawhide whip of the overseer, and the long rows of cotton, in his bare feet. But he also thought about the fact that one day he would have some shoes, and he could sing, "I got shoes, You got shoes, All God's chillun got shoes." "When I get to heaven gonna put on my shoes and start a-walkin' all

194. Martin Luther King, Jr., "Discerning the Signs of History," a sermon delivered at Ebenezer Baptist Church, Atlanta, Ga., (The King Center Archives, 15 November 1964), 4–5.
195. *Ibid.*

over God's heaven." It was religion that helped him sing like that.[196]

Apparently, King deemed it necessary for the black church of the present and the future to continue to hold spiritual values in high regard. The spiritual values of the black heritage—revealed most poignantly in preaching, prayer, testimony, and song—were for him the best possible source for keeping alive in his people a spirit of hope and struggle. In order to experience the fullness of freedom, black Americans, King thought, should also learn to hold in proper balance the spiritual and the intellectual, to couple deep intuition and feeling with the use of mind.[197]

There is much to be gained from the example that King himself left the black church. By forging a vital unity between intellectual concerns, spirituality, and social transformation, King gave new vitality and relevance to the black church during one of the most critical periods in national and world history.[198] The real power and genius of his campaigns, from Montgomery to Memphis, were evident in his ability to combine a simple but profound philosophy with the old-fashioned religiosity of the southern black church, thereby rekindling a passion for social justice that was already deeply rooted in the souls and in the history of the folk.[199]

In a real sense, the benefit of that legacy is not confined to the black church. As C. Eric Lincoln profoundly states, King challenged all Christians with a fresh vision of social responsibility—a vision the church must take

196. *Ibid.*
197. Lewis V. Baldwin, "Prayer and Testimony: The Spirituality of Martin Luther King, Jr.," *National Baptist Union Review*, 93, no. 2 (January 1989): 7.
198. Wilmore, *Black Religion and Black Radicalism*, 174. King's reference to the movement as "the Christian social struggle in which I am engaged" suggests a close connection between spirituality and social transformation in his perspective. See a letter from Martin Luther King, Jr., to Chaplain Vernon P. Bodein, 3 September 1960, The King Papers, Boston University.
199. Wilmore, *Black Religion and Black Radicalism*, 177; and Baldwin, "'Let Us Break Bread Together,'" 28.

seriously in order to be a vital force in the creation of a brighter future for humanity:

> The late Dr. Martin Luther King, Jr. did more than anyone in modern times to exemplify the spirit of Christianity and this tremendous benefit was to all of Christendom, not just the black church. Christianity itself was against the wall and King's moral leadership and eventual martyrdom did more to re-establish credibility and interest in the faith than all of the councils and pronouncements of the last hundred years. The late Dr. King demonstrated that being is more substantial than words, and doing is more convincing than good intentions.[200]

200. C. Eric Lincoln, "The Black Church and a Decade of Change," Part II, *Tuesday at Home* (March 1976); 7.

# UP, YOU MIGHTY RACE!
## THE BLACK MESSIANIC HOPE

4

> It is my solemn belief, that if ever the world becomes Christianized, (which must certainly take place before long) it will be through the means, under God of the *Blacks*, who are now held in wretchedness, and degradation, by the white Christians of the world. . . .
>
> David Walker, 1829[1]

> Up, you mighty race. You can accomplish what you will!
>
> Marcus Garvey, 1919[2]

> This may be the most significant fact in the world today—that God has entrusted his black children in America to teach the world to love, and to live together in brotherhood.
>
> Martin Luther King, Jr., 1964[3]

> We have lost our fear of our brothers and are no longer ashamed of ourselves, of who and what we are. . . . Let us now go forth to save the land of our birth from the plague that first drove us into the "will to quarantine" and to separate ourselves behind self-imposed walls. For this is why we were born. . . .
>
> Howard Thurman, 1971[4]

1. Charles M. Wiltse, ed., *David Walker's Appeal, in Four Articles, Together with a Preamble, to the Coloured Citizens of the World, But in Particular, and Very Expressly, to Those of the United States of America* (New York: Hill & Wang, 1965; originally published in 1829), 18.

2. Quoted in John H. Bracey, et al., eds., *Black Nationalism in America* (New York: Bobbs-Merrill, 1970), 187–91.

3. Martin Luther King, Jr., "Statement to the Press Regarding Nobel Trip," Sheraton-Atlantic Hotel, Atlantic City, N. J. (The Archives of the Martin Luther King, Jr., Center for Nonviolent Social Change, Inc., Atlanta, Ga., 4 December 1964), 1.

4. Howard Thurman, *The Search for Common Ground: An Inquiry into the Basis of Man's Experience of Community* (Richmond, Ind: Friends United Press, 1986), 104.

On January 10, 1958, a year after the successful Montgomery Bus Boycott, Martin Luther King, Jr., received a
letter from a black woman that stated in part:

> Rev. King, I do consider myself a Christian, and I do
> believe in God, but this is what I want to know: Why is
> it that God has let Negroes suffer so? Why from the
> beginning of time has He let us be dominated by other
> races? Why was it us that had to be in slavery? We have
> been taught from very early ages that God loves *every-
> body,* but as I take inventory of the Races, I can see
> something strange. Please think about this and help
> me find the answer.[5]

Although King's response to this letter is not known, it
is clear that he, too, like this woman, confronted the
central question of the meaning and significance of
the black experience in America. As he struggled with
this question, he dismissed the notion that black Americans, since slavery, had dreamed, struggled, bled, and
died in vain. Instead, King interpreted the suffering,
humiliation, and death experienced by his people under
oppression in light of some great divine purpose, an
interpretation that led him to propound a concept of
black messianism. Black Americans, he held, had a special redemptive role to play in American history and in
world civilization. King espoused this concept so consistently that it should be accounted a fundamental
component of his thought.[6] Studying King from this

5. A letter from Karolyn L. Trimble, to Martin Luther King, Jr., 10,
January 1958, The King Papers, Boston University, Boston, Mass.
6. Martin Luther King, Jr., *Stride toward Freedom: The Montgomery Story* (New York: Harper & Brothers, 1958), 224; Martin Luther
King, Jr., "A Proposed Statement to the South," presented at the Southern Negro Leaders Conference on Transportation and Nonviolent Integration, Atlanta, Ga. (The King Papers, Boston University, 10–11 January
1957), 3; Martin Luther King, Jr., "A Statement on the Black Mission"
(The King Center Archives, 17 April 1959), 1 ff.; Martin Luther King, Jr.,
"The Negro and the American Dream," a speech delivered at an NAACP
Public Meeting, Charlotte, N. C. (The King Papers, Boston University, 25
September 1960), 3; Martin Luther King, Jr., "Speech at a Rally," Savan-
nah, Ga. (The King Papers, Boston University, 1 January 1961), 5, 7, 9, 17;
Martin Luther King, Jr., "The Sword that Heals," *The Critic* (June–July
1964); 14; Martin Luther King, Jr., "Interview on World Peace," *Red Book*

angle can help us understand more fully his relationship to the black experience and black culture. This chapter analyzes King's view of the meaning and significance of the black odyssey in America. His views concerning the history, mission, and destiny of black Americans are examined against the background of similar views expressed by other black leaders and thinkers from the time of slavery to the present. The basic outline of this chapter is as follows: (1) King's black messianic vision; (2) King as a black messiah; (3) King and traditional black messianism; and (4) potential barriers to the fulfillment of King's black messianic hope.

## KING'S BLACK MESSIANIC VISION

King's struggle with the meaning of black history and the black experience began during his childhood. The experience of growing up in an atmosphere of pronounced racism made this struggle inevitable for him despite his early inability to understand it in logical and theoretical terms. While at Morehouse College and later at Crozer Theological Seminary and Boston University, King studied the writings of several thinkers and activists that led him to entertain this question of meaning on a deeper and more profound level. In Professor Walter Chivers' sociology classes at Morehouse College, he almost certainly read some of W. E. B. Du Bois' works, in which the messianic role of black Americans is a recurring theme. King's reading of Henry David Thoreau's "On The Duty of Civil Disobedience" (1848) during his Morehouse College years provided what would later be one of the central

---

*Magazine* (November 1964); 6–7; Martin Luther King, Jr., "The Negro Gains in Rights—1965," Atlanta, Ga. (The King Center Archives, November 10, 1965), 18–19; and Martin Luther King, Jr., "Address at a Mass Meeting," Laurel, Miss. (The King Center Archives, 19 March 1968), 4. King raised the question of *meaning* in a poignant way in his sermon, "The Death of Evil Upon the Seashore" but concluded that "I do not pretend to understand all the ways of God or his particular timetable for grappling with evil." See Martin Luther King, Jr., *Strength to Love* (Philadelphia: Fortress Press, 1981), 83.

ideas underlying his philosophy of black messianism—
the idea that history, in the final analysis, is saved by a
creative minority who resist an evil system with the goal
of improving it.[7] King found reinforcement for this idea
in the writings of the British historian Arnold J.
Toynbee, who concluded, in *A Study of History* (1947), that black
Americans had rediscovered "in Christianity certain original meanings and values" that rendered them capable of
bringing new vitality to Western civilization.[8]

It is also possible that King, during his studies at
Crozer Theological Seminary and Boston University, became quite familiar with Mohandas K. Gandhi's and
Reinhold Niebuhr's reflections on the meaning of the
black American experience. He almost certainly knew
of Gandhi's speculation that "it may be through the
Negroes that the unadulterated message of nonviolence
will be delivered to the world," a conclusion difficult
to avoid considering King's wide reading of the Indian
leader's works.[9] The same can be said of King with respect to Niebuhr's suggestion, stated as early as 1932,

7. See W. E. B. Du Bois, *The Conservation of Races* (Washington,
D.C.: American Negro Academy, 1897), 12; W. E. B. Du Bois, *The Negro*
(New York: Oxford University Press, 1970; originally published in 1915),
146; W. E. B. Du Bois, "What the Negro Has Done for the United States
and Texas," in Philip S. Foner, ed., *W. E. B. Du Bois Speaks: Speeches and
Addresses, 1920–1963* (New York: Pathfinder Press, 1970), 93; and John
Hope Franklin, ed., *The Souls of Black Folk in Three Negro Classics* (New
York: Avon Books, 1965), 215. Du Bois taught at Atlanta University for
many years, and his works were commonly used in sociology classes at
Morehouse College when King matriculated there. King apparently had a
broad knowledge of Du Bois's writings and the works of Thoreau. See
Martin Luther King, Jr., "Honoring Dr. DuBois," *Freedomways*, 8, no. 2
(Spring, 1968); 104–11; John J. Ansbro, *Martin Luther King, Jr.: The Mak-
ing of a Mind* (Maryknoll, N.Y.: Orbis Books, 1982), 111; and a letter from
Martin Luther King, Jr., to the Editorial Committee of *Dissent*, Salisbury,
Rhodesia (The King Papers, Boston University 1 June 1959). Thoreau's
contention that there is little virtue in the masses of people left an indelible mark on King's memory.
8. King, *Stride toward Freedom*, 224; and Arnold J. Toynbee, *A
Study of History*, Vols. I–IV (New York and London: Oxford University
Press, 1947), 129. Toynbee envisioned history not simply as the rise and
fall of civilizations but also in terms of the emergence of a creative minority to change the world for the better.
9. See Homer A. Jack, ed., *The Gandhi Reader* (Bloomington, Ind.:
Indiana University Press, 1956), 312–16.

that the liberation of black Americans probably depended on the adequate development of nonviolent strategy within their ranks.[10] These ideas undoubtedly came together in King's consciousness as he formulated his own thoughts regarding the history, mission, and destiny of his people.

In a speech at the Holt Street Baptist Church in Montgomery, Alabama, December 5, 1955, King publicly remarked perhaps for the first time that black people would play a messianic role in the life of the country:

> Right here in Montgomery when the history books are written in the future, somebody will have to say: "There lived a race of people, fleecy locks and black complexion, of people who had the moral courage to stand up for their rights, and thereby they injected a new meaning into the veins of history and of civilization." And we're gonna do that. God grant that we will do it before it's too late.[11]

This statement, given at the very beginning of the Montgomery Bus Boycott, became a motivating force for thousands of southern blacks engaged in boycotts, demonstrations, sit-ins, prayer vigils and other forms of nonviolent direct action. King consistently kept before his people a vision of black messianism as a way of motivating or inspiring them to greater heights in the struggle. In 1956 he spoke of the marvelous accomplishment blacks had made, largely through the Montgomery protest, in transforming "democracy from thin paper to thick action."[12] One year later he declared that "We have no moral choice but to continue the struggle, not for ourselves alone, but for all America. We have the

10. Reinhold Niebuhr, *Moral Man and Immoral Society: A Study in Ethics and Politics* (New York: Charles Scribner's Sons, 1932), pp. 252–54.

11. Martin Luther King, Jr., "Address to the Initial Mass Meeting of the Montgomery Improvement Association," delivered at the Holt Street Baptist church, Montgomery, Ala. (The King Center Archives, December 5, 1955), 4.

12. Martin Luther King, Jr., "Address at a Meeting of the Montgomery Improvement Association," Montgomery, Ala. (The King Center Archives, 22 March 1956), 1.

God-given duty to help save ourselves and our white brothers from tragic self-destruction in the quagmire of racial hate."[13] The essential point for King was that black America, through its struggle and suffering, was challenging white America with a new and greater sense of what it meant to be human by calling her back to the noble principles embodied in the Declaration of Independence, the Constitution, and the Judeo-Christian heritage. He believed that the special role of his people in shaping, by both critique and reformation, a prophetic vision of liberty was the most distinctive contribution any people could make to the American society and civilization.[14] By 1958, when King's first book appeared in published form, he was speaking in glowing terms about the rare opportunity blacks had to stand before the world as a model race—as an instrument through which America and the world could rise above hatred, materialism, and violence:

> This is a great hour for the Negro. The challenge is here. To become the instruments of a great idea is a privilege that history gives only occasionally. Arnold Toynbee says in *A Study of History* that it may be the Negro who will give the new spiritual dynamic to Western civilization that it so desperately needs to survive. I hope this is possible. The spiritual power that the Negro can radiate to the world comes from love, understanding, good will, and nonviolence. It may even be possible for the Negro, through adherence to nonviolence, so to challenge the nations of the world that they will seriously seek an alternative to war and destruction. In a day when Sputniks and Explorers dash through outer space and guided ballistic

13. King, "A Proposed Statement to the South," 3.
14. Martin Luther King, Jr., "Facing the Challenge of a New Age," *Fellowship* (February 23, 1957); 5; Martin Luther King, Jr., "Desirability of Being Maladjusted," a speech delivered to an unidentified congregation, Chicago, Ill. (The King Center Archives, 13 January 1958), 11; Martin Luther King, Jr., "A Statement on Segregation," Montgomery, Ala. (The King Center Archives, 24 May 1961), 1; and a letter from Martin Luther King, Jr., to Amin Mxowoya of Karonga Nyasaland, Central Africa (The King Papers, Boston University 12 October 1961).

missiles are carving highways of death through the
stratosphere, nobody can win a war. Today the choice
is no longer between violence and nonviolence. It is
either nonviolence or nonexistence. The Negro may
be God's appeal to this age—an age drifting rapidly to
its doom.[15]

King repeatedly made this point between 1958 and
1968, noting that his people were serving as a moral
force in awakening the consciences of America and the
world.[16] By this time the S.C.L.C. had adopted as a motto:
"To save the soul of America." This motto registered
heavily on King's thinking, as evidenced by his statement, in 1964, that "the thing that I am concerned about
more than anything is that it is our responsibility and our
great opportunity to teach the whole world something
through our humble efforts to make the United States a
better nation."[17] In 1965 he commented: "We feel that we
are the conscience of America—we are its troubled
soul—and we will continue to insist that *right* be done
because both God's will and the heritage of our nation
speak through our echoing demands."[18] King stated in
1968 that if black people did not assume a leadership role
in transforming America, "it's going straight to hell."
"Cities are burning down every summer," he continued,
"and there's war in Vietnam. Everywhere we look, things
are confused and messed up. And it's all because our
white brothers have not learned how to be just. And
we've got to make them just."[19]

King was convinced, however, that his people could
provide this transforming impulse only if they remained

15. King, *Stride toward Freedom*, 224. This statement also appears
in King, "A Statement on the Black Mission," 1 ff.

16. Martin Luther King, Jr., "The Negro in America: The End of Jim
Crow," (A transcription of a taped speech, The King Center Archives,
n.d.), 5; and Martin Luther King, Jr., *Where Do We Go from Here: Chaos
or Community?* (Boston: Beacon Press, 1967), 57.

17. King, "Interview on World Peace," 6–7.

18. King, "The Negro Gains in Rights—1965," 18–19; and Martin
Luther King, Jr., "Speech at a Rally," Crawfordsville, Ga. (The King Center Archives, October 1965), 1–2.

19. King, "Address at a Mass Meeting," Laurel, Miss., 4.

obedient to the spirit and teachings of Jesus Christ. It was at this point that the black church became immensely important for him. King's prophetic scenario suggested that that institution, with its reservoir of spiritual resources, was in an ideal position to bear witness to God's greatness and goodness, and to be a base from which the gospel principles of love and nonviolence could be shared with the world. He further suggested that the black church, by remaining an important channel through which feelings about society could be voiced and protest implemented, could possibly succeed in restoring credibility to and interest in the rapidly fading Christian faith, a mission that the white church had for so long failed to accomplish. King urged his people not to abandon Christianity simply because it had been prostituted by their oppressors. According to Coretta Scott King,

> . . . my husband felt that it was not the Christian ethic which must be rejected, but that those who failed Christianity must be brought—through love, to brotherhood, for their own redemption as well as ours. He believed that there was a great opportunity for black people to redeem Christianity in America.[20]

It would be unwise to dismiss King's black messianism as mere chauvinism or romanticism. Indeed, he felt he was being realistic about his people's capabilities. At the same time, with a boldness of vision characteristic of black leaders throughout American history, he admitted that black people were subject to the same frailties as all other human beings. "No one can pretend that

---

20. Coretta Scott King, *My Life with Martin Luther King, Jr.* (New York: Avon Books, 1969), 260. Cornel West includes King in what he calls "the exceptionalist tradition"—that black tradition in which the self image of Afro-Americans "is one of pride, self-congratulation, and often heroism." As an exemplar of this tradition, King held that blacks had "acquired, as a result of their historical experience, a peculiar capacity to love their enemies, to endure patiently suffering, pain, and hardship and thereby 'teach the white man how to love' or 'cure the white man of his sickness.'" See Cornel West, *Prophesy Deliverance: An Afro-American Revolutionary Christianity* (Philadelphia: Westminster Press, 1982), 72, 74–75.

because a people may be oppressed, every individual member is virtuous and worthy," King observed. He further remarked:

> Negroes are human, not superhuman. Like all people, they have differing personalities, diverse financial interests, and varied aspirations. There are Negroes who will never fight for freedom. There are Negroes who will seek profit for themselves alone from the struggle. There are even some Negroes who will cooperate with their oppressors. These facts should distress no one. Every minority and every people has its share of opportunists, profiteers, free-loaders and escapists.[21]

For all their shortcomings, many of them born of oppression, King considered black people generally more humane than their white oppressors. He saw in the great mass of black Americans dominant values and virtues—a vital and genuine spirituality, a humanitarian spirit, a prophetic vision of democracy, an incurable optimism, and a great toleration for human differences—values and virtues he considered extremely rare in the great mass of white people. In King's view, white Americans' obsession with racism, war, and wealth, and their historic quest for power and for domination over peoples of color had resulted in an incalculable loss of higher human values and genuine spirituality within the group. Consequently, whites were generally less congenial than blacks to the idea of meaningful, creative, and communal living among the various peoples of the world.[22]

Martin Kilson interprets King's brand of black messianism as a form of racism. Such an interpretation suggests that King's messianism was quite similar to the

---

21. King, "The Sword that Heals," 14.
22. *Ibid.* King believed that southern blacks, perhaps due to the depth of their oppression, were particularly endowed with a capacity for human feeling and service—a humanitarian spirit that represented the brightest hope for a transformed South, nation, and world. See King, *My Life with Martin Luther King, Jr.*, 260. King warned white America that its treatment of black Americans was symptomatic of "a basic spiritual problem." See King, "A Proposed Statement to the South," 4.

American "Manifest Destiny" concept, to Josiah Strong's vision of an "Anglo-Saxonized" world, and to much of the rhetoric of American Civil Religion.[23] This interpretation is erroneous, mainly because it misses the essential point of King's black messianic ideal. King saw black Americans' role in the world as that of a liberating force and as a spiritualizing and humanizing force; whereas the vision advanced through Manifest Destiny, Josiah Strong, and American Civil Religion has encouraged white control and domination over other peoples and cultures.[24] King was adamantly opposed to any notion that black people should control and dominate other peoples. He categorically stated that his people could never successfully fulfill their messianic vocation if they adopted the violence and racism so characteristic of white America:

> I am convinced that the black man cannot do it through hatred, he cannot do it through violence, he cannot do it through substituting one tyranny for another, he cannot do it by making a doctrine of black supremacy a substitute for white supremacy. But he can do it by committing himself to an action program, and by being sure that that action program is tempered with nonviolence and a powerful positive love, and a deep understanding and love for all mankind.[25]

23. Wilson J. Moses, *Black Messiahs and Uncle Toms: Social and Literary Manipulations of a Religious Myth* (University Park, Penn.: Pennsylvania State University Press, 1982), x–xi.

24. The idea of the Manifest Destiny and Josiah Strong's thoughts on the Anglo-Saxon Protestant mission of Americans, as set forth in his *Our Country* (1885), obviously contributed to the enslavement and oppression of peoples of color by whites and also to America's belated efforts at imperialism in this century. One source that fails to recognize this sufficiently is Ernest L. Tuveson, *Redeemer Nation: The Idea of America's Millennial Role* (Chicago: University of Chicago Press, 1968), 1–214. Considering the climate of race relations in late nineteenth-century America, and given Strong's firm belief in the superiority of the Anglo-Saxon way of life, it is difficult to accept Tuveson's contention that "it is unfair to call Strong a racist." Wilson J. Moses' suggestion that black messianism demonstrates that black Americans have not deviated significantly from the civil religion of the larger society is also highly questionable. See Wilson J. Moses, "Civil Religion and the Crisis of Civil Rights," *The Drew Gateway*, 57, no. 2 (Winter 1986); 24–42.

25. King, "Interview on World Peace," 3, 6–7.

King's insistence on the special role of his people in the shaping of a new humanity was based on several key concepts that are rooted in black thinking. First, it was based on what Lerone Bennett, Jr., calls "the providential view of a God-controlled history."[26] The idea here was that God controls the universe and its moral order and will ultimately bring the disjointed elements of humanity and of human society together in a harmonious whole. Drawing on the theological insight of the black church tradition, King held that the Bible is not only about how God pours the vial of wrath upon oppressors, but also about how God takes a particular oppressed people and uses them as instruments for achieving the divine will and purpose for humanity. This claim was clearly substantiated for King in the Exodus and Cross-Events, which afforded much of the symbolism on which he and his people drew for an interpretation of their own identity, mission, and destiny.[27] King's idea that God was preserving black Americans for a star role or a unique mission in the world was intimately linked to the traditional Christian optimism of the black church. This is why he could repeatedly say, with unshakable conviction, that "I believe in the future because I believe in God."[28] The future was bright and promising for him because of his conviction that God was with his people in their redemptive and transforming activity.[29]

King's black messianism was also based on a deep faith in his people's inclination to altruism. Always

26. Lerone Bennett, "Listen to the Blood: The Meaning of Black History," *Ebony*, 36, no. 4 (February 1981); 35. Bennett's essay is one of the best available concerning how blacks historically have interpreted the meaning and significance of their experience under white domination.

27. See William D. Watley, *Roots of Resistance: The Nonviolent Ethic of Martin Luther King, Jr.* (Valley Forge, Pa.: Judson Press, 1985), 26; James H. Smylie, "On Jesus, Pharaohs, and the Chosen People: Martin Luther King as Biblical Interpreter and Humanist," *Interpretation*, 34 (January 1970); 74–91; and Flip Schulke, ed., *Martin Luther King, Jr.: A Documentary . . . Montgomery to Memphis* (New York: W. W. Norton, 1976), 224.

28. King, "Desirability of Being Maladjusted," 17.

29. Martin Luther King, Jr., "An Address at the 47th Annual NAACP Convention," San Francisco, Calif. (The King Papers, Boston University, 27 June 1956), 8–9.

mindful of their shortcomings, he believed, nevertheless, that black people had powerful redeeming qualities
that suited them to be the vanguard in the struggle
to enlarge the reach of the human endeavor. King
spoke profoundly of the black American as representing
perhaps the greatest paradox on earth—as one who
was, at once, the symbol of liberty and limitation. He
held that in terms of material things and cultural values,
the black American had become a rich and irreplaceable
resource of the nation. The newest resource for King
was evident in the emergence of the "new Negro" in the
South, who was confronting his or her white overlords
with a new purpose and new courage. Although King
recognized in this "new Negro" the greatest possibility
for the fulfillment of the black messianic hope, he realized, at the same time, that black people, from the time
they first set foot on these shores, had consistently performed the noble mission of calling America back to the
moral and ethical principles of her democratic and
Judeo-Christian heritage. In this sense, blacks had been
far more "American" than their oppressors. This is how
King understood the historical role of black people in
America.[30] He regarded his own nonviolent movement
on behalf of the poor and oppressed as a part of this
ongoing mission to save the heart and soul of America
through the black church. In King's opinion, the "new
Negro" of the 1950s and 1960s, in his or her drive to
widen the structural channels defined by race, was of-
fering the greatest testimony to the validity and integrity
of his or her slave forebears' struggle.[31]

The traditional Christian belief in the redemptive
power of suffering was still another concept on which

30. Martin Luther King, Jr., "An Address to the National Press Club,"
Washington, D.C. (The King Papers, Boston University, 19 July 1962), 6–
16; Lewis V. Baldwin, "Martin Luther King, Jr., the Black Church, and the
Black Messianic Vision," *The Journal of the Interdenominational Theolog-
ical Center*, 12, nos. 1 and 2 (Fall 1984/Spring 1985); 105–8; and Lewis V.
Baldwin, "Understanding Martin Luther King, Jr. Within the Context of
Southern Black Religious History," *Journal of Religious Studies*, 13, no. 2
(Fall 1987); 22–26.
31. Baldwin, "Understanding Martin Luther King, Jr.," 26.

King's black messianic vision was based.[32] King constantly urged his people not to react with bitterness to their suffering, much of which stemmed from their involvement in the civil rights movement, but, rather, to transform that suffering into a creative and redeeming force:

> I pray that, recognizing the necessity of suffering, the Negro will make of it a virtue. To suffer in a righteous cause is to grow to our humanity's full stature. If only to save himself from bitterness, the Negro needs the vision to see the ordeals of this generation as the opportunity to transfigure himself and American society.[33]

Black people responded with mixed emotions to the challenge posed by King's black messianism. Some naturally recoiled from any interpretation of their historical mission that cast them in the role of "suffering servant" for the rest of humankind.[34] On the other hand, many blacks were motivated and inspired by this challenge. This was not a surprising development, especially since blacks had long looked with respect and admiration on persons who were willing to suffer and die for a righteous and just cause.[35] The idea that struck a responsive chord in the hearts of many blacks was that, through suffering, they could teach the world something profound about heartache and hope, and about the triumph of the human spirit in the face of seemingly invincible odds. It is noteworthy that much of the black theology that appeared in the late 1960s gave credence to the kind

32. Martin Luther King, Jr., "A Speech at the Southern Christian Ministers' Conference" (The King Papers, Boston University, 23 September 1959), 14; and Moses, *Black Messiahs and Uncle Toms*, x–xi.

33. King, "A Speech at the Southern Christian Ministers' Conference," 14; and James M. Washington, ed., *A Testament of Hope: The Essential Writings of Martin Luther King, Jr.* (San Francisco: Harper & Row, 1986), 41–42.

34. Wilson J. Moses gives the impression that black people generally recoiled from all interpretations of their historical mission that portrayed them as "a messianic redeemer race," a view that is not borne out by extant evidence. See Moses, *Black Messiahs and Uncle Toms*, xi.

35. Nathan I. Huggins, "Martin Luther King, Jr.: Charisma and Leadership," *The Journal of American History*, 74, no. 2 (September 1987); 480.

of "suffering servant" motif that undergirded King's
black messianic hope.[36]

King's black messianism implied the existence of an
ideal society, a kind of *earthly utopia*, a time when the
Christian spirit and principles would truly triumph. He
may have been terribly naive in thinking that such a vision would find fulfillment in human history, especially
given the human propensity for sin and evil. The extent
to which he maintained faith in the ultimate success of
the black messianic challenge is open to question. The
rising tide of the white backlash in the late 1960s, in both
the North and South, must have shaken his confidence in
the ability of black people to transform white America
through struggle and suffering. But King clung desper-
ately to his black messianic hope despite this development and despite the fact that riots, Black Power, and
other radical challenges to his ideal surfaced in the final
years of his life. As he looked back on the civil rights
movement in 1967, he could see that the challenge of the
black movement had forced many whites to re-examine
their ideas and values, a development he accepted with
great satisfaction:

> . . . the role of the Negro has been significant, forc-
> ing a re-examination of the true meaning of American
> democracy. The whole nation has for a decade given
> more inquiry to the essential nature of democracy,
> economically and politically, as a consequence of the
> vigorous Negro protest. Without writing books or ar-
> ticles that reached white America, by taking to the
> streets and there giving practical lessons of democ-
> racy's defaults and shortcomings, Negroes influenced
> white thought significantly.[37]

36. See Joseph R. Washington, Jr., *The Politics of God: The Future of
the Black Churches* (Boston: Beacon Press, 1969), 160, 166–68, 173–77;
and William R. Jones, *Is God A White Racist?: A Preamble to Black Theology* (New York: Doubleday Anchor Books, 1973), 79–97.

37. Martin Luther King, Jr., *Where Do We Go from Here?* (Unpublished draft (1967), The King Center Archives), 9–10. King's messianism
suggested the kind of "basic utopianism" discussed by Matthew Holden,
Jr.—a utopianism that holds that "if one can convert (or overcome) the

In a real sense, King's black messianism constituted a direct attack on white America's negative images of his people. Indeed, it was a reminder to whites that black America could not be logically excluded from their vision of the American mission and destiny.

## KING AS A BLACK MESSIAH

William R. Jones, the black philosopher of religion, has written the following concerning King's mystical authority as the black messiah:

> To be truthful we would have to admit that King has become, as it were, the black messiah, the singular and exclusive pattern not only for blacks in America to imitate but also for other liberation movements throughout the world.[38]

Jones's characterization of King as the black messiah is descriptive of how many black Americans viewed the civil rights leader in the 1950s and 1960s. King symbolized the hopes, dreams, struggles, and aspirations of his people during this period, and the high moral, spiritual, and political character of his leadership convinced them that he was on a special mission from God. This was evident as early as the Montgomery protest, when some of the women of the Dexter Avenue Baptist Church affectionately called King "Little Lord Jesus."[39] King was also called "the black Moses of Alabama" in some circles. Bernard Lee has reported that blacks in Montgomery virtually worshiped King, and "crowds just went wild whenever he spoke."[40] The feelings of profound awe,

---

sinful men exercising power, and get them to do the right thing, then a whole glorious future will open." Matthew Holden, Jr., *The Politics of the Black "Nation"* (New York and London: Chandler Publishing, 1973), 64.

38. William R. Jones, "Martin Luther King: Black Messiah or White Guardian?" (An unpublished paper presented before the First Unitarian Society of Minneapolis, Minneapolis, Minn. The William R. Jones personal collection, Florida State University, Tallahassee, Fla., 6 April 1986), 1.

39. Brady B. Whitehead, Jr., "Preaching Response to the Death of Martin Luther King, Jr." (Ph.D. diss., Emory University, 1972), 101.

40. A private interview with the Rev. Bernard S. Lee, Washington, D.C. 9 July 1986.

respect, and love that black Americans directed at King represented one important expression of black messianism in the 1950s and 1960s.

This image of King as a black messiah grew in proportion to his mounting involvements and fame. By the time of the freedom rides and the Albany, Georgia, campaign during the period 1960 to 1962, that image had become prominent throughout black America. After hearing King speak in the course of these activities, a black college student told a white researcher that "It's just like seeing Jesus up there."[41] Even King's detractors in the black community often referred to him as "De Lawd," a label to which he never reacted emotionally.[42] When King's efforts failed in Albany, critics spoke of him as a "fallen idol" and a "crucified Lawd," implying that the messianic role imposed on him by his followers was, in and of itself, insufficient to attain much-needed, positive advancement in civil rights.[43] But King's mistakes and failures did not change the general perception of him as "a Moses-figure" leading his people out of the Egypt of slavery, through the wilderness of segregation, and toward the Promised Land of freedom, justice, and equality.[44] Coretta Scott King recalled how her husband gradually assumed heroic proportions among his people, becoming for them the fulfillment of the black messianic hope:

> . . . it was very difficult for Martin to keep from being worshiped by the black masses. It was a great temptation to them, because they had never had the opportunity to acclaim a great leader of their own

41. Whitehead, "Preaching Response to the Death of Martin Luther King, Jr.," 101. For a poetic tribute that strongly suggests King's likeness to Jesus Christ, see Emery E. George, *Black Jesus* (Ann Arbor, Mich.: Kylix Press, 1974), 1 ff.

42. Moses, *Black Messiahs and Uncle Toms*, 180; and Washington, ed., *A Testament of Hope*, 348.

43. Malcolm X, *Malcolm X Speaks: Selected Speeches and Statements*, ed. George Brietman (New York: Merit Publishers, 1965), 13; and John A. Ricks, "'De Lawd' Descends and is Crucified: Martin Luther King, Jr. in Albany, Georgia," *Journal of Southwest Georgia History*, 2 (Fall 1984): 3–14.

44. Ervin Smith, *The Ethics of Martin Luther King, Jr.* (New York: Edwin Mellen Press, 1981), 181.

before. They felt that nothing was too good for Dr. King, that he should ride in Cadillacs behind motorcycles and have every sort of pomp and tribute usually paid to the great leaders of mankind.[45]

King's associates in the S.C.L.C. attached numerous labels to him that suggested a messianic role in the political-religious sense. They saw King as a co-worker with God, as a twentieth century prophet, as the "Moses" of the black freedom struggle, and as "De Lawd."[46] Hosea Williams, who was quite active in the S.C.L.C., once declared that King reminded him not only of Moses but of several other major personalities in the Bible:

> He reminds me of Job because he was a patient man. As Job heard the abuse of his friends when he fell into misfortune, so Dr. King heard the prophets of doom condemn nonviolence after the hot summers of 1966 and 1967. . . . He reminds me of David because he was a poetic man. His speeches are alive with a Psalm-like beauty of expression. Dr. King was like John the Baptist in that he was a "voice in the wilderness," a prophet with a message of urgency.[47]

The tendency to identify King with Jesus Christ was also quite strong among his closest advisors and associates. Hosea Williams insisted that King was very much like Christ in that he was humble, gentle, forgiving, partial toward the poor, and willing to die a martyr's death for the redemption and transformation of humanity.[48] Ralph Abernathy spoke of King as one "conceived

45. King, *My Life with Martin Luther King, Jr.*, 188.
46. Whitehead, "Preaching Response to the Death of Martin Luther King, Jr.," 86–97; and Jim Bishop, *The Days of Martin Luther King, Jr.* (New York: G. P. Putnam's Sons, 1971), 8. One author uses the title, "De Lawd," for a chapter he devotes to an analysis of King's role in the black struggle. See Carl F. Ellis, Jr., *Beyond Liberation: The Gospel in the Black American Experience* (Downers Grove, Ill.: Inter-Varsity Press, 1983), 62–85.
47. A letter from the Rev. Hosea Williams to Brady B. Whitehead, Jr., (The Brady B. Whitehead Personal Collection, Lambuth College, Jackson, Tenn., n.d.); and Whitehead, "Preaching Response to the Death of Martin Luther King, Jr.," 97.
48. Whitehead, "Preaching Response to the Death of Martin Luther King, Jr.," 106.

by God," and said in a letter he wrote to his friend posthumously:

> My dear friend, Martin, now that you have gone, there are some special thoughts that come to me during this Lenten season. There are so many parallels. You were our leader and we were your disciples. Those who killed you did not know that you loved them and that you worked for them as well. For, so often, you said to us: "Love your enemies. Bless them that curse you and pray for them that despitefully use you. . . ." And, in spite of the burning [after King's assassination], I think they are saying, "He died for us." It may seem that they are denying our nonviolence for they are acting out their frustrations. . . . That was the frustration of Jerusalem during this same season nearly 2,000 years ago. . . . There has been a crucifixion in our nation, but . . . we know that the Resurrection will shortly appear. . . . We promise you, Martin, just as the disciples tarried in the Upper Room, that we're going to wait until the power comes from on high. . . . When the Holy Ghost speaks, we're going to speak as Peter spoke. And others will be converted and added to the movement and God's Kingdom will come. . . .[49]

The identification of King as a kind of savior was only natural for a people who had had a "messiah complex" for so long. The idea that God raises up individual messiahs to challenge the Pharaohs of this world was deeply rooted in the religious traditions of the folk. This idea found expression in black songs, sermons, and tales, especially in the South, where the pain of oppression was so intense.[50] King was well acquainted with this idea and what it meant in terms of his own role as black America's most admired and prominent leader.[51]

49. *Ibid.;* and Ralph Abernathy, "My Last Letter to Martin," *Ebony,* 23 (July 1968), 58–61.
50. See Harold Courlander, *Negro Folk Music, U.S.A.* (New York: Columbia University Press, 1963), 42–43.
51. A letter from Martin Luther King, Jr., to Major J. Jones (The King Papers, Boston University 5 November 1960); and Washington, ed., *A Testament of Hope,* 41–42.

King did not consciously exploit feelings of messianic exuberance among his people for his own personal gain and satisfaction. His main concern was not to be worshiped by the masses but, rather, to inspire them to greater heights of responsible and militant nonviolent action. According to Coretta Scott King,

> Martin never took on the pretentious qualities of the leader of a large movement, nor did he ever feel the need to have people at his beck and call, as happens to so many men who rise in the world. When our staff tried to make him a person of importance who should have all sorts of attention paid him, he refused to allow it. He would much rather drive a Ford car than a Cadillac. I remember when he was coming back from the Birmingham Jail, our staff members were very excited and thought that he should have a real hero's welcome. It was even suggested that we use a motorcade of Cadillacs. When I told Martin about this, he said, "Now, what would I look like coming back from jail in a Cadillac? You just drive our car to the airport, and I'll drive you home."[52]

King's disapproval of his people's efforts to worship him did not change the fact that he viewed himself as the instrument of a special destiny. From the time of his "vision in the kitchen" in Montgomery, "King saw himself as a co-worker with God" and as a prophet "called to preach wherever evil and injustice lie."[53] He also identified his mission with that of Moses, as evidenced by his frequent references to the Biblical theme of the Exodus out of bondage to explain his people's movement toward civil rights and economic justice. Like Moses, King spoke of having gone through the wilderness and of having seen the Promised Land. Black Americans responded enthusiastically to this type of metaphorical language

52. King, *My Life with Martin Luther King, Jr.*, 187–88.
53. David J. Garrow, *Bearing the Cross: Martin Luther King, Jr. and the Southern Christian Leadership Conference* (New York: William Morrow, 1986), 123, 125; and Whitehead, "Preaching Response to the Death of Martin Luther King, Jr.," 86–88.

not only because it spoke to the depth of their own experience, but also because Moses had been a primary paradigm for black leadership since the days of slavery.[54]

Although King refused to compare himself to Jesus Christ, he did think of himself as acting in a Christ-like manner. Jesus' teachings became his teachings, and Jesus' suffering his suffering. King often said, humbly and proudly, that "I bear in my body the marks of the Lord Jesus," a statement he took from the Apostle Paul. Many times King spoke of having borne the Cross "with all of its tension-packed agony," knowing that "Good Friday comes before Easter," and that "before the Crown we wear there is a Cross we must bear."[55] Personal sufferings in the form of physical abuse, verbal attack, and jailings were for him a part of this Cross— "of the self-suffering that we must face in order to redeem the soul of America."[56] Such observations, when personalized by King, did suggest certain messianic overtones, and they help explain his successful appeal to both the millennial enthusiasm and the ethnic chauvinism of his people.

The Nobel Peace Prize in 1964 enhanced King's image as the black messiah among black Americans and among other peoples throughout the world. Oppressed peoples of various backgrounds increasingly attached messianic significance to his leadership and activities. The Jewish Rabbi Abraham Heschel spoke for many when he noted that "Martin Luther King is a sign that God has not forsaken the United States of America." "God has sent him to us," Heschel continued. "His presence is the hope of America. His mission is sacred, his leadership is of

54. Whitehead, "Preaching Response to the Death of Martin Luther King, Jr.," 93–96; and Smylie, "On Jesus, Pharaohs, and the Chosen People," 74–76.

55. Whitehead, "Preaching Response to the Death of Martin Luther King, Jr.," 98–104; Washington, ed., *A Testament of Hope*, 41–42; and Martin Luther King, Jr., "An Address to the Ministers' Leadership Training Program," Miami, Florida (The King Center Archives, 19 and 23 February 1968), 5, 19.

56. Washington, ed., *A Testament of Hope*, 41–42; and a letter from Martin Luther King, Jr., to Major J. Jones, (5 November 1960).

supreme importance to every one of us."[57] But King refused to view his Nobel Peace Prize and all of the other accolades that followed as a recognition and validation of his image as the black messiah. They were, for him, a symbolic recognition of the struggles of all peoples for justice and peace and, particularly, of "the gallantry, the courage and the amazing discipline of the Negro in America."[58] King's acknowledgment of this represented the very heights of magnanimity.

Significantly, King was able to transcend his role as a messiah in the black American community to become a symbolic messiah for the entire nation. Millions of whites came to see him as a leader in the effort to fulfill the American dream. As Wilson J. Moses has indicated, King "represented at once the militancy of black people and their willingness to get along with whites; he symbolized not only the rising aspirations of blacks but the democratic ideals that all Americans associated with their national destiny."[59] King's appeal to Americans in general stemmed largely from his ability to "blend the messianic themes in Afro-American thought with the strains of American millenarianism from which they were partially derived."[60] He convinced millions of Americans that freedom, justice, and equality for all people were not only consistent with black aspirations and traditions, but also with American democratic values and Judeo-Christian principles.[61]

The messianic significance of King's life and leadership reached a new level after his death. The assassin's bullet not only clothed him in martyrdom but also established him as a precious and irreplaceable symbol in the American mind. This is evident not only in the many monuments built as "living memorials" to King, but also

57. Abraham Heschel, "Conversation with Martin Luther King," *Conservative Judaism*, 22, no. 3 (Spring 1968); 1.

58. Washington, ed., *A Testament of Hope*, 224–26, 374–75.

59. Moses, *Black Messiahs and Uncle Toms*, 180.

60. *Ibid.*

61. King, "The Negro Gains in Rights—1965," 18–19; and King, "Speech at a Rally," Crawfordsville, Ga., 1–2.

in the scores of parks, schools, churches, streets, and other places named for him.[62] In 1970, the Holy Angels Catholic Church in Chicago canonized the civil rights leader by acclamation.[63] Nine years later, at the Black Theology National Conference at Cleveland State University, several theologians suggested that King's "Letter from the Birmingham City Jail" (1963) be included among the sacred writings of the Bible.[64] These and other forms of recognition have been based on the view that King was a special person ordained and inspired by God.

The Martin Luther King, Jr., Center for Nonviolent Social Change, Inc. is the most popular and visible symbol of the aura of messiahship that has developed around the civil rights activist over the years. Founded in Atlanta, Georgia, in 1968, and later erected on a forty-four acre national historic district, this monument provides a place where people can study King's philosophy and seek nonviolent solutions to racism, poverty, war, and other problems which impede human progress toward peace, justice, and community.[65] The King Center attracts millions of visitors from all racial and ethnic backgrounds across the world, many of whom literally worship the memory of King.

King's importance as a symbolic messiah in America led to the enactment of a federal holiday in his honor. On October 19, 1983, when the United States Senate voted overwhelmingly to designate the third Monday in January, beginning in 1986, as Martin Luther King, Jr. Day, the civil rights leader became institutionalized as an American icon.[66] This historic development confronted

---

62. "In Memory of Martin Luther King, Jr.: Streets, Buildings, Works of Art Honor Him Around the World," *Ebony*, 41, no. 3 (January 1986): 64, 66, 68, 72.

63. "Anniversaries: King Day," *Newsweek* (January 26, 1970); 24.

64. *Jet*, 56, no. 22 (August 16, 1979), 53. This suggestion has not been taken seriously by the black church community and the Christian community in general.

65. "Martin Luther King, Jr., Center for Social Change: A Monument to a Martyr," *Ebony*, 29, no. 6 (April 1974): 127–30.

66. Thomas R. Peake, *Keeping the Dream Alive: A History of the Southern Christian Leadership Conference from King to the Nineteen-Eighties*

all Americans with a new challenge—the challenge of preserving King's symbolic significance without diluting his message and distorting his dream. King's symbolic messiahship cannot be preserved if the holiday reduces him to "an American mascot," or to "just another plastic hero like Superman." Furthermore, this image will be lost if King's birthday commemoration becomes like all other national holidays—occasions for relaxation, picnics, and days off from work. King must be remembered as a gadfly to America's conscience and as a much-needed "countermainstream voice for justice," not as a flaming patriot who praised this country for its democratic standards.[67] If the integrity of King's commemoration is not upheld, Americans are doomed to what has been described as "simply another self-indulgent civil-religious holiday."[68]

It is difficult to avoid the conclusion that white Americans' adoration of King secures him more as a guardian of their interests than as a black Moses who tried to lead his people to the promised land of freedom and justice.[69] This explains why many black nationalists look with suspicion on King's mystical authority as the black messiah. William R. Jones has written of white Americans' attempts to consistently project King as a black Moses even to the detriment of black advancement:

> Black leaders are indexed as militant or violent, not on the basis of their actual thought and deeds, but by virtue of how far they strayed from King's footsteps. Because he localized nonviolence and vicarious suffering as the heart of Christian faith, other black interpretations of the gospel are suspect. Whites incessantly pressed his philosophy of nonviolence upon blacks—

(New York: Peter Lang, 1987), 311–18; and Kenneth L. Smith, "Equality and Justice; A Dream or Vision of Reality," *Report from the Capital* (January 1984); 4–5, 7.

67. Jerry Gentry, "How to Celebrate King's Birthday," *The Christian Century* (January 16, 1985); 36–37; and Smith, "Equality and Justice," 4–5, 7.

68. Gentry, "How to Celebrate King's Birthday," 37.

69. Jones, "Martin Luther King," 1.

when faced with the alternative of a Malcolm X—as the exclusive strategy for economic, social and political change. Yet when King was consistent and advanced the same policy for Americans in Vietnam, he was dropped like a hot potato. This ideological abuse of King's thought should be a hint to all to scrutinize carefully the heroines and heroes that those in seats of power place on a pedestal for us. Behind the facade of praise may be another Trojan horse to further the oppression of those for whom King gave his life to liberate. . . . All this generates for me the nagging suspicion that white America desires to perpetuate a black hero who fits its special needs of oppression and not those of black liberation. . . . Moreover, and here I must be blunt, there are serious, indeed, fatal defects in King's thought that sabotage any hope that he can be the theological alpha and omega for blacks. When these glaring faults are recognized, white America's recommendation of King as *the Black Messiah* becomes all the more suspicious.[70]

Most black Americans have not progressed beyond the point of calling on a Martin Luther King, Jr., to save them. King's philosophy and methods are still widely accepted among blacks as the *only* moral and practical way to liberation. Black America's models for a liberation ethic will not be significantly enlarged as long as such a perception remains dominant within its ranks.[71]

## KING AND TRADITIONAL BLACK MESSIANISM

Black messianic thought was almost two centuries old when Martin Luther King, Jr., emerged as a leader of his people. Although a black messianic consciousness was evident at least as far back as the late eighteenth century, the most crucial period in its formation was the nineteenth century—a period during which messianic, millennial, and apocalyptic ideas permeated American

70. *Ibid.*, 1–2.
71. *Ibid.*, pp. 1–2, 9.

thought.[72] Influenced by these ideas, black messianism assumed a character that was fundamentally *American* and *Christian*.[73] However, it differed from the more dominant conceptions of America's millennial role in that it embraced precise expressions of God's unfolding plan for black people. Early black messianic thought centered around the whole question of the meaning of black history and the black experience, thereby establishing a pattern that extended down to King, Jesse Jackson, and Louis Farrakhan in recent times.[74]

Most black slaves did not rise to the level of formulating precise definitions of God's plan for their people. However, many were haunted by the question of the meaning and significance of the black odyssey in America—a question that was seemingly inescapable in view of the brutal oppression and exploitation slaves were forced to endure.[75] It appears from the record that most slaves rejected the claim that slavery was consistent with God's providential plan for them. Frederick Douglass was among those who insisted that slavery was not a product of the divine will, but of "the pride, the power, and avarice of man," a point with which Martin Luther King, Jr., would hardly have taken issue.[76] But it was difficult for even slaves like Douglass to understand why God permitted a system in which the auction block, the slave-mart, the lash, and the shackles were so literally present in the black experience. In spite of this situation, the nature of black religion was such that slaves generally refused to question God's goodness, mercy, power, and justice.[77] The general view was that God had a plan to

72. Moses, *Black Messiahs and Uncle Toms*, 9–10.
73. *Ibid.*, 180, 226–27.
74. Bennett, "Listen to the Blood," 33–35.
75. *Ibid.*
76. *Ibid.;* and Leonard I. Sweet, *Black Images of America, 1784–1870* (New York: W. W. Norton, 1976), 69–71.
77. Bennett, "Listen to the Blood," 33–35; Sweet, *Black Images of America*, 70–71; and Frederick Douglass, *Frederick Douglass: An American Slave*, ed. Benjamin Quarles (Cambridge, Mass.: Belknap Press of Harvard University Press, 1971; originally published in 1845), 96. The reluctance on the part of most blacks to question God's attributes and plan for humanity is substantiated by a reading of Benjamin E. Mays, *The*

ultimately liberate His people—a plan that was hidden or beyond human understanding. This view was substantiated by the slaves' reading of the Old Testament, and it found eloquent expression in slave songs, tales, and sermons.[78] Furthermore, it was grounded in a Christian optimism that King would carry to new heights of clarity and power more than a century later.

It was uncharacteristic of slaves to think that they— through patience, long-suffering, and forgiveness— would eventually become a messianic redeemer people. However, they did tend to view themselves as morally and spiritually superior to their masters. Their sense of the parallels between their sufferings and those of the ancient Israelites in Egypt led them to believe that they were God's chosen people.[79] They found comfort and strength in the conviction that they were a people of destiny. Although the slaves believed firmly in the redemptive power of unearned suffering, as was the case with King generations later, they never envisioned themselves as possible saviors of the nation and the world.[80] But this did not prevent them from challenging

---

*Negro's God as Reflected in His Literature* (New York: Atheneum, 1968; originally published in 1938), 1–155.

78. Bennett, "Listen to the Blood," 35; and Lawrence W. Levine, *Black Culture and Black Consciousness: Afro-American Folk Thought from Slavery to Freedom* (New York: Oxford University Press, 1977), 33, 40, 43, 46, 48–49, 90–135.

79. Levine, *Black Culture and Black Consciousness*, 33–34. Although King believed that black Americans could be a vanguard in the quest for a new humanity, he was reluctant to refer to his people as "a chosen people." Of King, Wilson J. Moses has written: "He did not claim that black Americans were a chosen people or a master race, but he did feel that Providence had often made them pioneers in movements essential to the nation's development." See Moses, *Black Messiahs and Uncle Toms*, 180. Albert J. Raboteau has written of the slaves: "Identification with Israel could be so intense that the slaves in the ecstasy of the songs and dances of the praise meeting, collapsed present time with mythic past. They became Israel. The intensity of this identification blunted the sharp edge of the question, *Why does God permit slavery?* We are Israel; God frees Israel." Albert J. Raboteau, "'Ethiopia Shall Soon Stretch Forth Her Hands': Black Destiny in Nineteenth Century America," The University Lecture in Religion at Arizona State University, Tempe, Ariz. (27 January 1983), 4–5.

80. Thomas L. Webber, *Deep Like the Rivers: Education in the Slave Quarter Community, 1831–1865* (New York: W. W. Norton, 1978), 86; and Baldwin, "Understanding Martin Luther King, Jr.," 19–20.

their white overlords with a greater sense of spiritual and moral values. Throughout the seventeenth, eighteenth, and nineteenth centuries, Afro-American slaves consistently confronted their oppressors with a new vision of humanity, a new sense of human possibility, and a new conception of democratic and egalitarian values.[81] This heritage continued to challenge America in the life and work of King.[82]

Black thinkers and writers in the antebellum North had more freedom than their enslaved brothers and sisters in the South to frame their thoughts around the perplexing question: Why slavery? As early as 1808, Absalom Jones, pastor of St. Thomas African Episcopal Church in Philadelphia, proclaimed in a sermon that "It has always been a mystery why the impartial Father of the human race should have permitted the transportation of so many millions of our fellow creatures to this country, to endure all the miseries of slavery." Jones nevertheless speculated that perhaps God's "design was that a knowledge of the gospel might be acquired by some of their descendants, in order that they might become qualified to be the messengers of it, to the land of their fathers."[83] William Miller, the African Methodist minister, told his congregation in 1810 that his people's condition resulted from idolatry or disobedience to God, a position advanced later by the black nationalist David Walker, the black historian George W. Williams, and the African Methodist Bishop J. W. Hood.[84] The black

81. This point is supported by the many black petitions for freedom during slavery. See Herbert Aptheker, ed., *A Documentary History of the Negro People in the United States*, 3 Vols. (Secaucus, N.J.: Citadel Press, 1973), I, 1–459.

82. Baldwin, "Martin Luther King, Jr., The Black Church, and the Black Messianic Vision," 100–1.

83. Absalom Jones, "A Thanksgiving Sermon," in *Early Negro Writing, 1760–1837*, ed. Dorothy Porter (Boston: Beacon Press, 1971), 340; Sweet, *Black Images of America*, 79; Raboteau, "'Ethiopia Shall Soon Stretch Forth Her Hands,'" 7; and Gayraud S. Wilmore, *Black Religion and Black Radicalism: An Interpretation of the Religious History of Afro-American People* (Maryknoll, N.Y.: Orbis Books, 1983), 121–22.

84. Raboteau, "'Ethiopia Shall Soon Stretch Forth Her Hands,'" 6; and Sterling Stuckey, *Slave Culture: Nationalist Theory and the Foundations of Black America* (New York: Oxford University Press, 1987), 121.

Episcopal leader Alexander Crummell held in the 1850s
and 1860s that slavery was God's way of exposing
Africans to the healthy "influence of Anglo-Saxon life
and civilization," a view supported in the 1890s by Henry
McNeal Turner, the African Methodist Episcopal
bishop.[85] Other black leaders, like Martin Delany and Edward W. Blyden, wondered if God had not meant to
toughen black people for some great task on behalf of
humankind. Martin Luther King, Jr., would have found
all of these explanations unacceptable, mainly because
they assumed the inferiority of Africans and came fright-
eningly close to absolving whites of their guilt for slavery.[86] In any case, these various explanations are
illustrative of the tremendous struggle blacks had in resolving the question of the meaning and significance of
the black experience in slavery—a struggle with which
King would become well acquainted.

Despite the range of opinions on the question of meaning, black theoreticians in the North were essentially in
agreement with Sojourner Truth's idea that God had preserved His enslaved children for a special purpose and
destiny.[87] Many searched the scriptures for signs of God's
will for the race. In Psalm 68:31—which predicted that
"Princes shall come out of Egypt; Ethiopia shall soon
stretch her hands unto God"—black Americans discovered what they believed to be the answer to the question
of the meaning of black suffering and destiny, which explained why they so frequently quoted that verse. The
implication was that Africa's dark children would one
day rise to take their place among the great nations of
the world.[88] Some blacks found support for this conviction in the Exodus and in the Book of Job.[89] The famous

85. Quoted in Sweet, *Black Images of America*, 75, 81.
86. Wilmore, *Black Religion and Black Radicalism*, 122; and
Raboteau, "'Ethiopia Shall soon Stretch Forth Her Hands,'" 7.
87. Bennett, "Listen to the Blood," 35.
88. Raboteau, "'Ethiopia Shall Soon Stretch Forth Her Hands,'" 4–6;
and Wilmore, *Black Religion and Black Radicalism*, 105.
89. Raboteau, "'Ethiopia Shall Soon Stretch Forth Her Hands,'" 4–5.
The black minister William Miller interpreted the brutality of the slave

ex-slave Austin Steward noted in 1827 that black suffering in slavery had a redemptive value similar to that of
the Israelites in Egyptian captivity.[90] Frederick Douglass
and Henry Highland Garnet, the black abolitionist and
Presbyterian minister, moved beyond the scriptures
to assert, on a more practical level, that the destiny of
Africans was linked to America's destiny.[91] The fugitive
slave preacher and writer, James W. C. Pennington, insisted that the blood, bones, and souls of his people figured into God's plan to make America a great and
wealthy nation.[92] In a different vein, Martin Delany, the
prominent physician and proponent of black nationalism,
argued in 1852 that the greatness God had decreed for
blacks would be realized only after they broke commu-
nion with their oppressors and submitted wholeheartedly to the will of God:

> The time has now fully arrived, when the colored race
> is called upon by all the ties of common humanity,
> and all the claims of consummate justice, to go for-
> ward and take their position, and do battle in the
> struggle now being made for the redemption of the
> world. Our cause is a just one; the greatest at present
> that elicits the attention of the world. For if there is a
> remedy; that remedy is now at hand. God himself
> as assuredly as he rules the destinies of nations, and
> entereth measures into the "hearts of men," has pre-
> sented these measures to us. Our race is to be
> redeemed; it is a great and glorious work, and we are
> the instrumentalities by which it is to be done. But
> we must go from among our oppressors; it can never
> be done by staying among them. God has, as certain as

---

trade and the subsequent suffering of Africans in America as the literal
fulfillment of Isaiah 20:3–4. See William Miller, *A Sermon on the Aboli-
tion of the Slave Trade: Delivered in the African Church, New York, on the
First of January, 1810* (New York, 1810), 5–6.

90. Sweet, *Black Images of America*, 73.

91. *Ibid.*, 86.

92. James W. C. Pennington, *The Fugitive Blacksmith; or, Events in the
History of James W. C. Pennington, Pastor of a Presbyterian Church, New
York, Formerly a Slave in the State of Maryland, United States* (London,
1849), 76–77.

he has ever designed anything, designed this great portion of the New World, for us, the colored race; and as certain as we stubborn our hearts and stiffen our necks against it, his protecting arm and fostering care will be withdrawn from us.[93]

A century later, Martin Luther King, Jr., advanced the notion that blacks were the possible agents for the fulfillment of a special purpose and destiny on a higher level of sophistication. Frederick Douglass's and Henry H. Garnet's thoughts on the relationship between America's destiny and that of black Americans seemed very similar to King's. However, Delany's separatist ideology was quite inconsistent with this vision and would not have found affinity with King's black messianic hope.[94]

Nationalistic aspects of black messianism in the nineteenth century embraced a concern for the religious and socioeconomic uplift of Africa, a concern that had become classic among black leaders and thinkers by King's time. In the early 1800s, black churchmen such as Paul Cuffee, Lott Carey, and Daniel Coker traveled to parts of West Africa with the intention of Christianizing the natives and stimulating economic growth on the shores of the motherland, thus forging a connecting link between emigrationism, Christian messianism, and black nationalism.[95] From the 1840s to the end of the century, black nationalists and churchmen like Henry H. Garnet, Alexander Crummell, Edward W. Blyden, John E. Bruce, Henry M. Turner, and Emmanuel K. Love consistently taught that black Americans had a special or unique obligation to share the blessings of Christian civilization with their African brothers and sisters.[96] This same

93. Martin R. Delany, *The Condition, Elevation, Emigration and Destiny of the Colored People of the United States, Politically Considered* (Philadelphia, 1852), 183.

94. Martin Luther King, Jr., *Why We Can't Wait* (New York: New American Library, Inc., 1964), 93; and Moses, *Black Messiahs and Uncle Toms*, 180.

95. Wilmore, *Black Religion and Black Radicalism*, 99–109.

96. Ples Sterling Stuckey, "The Spell of Africa: The Development of Black Nationalist Theory, 1829–1945," (Ph.D. diss., Northwestern

message was proclaimed in various ways by leaders like W. E. B. Du Bois and Marcus Garvey in the early twentieth century.[97] However, the idea that God intended Africa for Afro-American missionaries had largely faded when Martin Luther King, Jr., emerged. King clearly saw that such an assumption was based on the arrogant and misguided notion that Africans were backward pagans who needed the guidance of those touched by Euro-American civilization. Although he expressed virtually no interest in Christianizing Africa, King did believe that blacks in America were in an ideal position to lead in preparing the way for the liberation and uplift of that continent and of people of color across the globe. In 1967, he wrote:

> The hard cold facts today indicate that the hope of the people of color in the world may well rest on the American Negro and his ability to reform the structure of racist imperialism from within and thereby turn the technology and wealth of the West to the task of liberating the world from want.[98]

Some black leaders attached a global significance to the messianic role of their people. In his celebrated *Appeal to the Coloured Citizens of the World* (1829), David Walker declared that Afro-Americans were better suited than whites not only to Christianize Africa but the entire world.[99] In striking ways, he anticipated King's message with regard to the potential of black Americans as a Christianizing force, though it is true that Walker, unlike King, felt that a divinely sanctioned violence would be necessary to free his people for such a task.[100] In the

---

University, June 1973), 172, 174–175; Sweet, *Black Images of America,* 69–124; and Raboteau, "'Ethiopia Shall Soon Stretch Forth Her Hands,'" 9.

97. Sweet, *Black Images of America,* 122; Stuckey, *Slave Culture,* 259; and Amy Jacques Garvey, ed., *Philosophy and Opinions of Marcus Garvey,* 2 Vols. (New York: Atheneum, 1973), I, 5, 11, 81, 96.

98. King, *Where Do We Go from Here?,* 57.

99. Sweet, *Black Images of America,* 113; Wiltse, ed., *David Walker's Appeal,* 18; and Stuckey, *Slave Culture,* 112–13, 132.

100. Baldwin, "Martin Luther King, Jr., the Black Church, and the Black Messianic Vision," 105–6; and Stuckey, "The Spell of Africa," 170.

whole history of black messianic thought, it is impossible
to find leaders and thinkers who were as adamant and
consistent as King in emphasizing love and nonviolence
as essential to the realization of the black messianic
hope.[101]

This idea of Afro-Americans as a Christianizing force
in the world also appeared in the writings of Alexander
Crummell, Edward W. Blyden, John E. Bruce, Alexander
Walters, Marcus Garvey, and other black nationalists in
the late nineteenth and early twentieth centuries, assuming the character of a more global, more millenialist messianism.[102] During the so-called "New Negro Movement"
of the 1920s, when black artistic and literary creativity
caught the attention of the world, Claude McKay concluded that God had put blacks on earth as a light for
true Christianity before white people destroy themselves
and civilization, an idea amazingly similar to King's.[103]
With W. E. B. Du Bois, and to some extent Paul Robeson,
the concept of a global, millenialist black messianism
reached its most brilliant expression prior to King's formulation of his own black messianism. As early as 1897,
Du Bois suggested that people of African descent had
their own unique contribution to make to humanity and
civilization, a contribution that would be essentially
spiritual in nature. "We are the first fruits of this new
nation," he argued, "the harbinger of that black tomorrow which is yet destined to soften the whiteness of the
Teutonic today."[104] By 1915 Du Bois had expanded his

101. Baldwin, "Martin Luther King, Jr., the Black Church, and the
Black Messianic Vision," 106.
102. Sweet, *Black Images of America*, 69–124; Raboteau, "'Ethiopia
Shall Soon Stretch Forth Her Hands,'" 9–11; Randall K. Burkett, *Black
Redemption: Churchmen Speak Out for the Garvey Movement* (Philadel-
phia: Temple University Press, 1978), 150–51; Philip S. Foner, ed., *The
Voice of Black America: Major Speeches by Blacks in the United States,
1797–1973*, 2 Vols. (New York: Capricorn Books, 1975), I, 489–91; and
Alexander Walters, *My Life and Work* (New York and Chicago: Fleming H.
Revell Company, 1917), 11 ff.
103. Earl E. Thorpe, *The Mind of the Negro: An Intellectual History of
Afro-Americans* (Baton Rouge, La.: Ortlieb Press, 1961), 37–38.
104. Du Bois, *The Conservation of Races*, 12; Stuckey, "The Spell of
Africa," 165; and Sweet, *Black Images of America*, 88, 120–121, 124.

messianism to include peoples of color throughout the world:

> Most men in this world are colored. A belief in humanity means a belief in colored men. The future world will, in all reasonable probability, be what colored men make it. In order for this colored world to come into its heritage, must the earth again be drenched in the blood of fighting, snarling human beasts, or will Reason and Good Will prevail? That such may be true, the character of the Negro race is the best and greatest hope; for in its normal condition it is at once the strongest and the gentlest of the races of men: *Semper novi quid ex-Africa!*[105] (Italics added.)

Paul Robeson envisioned "a unified, systematically developed black culture extending across geographical barriers" and aimed at "a global messianic objective."[106] "The world is full of barbarism," he wrote, "and I feel that the united Negro culture could bring into the world a fresh spiritual, humanitarian principle, a principle of human friendship and service to the community."[107] Both Robeson and Du Bois believed that black America's role in humanizing the world would be fulfilled only if it maintained and cultivated those artistic, spiritual, and aesthetic qualities so endemic to its culture—a view with which Martin Luther King, Jr., would have wholeheartedly agreed. Furthermore, Robeson and Du Bois knew, as did King and other proponents of black messianism throughout history, that such a noble role would necessarily require blacks to deal with the problems of self-hatred and disunity within the group, and to further develop cultural, economic, political, and moral force. Although Robeson, Du Bois, and King recognized how oppression kept blacks from developing their creative potential to the fullest, they believed, nevertheless, that blacks were eminently capable of interpreting their

105. Stuckey, "The Spell of Africa," 170; and Du Bois, *The Negro*, 146.
106. Stuckey, "The Spell of Africa," 266; and Stuckey, *Slave Culture*, 339, 345.
107. Quoted in Stuckey, *Slave Culture*, 345.

condition in ways that might be instructive to the whole
of humankind.[108]

King shared with Robeson, Du Bois, and other theoreticians of black messianism a deep love and a strong
desire for the salvation of humanity. Although King's
black messianic ideology did not include Robeson's concept of "a united Negro culture," it was consistent with
Robeson's idea of the vital spiritual and humanitarian
values blacks could bring to the shaping of a new humanity. Du Bois' black messianism found conceptual affinity
with King's views at many points. Du Bois' claim that
"Negro blood has a message for the world" was essentially identical to King's belief that blacks, through un-
merited suffering, could teach the world something
about the dynamism of the human spirit.[109] The two men
also tended to view the messianic role of their people in a
historical context, taking into account how blacks had
always challenged America with a prophetic vision of
freedom, justice, and community. In assessing the gifts
of black folk, Du Bois wrote: "It was the black man that
raised a vision of democracy in America such as neither
Americans nor Europeans conceived in the 18th century
and such as they have not even accepted in the 20th
century"—a "conception which every clear-sighted man
knows is true and inevitable."[110] Despite his critique of
the black church, Du Bois knew as well as King and
Robeson that it was the genius of religion that gave substance and shape to black people's vision of liberty and
democracy.[111]

    108. *Ibid.*, 325–26; King, *Where Do We Go from Here?*, 122–28, 134;
King, "Interview on World Peace," 6–7; and Vincent Harding, "W. E. B.
Du Bois and the Black Messianic Vision," *Freedomways*, 9, no. 1 (Winter
1969); 44–58.
    109. Stuckey, *Slave Culture*, 294, 344–345; Franklin, ed., *The Souls of
Black Folk*, 215; and King, "Interview on World Peace," 6–7.
    110. Baldwin, "Understanding Martin Luther King, Jr.," 26; and
W. E. B. Du Bois, *The Gifts of Black Folk: The Negroes in the Making of
America* (Boston: Stratford, Publishers, 1924), 135.
    111. Gayraud S. Wilmore, "Black Religion and the Concept of Lib-
erty" (An unpublished paper, 1976), 2–3; and Baldwin, "Martin Luther
King, Jr., the Black Church, and the Black Messianic Vision," 93–100.

The view that blacks, due to their history and suffering, were generally more humane than whites resounded through the writings of philosophers of black messianism long before King expressed it. The evils of slavery led David Walker to assert in 1829 that "The whites have always been an unjust, jealous, unmerciful, avaricious and blood-thirsty set of beings, always seeking after power and authority." He thought that the cruelty displayed by whites in dumping overboard whole cargoes of Africans during the slave trade was more than ample evidence that blacks, "take them half enlightened and ignorant, are more humane and merciful than the most enlightened and refined European that can be found in all the earth."[112] Henry H. Garnet shared this perspective, insisting that black people were less susceptible to "the besetting sins of the Anglo-Saxon race—the love of gain and the love of power." Alexander Crummell heralded blacks as "remarkably docile, affectionate, easily attached, and when attached, ardently devoted— a race with the strongest religious feelings, sentiments and emotion."[113] Edward W. Blyden characterized Europeans as "an imperial and conquering race," and described blacks as "the protege of the child, the attendant, the servant, if you like, of this dominant race."[114] The black scholar Kelly Miller declared in 1908 that "The aggressive, materialistic, and domineering qualities of the 'haughty Caucasian'" were considerably inferior to "the black man's natural 'meekness' and aptitude for Christianity."[115] W. E. B. Du Bois echoed this sentiment in

112. Wiltse, ed., *David Walker's Appeal,* 16–17, 24; and Stuckey, "The Spell of Africa," 8. Interestingly enough, Walker's comments call to mind those made by the Englishman John Wesley in 1774. Wesley characterized Africans as "fair, just and honest in all their dealings, unless where white men have taught them to be otherwise; and as far more mild, friendly, and kind to strangers than any of our forefathers were." See John Emory, ed., *Thoughts Upon Slavery in the Works of Rev. John Wesley* (New York: John T. Waugh, 1835; originally published in 1774), Vol. 6, 278–93.

113. Quoted in Stuckey, *Slave Culture,* 168; and quoted in Sweet, *Black Images of America,* 119.

114. Quoted in Sweet, *Black Images of America,* 120.

115. Quoted in *Ibid.,* 121.

1939 by boasting of black people's "spiritual joyousness" and "intense sensitiveness to spiritual values." "The black man has brought to America a sense of meekness and humility," he wrote, "which America never has recognized and perhaps never will."[116] "Are there no whites who believe that the meek shall inherit the earth?", Du Bois asked, in a tone which called to mind Martin Luther King, Jr.[117] These ideas struck at the heart of arguments in favor of white superiority and offered a strong challenge to the widely held notion that the salvation of the world depended upon the spread of Anglo-Saxon ideas and traditions. Moreover, they suggested that blacks, in assuming the role of a humanizing force in the world, had no need to turn to white Western cultures for example and imitation in matters of character.

From Walker to King, proponents of black messianism were so passionate in celebrating the special gifts of their people that at times they seemed to reinforce white stereotypes of blacks as childlike, docile, loyal, and long suffering. However, they avoided supporting these stereotypes by affirming the strength of the very qualities whites thought marked blacks as weak and inferior. While celebrating the redeeming qualities of blackness, these philosophers of black messianism acknowledged, at the same time, their people's shortcomings and failures. This aspect brought a high measure of integrity to ideologies of black messianism that was not so evident in white conceptions of America's millennial role.[118]

The history of black messianism from pre-Civil War years up to King would be incomprehensible apart from some consideration of the importance attached to individual messiahs. Black people's hopes for the coming of a "race leader" or "messiah" to lead them to the promised land of freedom and justice were evident

116. Du Bois, *The Gift of Black Folk*, 320, 339; and Sweet, *Black Images of America*, 120–21.
117. Quoted in Sweet, *Black Images of America*, 121.
118. Baldwin, "Understanding Martin Luther King, Jr.," 25–26; and Sterling Stuckey, ed., *The Ideological Origins of Black Nationalism* (Boston: Beacon Press, 1972), 3–27.

during the period of slavery, despite Eugene D. Genovese's suggestion that slave religion was not "essentially messianic in the political sense."[119] The slaves gave expression to these hopes in songs like "Go Down Moses" and "Joshua Fit the Battle of Jericho"— songs Martin Luther King, Jr., would quote generations later to inspire his people in the struggle.[120] These songs spoke of God's movement in history through messianic figures and of how God uses such figures as instruments of deliverance. There were undoubtedly those in the slave community, perhaps more than we will ever know, who attributed a messianic significance to Nat Turner, Gabriel Prosser, Denmark Vesey, Harriet Tubman, and other slave preachers, conjurers, and prophetic figures who may or may not be a part of the historical record. The fact that slaves rarely mentioned figures like Turner, Prosser, Vesey, and Tubman in their narratives and public conversations does not necessarily mean that they rejected the messianic claims and importance of these figures. The climate in which the slaves lived was not conducive for them to openly admit their admiration and respect for such leaders.[121]

The situation in the antebellum North was quite different, as evidenced by the many blacks who publicly advocated the rise of a black messiah. In 1808, Absalom Jones speculated that a "Joseph" would one day emerge to lead blacks in the salvation and uplift of Africa.[122] A year later, Joseph Sidney, described as "the black arch-federalist," envisioned the coming of a black "Wilberforce" for that same purpose.[123] Robert Alexander Young, the black New

119. Eugene D. Genovese, *Roll, Jordan, Roll: The World the Slaves Made* (New York: Pantheon Books, 1972), 272–73; and Lewis V. Baldwin, "'Deliverance to the Captives': Images of Jesus Christ in the Minds of Afro-American Slaves," *Journal of Religious Studies*, 12, no. 2 (Fall 1986); 35–37.

120. Harold Courlander, *Negro Folk Music, U.S.A.* (New York: Columbia University Press, 1963), 42–46; and Martin Luther King, Jr., "Address at the Chicago Freedom Movement Rally," Soldier Field, Chicago, Ill. (The King Center Archives, 10 July 1966), 3.

121. Baldwin, "'Deliverance to the Captives,'" 36–37.

122. Sweet, *Black Images of America*, 121.

123. *Ibid.*

Yorker who wrote *The Ethiopian Manifesto* in 1829, spoke of the rise of another "John the Baptist" who would liberate blacks from slavery and direct them in the establishment of a new black nation.[124] David Walker prophesied that God would provide "a Hannibal" to lead the slaves in battle against their enslavers. Edward W. Blyden hoped for a black Moses to bring to an end the American exile and lead an exodus to the promised land of Africa.[125] With the circulation of these ideas, which reached the South in some cases, it is highly possible that more than a few blacks were imbued with a messianic vision.[126]

This longing for a messiah did not fade among blacks with the abolishment of slavery. The tremendous violence visited on them during and after Reconstruction kept their expectation alive. In 1892, John W. E. Bowen, a black Methodist pastor from Washington, D.C., urged his people to set for themselves the highest standards in anticipation of "a black Alexander" to guide them in the amelioration of their condition:

> But the solution will not come until the Negro shall have reached his majority. And then will a black Alexander come forth, fortified by constitutional enactments and the moral sentiment of the nation; panoplied in the virtues of a Christian character; and with his own sword of courage and manhood, with intelligence, wealth and moral excellence, shall cut the Gordian knot and relegate to the dead past every vexatious problem. Believing this thoroughly, I am anxious that we do not stop at any half-way house and become a race of mediocres.[127]

124. *Ibid.*, 122; and Stuckey, ed., *The Ideological Origins of Black Nationalism*, 36–37.

125. Sweet, *Black Images of America*, 121–22; Wiltse, ed., *David Walker's Appeal*, 20; and Baldwin, "'Deliverance to the Captives,'" 36.

126. Baldwin, "'Deliverance to the Captives,'" 36; and Sweet, *Black Images of America*, 122.

127. John W. E. Bowen, *What Shall the Harvest Be?: A National Sermon; or, A Series of Plain Talks to the Colored People of America, on Their Problems* (Washington, D.C.: Press of the Stafford Printing Company, 1892), 26.

In 1907, several leaders of the African Union Methodist Protestant Church in Chester, Pennsylvania expressed anger over the increase of lynchings, and declared that "We pray the God of Nations to make bare his arm and in his appointed time raise up a deliverer as he did in the darkest days of slavery."[128] This kind of consciousness helps explain the advent of a considerable number of black messiahs in the four decades prior to the emergence of Martin Luther King, Jr., among them Marcus Garvey, Father Divine, Daddy Grace, and Elijah Muhammad. All of these messiahs inspired pride, self-confidence, and hope among black people, thus contributing to an atmosphere that made possible the rise of King.[129] The excitement generated by King in the black community has remained strong despite the emergence of Jesse Jackson, who has been referred to as "a black Moses" by the Black Muslim leader Louis Farrakhan.

Black messianic attitudes in the post-King era have remained essentially in the traditional mold. In 1970, the black writer Lerone Bennett, Jr., expressed the view of generations of black thinkers when he referred to the Negro as "a conservator of human values" and "a hewer of the human spirit." "Born into mission, ordained, as it were, from birth to advocate freedom," he continued, "the Negro is the only American who consistently makes an issue of democracy at home." For Bennett, the fact that "Hundreds of thousands of Negroes, from Bunker Hill to Vietnam, have died for an idea that was not real in their own lives," is the best indication of what the black presence has meant for America.[130] In the 1970s, the widely known professor Gayraud S. Wilmore wrote at some length concerning the prophetic vision of liberty with which black America continues to challenge the larger

128. See *Minutes of the 93rd Session of the Annual Conference of the African Union First Colored M. P. Church, of the Middle District, St. John's A.U.F.C.M.P. Church, Chester, Pennsylvania, May 15–20, 1907* (Wilmington, Del.: Hubert A. Roop, Printer, 1907), 22.

129. See Moses, *Black Messiahs and Uncle Toms*, 155–82.

130. Lerone Bennett, Jr., *The Black Mood and Other Essays* (New York: Barnes & Noble, 1970), 65–66.

society.[131] On a similar note, Martin Luther King, Sr., drawing on the insight of his famous son, stated in 1980 that America would discover its future through the black struggle.[132] Jesse Jackson repeated this idea in 1983, in the midst of his presidential campaign, and conjectured that maybe God "put us here to save the human race. It may be that our mission is greater than that recorded by historians."[133] In more precise terms, the black scholar C. Eric Lincoln observed in 1984 that in a society in which Protestantism, Catholicism, and Judaism have accommodated themselves to the status quo, the black church, due to its forced and historic exclusion from the inner circles of American religious pluralism, may well emerge as a vital moral and spiritual authority in resolving America's dilemma with respect to race.[134] The central question confronting black Americans in this last decade of the twentieth century is whether we can remain strong and dedicated enough to fulfill the humanizing role that Martin Luther King, Jr., and many other philosophers of black messianism envisioned throughout our history.

## POTENTIAL BARRIERS TO THE FULFILLMENT OF KING'S BLACK MESSIANIC HOPE

Black America confronts many problems that constitute potential barriers to the fulfillment of King's black messianic hope. One problem involves the male-dominated charismatic leadership model that was encouraged and exemplified by King. Although this

131. Wilmore, "Black Religion and the Concept of Liberty," 1–18; Gayraud S. Wilmore, "The New Challenge of Black Religion to American Christianity" (An unpublished paper, 1976), 1–19; and Gayraud S. Wilmore, "The Gifts and Tasks of the Black Church" (An unpublished paper, n.d.), 1–14.

132. Martin Luther King, Sr., written with Clayton Riley, *Daddy King: An Autobiography*, (New York: William Morrow, 1980), 94, 124, 179, 214.

133. Jesse L. Jackson, "Ministers as Apocalyptic Advocates for the Poor," *The Journal of Religious Thought*, 40, no. 1 (Spring–Summer 1983); 28.

134. C. Eric Lincoln, *Race, Religion and the Continuing American Dilemma* (New York: Hill and Wang, 1984), 60–86, 123–37, 228–60.

leadership model has inspired and motivated black people throughout American history, and has benefitted many from a psychological and spiritual standpoint, it has also been, and remains, in some ways counterproductive. As in the case of the civil rights movement, it has often stifled the creative energy and potential of the black masses by encouraging them to await a Moses figure to deliver them from oppression. The black female activist Ella Baker recognized this in the 1950s and 1960s, and concluded that the male-dominated charismatic leadership model is "unhealthy, unrealistic, and ideologically backward." In her view, mass movements are most effective when organized democratically, from the bottom up, with major attention devoted to the development of indigenous local leadership.[135]

This is the direction that black Americans must take today and in the future in order to be a vital and leading force in the humanization of America and the world. The resources of the black masses must be used to the fullest, and this will allow black people to assume more of a collective role not only in their own liberation but also in the liberation struggles of other poor and oppressed peoples.[136] Such a collective role will necessarily require a complete return to the communal values of the black heritage—values that respect personhood more than materialism, and that place the needs and aspirations of the community above those of the individual. To be most effective, black Americans should organize around issues and values rather than ideology, which is so often as fixed or rigid as the charismatic leadership pattern.

The ineptness of the male-dominated charismatic leadership model can also be seen in its exclusion of women.

135. Adam Fairclough, *To Redeem the Soul of America: The Southern Christian Leadership Conference and Martin Luther King, Jr.* (Athens, Ga.: University of Georgia Press, 1987), 50.

136. Although King expressed the belief that social movements must draw on the values and resources of the masses in order to be successful, he did not reject the male-dominated charismatic leadership model. See Garrow, *Bearing the Cross*, 141, 375–76; and Fairclough, *To Redeem the Soul of America*, 49–50.

Black female activists such as Rosa Parks, Ella Baker, Jo Ann Robinson, and Diane Nash Bevel made enormous contributions to the black freedom struggle in the 1950s and 1960s, but they always stood in the shadow of charismatic male leaders like Martin Luther King, Jr. King himself was a male chauvinist who did little to encourage female involvement at the highest levels of leadership in the movement.[137] This practice of exclusion was supported by the black church, and it stunted the movement in ways not evident to King and others who operated through major, male-controlled organizations such as the S.C.L.C., the NAACP, the Urban League, and C.O.R.E. Although King's leadership did much to free women and to give direction and momentum to the women's movement, the problem of discrimination against women remained.[138] This problem must be faced forthrightly and resolved before black Americans can effectively assume the messianic role King envisioned for them.[139]

137. Garrow, *Bearing the Cross*, 375–76; and Fairclough, *To Redeem the Soul of America*, 49–50. In all fairness to King, he did not hesitate to praise black women for their contributions to the movement. He called Ella Baker, the first Executive Director of the S.C.L.C., "a very able person and a stimulating speaker." Of Rosa Parks, who sparked the Montgomery Bus Boycott, King wrote: "She chose to stand her ground and say with those who have prophesied of old, 'Before I'll be a slave, I'll be buried in my grave, and go home to my Lord and be free.'" Concerning Diane Nash Bevel, King once said: "In the midst of student sit-ins in early 1960, Mrs. Bevel distinguished herself as the driving spirit in the nonviolent assault on segregation at lunch counters in her work as part of the Youth Division of the Nashville Christian Leadership Conference." King referred to the great gospel singer Mahalia Jackson as one who has "been fighting in the struggle so long." "It really has been difficult to say to you," he once told Mahalia, "how much you mean and have meant to the Negro revolution and especially S.C.L.C." King frequently exchanged letters with women, expressing gratitude for their "moral support and Christian generosity," and noting how this "renews my courage and vigor to carry on." See a letter from Martin Luther King, Jr., to Katie O. Whickam, 7 July 1958, The King Papers, Boston University; King, "Speech at a Rally," Crawfordsville, Ga., 1–2; a letter from Martin Luther King, Jr., to Basil Paterson 9 April 1962, The King Papers, Boston University; and a letter from Martin Luther King, Jr., to Mahalia Jackson, 10 January 1964, The King Papers, Boston University.

138. Fairclough, *To Redeem the Soul of America*, 49–50; and Ansbro, *Martin Luther King, Jr.*, xiv–xv.

139. See James H. Cone, *For My People—Black Theology and the Black Church: Where Have We Been and Where Are We Going?* (Maryknoll, N.Y.: Orbis Books, 1984), 122–39.

Another major threat to the fulfillment of King's black messianic hope is evident in the fact that increasing numbers of blacks are abandoning the spiritual values and emotive qualities of their heritage. This is especially true of the black middle class, many of whom are doing their utmost to achieve assimilation at all levels of the American society. Black Americans will have a better chance to be a model and inspiration for the world if they cultivate the emotive, intuitive, and aesthetic values that link them to their slave forebears and to Africa. King himself recognized that his people could never be a vital, creative, and transforming force in the world as long as they aspire toward white Western values—values undergirded by an abstract intellectualism, an excessive materialism, and a need to control the world through scientific, technological, and military advantages.[140]

Of equal importance is the need for black Americans to develop what King called "a world perspective."[141] Invariably, this means that the black American community must be educated to see that it shares a common condition and struggle with Africans, Asians, Latin Americans, and other oppressed peoples throughout the world. At this point in history, the masses of blacks are too preoccupied with their own survival issues and agenda to look beyond the boundaries of America, and this is to some degree understandable. Nevertheless, there is a need for black Americans to devote more time, energy, and resources to building bridges of communication and cooperation with others who are enslaved and colonized, and black churches should bear the major economic responsibilities for this development, especially given their advantaged financial condition when compared with so-called Third World peoples.[142] This is the vision

140. King, *Where Do We Go from Here?*, 167–91.
141. Martin Luther King, Jr., "What a Mother Should Tell Her Child," a sermon delivered at Ebenezer Baptist Church, Atlanta, Ga. (The King Center Archives, 12 May 1963), 4.
142. *Ibid.;* Martin Luther King, Jr., *The Trumpet of Conscience* (San Francisco: Harper & Row, 1967), 68–71; and Cone, *For My People*, 142–43.

Martin Luther King, Jr., had toward the end of his life.[143]
The resources of black Americans must be directed increasingly toward a global, messianic objective if they
are to become effective and recognized leaders in the
quest for a new humanity.

Despite its many shortcomings, black America is
still in a better moral and spiritual position than white
America to serve as a vanguard in the human struggle for
wholeness and harmony. This fact should be accepted
with humility and a deep sense of collective responsibility, not with arrogance and condescension. White Americans are still oppressed by their oppressing routine, and
are not as free to love and to practice nonviolence,
in accordance with the commands of Jesus Christ, as
black Americans. In fact, white Western society as a
whole is still gripped by an obsession with materialism,
war, and power—an obsession that deprives it of genuine
moral, spiritual, and aesthetic values. Moreover, blacks,
because of their history and suffering, are still, for
the most part, more sensitive than whites to issues and
concerns confronting the poor and oppressed worldwide. Blacks have always been forced to be more broad
visioned than whites, and are therefore more of a Renaissance people. When all is considered, however, the
messianic role envisioned by Martin Luther King, Jr.,
may be too heavy a cross for oppressed black Americans
to bear.[144] Nevertheless, it is black America's responsibility to make sure that King and the generations of black
martyrs and victims that came before and after him have
not bled and dreamed and died in vain. "There is no
meaning for the Black living or the Black dead or the
Black unborn," declares Lerone Bennett, Jr., "outside
the great Black chain of that hope."[145]

---

143. King, *Where Do We Go from Here?*, 57.
144. Moses, *Black Messiahs and Uncle Toms*, 234.
145. Bennett, "Listen to the Blood," 42.

# STANDING IN THE SHOES OF JOHN
## A BEARER OF THE BLACK
## PREACHING TRADITION

# 5

> The preacher is the most unique personality developed by the
> Negro on American soil. A leader, a politician, an orator, a
> "boss," an intriguer, an idealist—all these he is, and ever, too,
> the centre of a group of men, now twenty, now a thousand in
> number.
>
> W. E. B. Du Bois, 1903[1]

> The Negro today is, perhaps, the most priest-governed group
> in the country.
>
> James Weldon Johnson, 1927[2]

> I'm the son of a preacher, I'm the great-grandson of a
> preacher, and the great-great-grandson of a preacher. My fa-
> ther is a preacher. My grandfather was a preacher. My great-
> grandfather was a preacher. My only brother is a preacher.
> My daddy's brother is a preacher. So I didn't have much
> choice, I guess.
>
> Martin Luther King, Jr., 1967[3]

> Lord, bless the man who is gonna stand in the shoes of John
> this morning, to declare the truth between the living and the
> dead. Let him down into your storehouse of knowledge, and
> crown him with wisdom and understanding.
>
> from a traditional black prayer[4]

Martin Luther King, Jr., was a versatile individual,
talented in a great number of different endeavors. He

1. John Hope Franklin, ed., *The Souls of Black Folk in Three Negro
Classics* (New York: Avon Books, 1965; originally published in 1903), 338.
2. James Weldon Johnson, *God's Trombones: Seven Negro Sermons
in Verse* (New York: Viking Press, 1969; originally published in 1927), 3.
3. Martin Luther King, Jr., "The Early Days," excerpts of a sermon
delivered at Mt. Pisgah Missionary Baptist Church, Chicago, Ill. (The
Archives of the Martin Luther King, Jr., Center for Nonviolent Social
Change, Inc., Atlanta, Ga., 27 August 1967), 9.
4. These lines were taken from prayers given by my father, the Rev.
L. V. Baldwin, Sr., and others—prayers I heard as a boy while growing up
in Camden, Ala. Larry G. Murphy, "'God Got You Now': Conversion

has been presented in such diverse roles as social activist, agitator, ritual leader, political organizer, charismatic figure, world statesman, theologian, social ethicist, Personalistic philosopher, and orator. For all his multifarious activities, King was primarily and pre-eminently a Baptist preacher who drank heavily from the wellsprings of the black preaching tradition and who demonstrated great insight and unusual creativity in applying the resources of that tradition to public policy questions and to the practical problems of everyday life.[5]

This chapter treats King as an embodiment and a rich exemplar of the black preaching tradition, with a specific focus on two areas. First, it devotes attention to the range of religious, intellectual, and experiential sources that shaped and informed his ministry. The contention here is that King's understanding and practice of ministry were primarily, though not exclusively, influenced by the oral traditions of black folk, the prophetic heritage of the Bible, his exposure to liberal and progressive-minded black ministers and educators at Morehouse College, and his personal trials and sufferings as a social activist.[6] Second, the models of ministry that characterized King's activities as a clergyman and social activist are seriously considered. The treatment provided here reveals that King viewed the preaching, pastoral, priestly,

---

Narratives of Black Americans," *Explor: A Journal of Theology,* 5, no. 2 (Fall 1979): 30.

   5. Martin Luther King, Jr., "The Un-Christian Christian," *Ebony,* 20, no. 10 (August 1965): 77; William D. Watley, *Roots of Resistance: The Nonviolent Ethic of Martin Luther King, Jr.* (Valley Forge, Pa.: Judson Press, 1985): 17–18; Robert M. Franklin, Jr., "Martin Luther King, Jr. as Pastor," *The Iliff Review,* 42, no. 2 (Spring 1985): 4; Lewis V. Baldwin, "Understanding Martin Luther King, Jr. within the Context of Southern Black Religious History," *Journal of Religious Studies,* 13, no. 2 (Fall 1987): 3–8; and Gerald L. Davis, *I Got the Word in Me and I Can Sing It You Know: A Study of the Performed African-American Sermon* (Philadelphia: University of Pennsylvania Press, 1985), 11–12.

   6. Lewis V. Baldwin, "The Minister as Preacher, Pastor, and Prophet: The Thinking of Martin Luther King, Jr.," *American Baptist Quarterly,* 7, no. 2 (June 1988): 79; and Keith D. Miller, "The Influence of a Liberal Homiletic Tradition on 'Strength to Love' By Martin Luther King, Jr." (Ph.D. diss., Texas Christian University, Fort Worth, Texas, August 1984), 1–198.

and prophetic functions as *interrelated* and *interdependent,* and was able to maintain, in practical terms, a proper balance among them.[7] Thus, King fitted W. E. B. Du Bois's description of the traditional black preacher as a many-splendored figure and as a supreme embodiment of the union of the secular and sacred in black culture.[8]

This chapter begins with a discussion of King's early exposure to ministers in the black church. From that point, King's "call to preach," his early ministry, and the various ministerial roles he served are considered. The discussion ends with an assessment of his influence on ministers and perceptions of ministry since the mid-1950s.

## THE CALL TO PREACH

Martin Luther King, Jr., descended from a long line of Baptist preachers who mastered the modes of Afro-American oral expression and who wielded great influence among their people in the South. As noted earlier, King's maternal great-grandfather, the Reverend Williams, apparently exercised considerable power and influence as an exhorter in the slave community and later as a spiritual leader of ex-slaves in Greene County, Georgia. The Reverend A. D. Williams, King's maternal grandfather, was one of the few nationally known southern black preachers of the first three decades of this century—one who reflected the powerful, thundering style, the gestures, the cadences, and the deep emotive quality of his father and other preachers who came out of slavery.[9] These qualities were passed down to Martin

7. Baldwin, "The Minister as Preacher, Pastor, and Prophet," 79.

8. Franklin, ed., *The Souls of Black Folk in Three Negro Classics,* 338, 342.

9. Martin Luther King, Sr., Written with Clayton Riley, *Daddy King: An Autobiography* (New York: William Morrow, 1980), 27, 84–91; Frederick L. Downing, *To See the Promised Land: The Faith Pilgrimage of Martin Luther King, Jr.* (Macon, Ga.: Mercer University Press, 1986), 47; Coretta Scott King, *My Life with Martin Luther King, Jr.* (New York: Avon Books, 1969), 22, 72–73, 93, 98–99; and "Daddy King: 'There's No Hate in My Heart,'" *The Chicago Tribune* (December 23, 1980): Section II, 1, 4.

Luther King, Jr., whose rhythmic eloquence and poetic speech attested to the power of the preaching tradition that produced him.[10]

Very early, King developed a fascination for preachers and the art of preaching. As a boy, he found great delight in walking at his father's side as his father ascended the pulpit or moved among the people at Atlanta's Ebenezer Baptist Church. The youngster often witnessed, with a mixture of awe and respect, how the congregation danced, swayed, and cried under the impact of his father's powerful and emotional oratorical flourishes.[11] Martin Luther King, Sr., frequently recalled how his son enjoyed listening to, and being in the presence of, great preachers even before he was old enough to understand them:

> If he heard that some outstanding man was going to speak, he would ask me to take him. I remember after one such occasion when he was only about ten, he said, "That man had some big words, Daddy. When I grow up I'm going to get me some big words." As soon as he could read, he lived in dictionaries, and he made that saying come true.[12]

King's awe and respect for preachers were enhanced by his early exposure to some of the nation's best-trained and most widely known black preachers. The renowned William Holmes Borders and Sandy F. Ray were close friends of the King family. Young Martin was known to sneak down occasionally to Wheat Street Baptist Church, located a few blocks from his home on Atlanta's Auburn Avenue, to listen to Pastor Borders. Ray and Martin Luther King, Sr., had been classmates and friends at Morehouse College, and their friendship grew stronger in

10. "Daddy King: 'There's No Hate in My Heart,'" 1, 4; King, *My Life with Martin Luther King, Jr.*, 20, 22, 93, 98–99; and Hortense J. Spillers, "Martin Luther King and the Style of the Black Sermon," *The Black Scholar*, 3, no. 1 (September 1971): 15–16.

11. Stephen B. Oates, *Let the Trumpet Sound: The Life of Martin Luther King, Jr.* (New York: Harper & Row, 1982), 3–4; and King, *My Life with Martin Luther King, Jr.*, 93.

12. King, *My Life with Martin Luther King, Jr.*, 93.

later years, leading Martin, Jr., to refer to Ray as "Uncle Sandy."[13] William Holmes Borders, Sandy F. Ray, Joseph H. Jackson, Mordecai Johnson, Benjamin E. Mays, J. Pius Barbour, William H. Hester, James T. Boddie, Gardner C. Taylor, Howard Thurman, Lucius M. Tobin, and Samuel W. Williams were among that powerful and illustrious group of black Baptist preachers who occasionally spoke at Ebenezer church during King's childhood, and who were frequently guests in the King home. Some of these men took great pleasure in bouncing young Martin on their knees on such occasions.[14] All of these outstanding preachers, who skillfully combined an eloquent preaching style with a prophetic and socially relevant ministry, helped make Martin Luther King, Jr., possible. According to Philip Lenud, one of King's childhood friends, "these preachers loomed large in Martin's life. They were his fathom. He learned to worship these great preachers, these great minds who exalted the importance of education and who believed in a well-rounded ministry."[15]

King's early fascination for preachers and preaching was not shared by his brother A. D., who seemed determined not to be a preacher. This situation led Martin, Sr. to believe that young Martin would become a minister and would evolve more naturally than his brother to a

13. A private interview with the Rev. Ralph D. Abernathy, Atlanta, Ga., 17 March 1987; a private interview with Dr. Philip Lenud, Nashville, Tenn., 7 April 1987; and a letter from Sandy F. Ray to Martin Luther King, Jr., 24 March 1965, The King Center Archives.

14. A private interview with the Rev. Ralph D. Abernathy, 17 March 1987; and a private interview with Dr. Philip Lenud, 7 April 1987.

15. A private interview with Dr. Philip Lenud, 7 April 1987. Lenud has reported that "the old man King himself felt that he was not a great preacher, but he loved great preaching, and wanted to expose his people to great preaching. And he did that. The great preachers of the country, white and black, came to Ebenezer, and this went on the 1930s and 1940s. Daddy King had the great preachers of the world to come to that church. He spent $10,000 to bring a preacher from Scotland to Ebenezer, back then." Ralph Abernathy supports the view that black preachers like William H. Borders, Benjamin E. Mays, Sandy Ray, Mordecai Johnson, Howard Thurman, Lucius Tobin, and Samuel Williams "loomed large in King's life." A private interview with the Rev. Ralph D. Abernathy, 17 March 1987. Also see a private interview with Dr. Philip Lenud, Nashville, Tenn., 9 December 1986.

place in the pastorate of Ebenezer Baptist Church. This expectation was reinforced by the fact that Martin, Jr., could speak and sing well even before he reached age ten. This explains in part why Martin, Sr., began very early to guide the boy toward the ministry.[16]

The possibility of young King becoming a minister seemed to decline as he approached adolescence. At age thirteen, he began to experience some skepticism regarding the rigid fundamentalism to which he was being introduced at Ebenezer church and other black churches in Atlanta. That feeling increased as he focused more critically on the seemingly uninhibited emotionalism of certain black churches, and on the anti-intellectualism of certain old-fashioned black preachers.[17] But the continuing influence of Martin Luther King, Sr., and other black preachers who represented a more reasoned approach to the Christian faith kept young Martin from completely succumbing to skepticism.[18]

When King entered Morehouse College in 1944, he was determined to become either a lawyer or a physician. However, the Morehouse College experience, which brought him into closer contact with preachers and educators like Benjamin Mays, George Kelsey, and Samuel Williams, most of whom were his boyhood idols, led him to reconsider seriously the ministry.[19] These men helped King see that ministry could be both intellectually respectable and emotionally satisfying, and this opened the way for the young man to pursue that profession in

16. King, *Daddy King*, 127–28.
17. Martin Luther King, Jr., "An Autobiography of Religious Development" (Unpublished document, The King Papers, Mugar Memorial Library, Boston University, Boston, Mass., n.d., circa 1950) 9–10; King, *My Life with Martin Luther King, Jr.*, 98–99; and Zelia S. Evans and J. T. Alexander, eds., *The Dexter Avenue Baptist Church, 1877–1977* (Montgomery, Ala.: The Dexter Avenue Baptist Church, 1978), 69.
18. King, "An Autobiography of Religious Development," 15; and King, *My Life with Martin Luther King, Jr.*, 20, 28, 72–73, 98–99.
19. King, *Daddy King*, 140–41; Martin Luther King, Jr., "My Call to Preach," stated before the American Baptist Convention, (The King Papers, Boston University, 7 August 1959), 1; and King, *My Life with Martin Luther King, Jr.*, 96.

the black church. King's father was also a powerful force in turning him toward the ministry:

> I guess the influence of my father also had a great deal to do with my going into the ministry. This is not to say that he ever spoke to me in terms of being a minister, but that my admiration for him was the great moving factor. He set forth a noble example that I didn't mind following.[20]

In 1947, at the end of his junior year at Morehouse College, King returned to his summer job on a tobacco plantation in Simsbury, Connecticut, and at that point announced his decision to become a minister. He was only eighteen at the time, and his decision evoked friendly teasing from some of his classmates, as his sister Christine reported:

> Although everyone recognized that he was guided by admirable motivations, he still suffered good-natured ribbing about this decision from his classmates. They used to tease him that it was not the Lord but the hot sun of the tobacco fields that "called him" into the ministry.[21]

King's call to the ministry was somewhat different in structure and patterns of experience from that of the typical black preacher in his day. From the time of slavery, black preachers had established their right to "stand in the shoes of John" by turning back, in testimony, to transforming experiences that were as dramatic and existentially catastrophic as Saul's experience on the Damascus road.[22] From his earliest childhood, King had been in the presence of black preachers who frequently recalled such

20. King, "An Autobiography of Religious Development," 14.
21. Christine King Farris, "The Young Martin: From Childhood through College," *Ebony*, 41, no. 3 (January 1986): 58.
22. For important discussions of the "call to preach" as understood in the black church tradition, see Clifton H. Johnson, ed., *God Struck Me Dead: Religious Conversion Experiences and Autobiographies of Ex-Slaves* (Philadelphia and Boston: Pilgrim Press, 1969), 5–10; and Murphy, "'God Got You Now,'" 30–39.

experiences. However, he insisted that his own *call to preach* "was neither dramatic nor spectacular":

> It came neither by some miraculous vision nor by some blinding light experience on the road of life. Moreover, it did not come as a sudden realization. Rather, it was a response to an inner urge that gradually came upon me. This urge expressed itself in a desire to serve God and humanity, and the feeling that my talent and my commitment could best be expressed through the ministry.[23]

In one fundamental sense, King's call to the ministry did conform to the pattern so often described by generations of black preachers before and after him. Like the typical black preacher, his decision to preach resulted from an experience with God rather than from some casual choice on his part. He had a clear-cut conception of what constituted the call to the ministry in the black church tradition. The spirit of God lingered with King, causing the ministry to bear on his heart and mind even as he prepared for the possibility of becoming a lawyer or a physician. "As I passed through the preparation stages of these two professions," he remembered, "I still felt within that undying urge to serve God and humanity through the ministry." "I came to see that God had placed a responsibility upon my shoulders," he continued, "and the more I tried to escape it the more frustrated I would become."[24]

In the fall of 1947, King delivered his trial sermon at the Ebenezer Baptist Church in Atlanta. This event was symbolically important for a couple of reasons. First, King had grown up in Ebenezer and had received many of his earliest lessons in spiritual and moral values there. Second, his family history was intimately linked to that church. His father had pastored Ebenezer church for sixteen years, and, prior to that, his maternal grandfather had served the church as pastor for thirty-seven years.

23. King, "My Call to Preach," 1.
24. *Ibid.*

Furthermore, his maternal grandmother had been active at Ebenezer church until her death in 1941, and his mother had spent her entire life there, serving for many years as a musician.[25] Considering this close connection between family, church, and neighborhood, it is easy to understand why King's first sermon at Ebenezer church was greeted with enormous enthusiasm. Concerning that occasion, his sister Christine has written:

> To say that it was well received is an understatement. Generally, young ministers preached their trial sermons in the basement of the church. M. L.'s was delivered in the overflowing sanctuary because of the number of people who wanted to hear him speak.[26]

King's trial sermon evoked a hearty response, causing his father to burst with pride. The night after the sermon was delivered, Martin, Sr., fell to his knees and praised God for giving him such a son.[27] A few months later, on February 25, 1948, young Martin was ordained at Ebenezer church by a council of ministers that included his father, Lucius M. Tobin, Benjamin E. Mays, Paul A. Anderson, Samuel W. Williams, and eight other ministers.[28] King then began assisting his father at Ebenezer church, an experience that helped him polish his preaching style. After graduating from Morehouse College in the spring of 1948, he decided to enter Crozer Theological Seminary in Chester, Pennsylvania. That decision was enthusiastically supported by Martin, Sr., who was determined that his son would get the best training possible for the ministry.[29]

King was only nineteen when he entered Crozer Theological Seminary in the fall of 1948. His father made

25. King, *Daddy King*, 58–214.

26. Farris, "The Young Martin," 58.

27. *Ibid.*; King, *Daddy King*, 141; and King, *My Life with Martin Luther King, Jr.*, 99.

28. "Set for the Defence of the Gospel," a certificate of ordination awarded to Martin Luther King, Jr., Ebenezer Baptist Church, Atlanta, Ga. (The King Papers, Boston University, 25 February 1948).

29. Farris, "The Young Martin," 58; King, *Daddy King*, 144–47; and King, *My Life with Martin Luther King, Jr.*, 79, 100–01.

arrangements for him to work with J. Pius Barbour, a family friend who pastored Calvary Baptist Church in Chester. King remained with Barbour during the three years he studied at Crozer Theological Seminary. "His relationship with the Reverend Barbour was like a father-son relationship," according to Sara Richardson, an active member of Calvary Baptist Church. "The Reverend Barbour would call him up—'Mike, come out here, I want to talk to you,'" a request to which King always responded affirmatively.[30] "Mike was very fond of Reverend Barbour and Reverend Barbour was also fond of him," recalled Emma Anderson, another long-time member of Calvary church.[31] King spent many hours listening to Barbour's advice and wise counsel and engaging him in philosophical and theological discussions. He frequently accompanied Barbour in visiting and praying with church members who were sick or otherwise confined to their homes. At other times, King made his way to the church parsonage to eat soul food with the Barbours or to listen to the singing of the Reverend Barbour's wife, Olee Littlejohn Barbour.[32] These experiences recreated for King a sense of family not easily duplicated elsewhere in the North in the early 1950s. The Reverend Barbour permitted him to preach regularly at Calvary church and insisted that the young man work closely with children and teenagers. King's exposure to Barbour and to the membership at Calvary helped him develop skills that would prove useful when he emerged as a pastor and civil rights activist.[33]

King discovered a similar situation when he moved to Boston to pursue a doctorate degree in the fall of 1951. During his three years in Boston, he worked closely

30. A private interview with Sara Richardson, Chester, Pa., 29 May 1987.

31. A private interview with Emma Anderson, Chester, Pa., 29 May 1987.

32. A private interview with Sara Richardson, 29 May 1987; and a private interview with Emma Anderson, 29 May 1987.

33. A private interview with Sara Richardson, 29 May 1987; and a private interview with Emma Anderson, 29 May 1987.

with the Reverend William H. Hester of Twelfth Baptist Church, another close friend of the King family. At this point, Martin, Sr., was still very concerned about his son, "theologically and socially, and wanted to know that he was under the surveillance of someone who would guide him according to his father's dream and wishes."[34] According to the Reverend Michael Haynes, who associated with King as a student minister at Twelfth Baptist Church, "Martin was very special to Reverend Hester. Martin was the most popular among the Reverend Hester's seminary associates, and the one who preached the most regularly." "Twelfth Baptist became Martin's preaching station, his fellowship station, and feeding trough," continued Haynes. "This was his home away from home."[35] King was commonly referred to as "an adopted son" by the people of that congregation.[36] As had been the case in Chester, he preached at numerous black churches in Boston, developing and refining skills that would later benefit him immensely. His effectiveness at Twelfth Baptist Church was enhanced by the fact that he, as the Reverend Michael Haynes reported, "came naturally by the traditions of black preaching." "Martin's preaching reminded me so much of Reverend Hester—the same kind of mold and style," Haynes further observed. "A lot of this came down from his daddy and the previous generations."[37]

King demonstrated an intense interest in ministering to young people at Twelfth Baptist Church—an interest that had slowly developed as a result of his work at

34. King, *My Life with Martin Luther King, Jr.*, 72; King, *Daddy King*, 147–49; and a private interview with the Rev. Michael E. Haynes, Boston, Mass., 25 June 1987.

35. A private interview with the Rev. Michael E. Haynes, 25 June 1987. The Reverend Haynes noted that the Reverend Hester was "almost like an uncle" to King. "He favored Martin."

36. "The Twelfth Street Baptist Church of Boston, 1840: Celebration Two," *Program Booklet of the Threefold Celebration Year* (Boston: The Twelfth Baptist Church, 1985), 19.

37. A private interview with the Rev. Michael E. Haynes, 25 June 1987; a private interview with Dr. Philip Lenud, 9 December 1986; and King, *Daddy King*, 147.

Ebenezer church in Atlanta and Calvary church in Chester. Had he not been catapulted to leadership in the civil rights movement, King, according to the Reverend Michael Haynes, would have most certainly ended up working with youth:

> That was an area that Martin really wanted to look at—working with young black people. And had he not been thrust into the movement, I think he would have spent some time with a special focus on young black people. He was carried so fast into the broader arena that this very genuine interest never really had time to reach its fullest potential.[38]

The relationship King developed with the Hesters and the entire Twelfth Baptist Church family disciplined him tremendously and contributed substantially to the future course of his life. He spent a lot of time with the Reverend Hester and often took delight in eating large quantities of soul food prepared by Beulah Hester, the wife of the pastor. The young man dated one of the Reverend Hester's nieces, who was also doing graduate work in Boston. "Mrs. Hester was always concerned with what Martin and all of the other single guys at Twelfth Baptist were doing with the girls with whom they were going out," recounted the Reverend Michael Haynes. "It was like a family kind of thing."[39] Interestingly enough, it was through Twelfth Baptist Church that King met Coretta Scott, his future wife, who was studying music in Boston. The matchmaking resulted from a deliberate plan devised by Mary Powell, who was the Reverend William Hester's secretary. Powell had become well acquainted with the King family through her marriage in the family of Dr. Benjamin E. Mays, and this made her feel obligated to introduce young Martin to the most attractive and prosperous young ladies. "She thought she had all of these familial rights to Martin," reminisced the

38. A private interview with the Rev. Michael E. Haynes, 25 June 1987.
39. *Ibid.*

Reverend Michael Haynes, "and she didn't want him running around with all kinds of girls. So she deliberately plotted to bring him and Coretta together."[40] King's experiences at Twelfth Baptist Church were so rewarding and memorable until, years later, he would call or visit the Hesters every time he appeared in Boston.[41]

At Crozer Theological Seminary and Boston University King demonstrated many of the attributes of mind and spirit that were to characterize his later great ministry— an enthusiastic acceptance of liberal theology, a passion to make religion relevant to the human condition, a critical and questioning attitude toward the established order of things, and a personal charm that marked him as a leader of people.[42] Coretta Scott recognized that these attributes made King the instrument of a special destiny, and she was determined to be a part of that destiny.[43]

The reflections of Coretta Scott King reveal a great deal concerning her husband's early ministry. She was present on several occasions when he preached at Twelfth Baptist Church for the Reverend William Hester. "When he first started his ministry he leaned heavily on its theological aspect," Coretta observed, "for he was very self-conscious about anything that he considered too emotional." She further noted:

> Martin also altered his style of speaking to relate to his audience. In the sober, intellectual atmosphere of New England he talked quietly, with reasoned argument and little emotion. That was generally his style as a young minister. Later, when he preached in the South to more emotional congregations, he became less inhibited. He responded to their expectations by rousing oratory; and as they were moved, he would react to their excitement, their rising emotions exalting his own. The first thunderous "Amen" from the people would set him off in the old-fashioned preaching style.

40. *Ibid.;* and King, *My Life with Martin Luther King, Jr.,* 64–66.
41. A private interview with the Rev. Michael E. Haynes, 25 June 1987.
42. King, *My Life with Martin Luther King, Jr.,* 60–109.
43. *Ibid.,* 19, 26–27, 59, 68–69, 71, 77.

We called it "whooping." Sometimes, after we were married, I would tease him by saying, "Martin, you were whooping today." He would be a little embarrassed. But it was very exciting, Martin's whooping.[44]

During the period from 1948 to 1953, King spent the summers preaching and serving other ministerial functions for his father in Atlanta. This arrangement served the twofold purpose of giving his father a rest and of providing the young man with much-needed experience in ministry. Martin Luther King, Sr., was often in the pulpit at such times to monitor his son's progress in the ministry and to urge him to greater heights of rousing oratory. When young Martin preached, his father would frequently interject, "Make it plain, son! Make it plain!"[45] It was during the summer of 1953, when King assisted his father for the last time before assuming a pastorship in Montgomery, Alabama, that Coretta Scott King came to a better understanding of what it meant to be a minister in the black Baptist Church in the South. Previously, her image of preachers was restricted by her background in the African Methodist Episcopal Zion Church. By observing her husband and father-in-law, Coretta saw that the local, autonomous structure of the black Baptist Church shaped the character and style of ministers in ways uncharacteristic of the Methodist Episcopal structure. She came to appreciate the freedom and authority exercised by black Baptist pastors.[46] Her desire to share fully in her husband's role led her, in the summer of 1953, to accept baptism by total immersion at Ebenezer Baptist Church.[47]

Under the guidance of his father, King grew rapidly in the ministry, and made changes in his personal life that were obvious to his wife. When he first started his ministry in 1948, he still enjoyed dating and going to parties

44. *Ibid.*, 72–73, 98–99.
45. *Ibid.*, 22, 79; and King, *Daddy King*, 9.
46. Coretta Scott King, "An Address at the National Conference on Civil Rights," Fisk University, Nashville, Tenn., 5 April 1986, 1 ff.
47. King, *My Life with Martin Luther King, Jr.*, 73, 87.

on a regular basis, and this caused him to struggle a bit with the very strict Baptist discipline imposed by his father. On one occasion, Martin, Sr., made his son apologize publicly to the membership of Ebenezer church for attending a dance. For a while after that experience, young Martin stopped dating and going to dances. He spent considerable time alone, praying and reading the Bible, thinking that he had to purge himself.[48] When he met Coretta, King had become very serious about his image and believed that he had to always be on guard morally. "Martin felt that to lead people requires that your own life must be an example to them," Coretta recalled. Although he was always concerned about his moral standing and about how he was perceived by the people he led, King never really subscribed to strict Baptist discipline as understood and practiced by his father. Even after he emerged as a pastor and civil rights leader, he remained outgoing and fun loving, and was known to dance on rare occasions.[49] One writer said of him in 1964: "Martin Luther King has a subtle humor which is constantly operative, and upon occasion—for instance, a gathering of close acquaintances—he has broad humor which borders on the slapstick. A good mimic, he has been known to be the 'life of the party.'"[50] King's ministry, his leadership, and his relationship to people were significantly enhanced by his refusal to adopt the false piety and pretentious ways so typical of many black preachers in his time.

## A PREACHER AMONG PREACHERS

A turning point occurred in King's career as a preacher when he became the full-time pastor of the Dexter Avenue Baptist Church in Montgomery, Alabama, in 1954. From that point, he had to give greater attention to

48. *Ibid.*, 99.
49. *Ibid.*, 28–29, 75.
50. See Donald H. Smith, "Martin Luther King, Jr.: Rhetorician of Revolt" (Ph.D. diss., University of Wisconsin, 1964), 14.

preaching and to other responsibilities usually associated with a well-rounded ministry. King's development and role as a preacher, during and after his pastorate in Montgomery, must be understood in light of his views concerning the image of the preacher, the significance of the pulpit, and the meaning, content, structure, and purpose of the sermon—views that emerged primarily, though not exclusively, from the context of his black church experience.[51]

Some of King's most profound and inspiring sermons were delivered at the Dexter Avenue Baptist Church in the year prior to the Rosa Parks incident. He went to Dexter with the notion that sermonizing involved the proclamation of God's word in relationship to a myriad of human concerns, and with the idea that every sermon should have as its purpose the head-on constructive meeting of some spiritual, social, cultural, or personal problem that puzzles the mind, bears upon the conscience, and interferes with the complete flow of life.[52] King's first sermon at Dexter church, called "The Three Dimensions of a Complete Life," emphasized the necessity for individuals to move beyond personal concerns for their own welfare and goals in life to involve themselves in the universal concerns of humanity and in loving God with all their hearts, souls, and minds. This is how King explained the length, breadth, and height of life.[53] At other times, he challenged the members of Dexter church with sermons about forgiveness, community, and how to overcome the problem of fear—sermons that helped prepare the congregation for the role it would later play

51. One gets a sense of King's conceptions of the preacher, the pulpit, and the sermon from a reading of Spillers, "Martin Luther King and the Style of the Black Sermon," 14–27.
52. Martin Luther King, Jr., *Stride toward Freedom: The Montgomery Story* (New York: Harper & Brothers, 1958), 17, 25–36; King, *My Life with Martin Luther King, Jr.*, 112–16; and Martin Luther King, Jr., "Recommendations to the Dexter Avenue Baptist Church for the Fiscal Year, 1954–55" (Unpublished document, The King Papers, Boston University, 1954), 1–7.
53. King, *Stride toward Freedom*, 17; and John J. Ansbro, *Martin Luther King, Jr.: The Making of a Mind* (Maryknoll, N.Y.: Orbis Books, 1982), 29–34.

in the Montgomery Bus Boycott.[54] All of these sermons had a religious as well as a social message and were, therefore, consistent with King's belief that the minister should be a spiritual leader as well as an advocate for social justice. These sermons also conformed to his view that the pulpit should be an important single force in shaping public consciousness and in motivating and inspiring people to act responsibly in the social, political, and economic arenas of life.[55]

King developed the art of preaching not only as a vital part of his pastoral function at Dexter Avenue Baptist Church and later at Ebenezer Baptist Church, but also as an essential component of his role as a social activist. Over the course of the years, his sermons carried titles like "A Christian Movement in a Revolutionary Age," "A Knock at Midnight," "Remaining Awake through a Great Revolution," "To Serve the Present Age," "Standing by the Best in an Evil Time," "Making the Best of a Bad Mess," "Guidelines for a Constructive Church," "Love Your Enemies," "Transformed Nonconformist," and "On Being a Good Neighbor"—titles that spoke to social realities and the concerns of the social revolution in his day. Although the thematic spectrum of King's sermons included such theological topics as God, Jesus Christ, the Church, humanity, love, prayer, faith, and good and evil, his constant, general theme was the brotherhood and sisterhood of persons as a necessary precondition for a proper relationship with God.[56]

His favorite Biblical texts included the Sermon on the Mount, the Parable of the Good Samaritan, and the

54. King, *My Life with Martin Luther King, Jr.,* 115–16; a private interview with the Rev. Bernard S. Lee, Washington, D.C., 9 July 1986; and a private interview with the Rev. Ralph D. Abernathy, 17 March 1987.

55. King, *My Life with Martin Luther King, Jr.,* 115; and a private interview with the Rev. Ralph D. Abernathy, 17 March 1987. James Baldwin contends that the pulpit afforded King the best possible vehicle for expressing his love for the South. See James Baldwin, "The Dangerous Road Before Martin Luther King," *Harper's Magazine* (February 1961): 38.

56. Mervyn A. Warren, "A Rhetorical Study of the Preaching of Doctor Martin Luther King, Jr.: Pastor and Pulpit Orator" (Ph.D. diss., Michigan State University, 1966), 3–4.

prophet's call for Israel to seek righteousness and justice in Amos, Chapter 5. In sermons such as "Lazarus and Dives" and "Then My Living Will Not Be in Vain," King moved beyond a mere fascination with people's ideas to deal with what he called "the least of these."[57] He also frequently preached sermons with titles like "Dreams of Brighter Tomorrows," "Is the Universe Friendly?," and "The Meaning of Hope"—sermons designed to give his people hope in the midst of struggle.[58]

Much of King's genius was evident in the fact that he could preach effectively to any audience, black or white, with confidence and ease. This is what Benjamin Quarles had in mind when he noted that King "could quote Martin Buber to one audience and speak in the idiom of the ghetto to another, and be equally at home in both worlds."[59] Significantly, King planned and structured his sermons with particular audiences in mind, knowing, for instance, that a sermon that strongly appealed to whites was not likely to evoke enthusiastic responses from blacks. When preaching to whites, he employed reasoned argument with little emotion, and usually drew on Euro-American intellectual sources that were regarded as persuasive authorities in the white community. King's sermons before black audiences freely employed folk idioms and were expressed with high emotions and eloquence in order to reach the people, to move them, to uplift them, and to inspire them to act.[60]

57. A private interview with Dr. Philip Lenud, 7 April 1987; and a private interview with the Rev. Ralph D. Abernathy, 17 March 1987.

58. A private interview with the Rev. Ralph D. Abernathy, 17 March 1987. King had a habit of leaving his sermons on planes after he finished with them, which means that many of them were simply thrown into garbage cans. Unfortunately, this deprived us of many sermons that would have indicated more clearly the range of topics King used.

59. Benjamin Quarles, "Martin Luther King, Jr., in History," *The Negro History Bulletin*, 31, no. 5 (May 1968): 9.

60. James H. Cone, "Martin Luther King, Jr.: Black Theology—Black Church," *Theology Today*, 40, no. 4 (January 1984): 411. One writer referred to King as "a link between the fervid, old-time shouting religion of the Baptists of yesterday and the quiet, deep-thinking, measured philosophy of many of the modern Baptist standard-bearers and followers." See "The Martin Luther King Story," *Sepia Magazine* (March 22, 1957): 2.

In his sermons and speeches to blacks, King was also more apt to quote extensively from black folktales, from the poems of Paul Lawrence Dunbar and Langston Hughes, from the Negro National Anthem, and from slave spirituals and black gospel songs.[61] The structure of King's sermons always conformed to the tripartite partition of introduction, body, and conclusion.[62] The introduction for him involved reading a passage of scripture and choosing a theme or subject for the sermon. The body included the main points of his message. King's voice generally increased in pitch toward the end of his sermon, taking on a mournful, singing quality, and the conclusion usually raised the theme of hope in an inspirational manner. This structure and pattern had long been a part of the black preacher's sermon craft when King emerged.[63]

One way to understand more fully King's role as a preacher, and the manner in which he developed the sermon as a work of art, is to discuss his *art* within the framework of William R. Jones' five salient characteristics of black preaching.[64] These characteristics are *dialogical character, the use of parallelism, "cryptic" or "soul"*

61. Martin Luther King, Jr., *Strength to Love* (Philadelphia: Fortress Press, 1981), 64; and Martin Luther King, Jr., *Where Do We Go from Here: Chaos or Community?* (Boston: Beacon Press, 1967), 103. King made numerous references to the poems of Hughes and Dunbar in his unpublished, spontaneously delivered sermons and mass meeting speeches before black audiences. These sources reveal that "Free at Last," "Nobody Knows the Trouble I've Seen," and "There Is a Balm in Gilead" were among King's favorite spiritual songs, and "Precious Lord, Take My Hand," "How I Got Over," "Move on Up a Little Higher," "An Amazing Grace," and "Beulah Land" were among his favorite black gospel songs. Nothing moved him more than Aretha Franklin's version of "An Amazing Grace," Ben Branch's rendition of "Take My Hand, Precious Lord" on saxophone, and Mahalia Jackson's singing of "Move on Up a Little Higher," "Beulah Land," and "Take My Hand, Precious Lord." A private interview with the Rev. Ralph D. Abernathy, 17 March 1987.

62. Warren, "A Rhetorical Study of the Preaching of Doctor Martin Luther King, Jr.," 3–4.

63. Jon Michael Spencer, *Sacred Symphony: The Chanted Sermon of the Black Preacher* (Westport, Conn.: Greenwood Press, 1987), 4–5; a private interview with the Rev. Ralph D. Abernathy, 17 March 1987; and Johnson, ed., *God Struck Me Dead*, 5–10.

64. William R. Jones, "The Art of Preaching from a Black Perspective" (an unpublished paper, n.d.), 8–9.

*language, the union of body and soul,* and *a posture of freedom and fearlessness.* In the first place, King, reflecting the influence of his black heritage, understood preaching to be essentially *dialogical* rather than *monological* in character. He never wanted his hearers to be silent and passive receptors of his message, and he was never disappointed when preaching to black people. The cries of "Amen," "hallelujah," "that's right," "glory," "praise God," and "preach the word," which usually punctuated his sermons before black audiences, convinced him that his people perceived the spirit of God working through him, that they were in solidarity with him, and that they were willing to follow him wherever he led them.[65]

King was able to evoke enthusiastic responses from his people because he understood the emotional side of their religion and had a keen sense of the chemistry, dynamics, and rhythms that operated between himself and them. Hortense Spillers has elaborated at length about how King reflected the genius and ability of generations of black preachers before him in mastering the art of *preaching as dialogue:*

> The phenomenon was never absent when King spoke. Readers may recall King's Montgomery speech, "We're on the Move," and the unidentified man who stood at his side. ("Montgomery to Memphis" documentary.) After picking up the tenor of King's rhythm the man began to repeat the key words: "Yessuh, we're on the move!" Soon thereafter, the audience had been transformed into a vast echo chamber with King giving out the mainline, i.e., "We can't be dissuaded now . . . and no wave of racism can stop us," and the audience, spontaneous in its thrust, is highly technical and consistent; the speaker, with his innate sense of timing and rhythm, knows exactly which words will be prominent and what phrases an audience will respond

65. *Ibid.;* and Baldwin, "The Minister as Preacher, Pastor, and Prophet," 81–84.

to because he has seen the technique work for his elders time and again.[66]

Many of King's sermons were so improved by frequent repetition that every accent, every emphasis, and every modulation of the voice was so well timed and placed that one could not help being moved by his discourse. The approaches used by King to evoke lively and dramatic responses from his hearers varied. At times he reflected, in testimony, on his "vision in the kitchen" or on some other transforming event in his life. In language and in a tonality familiar to the folk, King would begin: "One day after finishing school I was called to a little church down in Montgomery, Alabama. Things went well for a while, but one day. . . ." The audience knew what was to follow, and would respond accordingly.[67] On other occasions King would tell humorous anecdotes, joke with the congregation, and make them laugh, thus "warming them up," relaxing them, and preparing them for active participation in the sermon. Oftentimes, he did it this way: He would announce his intention to be brief and "to the point," noting, in a joking manner, that "you know brevity for a Baptist preacher is a magnificent accomplishment. A Baptist preacher is always tempted to preach, and preach a long time, when he's before a very enthusiastic crowd."[68] Frequently, King would amuse his audience with references to the problems and uneasiness he and his associates experienced in flying to their

66. Baldwin, "The Minister as Preacher, Pastor, and Prophet," 82; and Spillers, "Martin Luther King and the Style of the Black Sermon," 19.
67. King, "The Early Days," 9–10. One gets a clear sense of how King skillfully used testimony to bring his people into full participation in his sermon by listening to a record album of excerpts from *Dr. Martin Luther King, Jr.'s Most Famous Speeches, With the Clara Ward Singers*, IXM-NIXMI, 809 (London: Benash Record Company, Limited, 1971).
68. Martin Luther King, Jr., "An Address at the Freedom Fund Report Dinner," 53rd Annual Convention of the NAACP, Atlanta, Ga. (The King Center Archives, 5 July 1962), 1; Martin Luther King, Jr., "Address at a Mass Meeting," Grenada, Miss. (The King Center Archives, 19 March 1968), 1; and Martin Luther King, Jr., "Address at a Mass Meeting," Augusta, Ga. (The King Center Archives, 22 March 1968), 3.

destination, as illustrated by his opening remarks in a
speech in Augusta, Georgia in March, 1968:

> . . . we did have those moments when our pilots had
> to make sure that the engine was working, and that
> held us up some; and I was agreeing that we certainly
> should take all care and be as scrutinizing as possible
> in attempting to deal with that problem, because
> when you get in the air, you want everything right.
> Now I don't want to give any of you the impression
> that I don't have faith in God in the air, its simply that
> I have had more experience with him on the
> ground.[69]

King was known to use humor at the beginning of his
message in order to establish a tone of down-home rap-
port, an approach his listeners generally liked. For example, after being introduced in glowing terms as the
guest speaker at the Canaan Baptist Church in New York
City, in March, 1968, by Dr. Richard Dixon, King told the
congregation:

> As he introduced me, I felt something like the old
> maid who had never been married. One day when
> she went to work, the lady for whom she worked said,
> "Mary, I hear that you're getting married." She said,
> "No, I'm not getting married, but thank God for the
> rumor." Well, I know all of these marvelous things
> that Richard Dixon said about me can't be true, but
> thank God for the rumor.[70]

69. King, "Address at a Mass Meeting," Augusta, Ga., 1; and Martin
Luther King, Jr., "Rally Speech on the Georgia Tour 'Pre-Washington
Campaign,'" Albany, Ga. (The King Center Archives, 22 March 1968), 1.
King sometimes concluded this anecdote by saying: "I would much rather
be Martin Luther King late than the late Martin Luther King." See Martin
Luther King, Jr., "Address at a Mass Meeting," Macon, Ga. (The King
Center Archives, 22 March 1968), 1. For a perceptive discussion of how
the traditional black preacher has used humor and other techniques to
arouse his hearers, see John Dollard, *Caste and Class in a Southern Town*
(New York: Doubleday & Co., 1957), 233–34.
70. King frequently told this story at the beginning of his sermons,
especially after he became famous. Martin Luther King, Jr., "A Knock at
Midnight," a sermon delivered at the Canaan Baptist Church, New York,
N.Y. (The King Center Archives, 24 March 1968), 1.

Although King's humor was almost always disconnected from the theme and general thrust of his sermons, it did not divert the attention of the people from the rich, profound, and serious nature of his message. On the contrary, it created among his listeners a responsive mood, thus making it possible for his sermons to become their sermons. King's skillful use of humor as a way of connecting with his audience was one indication of the high level of creativity he brought to his preaching art—creativity that established him, among other black preachers, as a fashioner and an exemplar of culture.[71]

The same can be said of King's use of parallelism in his sermons. He skillfully and effectively emphasized slavery in Egypt, the Exodus, the experience of the Israelites in the wilderness, Jesus' identification with outsiders, and other great Biblical themes as historical realities that paralleled the black experience.[72] This employment of parallelism was evident even in King's political speeches, which, in their poetic detail and structure, were sermons—"political sermons with King James replaced by current political idealogues, interspersed and peppered with Biblical allegory."[73] Although King rejected Biblical inerrancy and literal interpretations of scripture, he did affirm the truths and the authority of the Bible in ways that were existentially meaningful and liberating for his people. It was in his keen ability to weave Biblical allegory and analogy into his sermons, and to relate the Bible to more contemporary realities of black existence, that

71. Rich insights into the black preacher's role as a fashioner and an exemplar of culture are afforded in Johnson, *God's Trombones*, 1–56; Henry H. Mitchell, *Black Preaching* (Philadelphia and New York: J. B. Lippincott Company, 1970), 65–195; Davis, *I Got the Word in Me*, 49–113; and Spencer, *Sacred Symphony*, ix–xvi and 1–16.

72. Baldwin, "The Minister as Preacher, Pastor, and Prophet," 82; and Jones, "The Art of Preaching," 8.

73. Spillers, "Martin Luther King and the Style of the Black Sermon," 15–16. Mervyn A. Warren claims that King made a distinction between his sermons and his civil rights mass meeting speeches. However, the use of parallelism was common in both types of speeches. Warren, "A Rhetorical Study of the Preaching of Doctor Martin Luther King, Jr.," 3–4.

the prophetic dimension of King's preaching was prominently revealed.[74] In his use of parallelism, he masterfully combined the hermeneutics and sermonic structure of the scholar with the rhetoric, spontaneity, simplicity, dynamism, and storytelling art of the folk.[75]

"Cryptic" or "soul" language was a third essential element of King's preaching art. Steeped in the oral tradition of his elders, a tradition rooted in Africa, King used language that spoke to the heart out of the black pain predicament, and his message shifted immediately from heart to head.[76] The union between head and heart, between intellect and emotion, was what he strove to achieve in his sermons.[77] King's eloquence and brilliant use of imagery and the folk idiom help explain the ease with which he found a route to the hearts and eventually to the heads of his people. A sense of his people as a whole, and of their trials and sufferings, was reflected in the imagery and language of his sermons—sermons that amounted to speech music, with much of the sound, phrasing, and rhythms of black folksongs. It was these very qualities that compelled W. E. B. Du Bois, decades earlier, to refer to the black preacher as "one who rudely but picturesquely expressed the longing, disappointment, and resentment of a stolen and oppressed people."[78]

74. Baldwin, "The Minister as Preacher, Pastor, and Prophet," 82; and Jones, "The Art of Preaching," 8.

75. Quarles, "Martin Luther King, Jr., in History," 9.

76. Jones, "The Art of Preaching," 8–9; and Baldwin, "The Minister as Preacher, Pastor, and Prophet," 82–83.

77. King, *My Life with Martin Luther King, Jr.*, 98; and a private interview with Dr. Philip Lenud, 7 April 1987. King's effort to unite head and heart, the cognitive and affective, was actually his way of bringing together the resources of his heritage and the fruits of his academic training.

78. Baldwin, "The Minister as Preacher, Pastor, and Prophet," 82–83; and Franklin, ed., *The Souls of Black Folk in Three Negro Classics*, 342. What James Weldon Johnson said about the old-time Negro preacher may well be said of King: "He knew the secret of oratory, that at bottom it is a progression of rhythmic words more than anything else. . . . He was a master of all the modes of eloquence. He often possessed a voice that was a marvelous instrument, a voice he could modulate from a sepulchral whisper to a crashing thunder clap." See Johnson, *God's Trombones*, 5.

King believed that preaching was most powerful and effective when it involved the total being and personality of the preacher. This points to a fourth characteristic of his preaching; namely, the union of body and soul in the course of delivery.[79] The power of King's delivery, the deep sincerity that marked his facial expression, his raising and flinging of his hands, his moving of his head from side to side, and his standing on his tiptoes were indications that what he proclaimed was inseparable from what he believed. In his sermons, he brought together a range of emotions and thoughts—laughter, tears, compassionate pleading, and wrathful condemnation—elements that, according to William R. Jones, characterize black preaching as "a wholistic enactment of the divine encounter."[80]

A posture of freedom and fearlessness was still another characteristic of King's preaching style and manner. Time and time again he insisted on freedom and boldness in the pulpit. He refused to be inhibited with respect to what he uttered, especially when he was speaking the truth as he understood it. This posture was directly related to his prophetic role.[81] He was deeply disturbed by the fact that white preachers in the South were not free and courageous enough to speak the truth about racism and segregation from their pulpits.[82] It is impossible to understand King at this point apart from his background in the black church, where freedom and fearlessness on the part of the preacher "are expected, appreciated, and applauded."[83] The admiration and respect King enjoyed in the black community grew largely out of his willingness, as one called by God, to champion the rights of the poor and oppressed at all cost.

79. Jones, "The Art of Preaching," 9; and Baldwin, "The Minister as Preacher, Pastor, and Prophet," 83.

80. Jones, "The Art of Preaching," 9.

81. *Ibid.;* and Baldwin, "The Minister as Preacher, Pastor, and Prophet," 83–86.

82. Baldwin, "The Minister as Preacher, Pastor, and Prophet," 83.

83. *Ibid.;* and Jones, "The Art of Preaching," 9.

The foregoing discussion suggests that the five characteristics of King's preaching art were each the concrete expression and manifestation of the union and participation of the preacher with the congregation. This developed out of a conception of ministry that is unifying in the sense that it brings together the entire person (head and heart). The people become a community with the preacher and the past people of God (Israel), and thus become people of God; and as people of God, unified under God and with God, the people become a fearless community led by a fearless preacher. Since preaching involves bringing about the union and participation of the audience with the preacher, the preacher, in turn, becomes pastor, priest, and prophet, participating in the spiritual lives of individuals and in their services to the church and society. Therefore, preaching is a role that the pastor, priest, and prophet perform.[84]

King said very little about intellectual and preaching traditions that directly influenced his development as a preacher and homiletician. Apparently, his homiletical style and form resulted from a creative synthesis of various traditions, both white and black. King borrowed heavily from the sermons of liberal white preachers such as Harry Emerson Fosdick, George Buttrick, and Halford Luccock, and the content of his sermons also reflected the influence of various ethicists, philosophers, and theologians whose works he studied at Crozer Theological Seminary and Boston University.[85] However, King's greatest

---

84. Baldwin, "The Minister as Preacher, Pastor, and Prophet," 83–84.
85. Considerable attention is given to the influence of white pulpiteers on King's homiletics in Miller, "The Influence of a Liberal White Homiletic Tradition on 'Strength to Love,'" 1–207. In my view, Miller exaggerates the influence of the liberal white homiletic tradition on King. The influence was quite *indirect*. In the 1940s and 1950s, most educated preachers in America read sermon collections by reputable white preachers (e.g., Luccock, *Marching Off the Map*), and drew on materials from those sermons in developing their ideas—quotations, illustrations, and images. King did too. So there was some influence by some white preachers but not in style, delivery, or the structure of thought. King talked a lot about Fosdick, considering him one of the greatest preachers in the world. He also had a high regard for William Sloane Coffin, another liberal white clergyman, whose "courage, dedication, and unswerving devotion

indebtedness was to black Baptist sources, a contention borne out by his family, friends, and aides. Coretta Scott King has reported that her husband's "style of preaching grew out of the tradition of the southern Baptist ministers, with cadences and timing that he had heard from his father and other ministers as long as he could remember."[86] Martin Luther King, Sr., agreed, asserting that "Both of my boys learned preaching from me. We'd have lessons in the style. But they had the gift, too. I think Martin was a much better preacher than I was."[87] Ralph D. Abernathy has noted that young Martin's ability to "whoop" or "tune up" came from his father. "Martin seldom did it, but he could whoop," Abernathy said. "He could lift that robust, beautiful, and musical voice just like his daddy."[88] King's capacity to "whoop" or "tune up" clearly linked him in spirit and style to slave preachers like Harry Hoosier and John Jasper.

King's pulpit discourse was influenced in other significant ways by Vernon Johns, Benjamin Mays, Howard Thurman, and Sandy Ray, all of whom were reputable black preachers in the Baptist church. Johns' influence on King was most evident at the level of ideas. "Martin was just fascinated with Vernon Johns," according to Philip Lenud, because "Johns was such a theological genius." King felt that Johns "was complex, heavy, and funny," and he and his friend Ralph Abernathy spent many hours exchanging humorous stories about how the outspoken Johns used to rock the complacency of the middle-class, refined members at Montgomery's Dexter Avenue Baptist Church.[89] Much of the humor King

---

to the principles of freedom and justice for all people" greatly impressed King. A private interview with the Rev. Ralph D. Abernathy, 17 March 1987; and a letter from Martin Luther King, Jr., to the Rev. William Sloane Coffin, 13 June 1961, The King Papers, Boston University.

86. King, *My Life with Martin Luther King, Jr.,* 20.

87. "Daddy King: 'There's No Hate in My Heart,'" 1, 4.

88. A private interview with the Rev. Ralph D. Abernathy, 17 March 1987. King had great admiration and respect for great "whoopers" like Caesar Clark and C. L. Franklin and was touched in a special way by them.

89. *Ibid.;* a private interview with Dr. Philip Lenud, 7 April 1987; and King, *My Life with Martin Luther King, Jr.,* 107.

brought to his preaching art was inspired by Johns. Many of the idioms in King's sermons came from Benjamin Mays and Howard Thurman, men who equaled Johns in terms of intellectual depth and capacity. While at Morehouse College, King heard Mays say repeatedly during chapel services that if a person has "nothing worth dying for," that person is "not fit to live," and also that "it's not how long you live, but how well you live," and King included these sayings in his own sermons. He also adopted Mays' idea that "It isn't a calamity to die with dreams unfulfilled, but it is a calamity not to dream."[90] Many ideas in King's sermons were drawn from Thurman's *Deep River* (1945) and *Jesus and the Disinherited* (1949). King often quoted Thurman's reference to how black slaves straightened the question mark in the Prophet Jeremiah's sentence into an exclamation point by affirming that "There is a balm in Gilead."[91] Of Thurman's impact on King, Philip Lenud has commented:

> He loved and respected Thurman. I'd take him with me sometimes to hear Thurman speak in chapel when we were students in Boston (Thurman was Dean of Chapel at Boston). He always listened carefully when Thurman was speaking, and would shake his head in amazement at Thurman's deep wisdom. Martin didn't have a mystical orientation, and he didn't dwell too much on

90. King, *My Life with Martin Luther King, Jr.*, 327; a private interview with the Rev. Ralph D. Abernathy, 17 March 1987; a private interview with Dr. Philip Lenud, 9 December 1986; and William M. Philpot, ed., *Best Black Sermons* (Valley Forge, Pa.: Judson Press, 1972), 37. King once reported that "Dr. Benjamin Mays, President of Morehouse College, and Dr. George Kelsey, one of my teachers there, influenced me greatly because of their ability to interpret the Christian gospel. I admired them very much." See Martin Luther King, Jr., "A Talk to a Seventh Grade Class at George A. Towns Elementary School," Atlanta, Ga. (The King Center Archives, 11 March 1964), 1.

91. For examples, see Martin Luther King, Jr., "The Meaning of Hope," a sermon delivered at the Dexter Avenue Baptist Church, Montgomery, Ala. (The King Center Archives, 10 December 1967), 17; Martin Luther King, Jr., "A Knock at Midnight," a sermon delivered at the All Saints Community Church, Los Angeles, Calif. (The King Center Archives, 25 June 1967), 16; and Howard Thurman, *Deep River and the Negro Spiritual Speaks of Life and Death* (Richmond, In.: Friends United Press, 1975), 59–60.

metaphysics. He was concerned with the pragmatics of existence, and the relationship of people "with God in the valley." But he enjoyed Thurman and he loved him, because he knew that Thurman was saying some great things. The ontological meanings of what Thurman said went right over on many folks, including Martin.[92]

Lenud further observed that Thurman had "a personal, spiritual influence on Martin that was so lofty, and that helped him to endure. The spiritual and moral energy Thurman generated influenced him so much." In Lenud's opinion, Thurman's concepts of integration, community, and the interrelatedness of all life also influenced King significantly, "but when it came to the pragmatics of these things, Sandy Ray was more important."[93] When it came to the preaching art, the influence of King's father and that of Johns, Mays, Thurman, Ray, and others came together in his consciousness, and the ideals and examples of each reinforced those of the others in King's life.

King's links with the black preaching tradition reached all the way back to the slave preacher. King had a high regard for the artistic ability of this figure, who, despite physical enslavement and illiteracy, was able to achieve a high level of creativity in his sermon. The slave preacher's capacity to speak to the source of black pain and to uplift and unite his people struck King as particularly important.[94] This is why King, drawing on the insight of Howard Thurman, referred to the slave preacher as a symbol of unity and hope, a characterization equally fitting for himself:

> He didn't know anything about Plato or Aristotle. He never would have understood Einstein's theory of relativity if Einstein had been in existence at that time.

92. A private interview with Dr. Philip Lenud, 7 April 1987; and a private interview with Dr. Philip Lenud, 9 December 1986.

93. A private interview with Dr. Philip Lenud, 9 December 1986; and a private interview with Dr. Philip Lenud, 7 April 1987.

94. King, "The Meaning of Hope," 16–17; King, "A Knock at Midnight," 13; and Martin Luther King, "Is the Universe Friendly?," a sermon delivered at the Ebenezer Baptist Church, Atlanta, Ga. (The King Center Archives, 12 December 1965), 5–6.

But he knew God. And he knew that the God that he had heard about, and read about, was not a God that would subject some of his children, and exalt the others. And he would get there with his broken language. He didn't know how to make his subject and verb agree, you know. He didn't have that. But he knew somehow, that there was an agreement with an eternal power. And he'd look out and say, "You ain't no nigger. You ain't no slave, but you're God's children." And something welled up within them, and they could start singing, even though they didn't have any shoes, "I got shoes, you got shoes, all of God children got shoes. When I get to heaven, going to put on my shoes, and I'm just going to walk all over God's heaven." They thought about a chariot swinging low, because they dreamed of a better day.[95]

The slave preacher, according to King, gave his people "something on the inside to stand up amid the difficulties of their days." It appears that King, through his ability to articulate the dreams, hopes, and struggles of his people, had his most direct contact with the tradition of the slave preacher.[96]

A great deal can be learned about King's personality and image as a preacher through a study of how he related to other black clergy in his time. He enjoyed close friendships with some of the most dynamic and popular black preachers in the country, among whom were Caesar Clark, William H. Borders, Kelly Miller Smith, C. L. Franklin, Walter R. McCall, Dr. William H. Gray, Dr. James B. Cayce, Fred Shuttlesworth, Dr. Samuel D. Proctor, and Dr. Melvin H. Watson.[97] Ministers such as J. Pius Barbour, William Hester, Mordecai Johnson, Vernon Johns, Sandy Ray, Benjamin Mays, Gardner C. Taylor, and Howard Thurman were not only King's

95. King, "The Meaning of Hope," 16–17; and Thurman, *Deep River and the Negro Spiritual*, 17–18.

96. King, "Is the Universe Friendly?," 6.

97. Many of these preachers exchanged pulpits with King when he was pastor of the Dexter Avenue Baptist Church. See Evans and Alexander, eds., *The Dexter Avenue Baptist Church*, 82–83, 96–98, 109–12, 126.

friends but were some of his most trusted counselors. This was particularly true of Mays and Thurman, with whom King exchanged many letters. Mays constantly reminded King to "take every precaution as you move around," and to beware of those "who are trying to smear you."[98] On many occasions when King was faced with difficult and dangerous situations, he sought the advice of Mays instead of that of his parents, who were too emotionally tied to their son to be encouraging or objective in such situations. Mays was for King "a symbol of dignity, integrity, and dedicated statesmanship"—one who combined "the fact-finding mind of the social scientist with the far-reaching insights of the religious prophet."[99] King valued Mays's "interest in solving the moral and social crisis that confronts us amicably and nonviolently."[100] He held the same view of Thurman, whom he called one of "the outstanding Christian personalities of the nation."[101] Thurman was for King "a counselor concerned primarily with the younger man's spiritual life and emotional well-being."[102]

Some of King's most rewarding and memorable relationships were with black preachers who worked closely with him in the movement. Ralph D. Abernathy remained his best friend and closest colleague from the time of the Montgomery Bus Boycott until King's death in Memphis. The two men, known as "the civil rights twins," often teased each other, and sometimes wrestled in a playful manner. "He was the strongest little man I've ever seen in my life," Abernathy said of King. "He

98. A private interview with Rev. Ralph D. Abernathy, 17 March 1987; a private interview with Dr. Philip Lenud, 7 April 1987; and a letter from Dr. Benjamin E. Mays to Martin Luther King, Jr., 29 November 1963, The King Papers, Boston University.

99. A letter from Martin Luther King, Jr., to Dr. Benjamin E. Mays, 17 May 1960, The King Papers, Boston University.

100. A letter from Martin Luther King, Jr., to Dr. Benjamin E. Mays, 11 August 1958, The King Papers, Boston University.

101. A letter from Martin Luther King, Jr., to Dr. Howard Thurman, 7 July 1958, The King Papers, Boston University.

102. Walter E. Fluker, *They Looked for a City: A Comparative Analysis of the Ideal of Community in the Thought of Howard Thurman and Martin Luther King, Jr.* (Lanham, Md.: University Press of America, 1989), 197–98.

could out-box you, out-wrestle you, and out-run you."
The immediate families of King and Abernathy developed very strong bonds of friendship, often visiting and
dining with one another. King frequently said that
Juanita Abernathy, Ralph's wife, "could solve the race
problem in America, and especially in Montgomery, if
she would just serve George Wallace some of her home-
made ice cream."[103] Abernathy recounted that some of
his most thrilling moments with King occurred when
they swapped jokes and humorous stories. "He knew all
of my jokes," said Abernathy, "and he wanted me to tell
my jokes in the pulpit when we were together. Martin
would always say, 'Ralph, Ralph, tell the people that joke
about so and so.'" That kind of humor "relaxed us in the
midst of the tension and the frustration of the movement," continued Abernathy.[104]

King also shared many hours of serious reflection and
fun with other ministers who comprised the bulk of
S.C.L.C.'s executive staff and governing board, among
whom were James Bevel, Jesse Jackson, Bernard Lee,
Wyatt Walker, T. Y. Rogers, Hosea Williams, C. T. Vivian,
and Andrew Young. King once referred to this group as
"brilliant young men who could make, I'm sure, much
larger salaries elsewhere. But they stay here, and they
work because of their commitment to this struggle."[105]
On many occasions, and especially when they were in jail
together, King, Lee, Abernathy, Walker, and Young sang
freedom songs to keep their spirits high and as an
expression of their desire to continue the struggle together.[106] At other times, King teased and shared humorous anecdotes with his associates. Bernard Lee, who

103. A private interview with the Rev. Ralph D. Abernathy, 17 March
1987.
104. *Ibid.;* and King, *My Life with Martin Luther King, Jr.,* 107. According to Abernathy, King possessed the rare "ability to make people laugh
and cry at the same time."
105. Martin Luther King, Jr., "An Address to the Ministers' Leadership Training Program," Miami, Fla. (The King Center Archives, 19 and
23 February 1968), 2.
106. King, *My Life with Martin Luther King, Jr.,* 23; and a private
interview with the Rev. Bernard S. Lee, Washington, D.C., 9 July 1986.

traveled widely with King, was most often the object of his teasing. One day while King was addressing S.C.L.C.'s staff, Lee dropped something behind him, causing a crashing sound, and King teased: "What you been drinking, Bernard?"[107] "He could really tease you, or, as the fellows said, 'crack on you,'" Lee recalled. "And then he could be very serious. We'd sit and talk about the issues very seriously."[108] Lee remembered that one of the funniest stories King would tell "when the fellows were together" involved his parents, who got lost one Sunday morning while looking for a small, country church at which Daddy King was to preach. The rest of the story went this way:

> They stopped an old Negro man walking down the road and asked him for directions. He said, "Let's see, now. To get to that church, you go down this road about two miles, then turn right. . . . No, that's not right. What you do is, you turn around go up to the crossroads, then turn left and. . . . No, that's not right either. Let's see. . . ." The man scratched his head and said, "You know, I reckon I don't know where that church is." On that note, the Kings thanked the man for his trouble and pulled away. Suddenly, said Martin with a wide grin, Mama and Daddy King heard someone calling, and looking back, they saw the old man huffing and puffing down the road, trying to catch up with them. They stopped, backed up the car, and waited while he tried to catch his breath, and then listened expectantly. The man pointed out, "I just wanted to say—I just want to tell you—I just saw my brother, and I asked him, and he don't know where that church is either."[109]

107. Martin Luther King, Jr., "Why We Must Go to Washington," a speech delivered at the S.C.L.C. Retreat, Ebenezer Baptist Church, Atlanta, Ga. (The King Center Archives, 15 January 1968), 5; and a private interview with the Rev. Bernard S. Lee, 9 July 1986.

108. A private interview with the Rev. Bernard S. Lee, 9 July 1986.

109. *Ibid.* King's mother, Alberta King, also frequently told this story to amuse her hearers. See King, *My Life with Martin Luther King, Jr.*, 92. King's favorite tales were shared only with persons within the black community. King enjoyed telling stories but did not always tell them well.

This type of rich, raw humor strengthened King's relationship with his co-workers and gave him the kind of human spirit that brought him closer to his family and to the mass of his people. "But that was the way he was all his life—playful—even to the very last day," observed Coretta Scott King. "In the midst of the most serious times, Martin would bring fun into our lives with his ability to see the humor in even the most difficult situations."[110] Interestingly enough, King spent the final minutes of his life in Memphis telling stories and teasing the Reverend Samuel Billy Kyles, a local civil rights activist, and Jesse Jackson. Kyles, whose wife was preparing a soul food dinner for King and his staff, later recalled King's mood on that fateful day:

> On April 4, 1968, the day after he made that magnificent "Mountain Top" speech, I went to the Lorraine Motel to pick up Dr. King and Jesse [Jackson] and Ralph [Abernathy] to take them to my house for dinner. I'd gone by a bit earlier so we wouldn't be late, and we just sat around talking preacher talk. Dr. King was in a light mood rather than the somber mood he'd been in the night before. He started telling us a story about going to a friend's house for dinner. "We had cold potatoes, cold ham, cold bread and cool aid," he said. "You see, my friend was low on money because he'd just bought a new house." Well, I'd just bought a new house, also, and Dr. King said: "Now, Billy, if you've bought this big new house and you can't afford to feed us, I'm going to tell everybody in the country. Your wife can't cook anyway. She's too good-looking." As we started to leave, Dr. King leaned over the balcony and said to Jesse, "You aren't going to Billy's house looking like that are you?" Jesse, who had on a leather jacket, looked up and said, "Well, Doc, I didn't think a shirt and tie were prerequisite for an appetite." I had taken

---

There were times when he found only himself laughing at his anecdotes. In any case, he stood squarely in the tradition of great black southern storytellers. He knew the so-called "Negro idiom" and could tell stories with ungrammatical profundity.
110. King, *My Life with Martin Luther King, Jr.*, 105.

about five steps toward the stairs when the shot rang out. It was about a quarter to six.[111]

King made the ways of the black preacher a favorite target of his humor. Aware of the stereotype of the preacher as a lover of money, he often joked about the extremes to which his father went to save a dime. If chickens were on sale somewhere in Atlanta, Daddy King would drive across town to save ten cents, ignoring the cost of the gasoline used.[112] The black preachers who paraded through King's anecdotes not only loved money but also possessed ingenuity in dealing with difficult situations. One of his favorite stories involved a preacher he had called on to offer prayer during a street demonstration. A white mob surrounded the demonstrators, and the atmosphere got so tense and hostile that the brother prayed with his eyes wide open.[113] Another of King's favorite stories was about a Baptist minister in Atlanta who was untrained but blessed with wisdom and natural talents. One day the mayor of Atlanta called together all the top black ministers to discuss racial tensions created in the city as a result of the civil rights movement. "Let's see how many people in the Black community we have represented here today," the mayor said. According to King, one minister said he had 3,000 members, another said 2,500, another said 2,000, and so on. When the mayor got to the untrained preacher, who had a very small church and was hesitant about revealing the exact membership when the others had such large congregations, the preacher said, "Sir, I have a church *full*."[114]

Several of King's most commonly told jokes focused on this particular uneducated preacher, who was one of the King family's favorite people. This preacher "would mess up verbs, nouns, and sentences, and Martin really got a

---

111. "'I Remember Martin': Memories of M.L.K.'s Human Side," *Ebony*, 39; no. 6 (April 1984): 38.
112. King, *My Life with Martin Luther King, Jr.*, 91.
113. "'I Remember Martin,'" 40.
114. *Ibid.*

big charge out of that," Philip Lenud recalled. "He talked about how this preacher would announce," after extending the call to Christian discipleship during worship services, "that there are two seats up here—*are* there one?"[115] Ralph Abernathy remembered that King shared many anecdotes with him concerning this preacher. "Martin said that the Southern Baptists gave him a little stipend to teach preachers grammar, and this preacher was in his class," Abernathy recounted. "Martin said to the class one day, 'class, if you came home at about 2 o'clock in the morning and knocked on the door, would you say to your wife, *It is I, or it is me?*'" King's favorite preacher promptly raised his hand, requesting a chance to answer the question. With a sincere look on his face, the preacher said: "I would say, 'Baby, Baby, it is *me.*'" King spoke of another occasion when this preacher chose to preach a sermon on love. "I'm gong to preach on the text, 'God is Love,' and my subject is 'Love,'" the preacher declared. From that point, the preacher proclaimed in this manner, with his voice gradually taking on a mournful, singing quality:

> Love is no noun, and love is no pronoun, love is just love. Just like you love and I love—love is just love. Is you got your ticket? Love is just love, Oh Lord. You can't make it in unless you love, Oh Lord.[116]

One day this same preacher was driving his Cadillac in downtown Atlanta, according to King, and he mistakenly bumped a white man's car. Angered by the accident, the white man immediately emerged from his car and said: "Nigger, why did you hit my car? I have my mother

115. A private interview with Dr. Philip Lenud, 7 April 1987. The preacher who was the focus of these anecdotes carried the initials H. T. and was said to have had a great influence on King. King's jokes were not told to degrade the black preacher. His jokes were not "in bad taste," especially since he was putting his life on the line for the H. T.'s. For specific references to some of King's jokes about H. T., see Ralph D. Abernathy, *And the Walls Came Tumbling Down: An Autobiography* (New York: Harper & Brothers, 1989), 468–70.

116. A private interview with the Rev. Ralph D. Abernathy, 17 March 1987.

in this car." The preacher responded: *"Are* your mama hurt?" "No, nigger," the white man replied, "but you hit my car and almost knocked my mother out." "I said, *are* you mama hurt?," repeated the preacher. "Nigger, if you had hurt my mother, I would beat your brains out," the white man declared. At this point, the old preacher lost his temper, pointed his finger at the white man, and said in a loud voice: "Wait, let me tell y'all white folks something right now. If y'all don't get the hell away from here, mama's son are gonna be hurt."[117] "Martin was just rolling with these jokes," Philip Lenud recalled. "He knew so many humorous stories about this preacher."[118]

King's sense of humor was such that he often laughed at himself—at the way he ate, dressed, and looked. After a private audience with Pope Paul VI in 1964, he referred jokingly to the irony surrounding the meeting, noting that "things have really changed a lot when a Pope will agree to see a fellow by the name of Martin Luther."[119] King's ability to poke fun at himself and other preachers was evidence of his high level of maturity and self-confidence. He was very secure with who he was as a person, a preacher, and a social activist of international reputation. Furthermore, he had great faith in the power and potential of the black preacher as a leader in the black community, even as he criticized and joked about the shortcomings of that complex figure.[120]

King's great sense of humor was also proof of his spirited enjoyment of life even in the midst of danger and struggle. He refused to take life too seriously and had the capacity to actually stand back and laugh at life.

117. *Ibid.*
118. A private interview with Dr. Philip Lenud, 9 December 1986; and a private interview with Dr. Philip Lenud, 7 April 1987.
119. King, "An Address at the National Conference on Civil Rights," 1 ff.; and King, *My Life with Martin Luther King, Jr.,* 17, 25, 75, 86, 188.
120. King, "An Address at the National Conference on Civil Rights," 1 ff.; Martin Luther King, Jr., *Why We Can't Wait* (New York: The New American Library, 1964), 67; and a letter from Martin Luther King, Jr., to the Rev. Jerry M. Chance, 9 May 1961, The King Papers, Boston University.

It revealed the depth of the optimism with which he confronted life—an optimism essentially Christian in nature. A study of King's humor and playful manner seems to provide evidence against claims that he was a seriously guilt-ridden personality who, toward the end of his life, had surrendered himself to a bleak, enervating pessimism.[121]

## AS PASTOR, PRIEST, AND PROPHET

It is commonly believed in many circles that King's public ministry emphasized the prophetic role at the expense of pastoral and priestly functions.[122] However, a careful examination of King's books, sermons, speeches, interviews, and letters suggests that this view is not consistent with his self-understanding and his sense of his fundamental calling. King was essentially a Baptist minister who reconciled the pastoral, priestly, and prophetic roles through his preaching and his day-to-day tasks of ministry. For King, these roles were *interrelated* and *interdependent* in that each informed the others.[123] Furthermore, his normative understanding of the nature and function of the pastoral, priestly, and prophetic dimensions, individually and collectively, was

121. King, *My Life with Martin Luther King, Jr.*, 105, 179. This image of King as a guilt-ridden personality is emphasized in David J. Garrow, *Bearing the Cross: Martin Luther King, Jr., and the Southern Christian Leadership Conference* (New York: William Morrow, 1986), 11–624.

122. Sources that emphasize the prophetic ministry of King include Fluker, *They Looked for a City*, 162; William M. Ramsay, *Four Modern Prophets: Walter Rauschenbusch, Martin Luther King, Jr., Gustavo Gutierrez, Rosemary Radford Reuther* (Atlanta: John Knox Press, 1986), chap. 2; Peter J. Paris, "The Bible and the Black Churches," in *The Bible and Social Reform*, ed. by Ernest R. Sandeen (Philadelphia: Fortress Press, 1982), 140–44; and Richard Newman, "Martin Luther King, Jr.: A True Prophet," *Christianity and Crisis*, 47, no. 2 (February 16, 1986): 51–52. Sources that discuss how King combined the pastoral and prophetic roles are Baldwin, "The Minister as Preacher, Pastor, and Prophet," 79, 83–84; and Earl E. Shelp and Ronald H. Sunderland, eds., *The Pastor as Prophet* (New York: Pilgrim Press, 1985), 13, 15, 27.

123. Baldwin, "The Minister as Preacher, Pastor, and Prophet," 79, 83–84, 95.

grounded in the Biblical teaching of the common ministry and mission of Jesus, the Apostles, and the Hebrew prophets.[124] King's first and only experiences as the head pastor of a congregation began when he went to Dexter Avenue Baptist Church in 1954 and ended when he left that position in January, 1960.[125] He went to Dexter church with a traditional understanding of the pastoral role, an understanding shaped by his father, by his experiences at Atlanta's Ebenezer Baptist Church, and by his broader contacts with black Baptist pastors.[126] In his "Recommendations to the Dexter Avenue Baptist Church for the Fiscal Year 1954–1955," King insisted that the pastor's "authority is twofold." "First of all, his authority originates with God," he wrote. "Inherent in the call itself is the presupposition that God directed that such a call be made. This makes it crystal clear that the pastor's authority is not merely humanly conferred, but divinely sanctioned."[127] In King's view, the pastor's charismatic authority (divine gift directly from God in a personal religious experience) was affirmed and confirmed by that authority necessarily given through the intermediary of the church (institutional authority):

> Secondly, the pastor's authority stems from the people themselves. Implied in the call is the unconditional willingness of the people to accept the pastor's leadership. This means that the leadership never ascends from the pew to the pulpit, but it invariably descends from the pulpit to the pew. This does not mean that the pastor is one before whom we must blindly and

124. *Ibid.*, 79.
125. A letter from Martin Luther King, Jr., to the Dexter Avenue Baptist Church, 14 April 1954, The King Papers, Boston University; and Evans and Alexander, eds., *The Dexter Avenue Baptist Church*, 141.
126. A private interview with Dr. Philip Lenud, 9 December 1986; a private interview with the Rev. Ralph D. Abernathy, 17 March 1987; and a private interview with Dr. Charles E. Boddie, Nashville, Tenn., 1 December 1987.
127. King, "Recommendations to the Dexter Avenue Baptist Church, 1954–55," 1.

ignorantly genuflect, as if he was possessed of some infallible or superhuman attributes. Nor does it mean that the pastor should needlessly interfere with the deacons, trustees or workers of the various auxiliaries, assuming unnecessarily dictatorial authority. But it does mean that the pastor is to be respected and accepted as the central figure around which the policies and programs of the church revolve. He must never be considered a mere puppet for the whimsical and capricious mistreatment of those who wish to show their independence, and "use their liberty for a cloak of maliciousness." It is therefore indispensable to the progress of the church that the official board and membership cooperate fully with the leadership of the pastor.[128]

Despite his conviction that the church's ministry involved all the people of God, sharing their gifts and talents, King never really abandoned the authoritarian style of pastoring he inherited from his father and other mentors in the black church. Before going to Dexter church, he had been warned by a close friend of his father, who once pastored in Montgomery, that the deacons of that congregation had the reputation of running it and of being harsh with their pastors. King's father's friend said to him: "Mike, there's one man on the board at Dexter to watch out for. He may be dead by now, but if he is still alive, don't you go there, because he'll give you hell."[129] Discovering that this very man was the chairman of the deacon board at Dexter church, King went there prepared for trouble with him and the older deacons. "I'm going to be pastor and I'm going to run that church," said he to his wife Coretta. King apparently kept his promise, and the congregation embraced his ambitious program in the spirit of cooperation.[130] In

---

128. *Ibid.* This same perspective is advanced to some extent in King's recommendations to Dexter for the years 1956 to 1959.

129. A private interview with Dr. Philip Lenud, 9 December 1986; and King, *My Life with Martin Luther King, Jr.*, 114.

130. King, *My Life with Martin Luther King, Jr.*, 114; and King, *Stride toward Freedom*, 26.

any case, the Dexter church experience reinforced King's view of the pastor as the central, authoritative figure in the church.

The characteristics of King's pastoral role were determined primarily by the individual and collective needs of the membership of Dexter church. Although the membership was affluent for the most part, the people at Dexter faced common, daily problems such as internal dissension, premarital and marital difficulties, family conflict, sickness, and death. Furthermore, they constantly confronted the evils of racism and of unjust social structures. Fully aware of the needs of the members at Dexter church, King adopted a program designed to unite, uplift, and motivate them and to equip them to fulfill their ministries to each other and to the broader community. This is how he understood the pastoral role. He spent considerable time preaching and leading in worship, teaching and engaging the people in the study of the scriptures, supervising educational ministries, performing administrative duties, evangelizing, counseling, and fulfilling other caring functions associated with the pastoral role. Beside the weekly services, King's day-to-day activities included marriages, funerals, personal conferences, and appearances at the various auxiliary meetings of the church.[131] He also devoted much time to counseling bereaved families and to visiting and praying with members, especially the sick, aged, and others in need. The fact that King spent a minimum of fifteen hours a week preparing his Sunday sermon is suggestive of the tremendous importance he attached to preaching as a part of the pastoral task.[132] In every respect, King's work as a pastor at Dexter, apart from his nonviolent philosophy, reflected the overwhelming influence of his religious past.

131. King, "Recommendations to the Dexter Avenue Baptist Church, 1954–55," 1–7; and King, *Stride toward Freedom*, 25–27.
132. King, *My Life with Martin Luther King, Jr.*, 114–15; and King, *Stride toward Freedom*, 26–27.

Pastoral ministry for King carried responsibilities that extended beyond the needs and concerns of a particular congregation or parish. In other words, he believed that the pastor's task involved helping both his church and the larger community of persons to identify and struggle with those individuals and social evils afflicting them. This explains why King developed an immediate interest in the social, economic, and political life of the larger community of Montgomery, and also urged the members of Dexter church to do likewise.[133] As he moved into the broader arena of the nation's affairs, he began to see more clearly his role as an American pastor. Although he spoke out of the particularlity of the black experience in the South, King became, in the words of Patrick G. Coy, "An American pastor who cared deeply about the soul of his nation."[134]

The accuracy of this characterization was revealed in the pastoral manner in which King responded to the diverse needs and concerns of people across America. For example, in his monthly column in *Ebony* magazine, called "Advice for Living," printed from August, 1957, until December, 1958, he provided pastoral responses to questions of a personal and public nature submitted by blacks, whites, and other readers.[135] In these columns, King devoted considerable attention to articulating methods and norms for restoring marriages, reconciling family members, healing broken friendships, and resolving other problems that prevented wholesome and creative living.[136] By drawing on a range of sources and resources, King, according to Robert M. Franklin, spoke effectively "to a diverse public and modelled a style of

133. King, "Recommendations to the Dexter Avenue Baptist Church, 1954–55," 1–7; King, *Stride toward Freedom*, 27–34; and Evans and Alexander, eds, *The Dexter Avenue Baptist Church*, 68–145.

134. Quoted in Shelp and Sunderland, eds., *The Pastor as Prophet*, 15.

135. Franklin, "Martin Luther King, Jr. as Pastor," 6. This approach to pastoring is also evident in King's letters, especially those addressed to children and prisoners. Many of these letters can be found at both Boston University and the King Center.

136. *Ibid.*, 6, 8–10.

Christian discourse, critical reflection on faith and society, and practical moral teaching which was accessible to large numbers of persons":

> King was that finest of pastors who brought to bear on the practical problems of everyday life, the resources of the Christian tradition along with other religious perspectives, insights from the social sciences, philosophy, Afro-American music and culture, and his own personal faith journey. He correlated insights from a wide host of disciplines, integrated, refined, and translated them into a language familiar and compelling to his listeners.[137]

King has been described in some circles as a pastor to pastors. This image was clearly evident in the way he related to and nurtured those preachers and pastors who worked with him in S.C.L.C. As the central figure in that organization, King's mediating influence helped the preachers and pastors to resolve conflict and dissension and to find commonality. Bernard Lee recalled King's amazing pastoral ability in this area:

> Ego-clashes and arguments would take place in S.C.L.C. meetings. Martin would listen carefully, and would later take that chaos and smooth it out and bring it into focus—into perspective. That pastoral ability would just come out. That was a part of his genius. This happened quite a bit because we had some "reindeer personalities" in S.C.L.C.[138]

King's role as a pastor to pastors was also reflected in his "Letter from the Birmingham City Jail," addressed to eight white Alabama clergymen in April, 1963. This

137. *Ibid.*, 4–6.
138. A private interview with the Rev. Bernard S. Lee, 9 July 1986. King's pastoral role in S.C.L.C. has not been sufficiently treated even in major works such as Garrow, *Bearing the Cross*, 11–624; Adam Fairclough, *To Redeem the Soul of America: The Southern Christian Leadership Conference and Martin Luther King, Jr.* (Athens, Ga.: The University of Georgia Press, 1987), 11–383; and Thomas R. Peake, *Keeping the Dream Alive: A History of the Southern Christian Leadership Conference from King to the Nineteen–Eighties* (New York: Peter Lang Publishing, 1987), 13–321.

piece was in large measure a pastoral letter written to pastors about genuine pastoral concerns and interests. It spoke brilliantly to the need for persons to move beyond segregation as a social evil to bring about healing, reconciliation, and community. King's Birmingham letter affords a perfect illustration of how the pastoral and prophetic dimensions converged in his consciousness.[139]

Some of King's most interesting and unforgettable pastoral experiences occurred while he served with his father as co-pastor of Atlanta's Ebenezer Baptist Church. He served in that capacity from 1960 until his death in 1968, the period during which he was most heavily involved in the broad human struggle for justice, peace, and community. This new situation allowed King to fulfill his dream of maintaining a pastoral role in the black church, even as demands on him as a social activist mounted. It also gave him an opportunity to combine his pastoral concerns at Ebenezer church with his broader pastoral concerns in the larger world. He said in 1960 that "In order to be true to my work in the South, and my position as co-pastor of Ebenezer Baptist Church in Atlanta, I have had to adopt a policy of not being out of the pulpit more than twice a month."[140] Although increasing responsibilities sometimes prevented King from maintaining this policy at Ebenezer church, he was still able to rearrange his schedule "in order to adjust to the program of the Church."[141]

King's pastoral role at Ebenezer church was essentially what it had been at Dexter Avenue Baptist Church. The difference was that he brought a higher level of experience and insight to his work at Ebenezer church, qualities developed as a result of his involvements in Montgomery. In keeping with his father's wishes, King preached at least once a month at Ebenezer church, on the average, and devoted limited time to teaching,

139. King, *Why We Can't Wait*, 76–95.
140. A letter from Martin Luther King, Jr., to the Rev. W. H. McKinney, 31 March 1960, The King Papers, Boston University.
141. A letter from Martin Luther King, Jr., to the Rev. H. Beecher Hicks, 18 May 1960, The King Papers, Boston University.

counseling, weddings, and funerals. There were times when he interrupted his busy schedule abroad and returned to Atlanta to either attend or officiate at the funerals of distinguished members. King's warm relationship with his father and his brother, A. D., who also became a co-pastor at Ebenezer church, made it possible for him to function well as a co-pastor in that church, and to use it as a platform for his broader activities. However, Daddy King was known to assert his authority as head pastor when he felt challenged by his sons. "Well, he makes it clear, sometimes consciously and sometimes unconsciously, that he is the pastor and I'm the co-pastor," King said of his father on one occasion.[142] At times King became slightly irritated with his father's pulpit manner, according to Bernard Lee, but he still exercised patience and humility:

> Daddy King was one of those preachers from the old school. He would often get up and ramble for ten minutes after he preached, saying nothing, but Martin understood. That spirituality just entered into their relationship.[143]

King used the terms *pastor* and *priest* interchangeably in reference to a particular aspect of his ministry, suggesting that there was no distinction between these two categories. For him, the essential role of the pastor or priest consisted of nurturing and caring for persons, individually and collectively.[144] However, these categories must be clearly distinguished if the significance of this collapsing for King is to be understood. The pastoral function imposed on King the role of *religious leader* primarily, whereas the priestly function established him essentially in the role of *ritual leader*. As a priest or ritual leader, he constantly established and

142. Martin Luther King, Jr., "Transcript of an Interview on the Merv Griffith Show," New York, N.Y. (The King Center Archives, 6 July 1967), 2.
143. A private interview with the Rev. Bernard S. Lee, 9 July 1986.
144. Martin Luther King, Jr., "Transcript of an Interview with Local Newscasters," KNXT T.V., Los Angeles, Calif. (The King Center Archives, 10 July 1965), 2; and Martin Luther King, Jr., "Transcript of an Interview on 'Face the Nation,'" Broadcast of CBS Television Network (The King Center Archives, 29 August 1965), 3.

re-established his people's relationship with one another and with God, so that they might perceive themselves more clearly as the people of God. In this sense, King's ritual role was practically identical to that of the slave preacher, as described by W. E. B. Du Bois and James Weldon Johnson.[145] In other words, King became a mediator between God and the people—one who pointed out where, when, and how the divine was present for them (e.g., Scripture, worship, the black experience, society, the world); who demonstrated the divine presence and will (in his attitude, actions, sacrifices, and ways of preaching and ministering); and who allowed his people (the community and individuals) to participate with him in this relationship with God.[146]

The characteristic of "priesthood" in King's ministry was revealed specifically and most prominently in the way he exercised the ministry of the word, the eucharistic function, and prayer. Through his ministry of the word, as expressed through his preaching and teaching, King sought to enlighten and to nurture his people as they grew in the faith. In this way, he was a stepping stone to the faith and to God for black people who were spiritually insecure and inadequate, who felt alienated from friends and family, and who experienced frustration and despair in the midst of struggle. His ministry of the word had more of a comforting and healing effect when tragedy occurred among his people because, in such times, the community needed reaffirmation and reinforcement. For example, when a bomb exploded at Sixteenth Street Baptist Church in Birmingham, Alabama, in September 1963, killing four little black girls and injuring some other worshipers, King dealt with the crisis of grief and despair by skillfully combining the comforting words and presence of the priest with the wise

145. Baldwin, "The Minister as Preacher, Pastor, and Prophet," 84–85; Franklin, ed., *The Souls of Black Folk in Three Negro Classics*, 342; Johnson, *God's Trombones*, 2; and Sterling Stuckey, *Slave Culture: Nationalist Theory and the Foundations of Black America* (New York: Oxford University Press, 1987), 255, 257.
146. Baldwin, "The Minister as Preacher, Pastor, and Prophet," 84.

counsel of the pastor and the boldness and inspiring vision of the prophet. In his "Eulogy for the Martyred Children," King declared before the bereaved families and the larger community:

> These children—unoffending, innocent and beautiful—were the victims of one of the most vicious, heinous crimes ever perpetrated against humanity. . . . Yet they died nobly. They are the martyred heroines of a holy crusade for freedom and human dignity. So they have something to say to us in their death. . . . They say to each of us, black and white alike, that we must substitute courage for caution. They say to us that we must be concerned not merely about who murdered them, but about the system, the way of life and the philosophy which produced the murderers. . . .
>
> So in spite of the darkness of this hour we must not despair. We must not become bitter; nor must we harbor the desire to retaliate with violence. . . .
>
> It is almost impossible to say anything that can console you at this difficult hour and remove the deep clouds of disappointment which are floating in your mental skies. But I hope you can find a little consolation from the universality of this experience. Death comes to every individual. There is an amazing democracy about death. It is not aristocracy for some of the people, but democracy for all of the people. . . . I hope you can find some consolation from Christianity's affirmation that death is not the end. Death is not a period that ends the great sentence of life, but a comma that punctuates it to more lofty significance. Death is not a blind alley that leads the human race into a state of nothingness, but an open door which leads man into life eternal. Let this daring faith, this great invincible surmise, be your sustaining power during these trying days. . . .[147]

147. James M. Washington, ed., *A Testament of Hope: The Essential Writings of Martin Luther King, Jr.* (San Francisco: Harper & Row, 1986), 221–23. King's sermon at the funeral of Jimmie Lee Jackson in Marion, Ala., in early 1965 affords another example of how he served as a comforter of the afflicted. See Charles E. Fager, *Selma, 1965: The March that Changed the South* (Boston: Beacon Press, 1985), 85–86.

Through his ministry of the word, King had the capacity to mediate between the living and the dead, to relate this world to the otherworld, in order to ease the pain of the living. This priestly function was deeply grounded in his black church experience and heritage. Thus, what W. E. B. Du Bois said concerning the slave preacher as priest—as "the interpreter of the Unknown, the comforter of the sorrowing, the supernatural avenger of wrong"—also applies to King.[148] Through the priestly role, King, like black preachers historically, forged a unity with his people that extended beyond a simple identification with a particular religious community to include the total experience of living.

King's participation in the Lord's Supper always carried a special meaning in his priestly role. The administration of this sacrament became a vital part of his pastoral and priestly functions at both Dexter Avenue Baptist Church and Ebenezer Baptist Church. His life and work became a testimony that the breaking of bread within the church's sacramental ministry must be directly related to the sharing of bread with the poor and the oppressed in the larger world. King demonstrated that the drinking of wine was not only symbolic of Christ's sacrifice on the Cross, but also indicative of the sacrifice people had to make, individually and collectively, for the cause of human dignity, freedom, and community. It was impossible for King, given his intellectual and spiritual depth, not to see the relationship between redemptive suffering on Calvary and the unearned suffering he and his followers were forced to endure in the jails, courthouses, and streets. After a near-fatal stabbing in Harlem in 1958, King spent a lot of time thinking about the meaning of redemptive suffering, and he often said in later years that he viewed his personal ordeals as an opportunity to

148. Washington, ed., *A Testament of Hope*, 221–23; Baldwin, "The Minister as Preacher, Pastor, and Prophet," 84–85; and Franklin, ed., *The Souls of Black Folk in Three Negro Classics*, 342.

transform himself and to heal the people involved in the struggle.[149] Through the Lord's Supper, he and his people not only witnessed the divine presence but also manifested and participated in that presence through the blood they shed to redeem and transform human society. At this point, the priestly, pastoral, and prophetic came together for King.

The importance of prayer in King's life and ministry also reveals much about his priestly function. After his "vision in the kitchen" in 1956, prayer took on a special meaning for King, becoming not only a vital part of his interior life, of his life in Christ, but also "an undergirder" of his people's liberation efforts under his leadership.[150] In his church and in the streets, King became a prayer leader—one who exercised prayer as intercession, adoration, and thanksgiving. He often prayed for the dignity, freedom, and well-being of the black community; for the health and welfare of family; and for the realization of a new human spirit in the nation and the world. Furthermore, he thanked God for life, health, strength, courage, and the willingness on the part of many to struggle for peace, justice, and righteousness.[151] Within the movement, prayer became largely a communal activity and experience for King and his people—an experience that included talking to God and sharing in the divine presence. As was the case with the sermon and the Lord's Supper, prayer for King became an experience through which the community constantly re-established and reaffirmed itself as the

149. Washington, ed., *A Testament of Hope,* 41–42; and "Martin Luther King, Jr.: A Personal Portrait," a video-taped interview (Goldsboro, N.C.: Distributed by Carroll's Marketing and Management Service, 1966 to 1967).

150. King, *Stride toward Freedom,* 178; Harold A. Carter, *The Prayer Tradition of Black People* (Valley Forge, Pa.: Judson Press, 1976), 21, 65–67, 94, 106–13, 129–30; and O. Richard Bowyer, et al., eds., *Prayer in the Black Tradition* (Nashville: The Upper Room, 1986), 64–66.

151. King, *Strength to Love,* 131–33; and a private interview with the Rev. Bernard S. Lee, 9 July 1986. Lee reported that "We always opened and closed S.C.L.C. meetings with prayer. Prayer was very much a part of our existence."

people of God and as co-sufferers with God for the improvement of humanity.[152]

King did not set the pastoral and priestly functions in opposition to the prophetic function, and neither did he rank one higher than the others. In July, 1965, he emphatically stated that his ministry embraced all of these functions:

> I'm the pastor of a church and in that role I have a priestly function as well as a prophetic function, and in the prophetic role I must constantly speak to the moral issues of our day far beyond civil rights.[153]

A month later, in an appearance before a panel of newsmen on CBS's "Face the Nation," King reiterated this point in more specific terms:

> I happen to be a minister of the Gospel and I take that ministry very seriously, and in that capacity I have not merely a priestly function but a prophetic function, and I must ever seek to bring the great principles of our Judeo-Christian heritage to bear on the social evils of our day.[154]

King's view of the prophet and the prophetic role coursed through these statements. He held that the prophet was one called by God to speak the truth in love at all cost. After his "vision in the kitchen," which was a major breakthrough in his religious consciousness, King came to see himself as a prophet, as a mouthpiece for God, commissioned to speak clearly and boldly concerning arrogance, greed, pride, racism, war, and other individual and collective sins and evils that kept people alienated from themselves, from one another, and from God. Thus, he became a transgressor, a disturber of the status quo, a transformed nonconformist, one who combined a tough mind and a tender heart. This kind of

---

152. Carter, *The Prayer Tradition of Black People*, 65–67, 106–13, 129–30; and a private interview with the Rev. Bernard S. Lee, 9 July 1986.
    153. King, "Transcript of an Interview with Local Newscasters," 2; and Baldwin, "The Minister as Preacher, Pastor, and Prophet," 85.
    154. King, "Transcript of an Interview on 'Face the Nation,'" 3.

prophetic consciousness permeated King's sermons.[155] He not only had a vision of prophetic preaching but also the valor to sustain that vision through nonviolent action. He did not say anymore at eleven o'clock on Sundays than he was willing to die for during the other six days of the week. The significance of King's prophetic role rested precisely on his work as a working minister with real parish responsibilities, both priestly and pastoral.[156]

King's role as prophet required him to take positions on issues often misunderstood and unappreciated even by fellow Christians. When he launched an attack against racism and unfair business practices in Birmingham in 1963, he was called an "outsider" and his actions were labeled "untimely" by fellow clergymen. King answered with the powerful claim that the work of the true prophet is not restricted to certain seasons and geographical boundaries:

> I am in Birmingham because injustice is here. Just as the prophets of the eighth century B.C. left their villages and carried the gospel of Jesus Christ to the far corners of the Greco-Roman world, so am I compelled to carry the gospel of freedom beyond my own home town. Like Paul, I must constantly respond to the Macedonian call for aid.[157]

In King's view, the glaring reality of sin and evil in the world demanded that the prophet be universal rather than parochial in his concerns and activities. His attacks on the involvement of the United States in Vietnam between 1965 and 1968 grew out of this perspective:

> I must make it clear that my expressions on the war in Vietnam grow out of something much larger than my participation in the Civil Rights movement. . . . I happen to feel that war is obsolete and that it must be cast into unending limbo, and that if we continue to escalate this war, we move nearer to the point of

155. See the sermons in King, *Strength to Love*, 10–155.
156. Baldwin, "The Minister as Preacher, Pastor, and Prophet," 79–86.
157. King, *Why We Can't Wait*, 77.

plunging the whole of mankind into the abyss of anni-
hilation. I will continue to speak when I deem it
timely and necessary on this issue, not as a civil rights
leader.[158]

King's public expressions on foreign policy issues like
Vietnam ultimately developed out of his perception of his
calling as a minister of the Gospel. It was his understanding of his authority and role as a minister, not as a civil
rights leader, that kept him from becoming absorbed into
a conspiracy of silence on the issue of Vietnam:

> I cannot stand idly by and not raise my voice against
> something that I see as wrong. Now there are those
> who say, "You are a civil rights leader. What are you
> doing speaking out? You should stay in your field."
> Well, I wish you would go back and tell them for me
> that before I became a civil rights leader, I was a
> preacher of the Gospel. And when my father and oth-
> ers put their hands on my head, and ordained me to
> the Christian ministry, it was a commission. And
> something said to me that the fire of truth is shut up
> in my bones, and when it burns me, I must tell it.[159]

Given the unpopularity of the Vietnam War, King's
stand on that issue presented a powerful prophetic challenge to American pastors and churches in the 1960s. As
his attacks on Vietnam mounted, he became increasingly
aware of the difficulties and dangers involved in being
a true prophet of God. Ministers castigated him, the
federal government became less supportive of his campaigns, black conservatives questioned the wisdom of his
position, and threats against his life increased.[160] Yet,

158. King, "Transcript of an Interview on 'Face the Nation,'" 3.
159. Martin Luther King, Jr., "To Serve the Present Age," a sermon
delivered at Victory Baptist Church, Los Angeles, Calif. (The King Center
Archives, 25 June 1967), 7.
160. David Halberstam, "When 'Civil Rights' and 'Peace' Join Forces,"
*Martin Luther King, Jr.: A Profile*, ed. by C. Eric Lincoln (New York: Hill &
Wang, 1970), 188, 206–7; Martin Luther King, Jr., "Transcript of a Press
Conference," The Biltmore Hotel, Los Angeles, Calif. (The King Center
Archives, 12 April 1967), 3; and Edward Brooke, "Statement Regarding
M. L. King, Jr.'s Anti-Vietnam Stand," Washington, D.C. (The King Center
Archives, 16 April 1967), 1.

King refused to soften his criticisms. When his black associates and supporters warned that his position on Vietnam would diminish the flow of financial support for S.C.L.C., King, in the spirit of a prophet, rejoined:

> I don't determine what is right or wrong by looking at the budget of the Southern Christian Leadership Conference, or by taking a Gallup Poll of the majority opinion. Ultimately, a genuine leader is not a searcher for consensus, but a molder of consensus. On some opinions, Cowardice asks the question, "Is it safe?" Expediency asks the question, "Is it politic?" And Vanity comes along and asks the question, "Is it popular?" But Conscience asks the question, "Is is right?" And there comes a time when one must take a position that is neither safe nor politic nor popular, but he must do it because Conscience tells him it is right. And this is where, I believe, we must go as ministers of the Gospel. . . . We are prophets and if we are going to have a creative ministry, we must have a prophetic ministry. . . . I came to the conclusion that I had to tell the truth, knowing that it would hurt my budget.[161]

As a prophet, King did not stand alone over against the world. He was able to deal with the storm of critical responses to his struggles against racism, economic injustice, and war because he was convinced that God struggled and suffered with him. Furthermore, King saw himself as a representative of the black community, and this meant that that community as a whole, and not merely the prophet, had this prophetic role. This aspect helps explain the complexity of King's ministry in terms of the prophetic function.[162]

King's prophetic consciousness and role were shaped, informed, and inspired by a range of religious, intellec-

161. King, "An Address to the Ministers' Leadership Training Program," 2 ff.; and Baldwin, "The Minister as Preacher, Pastor, and Prophet," 86.

162. Daniel Patte, "Notes on 'The Minister as Preacher, Pastor, and Prophet,'" (Unpublished paper, Vanderbilt University), 4–5; and Baldwin, "The Minister as Preacher, Pastor, and Prophet," 83–84.

tual, and experiential sources. Peter J. Paris persuasively contends that King was representative of "the prophetic strand of the black Christian tradition," which is "rooted in antebellum opposition to slavery that predates the official abolitionist organizations."[163] As a prophet, he was nurtured by the strength of an ethnic heritage and idiom that reached at least as far back as Richard Allen in the late eighteenth century. The moral and ethical dilemma that King pointed to in the churches and in the society as a whole had been targeted by black preachers such as Richard Allen, Jarena Lee, Peter Spencer, Henry H. Garnet, and Henry M. Turner from antebellum times. King's father and maternal grandfather had drawn heavily on this prophetic heritage, a fact that accounted in part for the sense of anger and urgency in his own prophetic consciousness. This heritage made it possible for King to speak forthrightly and relevantly concerning the evils of the white Western world.[164]

King combined what he inherited from the prophetic stream of the black Christian tradition with what he got from the Evangelical Liberalism of George W. Davis, the Social Gospelism of Walter Rauschenbusch, and the Personalism of Edgar S. Brightman and L. Harold DeWolf. His genius in creating a dynamic complementarity of these sources was one of his most distinctive contributions as a prophet. Davis, Rauschenbusch, Brightman, and DeWolf provided King with a theological foundation for the kind of prophetic ministry he had inherited from his father and others in the black church.[165]

King's personal trials and sufferings informed his prophetic ministry in a special way. Although he was always hesitant to talk about his personal struggle, realizing the danger "of developing a martyr complex and of making others feel that he was consciously seeking

---

163. Paris, "The Bible and the Black Churches," 140–44.
164. Baldwin, "The Minister as Preacher, Pastor, and Prophet," 88–89; King, *Daddy King*, 82; and Halberstam, "When 'Civil Rights' and 'Peace' Join Forces," 203.
165. Baldwin, "The Minister as Preacher, Pastor, and Prophet," 92–93.

sympathy," King admitted at times that his trials and sufferings strengthened him as a minister of the gospel. They made him more courageous and committed as a prophet. Moreover, they enhanced his effectiveness as a priest because he could share his wounds as a source of comfort, growth, and healing for others.[166]

The Bible provided the model for King's prophetic role. His understanding of the prophetic posture largely resulted from his reading of Amos, Micah, Isaiah, Hosea, Jeremiah, and other Old Testament prophets in whose tradition Jesus and the Apostles stood. Although King spoke out of a twentieth-century American orientation, and especially out of the black experience, his words and actions were in many ways reminiscent of those of the Hebrew prophets. Like the prophets, King was a public figure concerned with public affairs.[167] The social and political message he shared with America and the world called to mind the prophets. In Hebrew society in the eighth century B.C.E., prophets such as Amos, Hosea, and Micah recognized the problems of social dislocation, of the mistreatment of the poor and humble by the privileged, and of idolatry, and they urged the people to seek God and not evil in the face of the coming judgment.[168] King discovered in these prophets the echoes of the same concerns he had as he spoke out against America's

166. *Ibid.*, 92; and Washington, ed., *A Testament of Hope*, 41–42.

167. Shelp and Sunderland, eds., *The Pastor as Prophet*, 15, 33; and Thomas Hoyt, Jr., "The Biblical Tradition of the Poor and Martin Luther King, Jr.," *The Journal of the Interdenominational Theological Center*, 4, no. 2 (Spring 1977): 12–32. Benjamin Mays linked King to the Old Testament prophetic heritage, noting that "Surely this man was called of God to do this work. If Amos and Micah were prophets in the eighth century, B.C.E., Martin Luther King, Jr., was a prophet in the twentieth century." See Benjamin E. Mays, "Eulogy of Martin Luther King, Jr.," Atlanta, Ga. (April 9, 1968), reprinted at the request of State Representative Matthew McNeely, 4–5. One important study, which compares the work of King with that of the canonical Hebrew prophets, concludes that King was not prophetic in the biblical and theological sense. See Joseph M. Thompson, "Martin Luther King, Jr. and Christian Witness: An Interpretation of King Based on a Theological Model of Prophetic Witness" (Ph.D. diss., Fordham University, Spring, 1981), 3 ff.

168. Walter Harrelson, "Martin Luther King, Jr. and the Old Testament Prophets," a lecture given at Vanderbilt University, Nashville, Tenn. (February 6, 1986), 1 ff.

racism, her idolatry, her militarism, and her mistreatment of the poor and oppressed.[169]

Religion in America in King's time was strikingly similar to religion in Hebrew society in the age of the prophets. In both cases, it appeared healthy in all its external ways but was rotten at the core. This is why King frequently quoted Amos 5:24: "But let justice run down as waters, and righteousness as a mighty stream."[170] Generally speaking, the message that the Hebrew prophets and King so eloquently proclaimed was twofold. The first part was that God would not long endure the cruelty and destructiveness of people against people. The second part held that God would not continue to allow devoted people not to practice what they affirmed in creeds and ceremonies, because there had to be continuity between what was affirmed and celebrated in worship and what was practiced in daily life.[171]

The manner in which the Hebrew prophets and King turned their attention inward, to keep themselves true to their calling and purpose, also suggests a point of similarity. They knew that they, too, were under the judgment of what they preached. They presented their messages forcefully, knowing that they were bearers of God's prophetic word for their respective times, and that they had to apply their concerns for justice and righteousness to their own specific contexts. Furthermore, the prophet's claim that God had called Israel to be a comforting and redemptive community for herself and other nations clearly corresponded to King's notion that God had assigned a messianic role to black Americans.[172]

169. *Ibid.*; and Baldwin, "The Minister as Preacher, Pastor, and Prophet," 86–87.

170. Baldwin, "The Minister as Preacher, Pastor, and Prophet," 87.

171. Harrelson, "Martin Luther King, Jr. and the Old Testament Prophets," 1 ff.

172. *Ibid.*; Shelp and Sunderland, eds., *The Pastor as Prophet*, 17; and Baldwin, "The Minister as Preacher, Pastor, and Prophet," 87–89. King inherited from his slave forebears not only the capacity to look critically at white society and the conventions of authority but also the capacity to look critically at his own life. Like the Hebrew prophets of old, the slaves knew that they were not excluded from the judgment of what they

Although the Hebrew prophets were not in complete agreement on what was the divine purpose, they were hopeful for the world. They knew that a just and merciful God was at work in the world to bring some purpose to full realization, and that this God would find vindication.[173] King shared this hope, and this is why he accepted suffering without retaliation. When he spoke of the ultimate triumph of the moral order, and when he sang "Free at Last," King was affirming the existence of a God who punishes the wicked and replaces evil with good.[174]

The Hebrew prophets and King were also similar in that they died before accomplishing their goals, which involved the redemption and transformation of their respective societies. During their life pilgrimages, they experienced one failure after another and were often unpopular, but they were sustained by the belief that though they had failed in some ways, God would not fail.[175] On April 3, 1968, the night before he was assassinated, King expressed this conviction in a statement inspired by the prophetic heritage of the Bible:

> Well, I don't know what will happen now. We've got some difficult days ahead. But it really doesn't matter with me now, because I've been to the mountaintop. And I don't mind. Like anybody, I would like to live a long life. Longevity has its place. But I'm not concerned about that now. I just want to do God's will. And He's allowed me to go up to the mountain. And I've looked over. And I've seen the promised land. I may not get there with you. But I want you to know tonight, that we as a people will get to the promised

preached. This is why they sang songs like, "Oh duh fault een me, eh Lawd." For brilliant insight into how the slaves turned their prophetic genius inward, see Gardner C. Taylor, "A King Day Sermon," delivered at Colgate-Rochester Divinity School, Rochester, New York (January 15, 1974), 1 ff.

173. Harrelson, "Martin Luther King, Jr. and the Old Testament Prophets," 1 ff.

174. *Ibid.;* and Baldwin, "The Minister as Preacher, Pastor, and Prophet," 87.

175. Harrelson, "Martin Luther King, Jr. and the Old Testament Prophets," 1ff.

land. And I'm happy, tonight. I'm not worried about anything. I'm not fearing any man. Mine eyes have seen the glory of the coming of the Lord.[176]

## KING'S IMPACT ON MINISTERS AND PERCEPTIONS OF MINISTRY

King's rise to prominence in 1955 generated much excitement and hope among scores of black Americans who had become disillusioned with the reactionary traditionalism of their ministers and churches. King brought a new image, a fresh message, and a renewed zeal to the black pulpit, thereby giving new vitality and relevance to the black church.[177] Because of his high moral and spiritual leadership, ministers and churches throughout America and the world became more sensitive to the need for new and more vital forms of ministry—pastoral, priestly, and prophetic.

A significant part of King's legacy is evident in the ways in which he influenced the small group of black ministers who were his closest aides and lieutenants in S.C.L.C. Ralph Abernathy, James Bevel, Bernard Lee, C. T. Vivian, Wyatt T. Walker, Hosea Williams, Andrew Young, and Jesse Jackson have all been inspired by King's leadership and message and have enhanced their own ministries by projecting images of association with him.[178]

176. *Ibid.*; and Flip Schulke, ed., *Martin Luther King, Jr.: A Documentary—Montgomery to Memphis* (New York: W. W. Norton, 1976), 224.

177. Gayraud S. Wilmore, *Black Religion and Black Radicalism: An Interpretation of the Religious History of Afro-American People* (Maryknoll, N.Y.: Orbis Books, 1983), 174. It has been argued in some circles that King's leadership represented a break from that of the traditional black preacher in the South, whose role "was often to tranquilize the black community and placate the white." This argument contains some truth, but it must be critically assessed in light of the contributions of preachers like Nat Turner and Henry M. Turner, who employed radical and sacrificial forms of ministry in the South long before the emergence of King. See Matthew Holden, Jr., *The Politics of the Black "Nation"* (New York and London: Chandler Publishing, 1973), 12.

178. "Where Are The Keepers of Dr. M. L. King's Dream?," *Ebony*, 38, no. 6 (April 1983): 31–32, 34, 38, 40; "Poll Power: The New Black Politicians," *Life*, 11, no. 5 (Spring 1988): 34–39; "His Truth Is Marching On: Dr. King's Aides Continue Crusade in Politics, Religion and Education,"

Furthermore, these ministers have assumed the task of continuing King's crusade for a more just and peaceful society through the various arenas of religion, politics, and education.[179] Abernathy, who succeeded King as president of S.C.L.C. in 1968, was, until his death in 1990, still an active supporter of that organization, and, as pastor of the West Hunter Street Baptist Church in Atlanta, continued to preach a socially relevant gospel. Lee, formerly a field secretary for King, currently serves as an assistant pastor at Trinity Baptist Church and as an active participant in social ministries in Washington, D.C.[180] Vivian, once a field coordinator of S.C.L.C., heads the Atlanta-based Black Action Strategies and Information Center (also called Center for Democratic Renewal), which helps communities respond to hate groups in nonviolent ways. Walker, an Executive Director of S.C.L.C. in the early 1960s, pastors the Canaan Baptist Church in Harlem and is involved in the struggle for decent housing and a drug-free America. Williams, who served as Voter Registration Director of S.C.L.C., is now an Atlanta city councilman. Young, the Executive Director of the S.C.L.C. at the time of King's death, is mayor of Atlanta, and was a candidate for governor of Georgia in 1990.[181] Jackson, the Director of Operation Breadbasket under King, continues to wield considerable influence as the founder of People United to Save Humanity (P.U.S.H.), as the organizer of the Rainbow Coalition, and as a presidential candidate.[182] The works of all of these men attest to the power of King's legacy. However, "the most

---

*Ebony*, vol. 45, no. 3 (January 1989): 44, 46, 48; and Adolph L. Reed, Jr., *The Jesse Jackson Phenomenon: The Crisis of Purpose in Afro-American Politics* (New Haven: Yale University Press, 1986), 28, 37.

179. "His Truth Is Marching On," 44, 46, 48.

180. *Ibid.*; "Where Are the Keepers of Dr. M. L. King's Dream?," 32; a private interview with the Rev. Ralph D. Abernathy, 17 March 1987; and a private interview with the Rev. Bernard S. Lee, 9 July 1986.

181. "Where Are the Keepers of Dr. M. L. King's Dream?," 34, 38, 40; and "His Truth Is Marching On," 44, 46, 48.

182. Reed, *The Jesse Jackson Phenomenon*, 1–122; and Roger D. Hatch, *Beyond Opportunity: Jesse Jackson's Vision for America* (Philadelphia: Fortress Press, 1988), 7–130.

detrimental thing about the King legacy," says Hosea
Williams, "was that people close to him didn't have the
wisdom and the ability to remain a united force."[183]

Jesse Jackson affords perhaps the most striking example of how King's ideas and work continue to challenge the nation and the world. Both P.U.S.H. and the
Rainbow Coalition—designed to unite people across
racial, ethnic, class, religious, and sexual lines in the
interest of social justice and peace—are modeled on
King's beloved community concept. Like King, Jackson
relies on the black church as a platform for his activities. In 1984 and 1988, he went to black congregations to
legitimize his intention to run for president of the
United States, and to solicit moral, spiritual, and financial backing for that initiative.[184] In the tradition of
King and scores of black preachers before him, Jackson
has made an art of fusing politics and religion, a technique that accounts for the significant increase in black
voter registration for the 1980s. As the prime mover of
contemporary black political life, Jackson has forged a
unity among his people not seen since King.[185] As
Adolph L. Reed, Jr. has suggested, Jackson has accomplished this unity mainly by draping "himself in the cultural authority of King's image. . . ."[186]

The magnitude of King's influence on black preachers
and forms of ministry in the black church is difficult to
assess. It is certain, however, that he inspired many black
ministers in America toward a career of service to

183. "Where Are the Keepers of Dr. M. L. King's Dream?," 40.
184. Reed, *The Jesse Jackson Phenomenon*, 9, 11, 26, 70, 85–86, 112–
15, 129; and Hatch, *Beyond Opportunity*, 21, 25, 77, 91, 95.
185. Reed, *The Jesse Jackson Phenomenon*, 9, 42–48.
186. *Ibid.*, 37. King's relationship with Jackson in the late 1960s was
marked with some tension. King felt that Jackson, a young seminarian,
was "too ambitious," and the two men exchanged harsh words on at least
one occasion. See "Jesse Jackson: The Power or the Glory?," *Vanity Fair*,
51, no. 1 (January 1988): 100. King's influence courses through Jackson's
speeches and writings. See Jesse L. Jackson, *Straight from the Heart*, ed.
Roger D. Hatch and Frank E. Watkins (Philadelphia: Fortress Press,
1987), 1 ff.

humanity. Fred Shuttlesworth, who was heavily involved with King in the Birmingham campaign in 1963 and who currently pastors the New Life Baptist Church in Cincinnati, is among the most well-known black preachers inspired by King. Shuttlesworth still pursues King's dream on a practical level by pushing for better services for the poor and the elderly in his city.[187] Joseph E. Lowery, who followed Ralph Abernathy as president of S.C.L.C. in 1977 and who presently serves in that same capacity, has vowed to revitalize the work of King through his organization. Lowery, who also serves as pastor of the Cascade United Methodist Church in Atlanta, is convinced that King's idea of building pluralistic coalitions and protesting in the streets is still relevant.[188] The same holds true for Walter E. Fauntroy, who was the liaison between federal agencies and S.C.L.C. when King died. As a congressional delegate in Washington, D.C. and as pastor of the New Bethel Baptist Church in that city, Fauntroy remains quite active in movements against *poverty and South African apartheid. John Lewis, who worked closely with King in the Selma movement in 1965, is not a pastor, but he still employs his gifts and talents as a minister and a Georgia congressman to make the political process more sensitive to the needs and concerns of the poor and oppressed.[189] The same can be said of Congressman William Gray of Pennsylvania and Congressman Floyd Flake of Queens, New York, both of whom are black pastors influenced and inspired by the King legacy. In fact, it is virtually impossible to find socially and politically active black preachers in America today who have not been touched in some way by the spirit and work of King. Because of King, black preachers throughout

187. "Where Are the Keepers of Dr. M. L. King's Dream?," 40; and "His Truth Is Marching On," 46.
188. "Where Are the Keepers of Dr. M. L. King's Dream?," 34; and Peake, *Keeping the Dream Alive*, 323–51.
189. "Where Are the Keepers of Dr. M. L. King's Dream?," 38; and Simeon Booker, "Black Ministers: A New Force in U. S. Politics," *Jet*, 71, no. 19 (February 2, 1987): 14–16.

America have a renewed sense of the vital link between the pastoral, priestly, and prophetic functions.[190] At the same time, the extent to which King himself was influenced by black preachers must be recognized.

The profound influence King had on white preachers and their perceptions of ministry, particularly in the South, has been almost completely ignored. In the 1950s and 1960s, white fundamentalist preachers such as Jerry Falwell and Billy Graham challenged the confrontational nature of King's prophetic ministry and urged their hearers to deal with the evils of "this world" by isolating themselves from them. However, the powerful challenge King presented to white preachers helped alter their consciousness. After King's death, many of these same preachers issued a stern call to social and political action and sought to influence political elections and the shaping of the national agenda on a range of domestic and foreign policy issues.[191] The emergence of Jerry Falwell, Billy Graham, Pat Robertson, James Robison, and other politically oriented preachers of the so-called electronic church in the 1970s and 1980s cannot be fully understood apart from the challenge presented by King.[192] Racism accounts for the failure of most whites to understand this concept.

The vitality of King's personality and leadership in the human struggle has caused many black churches to

190. "Where Are the Keepers of Dr. M. L. King's Dream?," 31–32, 34, 38, 40; "Poll Power: The New Black Politicians," 34–39; "His Truth Is Marching On," 44, 46, 48; and Booker, "Black Ministers: A New Force in U. S. Politics," 14–16.

191. Gabriel Fackre, *The Religious Right and Christian Faith* (Grand Rapids, Mich.: W. B. Eerdmans, 1982), 14, 27–28; and Edward L. Moore, "Billy Graham and Martin Luther King, Jr.: An Inquiry into White and Black Revivalistic Traditions" (Ph.D. diss., Vanderbilt University, May 1979), 453–68. King exchanged many letters with Clarence Jordan, who founded Koinonia Farm in Americus, Ga., a pioneering interracial farming community. These letters, which are among the holdings at the King Center, are useful for studying King's relationship with preachers in the South.

192. This subject still awaits full exploration. A fleeting reference to Falwell's possible admiration for King appears in George Marsden, ed., *Evangelicalism and Modern America* (Grand Rapids, Mich.: W. B. Eerdmans, 1984), 60.

reconsider the potential resources, gifts, and talents that young, promising, seminary-trained ministers can offer. King brought a youthful energy and creativity to ministry unprecedented in American history. Furthermore, he challenged the American churches, both black and white, to produce young ministers capable of revitalizing ministry as the vital center of Christianity.[193] In 1961, King and S.C.L.C. planned, along with the Student Interracial Ministry Committee of the National Student Christian Federation in New York, a summer project designed to prepare young black and white seminarians for ministry in interracial situations in the South. The idea was to expose black seminarians to white churches and white seminarians to black churches as "ministerial interns." King called the proposed project "a bold and creative venture in human relations" and assessed its possible impact in these terms:

> For a period of 10–12 weeks, the white seminarians will have the opportunity to live and work within the framework of a Negro church community; to know them intimately, sense their hopes and fears, their joys and sorrows. This will aid inestimably in preparing them to serve the church and to give clear Christian witness. For Negro seminarians, it will provide for them the kind of exposure to a white community that they have never had, and in the same will produce a broader and more sympathetic understanding to the very deep problems with which the white church has now to grapple in the face of the South's severe social change. Thusly, by common sharing, the two church communities will be building significant bridges of mutuality which will better equip both for resolving the troublous times in which we live.[194]

193. A letter from Martin Luther King, Jr., and Wyatt T. Walker to the Student Interracial Ministry Committee of the National Student Christian Federation, 29 March 1961, The King Papers, Boston University; and a letter from Martin Luther King, Jr., to Thomas E. Jordan, 31 July 1963, The King Papers, Boston University.

194. A letter from Martin Luther King, Jr., and Wyatt T. Walker to the Student Interracial Ministry Committee of the National Student Christian Federation, 29 March 1961.

This proposed summer project, planned at a time when southern resistance to integration was still strong, did not meet with success. Nevertheless, King continued to push the idea that creative witness in both black and white churches depended greatly on the contributions that sincere and enlightened young ministers could bring to the ministerial task. In 1963 he wrote:

> It goes without saying that one of the great needs of this hour is for more dedicated, sincere, and intelligent young men to enter the Christian ministry. The opportunities for leadership in the Christian community are greater than ever before. No one has the ears of as many people as the man who occupies the pulpit.[195]

King's idea of a creative, well-rounded ministry commends itself to preachers and pastors now grappling with the many troubling developments in our society, from racial polarization to nuclear proliferation.[196] His prophetic voice deserves a special hearing because it spoke out of a deep sense of pastoral and priestly concern for the whole of creation.[197] The failure of American churches to produce ministers of King's quality has led to a serious leadership crisis in the last two decades, a crisis that must be resolved if the integrity and vitality of the Christian faith is to be preserved. Black preachers and the black church can make a special contribution to the resolution of this crisis by promoting a deeper understanding and appreciation for King's prophetic message and zeal, and by keeping alive and building on the preaching tradition that produced him.

195. A letter from Martin Luther King, Jr., to Thomas E. Jordan, 31 July 1963.
196. Franklin, "Martin Luther King, Jr. as Pastor," 4–5; and Shelp and Sunderland, eds., *The Pastor as Prophet*, 15.
197. Shelp and Sunderland, eds., *The Pastor as Prophet*, 15.

# CONCLUSION

This work has sought to uncover those central threads that gave shape, vitality, and unique significance to King's life, thought, and vision. More specifically, it has focused on King as essentially a product of black culture and the black experience in the South. Special attention has been devoted to his sense of regional identity and regional responsibility as a black southerner, and also to his nourishing foundation in the contexts of family, church, and the larger black community of Atlanta, Georgia. It has been argued that the black experience and the black Christian tradition were the most important influences in the shaping of King's life, thought, vision, and efforts to translate the ethical ideal of the *beloved community* into practical reality.

Much of the writing about King has been intensely biographical, with particular attention to the significance of his studies at Crozer Theological Seminary and Boston University. Such works have merit, but their failure to attach primary importance to King's cultural context suggests both a racial bias and an antisouthern bias. This volume should serve as a corrective to this misguided approach. This work effectively shifts research from the usual configuration of the sources of King's life and thought to a greater appreciation of the decisive influence of his roots in the institutions, values,

and traditions of the black South. Thus, it should constitute a genuine advance in our understanding of King.

This study has identified and emphasized three central themes that lead to a fuller understanding of King's
essence, power, and unique significance. One is *sense
of place* in a southern context, a notion that can be understood only by those who are willing to concede the
possibility of sentiment connected with *place*. King's
ambivalent feelings about the South—his dislike of the
region's virulent racism on the one hand, and his belief
in its potential for positive growth and development on
the other—have been discussed at great length. It has
been suggested that the very metaphors King used in
the southern context—metaphors of progress, growth,
development, rebirth, freedom, and "new South"—
carried optimistic connotations that gave way to the
possibility of a revitalized and racially inclusive South
in the present and future.

The communitarian ideal has been examined as a
second central theme essential for understanding King.
This study has shown, explicitly and by implications,
that *community* was one of the most pervasive themes in
King's thought, speeches, and writings—that all other
important concepts (i.e., love, nonviolence, forgiveness,
reconciliation, freedom, justice, human dignity) coursing through his works are intimately related to his understanding of and quest for community. Further, the study
has revealed that King challenged the South, the nation,
and the world with a positive and compelling communal
vision that transcended human categories and immediate historical realities and experiences. The depth of
King's communal vision will become clearer with the
publication of the companion volume to this work, which
will be issued soon under the title, *To Make the Wounded
Whole: The Cultural Legacy of Martin Luther King, Jr.
There Is a Balm in Gilead* and *To Make the Wounded
Whole*, when considered jointly, aim to reveal how King's
understanding of community gradually transcended

family, the black church, and the larger black community of Atlanta to embrace the entire South, the nation, and eventually the world.

*Christian optimism* has been treated as a third central theme fundamental to an understanding of King. King affirmed that in spite of the tragic ambiguities and vicissitudes of life, especially as revealed in the history of human suffering and fragmentation, God will ultimately emerge triumphant over evil and bring liberation, wholeness, and salvation to people. Some would undoubtedly describe this spirit as one of *Christian hope* rather than *Christian optimism*, suggesting that the two are in some ways different. This study has moved from the premise that *Christian hope* and *Christian optimism* are virtually synonymous in King's rhetoric, and can therefore be used interchangeably to describe his vision concerning the future of humanity and human society.

Vast and often subtle fundamental historical and cultural elements were at work in King's life—elements that explain him as a person, a thinker, a preacher, and a social activist. Unless one understands them, then one cannot possibly understand the spirit of Martin Luther King, Jr.

# INDEX

83154